A Different Christianity

SUNY Series in Western Esoteric Traditions
David Appelbaum, editor

A Different Christianity

*Early Christian Esotericism and
Modern Thought*

Robin Amis

STATE UNIVERSITY OF NEW YORK PRESS

Published by
State University of New York Press, Albany

For information, address State University of New York Press,
State University Plaza, Albany, N.Y., 12246

Production by Marilyn P. Semerad
Marketing by Bernadette LaManna

Library of Congress Cataloging-in-Publication Data

Amis, Robin
    A different Christianity : early Christian esotericism and modern
thought / Robin Amis.
        p.   cm. — (SUNY series in Western esoteric traditions)
    Includes index.
        ISBN 0-7914-2571-1 (alk. paper). — ISBN 0-7914-2572-X (pbk. :
alk. paper)
        1. Spirituality—Orthodox Eastern Church.   2. Mysticism—History–
–Early church, ca. 30–600.   3. Monastic and religious life.
    4. Occultism—Religious aspects—Orthodox Eastern Church.
    5. Orthodox Eastern Church—Customs and practices.   I. Title.
    II. Series.
    BX384.5.A39   1995
    248—dc20   94-40813
                                                         CIP

10   9   8   7   6   5

*Now seekers after knowledge must know exactly
how to make out true orthodoxy for themselves
by using natural examples; and especially such
as are drawn from our very selves, for they are
surer and are a true means of proof.*

—Saint Gregory the Sinaite,
Discourse on the Transfiguration

Contents

PREFACE. The Forgotten Christian Inner Tradition   xiii

    An Accident of History   xiv

    The Modern Situation   xvi

ACKNOWLEDGMENTS   xxi

INTRODUCTION. Searching in the Ruins   1

    A Research Report   4

    A Method of Therapy   9

    Saints Are Always Somewhere Else   11

    From Investigation of the Past, a New Vision   13

CHAPTER 1. The Royal Road of the Early Church   19

    The Path of Heart   20

    Pray for Help   23

    The General Resurrection   25

    Unchanging Truth   26

    Loss of Ancient Knowledge   27

    The Sources of My Investigation   30

       The Teachings of the Bible   32

       The Apocrypha   32

       The Fathers of the Church   33

       Eastern Monastic Practice   36

       Monastic Rules   37

       Church Liturgies   38

       Great Spiritual Texts   38

       Alchemical and Mystery Teachings   39

CHAPTER 2. The Burning Bush   41
  A Hermit Speaks   43
  Trial by Fire   44
  Symeon the New Theologian on Inner Experience   47
  Saint Maximos on the Fall   48
  Our Nature Is Fundamentally Good, but Has Been Distorted   51
  Modern Man's Inability to Remember Inner Experience   54
  A Theory of Knowledge Is a Barrier to Faith   55
  Gregory of Nyssa's View   58

CHAPTER 3. The Rediscovery of Spirit   61
  The Christian Overcomes the Fall   63
  The *Life of Moses*   64
  Philosophy in the Early Church   65
  Saint Isaac's Prayer for Gnosis   69
  Two Very Different Kinds of Knowledge   70
  The Inner World as a Window onto the Invisible World   71
  The Role of Knowledge in Spirituality   75
  Saint Maximos on Contemplation   77

CHAPTER 4. The Wise and Foolish Virgins   79
  The Quest for Energies   80
  The Wedding Garment   82
  Shining Faces   85
  "Ask, and it shall be given you."   89
  Christianity as a State of Being   90
  The *Startsi*   91
  The Prayer of Joseph the Visionary   92
  The Control of the Senses   93
  The Five Virgins as the Senses   94
  Koinonia as Communion   96

CHAPTER 5. Gnosis Is Not Gnosticism   101
  An Experiential Gnosis   102
  Different Worldviews   103
  False Gnosis   105

The Alexandrian Tradition 107
Knowledge of God's Omnipotence 111
A World Without Gnosis 114
The Question of Education 115
Paideia and Catechism 116

CHAPTER 6. The Work of God **119**
The Working of the Word 120
Surrender into the Hands of God 121
Doing the Will of God 123
Gregory of Nyssa and the Chariot Parable 126
Work on Oneself 130
Modern Solutions 131
The Biblical Paradox of the Knowledge of God 134
Ascesis as Work on Oneself 137

CHAPTER 7. Three Renunciations **141**
Three Renunciations Defined 143
The First Renunciation: "Dying to the World" 145
The Turn Toward Reality 145
The Two Nights 147
Bitter Waters 150
The Second Renunciation 154
"Transcending Knowledge with My Thought" 157
The Third Renunciation 158
The Parting of the Ways 164
A Fourth Stage 165
Theosis: Deification 165
A Modern Understanding of the Three Renunciations 167
Saint Silouan of Mount Athos 169

CHAPTER 8. Faith and Assent **171**
The Philosophy of Assent 172
The Psychology of Assent 175
Two Stages of Faith 176
Faith Without Works 178

Faith of Consciousness   179

The Common Ground of Faith   181

CHAPTER 9.   The Eye of the Soul   **183**

Transformation of the Heart   184

The New Man as the Prodigal Son   186

Mneme Theou   189

The Struggle for *Metanoia*   191

"The love of the soul is its salvation"   193

Recognition   198

CHAPTER 10.   *Metanoia* and Ascesis   **203**

Modern Views of *Metanoia*   204

Metanoia as Change of Being   206

Saint Paul and the Ascetic Struggle   213

Monastic Forms of Ascesis   214

    Agrypnia: The All-Night Vigil Service   217

    Fasting   220

    Obedience and Cutting off the Will   224

    Obedience to the Commandments   225

    The Struggle with Eroticism   227

    The Passions   229

A Transformed Eros   231

The Hospitality of Abba Moses   232

CHAPTER 11.   Prayer   **235**

The One Thing Needful   236

Theocentric Selflessness   239

The Just   240

Epiousion   242

Prayer as Relation to God   242

Degrees of Prayer   246

The Inner Room   249

The Jesus Prayer   254

Noetic Prayer   257

Non-Doing   258

CHAPTER 12. A Nonmonastic Path   **261**

Monastic and Nonmonastic Ways   263

The Difficulty of Monastic Methods   264

Renunciation of Inner Possessions   268

Yoga and Discrimination   271

The Two "Legs" of the Tradition   273

Mouravieff's Method   274

Watchfulness (*Nepsis*)   276

Presence   280

The Ark As Separation from the World   282

Magnetic Center   285

    Passive Unconscious Stage: Attraction to the Way   286

    Active Stage: The Struggle   287

    Through Knowledge to Detachment   288

    Second Passive Stage: Magnetization to God   291

CHAPTER 13. Memory and Discrimination   **295**

What We Think Determines What We See   296

The Garden, a Model of Memory   297

Plato's Wax Tablet Model   300

The Parable of the Sower   301

Illusory Memories   302

The Nature of *Diakrisis*   304

Cassian on *Diakrisis*   307

Meat Diet and Milk Diet   314

CHAPTER 14. Provocation   **317**

Stages of Provocation   318

    1. Provocation (Russian *prilog*)   320

    2. Conjunction (Russian *sochetanie*)   321

    3. Joining (Russian *slozhenie*)   322

    4. & 5. The Struggle Against Habit   323

    6. Captivity (Russian *plenenie*)   324

Observation of Provocations   325

Resisting Provocation   327

First Provocation: Gluttony   329

Second Provocation: Lust   330

Third Provocation: Avarice   330

Fourth Provocation: Sadness   331

Fifth Provocation: Anger   332

Sixth Provocation: Accidie   333

Seventh Provocation: Vanity   333

Eighth Provocation: The Demon of Pride   334

The Fear of Opening Ourselves to God   335

**POSTSCRIPT.   Healing the Soul: Some Conclusions
from Matthew 13**   **337**

The Barbarians Within   338

Need for Christian Teaching   340

Taking up the Cross   341

Reports of a Lost Esotericism   342

The Psychological Method   344

A Method for Today   346

A Christian Origin   347

If Thine Eye Be Single   348

A Different Kind of Concentration   350

NOTES   **353**

INDEX   **381**

Preface

The Forgotten Christian Inner Tradition

"The tradition is one," says Boris Mouravieff in his book *Gnosis: Study and Commentaries on the Esoteric Tradition of Eastern Orthodoxy.* And today, despite claims to the contrary, my observations have convinced me that this links with the fact that Christianity possesses and always has possessed an *inner tradition:* not a system, but what might be called a discipline. To those with sufficient experience in investigating this field, I believe that this book will convey the same conviction. In addition, I would add to the idea that the inner tradition is one—although with local variations—certain other observations about it:

1. All the major religions of the world possess a complete tradition of inner knowledge (or a version of the one tradition), although it has only reached a small percentage of the most able individuals within that faith.
2. Many or all of the great civilizations of the world are formed by the great faiths of the world.
3. In each case of a civilization formed by one of the great faiths, the inner tradition is a fundamental element in the structure of the associated civilization.

Yet today there are fundamental differences between the attitude of Christianity to its inner tradition and that of the other great faiths to theirs. For example, faiths such as Hinduism, Buddhism, and Islam are today attempting to make their inner tradition better known, yet the Western churches either claim that there is no tradition of inner or esoteric knowledge, or reserve it to a clergy who themselves are not expected to give too much credence to it. This has forced countless thousands to turn to Eastern faiths for no other reason than because their inner teachings are more accessible than our own: because although Christianity has always possessed its own tradition of inner knowledge, looked at through intellectual eyes, that tradition has been relegated to the status of an intellectual curiosity. As a result some of it has been irrevocably lost, much mislaid, and the remainder has reached only a very small proportion of the population. Consequently—because knowledge acts only through being known—it has had little effect on our civilization.

This is one reason why many people no longer regard ours as a Christian civilization. But the truth is not Nietzsche's 'death of God,' nor has Christianity failed. What actually happened was that, due to the difficulties of conveying the inner tradition through the barbarous centuries following the decline of the Roman Empire, and due to the limited classical education of most Westerners, this key element of Christian teaching has never been common knowledge in the Western world.

An Accident of History

The focus of the problem exists at the point where the Roman Empire split. Physically, this is represented by a line that passes through the Balkans and to this day marks an area of recurrent conflicts,[1] which have now emerged again after a few decades of uneasy peace. Let me risk here a complex image for what has occurred by describing it as a "balkanization of the mind." This inner balkanization has entailed several successive stages of psychological and spiritual fragmentation, beginning in the Roman era but bearing problem fruit today. It is this fragmentation, this "balkanization of the mind," that concerns this book, and it is this that has led to our times being described as "the age of specialization." And each of these stages was as catastrophic as that described in the following paragraph:

> When bishops, a generation after Hobbes's death, almost naturally spoke the language of the state of nature, contract and rights, it was clear that he had defeated the ecclesiastical authorities, who were no longer able to understand themselves as they once had. It was henceforward inevitable that the modern archbishops of Canterbury would have no more in common with the ancient ones than does the second Elizabeth with the first.[2]

At that time, the emergence of science against the opposition of the church led to an intellectual worldview that shaped the thought of an age, resulting in a massive change of thought in the Christian religion. Instead of the sciences, law, and morality fitting into the Christian worldview as once they did, Christian thought was relegated to a form of specialization that was expected to fit into the scientific worldview. Observation suggests that two ideas that developed in the biological sciences can be applied to this: one, that specialization limits adaptability, and two, that ability to adapt defines intelligence. If this is so, then this specialization can be seen as limiting the adaptability of the faith, and even as limiting human intelligence. This situation, I believe, is directly responsible for many of the problems of the churches today, and if we accept that religion does have a function in human society we may see that its narrowing is also responsible for our inability to adapt to the problems of our present time. Even more it explains our inability to understand ideas that were greatly valued by past ages.

One of the implications of this is that if Christianity is a single coherent truth, as the early Fathers would have said it is, one of the signs that a book like this is genuinely Christian would be its ability to convey its central message to different types of people with very different questions, with very different specializations, and coming from very different places in themselves. This book intends to do just that, but faces the problem, already met in discussing the draft with different people, that to satisfy so many different types of individual, the book has to offer something meaningful to each—and offer it right at the beginning of the book. Otherwise readers will assume that this text has nothing for them, and, sensibly enough, will set the book aside.

To develop this, let me try to describe how I imagine certain of the most important specializations of our contemporary Western world might come to discover what this different Christianity means to them:

— Devout Christians of all denominations who have shown an inclination to seek a deeper understanding of inner Christianity, many of whom today can understand that an inner tradition might have therapeutic aims

— Seekers after truth, whatever form their search has taken, if they are sufficiently rigorous and careful in their search, as long as they take the special kinds of care necessary to keep their search free of the prejudices formed in early life

— Those who have joined in earlier attempts to recapture the inner spirit of their faith, or simply to find expression for their own inner impulse in organizations studying material that—as we have discovered—was once the subject matter of Christian thought and discipline, but now is more often studied in forms that are externally very different from its early Christian forms.

The Modern Situation

S ince the meaning of esotericism is "inner," this book necessarily touches
on personal and psychological questions which individuals must face
in their lives, but which—for a century or more—they have had to face
in private, since the study of such questions has for a while not been the
open and accepted discipline it once was. It touches on the historical, in
order to show that in early stages of our history there existed a detailed
knowledge of these inner questions which we in our time have been
taught to ignore, and because, as I suggested, by uncovering this history
we rediscover the lost or balkanized territory in our own inner lives as we
expose to view the inner truths and inner struggles of those earlier times.
Past struggles toward unity, especially when successful, can help us toward
inner unity today. This clearly relates to a particular idea in spiritual history, the idea of the periodic reemergence of an inner tradition that is
repeatedly lost. It touches on the philosophical, in the sense that it touches
on the roots of the new or reconstituted doctrines that, in the past century
or so, have emerged on the borderline of philosophy, theology, and psychology, in that balkanization[3] of the mind to which I referred earlier, in
which the original terms coined in that ancient world have become a
direct cause of certain present-day confusions.

My investigations have uncovered previous searches of the same kind,
some of which have led me to individual successors of ancient streams
whose knowledge and capabilities still survive. I have identified certain
groups and schools—some of them in the West—that have come from such
studies, but which seem in every situation to have reached the same point
of obstruction: a stage, always the same or very similar in character, where
their progress, the progress of all their participants, appears to go no further;
a threshold, a point of decision they are not motivated enough, nor well
enough equipped, to pass; a barrier between change of mind and change of
heart. As my later researches have made clear, there was good reason why
seekers like ourselves—as a whole, and not only advanced students—needed
to make further contact with the Tradition . . . the Tradition of the light
referred to in Matthew 6: "The light of the body is the eye: if therefore thine
eye be single, thy whole body shall be full of light. But if thine eye be evil,
thy whole body shall be full of darkness. If therefore the light that is in thee
be darkness, how great is that darkness!" (Matthew 6:23).

At this point it appears necessary to me to deal specifically with
the relation of esoteric forms of Christianity to certain events earlier in
this century, especially the ideas of Gurdjieff, Ouspensky, and those who
have followed their lead, teachings whose sources are difficult to trace
but in which the first hinted and the latter openly stated, more than
once, that they in fact formed a reemergence of a lost ancient tradition

or traditions of inner truth several times described as esoteric Christianity.[4] The Postscript at the back of the book gives additional information about the recent history of those ideas for those who lack basic information.

Either to study this tradition in order to regain our own inner tradition as Christians, or to discover that esoteric Christianity referred to by Gurdjieff and Ouspensky and not easily visible in the Western churches and so to make use of its great armory of practical methods, we find that we have to adopt what will be, to most modern individuals, an unfamiliar way of thinking about the world. This unfamiliar way of thinking about the world is itself part of Christian tradition. Because of this way of seeing the world, Christianity had, in its first century or so, the power to enlighten and transform; it then answered just those questions that today take people to other lands, other times, other faiths for their answers. It is now unfamiliar because today most people judge by intellectual criteria and expect to verify everything against what can be weighed, measured, or in some way perceived by the senses.

In such a world, it would be foolish to expect everyone to see, behind the troubles of our times, the need for a new spiritual vision, and even more unrealistic to expect them to adopt that new-old vision. But because it is such a world, a whole class of knowledge has been almost entirely lost to modern man. Yet inner and spiritual problems can only be resolved by inner and spiritual interpretations, and because of this the tradition of which I speak is a tradition of interpretation, a way of distilling the meaning from the gospel teaching, using the tools of understanding provided by that tradition itself. Many people who are aware of the need for them will find both personal solutions and general answers not in the religions of other civilizations, where so many have already searched without success, but in the roots of our own world. They will make this discovery if they take a new look at an ancient and transforming interpretation of the Christian faith, an interpretation that is little known and even less valued today. As this book will show, there is also little doubt that most of those answers still exist—within Christendom, but tucked away in its inaccessible corners—and I have slowly become certain that with sufficient effort these answers can be rediscovered and restored to use for modern man, as part of a spiritual reawakening that has already begun but has not yet taken definite form.

This book is written for the many who have become aware that the most viable solution may not be to invent or reinvent a new religion, nor to explore the religions of other civilizations and import them to our shores as seeds of future division, but to take a look at some other aspects of Christianity that are little known today.

To understand this and the possibilities it offers, we need, as suggested earlier, "new eyes," a new yet very old way of thinking about the
world. To approach this, I must first write of experience, as I shall do from
time to time throughout the book, for in our times, experience, and a
strange and little-known relation between experience and faith, form the
latchkeys to new insights and even to the rediscovery of the inner meaning
of the old. From direct experience, we can pass to ways of drawing on
traditional sources for our own spiritual needs, and through this we may
not only discover ourselves, but rediscover the seedbed of certain aspects
of Western civilization which have long been in decline, and perhaps learn
how these key streams in the river of our life can be restored for use by
modern man.

To understand, we also need to recognize the existence of a contemporary
obstacle to research of this kind. Like so many of our problems, this is a
result of modern thought, perhaps exacerbated by modern methods of
funding research. The sheer difficulty of gaining acceptance now means
that to establish the value of a single document may take a person half a
lifetime or even almost a whole lifetime's work. This has created a situation
where almost everybody is afraid to draw general conclusions, or to publish a general study of the whole subject area, unless they can join it
seamlessly to what has been said before.

    Yet under such conditions, when people are forced to conform to
outside opinion rather than their own insight, a slight deviation from
accuracy can become compounded over the years and, because no alternative view will be acceptable as a basis for comparison, this deviation may
remain unrecognized until the situation has gone so far that everyone
outside the field can see the inaccuracy, although it remains invisible to
those within the "charmed circle" of the discipline in question. This is a
double bind: in any discipline there have got to be criteria and detailed
investigations, which must contribute to the shaping of a consensus, and
there must be work on the broader outline. All these together create the
climate for further studies. When both become too insistent, and Western
thought itself tends to be insistent by its very nature, how does one free
oneself from such a trap?

    This is the situation in which this book was written: the twelve
years of exact research on which it has been based are a distillation of
those longer and slower researches of others on the many separate subjects, and yet the book is based on a clearly seen need at this time to
look in from outside, by taking certain tools of modern reason and the
lessons learned from other, non-Western spiritual traditions, by looking
to previous researches of the same kind, some of them previously re-

jected, and finally, by standing not on the platform of scientific objectivity, but instead on that different platform of the attitude of faith and of
knowledge derived from faith, in which these ideas were originally written down or passed on.

Specifically, it is an attempt to use an awareness of the *intentions* of
the texts as a tool for the interpretation of those texts.

In other words, this work is an effort not of analysis, nor of proof,
but of understanding: an attempt to understand, in modern terms, the
ancient ideas that have been rediscovered over the past century or so.

After all, an inner tradition that cannot speak for itself when necessary cannot expect to be recognized. To put this differently, there is little
doubt that the same inner tradition has been expressed in certain texts
such as the recently discovered text known as the *Gospel According to
Thomas*, from which the following passage could well set the correct tone
for this study:

> These are the secret words which the Living Jesus spoke and
> Didymos Judas Thomas wrote: And He said: Whoever finds
> the explanation of these words will not taste death. Jesus said:
> Let him who seeks, not cease seeking until he finds, and when
> he finds, he will be troubled, and when he has been troubled,
> he will marvel, and he will reign over the All. Jesus said: If
> those who lead you say to you: "See, the Kingdom is in heaven,"
> then the birds of the heaven will precede you. If they say to
> you: "It is in the sea," then the fish will precede you. But the
> Kingdom is within you and it is without you. If you will know
> yourselves, then you will be known, and you will know that
> you are the sons of the Living Father. But if you do not know
> yourselves then you are in poverty and you are poverty.

Acknowledgments

I would like to record my indebtedness to the Abbot and the monks of the monasteries of Grigoriou and SimonoPetra on Mount Athos, and to the Abbot and nuns of the convent at Ormylia in Northern Greece, as well as to the many pupils of Ouspensky, Gurdjioff, and Boris Mouravieff who have also helped over the years to shape whatever understanding has found its way into these pages, and to the Hermit Father P—now deceased—without whose influence nothing new would have come into being. Last, but certainly not least, to my wife Lillian, without whose encouragement, physical assistance and perceptive reading this text would never have been finished.

Introduction

Searching in the Ruins

In investigating ancient traditions, the question is always, How can one begin? Some ancient ideas can first be understood only by seeing the reality behind them—one can learn much even by seeing the physical changes that have occurred alongside the changes in ideas. So first I shall write of how our world has changed, of how our faith has changed, and for this it is certainly better to speak of experience, for at this moment we begin to build a bridge over the very boundaries of the world of ideas.

This was what took me to the great monastery of Saint Andrew, beside the road into Karyes, capital town of the monastic republic of Mount Athos (known as the Holy Mountain), a forty-kilometer peninsula off the mainland of northern Greece, which is still today an autonomous monastic republic, although under the protection of the Greek government. When I walked into the courtyard, the monastery lay empty of monks, as it has since a plague in 1926. Greek schoolboys in black monastic robes came and went to one wing. Elsewhere, nobody stirred. Earlier that week, the first liturgy since the monastery had closed in 1926 had been held in the enormous Katholikon church. With my friend, the American monk Germanos, I walked up to the marble portico and hammered on the rusted iron-framed glass doors. Nobody answered. Eventually, one of the boys came over to see what we were doing there, and explained that in

---

The reader will note that in the text of this book certain monks are referred to by name, while others are given only an initial. There is a reason for this: out of respect for the Fathers of Mount Athos we have agreed with certain of them to avoid giving names of living monks whose anonymity might thereby be threatened. Monks (and abbots) whose names are given are either deceased or already publicly known.

all that enormous complex there were only two caretakers. Often they would not answer the door. Often they were out.

The marble portico was badly cracked. Once it had been magnificent. Now it was heading for ruin. Carved into the stone was the date of its building: 1910. Although I failed to get into the monastery, in the fallen roofs, the neglected, empty buildings I gained a sense of something hidden everywhere else. This was the visible result of what had happened in 1918, since frozen in time. That was when a world had come to an end, and here at the monastery of Saint Andrew, nothing has really happened since, except wind and weather; here time has done its work unstayed by human hands. Here you can see the end of that world, the tremendous change whose form has been hidden elsewhere by renewed activity.

Here the disaster that everyone ignores, the collapse of an age, is clearly visible to the eye, giving an image that is a surprisingly appropriate introduction to the detailed study that follows, a summary of years of investigation into the esoteric Christian tradition. It will help to set the scene and to give depth of meaning to our theme. For this book summarizes investigations that I have now been working on almost full time since the beginning of the 1980s. In that time, my investigations have led me to certain places where ancient truths still dwell, as well as to connections with surviving students of those who have sought the same knowledge in the same way, in faraway places. In time they led me to certain important sources in which this ancient tradition survives, at least in part, to the present time—particularly around the eastern end of the Mediterranean, in Greece and Egypt.

By now the conceptual and psychological climate of the West has gone so far from the inner meaning of early Christianity that to restore these ideas to their original meaning at first seems almost impossible. Speaking on television at the New Year heralding 1994, Archbishop Carey (of Canterbury, primate of the Anglican Church) clearly interpreted one of the many scriptural passages promising peace of mind to those who turn to God as a promise to be kept after death. In so doing, he denied one of the great promises of the inner church, the promise of *present help,* specifically defined throughout the early Fathers, although admittedly often referred to in the Bible with the kind of ambiguity that allows such mistakes.

Yet the inner truth and its psychological components, which find their justification in the gospel passage that says "They that are whole have no need of the physician" (Mark 2:17) survives, or persistently reemerges. This therapeutic view survived in medieval Europe in the attitude that treated Christ as the "doctor of souls." It survives in Greece today in the mountain fastnesses where hermits hide. One Athos hermit once explained his role to me by saying that his work was like that of a doctor, but not a doctor for the body. Today this attitude is reemerging as a growing movement[1] that seeks to distinguish between inner and outer interpretations of Christian doctrine, and refers to the outer form as "moralistic" or sometimes "legalistic." By this they mean a faith that judges, that asks things of us, without giving us the means to achieve those things. The ancient inner tradition took a view opposite this; it gave people the means to be moral, then allowed the form of that morality to emerge naturally. It survives in the Orthodox Church, dispersed from its homelands into the West, custodian not only of the empty monastery of Saint Andrew on Mount Athos, but of many still active monasteries on the same peninsula, and of the true keys to the forgotten tradition that was once taught there. Truth it may have, but its resources and its capabilities were and still are generally swamped by lonely exiles, who ask it to speak not primarily of God but of some inexpressible motherland.

It began to reassert itself almost spontaneously in the 1930s but failed to do so because of war. The German phenomenologists asked the right questions, but the breakdown of their world stopped them short of finding a resolution to the desperation inherent in their formulation, and this robbed them of any coherent answer that would have broken them out of their subservience to the subjective images of phenomena, any hint of something out of sight of the mind, of something more than an image, a genuine hint of which might have ended their ridiculous assumption that the ego is no more than an image of an image. There was the impasse of the physical sciences, in which Eddington, in the 1920s, could already see the need for a "new epistemology" that might reconcile human thought with the paradoxical perceptions of quantum physics. By the late 1930s, quantum physics was to have a more sinister role, and it was the late 1960s before this arcane knowledge again began to interest the postwar world in implications other than weapons technology. By then, Eddington's question had been forgotten . . . and little did Eddington know, anyway, that the key to this enigma—a new epistemology that encompasses our contemporary view without being limited to it—had already been provided more than a thousand years before, in the second-century works of Gregory of Nyssa, an ancient Christian author totally ignored by modern philosophy. Even the great physicist and philosopher Erwin Schroedinger and the highly religious Albert Einstein remained unaware that the questions they debated had been answered by Fathers of the church long before the fall of Byzantium. Even now, few can see the direct connection between the paradoxes of particle physics and the ancient Russian philosophical method of antinomies, a philosophical tradition preserved intact to the present but finding its roots in the gospel itself.

The First World War ended an age, and cutting off the prime of our youth it cut off our innate access to the strengths of the past. The time before the Second was too brief for new growth to go deep enough to root itself. After the war, the unfinished new growth that had begun in the thirties but never come to term was rooted out and cast aside, to be forgotten by the generation that followed. Only now, sixty years later, can we begin again to repair the ruins of even the recent past, to pick up the pieces of that era in relation to the deeper questions of life. Only now can we say a prayer for those forgotten pathfinders of the thirties, and only now can we make yet another attempt to cultivate the soil of the human spirit—remembering that we are ourselves children of our century, so that in any such cultivation we must begin with ourselves.

So, as with others before us, it was from an awareness of that situation that my researches into the early church and the survival of its ideas began shortly after 1980, and it is a few of the surprisingly large number of discoveries made during those researches that I am going to describe in this book—as well as drawing on some of the less well-known discoveries of those who have preceded us in this search, particularly those of Boris Mouravieff, Russian émigré, historian, and little known teacher of esotericism who worked in France and Switzerland at the time of Gurdjieff and Ouspensky, and whose three-volume work *Gnosis*—although for many still difficult to understand—provides the most comprehensive and precise primer on this difficult subject.

A Research Report

This book, then, is a report on the researches I have just introduced so dramatically, a study of certain ideas and methods known in the early church but lost, in one way or another, to modern Christianity. (This loss is, of course, at the root of the idea that *esoteric* means *secret*. Nothing could be further from the truth.)

At the same time as being a properly documented study of these lost ideas, this is also of necessity the summary of a personal search, and links the discovered ideas to personal experience. It does this not so much to provide a final definition as to suggest to readers how they should develop their own understanding of the same ideas. This is because the esoteric tradition is so easily misunderstood that, to avoid dangerous mistakes, actions should only be taken on the basis of recognition, of a clear personal understanding in which the teaching is verified by direct experience. I should also add that although these researches have been supported to a degree unusual in such a work, sometimes by taking them to a point of academic accuracy, it is in large part a study of an unwritten tradition, and it has been found—not surprisingly—that documentary evidence of an unwritten tradition is not always available.[2]

It began with a search for the springs of Christian sanctity, a search for the source that I believe is found in the esoteric or inner teachings of the early church. Not for a different gospel, but for a different way of understanding the gospel.

So what do I mean by sanctity? At a workshop in New York recently, I asked about this in the form of a question that now provides the basis of this book.

My question was this: Which of you has ever met a saint?

This is how my own investigation began. But the question has of course been answered, and even evoked answers, many times in the past, and I must have something more to say about how those have emerged over the years. Before you buy the animal, you must read the pedigree.

Several centuries ago, there was a move in the West, probably not the first, to rediscover in the writings of the Fathers of the church—writings that then were inaccessible to most of those who sought—Christian truths that were no longer a part of Western Christian teaching. Again in Europe, in the nineteenth century, some of these works were translated and made generally available, and were clearly valued by a few souls who glimpsed the treasures hid in them. But none of these attempts succeeded in restoring this knowledge to the "mainstream." The time was not right, and what these texts contained was so different from what is now generally understood as Christianity, that by that time, practically nobody possessed the tools with which to grasp those ancient truths.

In Russia, the story was different, because "the times" were different. In the nineteenth century, Russia was still in the throes of the Westernization forced on her by Peter the Great; Western or at least Westernized philosophical and scientific thought existed alongside surviving streams of thought and spirituality in an Eastern Church that later survived the revolution itself. The interaction between these two powerful rivers gave rise to similar investigations and these, the discovering of these ideas by people in active contact with the spiritual practices that endure, almost unchanged over the centuries, in certain corners of the Eastern Church, bore different fruit: a greater valuation of the ideas discovered, which led as a result to more active and sometimes more successful attempts to apply this ancient knowledge. In the nineteenth century certain teachers appeared to transmit this knowledge; some of them, such as Saint Theophan the Recluse, were conventional, others, laymen with more Western backgrounds, were highly unconventional both by the standards of Eastern Christendom and Western humanism.

An important work in the esoteric tradition is the *Philokalia.* Its origin came from a key event during the history of this path. Part of the meaning of these teachings has been lost more than once even by the monasteries. Then it has had to be restored. The major example is that of Paisious Velitchkovsky, who restored the original meaning of the text in the eighteenth century, long before this work was translated into English. The text used in the earliest version of this work sparked a major renewal in the inner tradition that shaped the form it now takes in Eastern monasticism. This renewal of the inner tradition, led by Velitchkovsky, began on Mount Athos and then spread, carried by Velitchkovsky, first to Moldavia and afterwards to Russia. The Greek version of the *Philokalia,* formed by Nicodemus of the Holy Mountain primarily from the texts collected by Velitchkovsky, provides a primary technical instruction for the monks of the Eastern Church who carry on the same tradition to this day on Mount Athos, as well as in many other parts of the world.[3]

Since then, the parallel volume to the *Philokalia,* the *Gerontikon*—teaching-stories about the same early Fathers, in very Middle Eastern style—has been translated several times with varying degrees of success. Thomas Merton selected from this collection stories that are meaningful to modern man.[4] Another émigré, almost certainly a direct successor to the Russian seekers of the nineteenth century, Boris Mouravieff, wrote in the 1960s, in French, his own attempt to summarize his own discoveries in this field and discoveries unpublished by those who had gone before him. I myself have had the honor to publish the three volumes of his main work between 1990 and 1993.[5]

Other key texts have been published recently, as a result of an initiative by Father Nikon, P. D. Ouspensky's friend who was a hermit on Mount Athos: *Unseen Warfare,* also by Nicodemus of the Holy Mountain, later reedited by Saint Theophan the Recluse (see list on pp. 11–12) one of the greatest spiritual teachers of the Russian church who died as recently as the 1890s—and the *Art of Prayer,* by Abbot Chariton of the monastery of Valamo, an ancient and at one time enormous monastery which preserved its spirituality in difficult times by moving across the border from Russia to Finland.

Thus, many of the ancient texts are now more readily accessible. Their readership is increasing, because many, many readers obtain sudden insights from within their pages. But their message in full nobody in the West can read, for it is a message of repentance, *metanoia,* and it cannot be read in any depth and then ignored. So the gap in understanding still remains between Christian East and Christian West. All of this great effort has not yet revealed anything clearly, but it has definitely shown that there is something here to discover, although it is very difficult to discover it in full. The *idea of metanoia,* of the possibility of such a change, as far as I know was first reintroduced to the West in the 1930s by Maurice Nicoll.[6] The meaning and specific methods were described in a fragmentary way,[7] in the *Philokalia* translations among other places,[8] but *metanoia*—repentance—is the essence. This one word is not understood until we realize that it distills the underlying principle, the practical objective, of a complete discipline, one that reaches its goal through a myriad of variations and alternative methods.

Although today *metanoia* still forms the basis of the practical work of the monks of the Eastern Church, few even of the more important methods of approaching it are understood in the West, and the basic principles, in the form of a complete Christian worldview—based on faith, but not on blind belief—seem to have been almost entirely forgotten.

Once read, understood, *and accepted*, these basic principles, and the commandments or rules that accompany them, form the foundation of the whole process. They lead—although normally not without a *struggle,* not without a strong resistance from past habits—to a true reversal of direction in the reader, bringing the catechumen to the threshold, the point of entry, of the path of transformation, the path of *metanoia.* But to enter the path of *metanoia* is to seek to pass through the strait gate of the gospel, and "It is easier for a camel to go through the eye of a needle, than for a rich man to enter into the kingdom of God" (Matthew 19:24). Its import is so difficult, it demands such efforts, such struggles by those who try to apply it, that instead it is often rejected. If this principle were accepted by enough people, so that we could say that it was once again understood by the churches, especially at the present time, it could only lead to a true change of direction by those churches. If understood at the basic level, it could lead to the creation of methods suited to modern individuals and to the situation in which we live. If assimilated by Western civilization at large, which would only happen if many individuals came to understand it and its importance, it might even change the direction of that civilization. (But what kind of change that might be is the subject of my Postscript, and should rest for the moment.)

The purpose of this book, then, is not simply to introduce valuable texts, but to explore the meanings that occur, often many times and expressed in many ways, not only in texts now being translated into English, but in early texts that have already been made available. I also hope to show, where possible, how these early meanings link with *and very often answer* our own questions about ourselves and our world, and how they relate to modern thought on this same subject.

In the time of growth from those early beginnings something changed, and the idea behind this book is that this change must concern us now. As our relation to Christianity has changed, our Christian worldview and our idea of Christianity have both also changed until we can no longer recognize their original forms in them. If we look at the great faiths of the world all the major faiths have an inner tradition except—at first sight—Christianity.

But is this true? The thesis of this book is that Christianity too has or had such a tradition, but that in the development of reason, humanism, and then the physical sciences, that inner tradition has been effectively forgotten or lost.[9] I should expand too on the idea that this tradition has been *effectively lost*. The fact is that the Christian inner tradition is not entirely lost, but its significance has been lost to sight and, as a result, its actuality has been neglected or reduced to a curiosity. Its practical application has been restricted to a few hundred monks, most of them in Eastern Christendom; its texts are few of them translated with their original practical significance in mind; its exercises are mostly forgotten; even its usefulness is no longer understood; its importance to society as a moral restorative is entirely unknown to the majority of thinking men and women.

This, as we understand it, has been the fall of Christendom. This tradition that has fallen or been lost in fact forms the context of the personal fall and the personal resurrection to which we referred above, the background against which monastic writers of the Eastern Church speak continually of the monk's many falls. As Saint John of the Ladder says, "He falls, and gets up again, falls and gets up again."

This book, then, is an attempt to rediscover that tradition of consciousness and make it generally known. As it refers to consciousness, it applies even to those who, unable to follow the way of the monk, walk the esoteric path by methods generally unknown to the monks: they will fall, and they must get up again, day after day and year after year. Those who regard a single rising of this kind as being born again must realize that to be Christian in the full sense of the word, to be Christian as the Fathers understood the word, they must reach the point where they are born again not once, nor even many times, but many, many times each day . . . and then must pass this point. These many awakenings, many little rebirths, are part of the process by which we can eventually be "born from above."

With the Fall, man was cast out of the "garden" of the inner life to till the earth. As the higher faculties are lost, the higher vision, the higher consciousness, is lost to sight, as a recent commentator says about the Fall something that we should perhaps memorize, so clearly does it define our times: that today "The heavenly world has disappeared from man's field of vision and has become an invisible world. There remains only the sensory, material, visible world, like an island in the ocean of the invisible world."[10]

A Method of Therapy

What we can say, at this point, is that in studying the inner life of man, this material constitutes a true psychological science—and an effective system of therapy—that is older by many centuries than anything that passes today by that name. More to the point, as I hope I shall show in this book, once adapted to the different conditions of modern life, it is also a very precise and workable science, despite certain basic differences from modern psychology. All the great religions of the world have a tradition that exists just to meet man's need for inner renewal, for healing of the soul—what has been called a therapeutic tradition, a means of making saints. Hinduism has its Yoga. Islam has Sufism. Buddhism has a number of meditation traditions including Zen. Only Christianity, at first sight, lacks such an "organ."

But that is not so. Christianity has its ways, an almost forgotten mystical science, a *science of metanoia* sometimes called "the Royal Road," that is akin to psychological means of therapy yet more than merely psychological in character, and this ancient and forgotten science not only parallels these Eastern traditions, but it is entirely Christian in character.

This early Christian psychology reflected the gospel statement that: "They that are whole have no need of the physician, but they that are sick: I came not to call the righteous, but sinners to repentance" (Mark 2:17).

The problem is that this therapeutic tradition has been suppressed as a result of the pietism and moralism that dominate modern Christianity. These tendencies to *externalize* the faith exist in all churches and all faiths. They are characteristic not of one religion but of a particular type of human immaturity; they belong to the lower stages of spiritual life, when people are using only one of the functions of their psychological life—they are driven by the senses and by what has been formed within us through the senses.

But this practical method creates a true or spiritual morality by developing *conscience*.

The therapeutic interpretation is not any moralistic or legalistic doctrine, but a practical method aimed at specific results. This interpretation is exact and has its own scientific method.

One Greek author wrote: "Sanctity does not have a moral meaning, but an ontological one."[11] In this the truthfulness of what is believed is subject to the test of praxis, the test that asks: Does it work? This uses an essentially Christian definition of sickness, for Christ was concerned with the spiritually sick, with man in his fallen state. Directly because of this difference, it aimed not at manipulation but at *liberation*. This Christian psychology was very different, and its morality was not enforced but emerged naturally from within the individual,[12] whereas the modern equivalent frequently views ethical activity as having to be imposed on individuals from outside.

It was P. D. Ouspensky who pointed out that modern psychology is primarily a tool of a medicine which studies pathologies, so that it sometimes calls itself "abnormal psychology," or of the "social sciences" which have sprung from this stream.

This ancient psychological method, then, was a form of *traditional knowledge,* having different rules for verification from those of modern psychological science, but they are genuine working rules. In its time, it had its own *consensus,* and this evolved over time as does any modern scientific consensus, but was very different from that of contemporary psychology because it had very different goals. The esoteric tradition necessarily used words with quite specific meanings different from their general usage. Divergence from this tradition led to these meanings being forgotten. Once this point is reached, and it was reached more than a millennium ago, a new process enters in: readers find themselves faced with words in a context in which these words appear meaningless. The result is that people regard such words as superstitions, in the sense that they seem to have no recognizable meaning. Thus what is first forgotten is afterwards discredited.

Words can be transmitted in writing, and this can be a dead process, but the meanings must also be transmitted, and this must be a living process.

Without the transmission of meaning from the same source, the particular meaning of the words is lost, and then, in that context, the words themselves become meaningless.

This was the reason for the researches that led to this book, and the purpose of this book is to restore some of those lost meanings.

This whole concept leads to a practical way of presenting these ideas. This can be put in modern terms by utilizing the word *recognition.* The goal of texts in this tradition, and the characteristic by which texts that genuinely belong to this tradition can be identified, is that they are written for recognition. The meaning of an idea must be understood and recognized (and the meaning of this particular idea too must be understood and recognized). We are not using the word *recognition* here in the sense of *public recognition.* Usually nothing was further from the minds of practitioners of this ancient science. They taught a traditional knowledge, and in it, their scientific method depended on the student's accepting the truth of what they taught, by discovering for himself and then *recognizing* what it was they were describing. The fact that they had in general a consensus about what was true makes it clear that they all in fact—although step by step, not immediately—came to recognize the same things. Experience will enable the present-day student who strives for such a level of accuracy to recognize that this situation, carried out rigorously, eliminates all possibility of doubt.

Saints Are Always Somewhere Else

For Westerners, the visible sign of the loss of the early kind of Christianity, of the loss of *metanoia* as a way of spiritual life, especially for those belonging to Protestant churches who today do not formally recognize new saints, is that saints always seem to live somewhere else or to have lived in some other time. Many of us, indeed, see this fact simply as a sign that we have outgrown such ideas as religion and sanctity. But this tells more about the person who believes it than about any wider reality. In this, young children often know better than their elders, for this mystery of the missing sanctity is really a most serious question for us all, and the sophistication, the cynicism that hides the question, is no more than a tissue of self-deception.

But to go back to that question with which I began. If you answer no, you have never met a saint, my next question for you would be: Why not? If you honestly believe you can answer "yes"—not "almost," or "there's someone I think is a saint," but an unequivocal "yes" to this question—my next is instead to ask you: How many saints have you met? The point of all this is to take a serious look at this question. Many of us will already realize that, whatever their own answer, many people now believe that the time of saints is past, that they do not occur any more, and have not occurred for many centuries. This is almost but not entirely true.

What did I know when I began my researches? I knew that some genuine saints have been recognized within the last century, more since 1800, particularly in Russia but also in Greece. But many of the list below were only canonized in 1988, with the millennium celebrations of the Russian Church. In fact, in this world the list of recent saints is actually considerably longer than one might expect . . . it is not the reality, but our view of it, that I am questioning. An incomplete list of recent saints includes:

— Saint Theophan the Recluse, born 1815, died 1894, canonized 1988 as part of the millennium celebrations of the Russian Church. As a young man he became a monk, then hieromonk (priest-monk), bishop, abbot, and finally anchorite. He guided thousands by mail and edited two of the world's greatest books on the life of prayer, as well as writing several other important works. His teachings help to clarify the inner tradition in modern terms, and are referred to frequently in this book.

— Saint Seraphim of Sarov, died 1833, whose teachings help to clarify one important factor of the inner tradition, so that they too are referred to in this book.

— Saint Therese of Lisieux, died 1897, who was called to the life of prayer as a child and became one of the great spiritual inspirations of the Roman Church. Her writings are referred to in this book.

— Saint John of Kronstadt, died 1908, a priest in the Russian naval town of Kronstadt, whose ability to help people reached so many that a series of guest houses had to be built to accommodate those who came to him.

— Saint Nektarios, died 1920, whose shrine on the Greek island of Aegina has in the past few years been the scene of many miracles, including miraculous conversions.

— Saint Arsenios of Cappadocia, died 1926, a saint who said very little, but who, over many years, worked a great number of miracles to assist those living around him.

— Saint Silouan of Athos, died 1933, a massive Russian peasant who nearly murdered someone in Russia, became desperate about his lack of self-control, and went to see Saint John of Kronstadt. From there he went to Athos on the advice of Saint John, and became a man of impressive abilities and very great spirituality. His teachings are referred to in this book in order to clarify one inner aspect of Christian tradition that is difficult to understand by drawing only on earlier sources.

Several saints have also been canonized by the Roumanian Church, but we have listed enough examples of recent Eastern saints.

In particular, you will notice that in this list there are no Protestant saints. It would be interesting to ask the Protestant churches whether, indeed, they believe that saints are created today or, more specifically, whether they have under consideration the canonization of any of their recent members. One might even ask what they imagine the significance of saints to be, beyond the obvious: that they are often very good role models, if only they weren't so impossible to follow. Certainly the Protestant churches have some very splendid people, but in the early church, that was not quite what the word *saint* meant; to the early Christians, a saint was "something else."

In fact, all the individuals listed above were in some sense direct followers of the early Fathers of the church. Nearly all of them (as well as certain others who will appear later) referred at some time to the Royal Road or Royal Way. The significance of both these facts will become increasingly apparent the further we read into this book.

When I asked my original question, I turned the question toward the audience as individuals, asking them another question that every sincere seeker should ask himself or herself. I asked them then, as I ask you now, which of you who think of yourselves as Christians has not asked the catch question: How can I be more Christian than I am now?

Or to put it another way:

— How can I free myself from my own bad habits?
— How can I learn to live to my own highest principles?
— How might I feel growing in my own heart the qualities described in the Sermon on the Mount?
— How can I learn to turn the other cheek?
— How can I love my enemies?

Behind this is a basic answer given by my researches. If people understood what my researches have confirmed—that saints are made holy, not born holy—then it would be possible at least to begin to answer these other questions, and that in such a way that we could understand how we ourselves might change if we wanted to.

Saints are made: with the help of our Lord, certainly, but made, not born holy. Those of us who want to see a better world might be well advised never to forget this.

From Investigation of the Past, a New Vision

As the Abbot of an Athos monastery wrote recently: "When the monk possesses the grace of repentance he knows the true God, not some idea of God."[13] In actual fact, the Christian esoteric or inner tradition is in every respect a true tradition that is the equal of the great inner traditions of the East. Unfortunately, due to certain accidents of history, the texts of the tradition have been so long unknown in the West that although they are now becoming available, their special meanings have failed to reach us. This has left them meaningless, which in turn has seemed to confirm the facile idea that they have now been disproved by science. Diluted to the point where it lost its power to produce results, and with its credibility weakened because its meaning has been lost, the inner tradition has proved an embarrassment to churches who wanted to appear "scientific," wanted to be accepted in circles that also *appeared* scientific. Because of this, the very idea of an inner tradition has been swept under the carpet when nobody was looking.

Yet it was the strength of psyche this part of Christian tradition gave to many individuals that explains the way the early martyrs of the church[14] made such an impression on those who saw them, so that the Christian church in its early centuries—before it became divided—almost entirely supplanted competing faiths.

The initial growth of the early church was the direct result of its inner power to transform the individual. As this ability has declined below a certain point, the church itself has begun to lose membership.

Whether we believe that, as I shall suggest later in the book, a spiritual reawakening is now taking place, or believe only that it *should* do so, with either of these viewpoints we will see the value of recovering a lost Christian tradition of knowledge about the inner experience that some of the most valued members of the church—among them saints, bishops, abbots, monks, hermits, and "learned doctors"—have accumulated over nearly twenty centuries, but particularly what they learned in the early days of the church, when the initial energy given by gospel and resurrection was still at its most intense.

The background to the loss of this great reservoir of truth is that, in two thousand years, Christianity has built up an enormous corpus of knowledge and ideas. Nobody can know all of this, and so everybody has had to be selective. More than this, there are both historical and psychological reasons why this selective process has developed a particular bias over the centuries, so that some of the knowledge acquired by the church during its early years has for long been forgotten—either it has been totally forgotten, or in other cases the words are remembered, but part of their meaning, their significance, has been forgotten, so that they are effectively *misunderstood*. The criteria for interpretation have changed with the times, until what is believed now as a result of reading the gospel is entirely different from what was believed in the early days of Christianity. Now, if the early meanings are made available again, we find them difficult to understand, and if we do get close to them, we discover that it is even more difficult for us to see their value to us, their relevance to our personal questions and to the main questions of the civilization of which we are part.

The connections have worn thin with time, although the problem of the misunderstanding of inner knowledge is not a new one. We no longer have the intellectual tools to recover that early knowledge; we have replaced them with a "newer model." As long ago as the third century Origen, head of the Alexandrian catechetical school previously led by

Clement of Alexandria, wrote that the Bible should be interpreted in ways other than historical, because in the historical interpretation, the inconsistencies of the text make it look foolish. Sixteen centuries later, vast numbers of scholars now study the Bible simply as a history text and, in the attempt to maintain "scientific objectivity," regard it is misleading to study it against criteria other than those of history.

But nobody asks the question, If this is only history, why is it studied so much more than other historical texts?

A commentator in the 1993 issue of *Bible Review* claims that to follow the historical interpretation conscientiously it is necessary to disbelieve in basic tenets of Christianity, such as the Resurrection. One can only say of such people that they may believe something, but they have no Christian faith, for Christian faith is not blind belief in all and everything, but only in what Boris Mouravieff would call the objects of faith, objects outlined if not exhaustively defined in the Creed and, for inner Christianity, particularly in the Nicene Creed. "If you do not believe," nor will you understand the writings of men of faith: this kind of modern interpretation ignores the intentions of the authors of works such as the books of the Bible, assuming that you can interpret a passage in the same way whatever the intentions of those who originally wrote it. It sometimes even assumes that you can interpret it idiosyncratically, from your own personal point of view, and still consider that you are passing on to others a valid view of the text that you are interpreting. Such an approach is only credible to those who are completely ignorant of the process of writing in a conscientious way, or who imagine that earlier authors were such fools that the content even of the great books of the Bible is *accidental*, and that no specific purpose existed for them other than the today fashionable objective of "self-expression." Those with experience of *intentional* writing, writing for a specific aim, will realize that in such work the aim determines the method of expression, and that only an awareness of that original aim can accurately reveal the *intended* meanings of certain words whose interpretation is determined by their context.

In particular, very great care is needed when interpreting even the most open text about inner teachings. As parables to illustrate inner truths the early Fathers of the church repeatedly used biblical texts that appear to have a purely outer meaning. We must also realize that since the second century, when the inner teaching went underground, those texts which illustrate some spiritual lesson with examples from the lives of those who had passed through the relevant experience in the past—as in Gregory of Nyssa's *Life of Moses* and other works on the same theme—actually were intended to be misinterpreted by anyone who had insufficient inner experience to understand their deeper meaning. The effects of taking such texts to have merely historical significance is just the confusion we observe in modern theology.

One problem group of Greek words used throughout the history of the early church—in the Gospels (particularly Saint Mark), in the epistles of Paul, and in the writings of the early Fathers of the church—was that whose common modern form is *gnosis*. We can find records of the use of this word not remotely linked to what is now popularly called Gnosticism, as *gnosis* was originally simply a term for a special kind of *knowledge*, one of the properties of which is that it is not obtained through the senses.

This idea, which will be discussed further in chapter 11, was summarized by the translator of Clement's *Stromata* thus: "By 'gnosis,' Clement understood the perfect knowledge of all that relates to God, His nature, and dispensations. He speaks of a twofold knowledge, one, common to all men, and born of sense; the other, the genuine 'gnosis'. . . .[15] This latter is not born with men, but must be gained and by practice formed into a habit. The initiated find its perfection in a loving mysticism, which this never-failing love makes lasting."[16] And Clement himself wrote: "And the gnosis itself is that which has descended by transmission to a few, having been imparted unwritten by the apostles. Hence, then, knowledge or wisdom ought to be exercised up to the eternal and unchangeable habit of contemplation."[17]

But then, this book exists to help us recreate those old interpretive tools and with them again to make connection with that ancient knowledge, through just those channels used by those holy men of old, through three processes:

— To draw on personal observation and direct experience, related to the comments of others, so as to discover certain current concerns, personal as well as those concerning our whole civilization; to take cognizance of the experiences that give rise to them; to give an idea of why they have been forgotten or *ignored* for so many centuries; and finally to show how they are fundamental concerns that have lasted as long as Christendom, and are often rooted in inner and often mystical experiences that have recurred since the earliest days of the Christian era

— To illuminate this by study of the esoteric tradition, so as to show how the early Christian tradition of inner knowledge relates to both personal and social concerns and experiences that have become important in our contemporary life

— Finally, to comment as necessary on the relation of the two, in keeping with the methods of that early tradition, and analyze them with tools of contemporary but not purely intellectual understanding

It should be noted in this last that this kind of understanding must include a full intellectual content, and with this there is always a danger that, to the untrained mind, such a text will look as if it is pure intellectualism.

As Saint Nilus of Sora once did, I must ask pardon of my reader if anything appears in this work that is "inconsistent with the sense of truth." To me, this means that if you do not *recognize* something from my description, I would ask you to classify it as untested, until experience makes its accuracy—or inaccuracy—clear to you. But this is a good point to introduce an ancient practice sometimes described in odd corners of the tradition, known today as *pondering*. To understand this book, certain parts of it—and there may be many of them—need to be *pondered*. Today we are so used to speed-reading and other methods of reading superficially, that we need to know a technique that most people perhaps once knew: what it means to ponder a statement.

To ponder a passage of a book we should first read it with great care, making sure that we have clearly dealt with each of its statements separately. Then we should ponder each statement on its own, comparing it with our own experience, until we *recognize* what it describes. When we have *recognized* what is described in each statement, we may reconsider the passage as a whole. At this point a characteristic sign is that it will seem less interesting. After all, it is not "news," it is telling only things we already know. This sensation is a sign of success in our pondering.

Without having learned to ponder, one should not read serious esoteric texts.

Chapter 1

The Royal Road of the Early Church

The inner tradition is a Christian equivalent of Zen or Raja Yoga, both of which contain extensive psychological teachings, but the technicalities of this Christian equivalent, known in the gospel as the Way,[1] have never been known in the West. Now modern travel and scholarship have given us access to some of the most important of the forgotten psychological teachings of this Christian tradition, but it is almost too late. The very words have lost their meaning, so that new methods of research are now needed to rediscover the inner sense of these texts, the ambitious aim that forms the subject matter of this book. In its full form, the psychological method to which I refer represents what was known in the early church as the Royal Road. This name was once given to certain therapeutic psychological and psycho-spiritual techniques developed by Christians who followed Christ's narrow way.[2] The Royal Road was a science based on the gospel teaching about the cure of the soul—by curing the *nous*, sometimes known as the eye of the soul. This leads to what was then known as the illumination of the nous, and so develops the hidden potential or talents of the individual, once described by Saint Paul as the Gifts of the Spirit.

The first part of this book gives us glimpses of this Royal Road, as it was described by the church's great masters of spirituality, from Clement of Alexandria in the second century, to Pierre Caussade in the eighteenth and, in our own time, to the enigmatic figure of Boris Mouravieff. Here we will discover that this ancient path is not simply a Christianized form of India's Rajah Yoga, and that the early Fathers of the church regarded the name Royal Road as a direct synonym for the Narrow Way of the gospel.

The similarities and differences between this way and Yoga are important. One is that this Christian Royal Way is entirely in keeping with Christian theology, at least on the level where it is justly said that, whatever their differences in doctrine, the churches are charismatically one.[3] Its most fundamental technique is very different from Yoga, being based on the gospel idea that what is impossible to man is possible to God. More important today, although its practical work is entirely dependent on holding a traditional prescientific Christian worldview, yet it contains a detailed spiritual psychology as great and as precise as any belonging to the religions of the East. It is in truth an ancient science, and the great hesychast master Saint Gregory Palamas wrote about it that "truly this seems to me to be a craft above all crafts, and a science above all sciences, to lead a man, the wiliest and most changeable creature."[4] This craft is said to introduce us to the kingdom of heaven, in the bliss of the uncreated light of God: in the Greek this is *theoria*. So, say the fathers, on this Way the vision of God becomes light, and not fire for us.

The chapters that follow this describe certain practical aspects of this Royal Road and show how certain ideas in Christian doctrine have been misunderstood, a misunderstanding that has had serious consequences for what was once a Christian civilization.

The Path of Heart

In certain monasteries that are dead to the world yet infinitely alive within, an old kind of Christianity is still understood. It does not speak to us of how to get what we want. It does not offer us heaven in return for taking out membership. It is entirely deaf to our everyday desires. So, against a background of television and consumer goods and easy living, what it offers seems meaningless to most of us, just as it seemed when Jesus offered it in Palestine almost two thousand years ago. But in stillness, in the shade of the Tree of Life, when we begin that inner dialogue with God that is our birthright, but which exists in its pure form only in the garden of the heart—in openness of eye and mind, there we will find the meanings and the joyfulness of those old texts, those doctrines that involve the heart, so that what they convey is not only thought, but felt. This reuniting of the thinking faculty to the heart might be described as the great secret of Inner Christianity, only it is not really a secret so much as something unnoticed because of our lack of understanding.

To read about these things and enjoy, to ponder them and understand, we have to declare a moratorium on analytical methods and avoid debate, even with ourselves. As Socrates once discovered, only when we recognize that in a special sense ideas are not knowledge—and in what sense this is true—can we link the mind to the heart. It was just these motivations which led monasticism to emerge in the Christian world as a reaction to the establishment of the church. Metropolitan Anthony of Sourozh once described this beginning of monasticism in a talk:

> . . . the monastic movement began as a reaction of men and women of depth and spiritual intensity against the lukewarm . . . Christian society that had evolved as a result of the imperial edict giving a right of existence and later predominance to the Christian Church. These people left the city, left the countries of their origin to go to places where Christianity was not watered down, and where they could create communities full of ascetic endeavor, of ruthless determination, of radicalism that allowed them to make of the gospel nothing else than the total of their lives.
>
> Some on the other hand left their place of origin, whether it was the great cities of the empire or small villages, because danger had come upon them, physical danger or moral danger, danger of personal corruption or danger of physical destruction. These people left in a state of frailty, but a frailty which, aware of itself, was not prepared to be used by the surrounding world of people who had authority or power over them to destroy them as human beings, as Christians. Others left their places of origin because, surrounded not only by lukewarm Christians but also by a largely pagan society, they fell into despair at the emptiness of life. This is something which we find now in all the countries where atheism predominates, people who are confronted with despair and therefore move onwards and try to find either an interior situation, the kingdom of God within them, or an outer situation, be it prison, concentration camp, or monastery, where they can find another kind of safety—not the safety of the body, not the comfort of the mind and their emotions, but the safety of knowing that they are anchored in God, and that life has a meaning . . . and they went into the desert . . . into solitude, into the unknown . . . into a desert still unknown or still unexplored by others.[5]

To this day, a gentle—and occasionally not so gentle—conflict between monasticism and the moralistic element in the church shows that the forces that led to monasticism as a reaction have not yet disappeared. In fact, they have grown stronger, and in this century of politics, communication, and tourism,[6] the inmost heart of monasticism may not survive this intensified pressure. P. D. Ouspensky, in his early lectures, wrote of this path: "We shall now speak about the conditions necessary for development because it must be remembered that although development is possible, it is at the same time very rare and requires a great number of external and internal conditions. The first is that a man must understand his position, his difficulties, and his possibilities, and must have either a very strong desire to get out of his present state or a very strong inclination for the new, for the unknown state which must come with the change."[7]

Even today, in the monasticism of the Eastern Church, much is conveyed in unwritten ways. I was once talking to a monk about where they had learned the traditional methods. He listed a few books in Greek. I asked if any of these described the complete tradition. "No," he replied. I asked again what book contained the basics of the tradition. "None," he replied. "Where do you obtain these basics?" I asked him, somewhat frustrated. "It's the tradition," he replied, and would say no more on the subject.

What is this tradition, and what does it tell those who follow it? Many things, but here is an example of great practical merit from Saint John Cassian, who came from the African deserts to found some of the earliest monasteries in Western Europe. He wrote that to remain on this Royal Road was possible only through persistent efforts to discriminate.[8] He also wrote of many monks he knew who had lost the Way, asking: "What was it, then, that made them stray from the straight path? In my opinion it was simply that they did not possess the grace of discrimination; for it is this virtue that teaches a man to walk along the Royal Road, swerving neither to the right through immoderate self-control, nor to the left through indifference and laxity."[9]

Throughout the centuries, this path known as the Royal Way has been a common but barely recognized thread in Christianity. A typical example is how Clement of Alexandria linked this Royal Way to the classical narrow way of the gospel, writing: "And as, while there is one royal highway, there are many others, some leading to a precipice, some to a rushing river or to a deep sea, no one will shrink from traveling by reason of the diversity, but will make use of the safe, and royal, and frequented way." And he also wrote elsewhere: "Whence, 'Seek and ye shall find,' holding on by the truly Royal Road, and not deviating.' "[10]

When we look for it, we will discover that often the term *Royal Way* or *Royal Road* is not capitalized, nor treated as a proper noun by translators, suggesting that in a time of secrecy, some effort was made to put this term in such a way that only those familiar with it would recognize its significance. But what, in essence, is this Royal Way? Certainly there is "one way," but there are many "ways" of walking it. Gurdjieff talked about what he called the "sly man's pill." To find salvation, he tells us, the fakir, the man who works with physical exercises, spends sixteen hours a day on them; the monk, taking the way of the heart, spends twelve; the sly man, the man of understanding, simply takes a pill each day. The pill is one of a selection of methods—described in a later chapter—referred to as noetic ascesis.

Pray for Help

A major element in the esoteric tradition takes the form of teachings of different kinds. Oral teachings help to eliminate error, and at one time these were conveyed by those called to be teachers of whom Saint Paul spoke. Sometimes they are embedded in the liturgies of the early church. And because language is limited in what it can convey, there is a whole unwritten doctrine, much of which is not even spoken. The non-verbal teaching is more difficult to find and to understand, but when found, it greatly reduces the possibilities of error.

Similar methods are described in India in a parable in which a man with a thorn in his foot finds a second thorn with which to extract the first. Once successful in this, both thorns are thrown away. This parable can be understood on several levels, but is not normally presented with any indication that deeper levels of meaning exist, so it conveys only the idea that good ideas or doctrines remove bad ideas; this, although valuable for its breadth, does not have the depth of Macarius's presentation (see p. 95) and the Christian interpretation he gives. And of course the whole point of this Christian method is that it uses two new thorns, the Word and the Spirit, to extract the single unwanted thorn. The second thorn, the action of the Spirit, is not to be thrown away; the whole aim is to make it *permanent*. If it stays with us, it keeps us free from involvement in externals.

But in the Christian tradition, there is also a quite different way of looking at this question. At a certain point on the journey—as described in the parable of the prodigal son, where his father comes out to meet the returning prodigal—God will take us by the hand, as it were, and begin to show us the correct meaning of the teaching. In the West, this is called "infused contemplation": "It is He [Christ] who truly shows how we are to know ourselves. It is He who reveals the Father of the universe to whom He wills, and as far as human nature can comprehend. 'For no man knoweth the Son but the Father, nor the Father but the Son, and he to whom the Son shall reveal Him.' "[11]

When we talk about the Royal Way, then, we are talking about an *oral tradition* based on a psychology of prayer; not prayer used simply as an exercise for the mind, but practiced for transcending the mind through a true *synergy,* the core of which is a request for the help of an all-powerful God to change in ourselves what we cannot change by our own unaided efforts. Properly practiced, this expands into a two-way flow expressed in the classic formula in which "it is not I who prays, but Christ who prays in me."

This is well understood in the Eastern Church, where the interpretation and expression of the written teachings have always been shaped by an unwritten tradition coming down through the centuries. Although it is commonly believed that there is a divergence between these methods in Eastern and Western churches, this divergence is more in terminology and contemporary practice than in basic principles. At least one of those who refers to the Royal Road is Roman Catholic in background,[12] although I have not often seen it named in this way outside the Eastern Church. The teachings of Saint John of the Cross, of the Western authors in the tradition of Saint Denys, Thomas à Kempis and Jan van Ruysbroek, and the anonymous author of the *Cloud of Unknowing,* among others, basing their teachings on those of Dionysius the Areopagite,[13] also clearly belong to this type of prayer teaching.

Over the many centuries of its currency, different authors have associated the Royal Way specifically with different aspects of practical esotericism, and in Pierre Caussade's marvelous book *Abandonment to Divine Providence,* it is abundantly clear that he understood this same Way, by name, where he writes: "O Love eternal, adorable, ever fruitful, and ever marvelous! May the divine operations of my God be my book, my doctrine, my science. In it are my thoughts, my words, my actions and my sufferings. Not by consulting your former works shall I become what You would have me to be; but by receiving You in everything. By that ancient road, *the only Royal Road* [emphasis added], the road of our fathers, shall I be enlightened, and shall speak as they spoke. It is thus that I would imitate them all, quote them all, copy them all."[14]

Others in this century have uncovered evidence of this Way: in 1973 a Harvard scholar named Morton Smith summarized certain ideas he said had been described by Clement of Alexandria, both in his *Stromata* and in a letter which Smith attributed to Clement partly on the basis of the extremely close coincidence of such elements. He tells us that this second-century author claimed that, for prepared students, Christianity should:

> develop or improve certain psychological qualities of human individuals;
> include "development to perfection of gnosis," which term is

used specifically by Clement and reported by Morton Smith: lead to what the Eastern Church calls *theosis* or deification. This result of gnosis can be obtained in this life.

And finally, he added that this gnosis is "a result of instruction in three stages." In all of this, Smith seems to have quite accurately defined the practical aims of esoteric teaching. It is worth noting that he also says in this book that "Progress in this 'gnosis' or inner knowledge is then said to be a condition for admission into the 'greater mysteries.' "[15]

The General Resurrection

Here we come back to the question of the Fall of Adam. In their inner meaning, the Fall and the Resurrection of the dead relate to consciousness. Genesis tells how Adam fell as a result of eating the fruit of the tree of the knowledge of good and evil. This makes it clear that knowledge played a part in the Fall of man. The idea of the Fall is exactly like the idea of the Resurrection in one way. To external religion it has only one meaning: the Fall happened *once,* the "General Resurrection" will come on one particular day in the future. But if this is so, then it is a purely external event. Yet certain of the early Fathers of the church, giving an esoteric view of Christianity, have made it clear that, to them, the Resurrection exists in three ways: it does exist outside us, in the past as a single event, and in the future as a universal event, but it also exists *now,* in any moment, always accessible, always possible if rarely actual *within us.* The same is true of the Fall, which happens to us time after time. One of the Fathers in the *Philokalia* wrote of the life to come that:

> In saying this (that we must seek to enter the Kingdom while we are still alive), we are not forgetting the blessings of the life to come or limiting the universal reward to the present life. We are simply affirming that it is necessary in the first place to have the grace of the Holy Spirit energizing the heart and so, in proportion to this energizing, to enter into the kingdom of heaven. The Lord made this clear in saying: "The kingdom of heaven is within you" [Luke 17:21]. The Apostle too said the same: "Faith is the substance of things hoped for" [Hebrews 11:1]. "Run, that you may reach your goal" [I Corinthians 9:26]. "Examine yourselves whether you are in the faith. . . . Do you not know . . . that Jesus Christ is in you unless you are worthless [2 Corinthians 13:5]."[16]

Experience is closely linked with consciousness. The Resurrection is also a raising of consciousness, and the inner meaning of the Fall of man

is a description of a universal fall in our state of consciousness. (But this
idea of consciousness is an idea that is easily misunderstood.) It is possible
to experience these inner meanings in our own lives; resurrection in fire
is an uncommon experience, but to fall again into inner darkness is common enough. Here is the Christian view of the transformation of consciousness, hidden in mythological language.

This view is confirmed by the way Macarius the Great, whose works
are of the highest importance to monastics of the Eastern Church, describes how, in the tradition, Moses is used as an example of a resurrection
in life:

> In a double way, therefore, the blessed Moses shows us what
> glory true Christians will receive in the resurrection: namely,
> the glory of light and the spiritual delights of the Spirit which
> even now they are deemed worthy to possess interiorly. Be-
> cause of this, these gifts of the Spirit will then redound also in
> their bodies. The saints even now possess this glory in their
> souls, as said above, but it will then cover and clothe their
> naked bodies. It will sweep them up into heaven and we will
> at last come to rest, both body and soul, with the Lord forever.
>
> When God created Adam, he did not furnish him with
> material wings as birds have, but he prepared for him the
> wings of the holy Spirit. The same he plans on giving him at
> the resurrection, to lift him and direct him wherever the Spirit
> wishes. These wings the saints already now are deemed wor-
> thy to possess to fly up mentally to the realm of heavenly
> thoughts.
>
> For Christians live in another world, eat from another
> table, are clothed differently, prefer different enjoyment, differ-
> ent dialogue, and a different mentality. . . . Therefore, also in
> the resurrection their bodies will be worthy to receive those
> eternal blessings of the Holy Spirit. They will be permeated
> with that glory which their souls in this life have already
> experienced.[17]

Unchanging Truth

The idea of unchanging truth, encapsulated in the concept of the
Perennial Philosophy, has at least three different but related meanings.
One reflects the insights of Plato that the truth of the spirit refers to that
which is eternal and timeless and hence unchanging. This concept has

gained a special meaning in the Christian Church, whose God—according to the Bible but more clearly in the words of the early Fathers—is eternal and unchanging yet loving and in a special sense personal. The second meaning is that those facts about human life that have to do with the approach of that life to the eternal also tend to show very little change over the centuries. Our spiritual potential changes little, if at all, reflecting the unchanging center of the inner world, while our everyday, worldly nature changes through the years and reflects the changeability of the outside world.

The third meaning is that the true teaching, the esoteric tradition, changes very little—and does so, when it changes, *organically.* Unlike modern scientific thought, esoteric truths are never replaced by new paradigms. The occasional new discoveries that do occur in esotericism are added to those that have gone before.

Those alive today whose experience confirms the conclusions of the inner or esoteric teaching will accept that, as Huxley suggested in the title to his *Perennial Philosophy,* truth does not change, and that the original form of the inner teaching in the early days of the Church was little different from that which appears to be necessary today. The small changes that are needed are due almost entirely to changes in educational and other factors, perhaps evolutionary, that modify human character in different historical epochs.

At the risk of appearing Platonic, one can say that the goal of the spiritual life in the Eastern Church, *theosis* or deification, is the establishment of a living relationship with the unchanging. But it is necessary to understand this in a way that is both experiential and Christian: not to attempt to define or limit the Lord by this term, nor to demand to see Him "face to face," but simply to "locate" Him, to describe the "direction" in which one can relate to Him—a direction more dependent on human limitations than on any illusory possibility of restricting or "placing" the divine in some human scheme. And the New Testament tells us: "If ye fulfill the royal law according to the scripture, Thou shalt love thy neighbour as thyself, ye do well" (James 2.8).

Loss of Ancient Knowledge

How did it happen that this psychological knowledge, which was a mature science in the Christian world long before the development of our modern physical sciences,[18] became lost?

Often the inner changes of history have the simplest causes. In this case, for example, with the decline of the Roman Empire, book learning became the almost exclusive concern of the clergy. This had the effect of an unplanned but effective censorship. To this was added mistranslation and careless copying, and there is frequent evidence as well of deliberate distortion. By the late medieval era these causes had led to an almost total loss of the psychological knowledge of the previous era. The fact of the matter is that most of these teachings never reached the West in usable form. The Christianity of the Fathers has never been tried in the Western world. In summary:

1. What is now known as Gnosticism—different from the Christian concept *gnosis*—survived only as a few short-lived sects with conflicting teachings.
2. Much pre-Christian Greek thought was lost by accident or by monastic censorship, although other elements were preserved to the present day in the writings of the early Fathers and those who have followed in their spiritual footsteps.

What survived was understood only by a few. Psychology in those days was regarded as a form of philosophy, and this was so thoroughly lost in medieval times that one of the great scholars of this century, Etienne Gilson, speaking particularly of the Greek form of philosophical thought, wrote that: "there is no philosophy between the end of the 3rd century after Christ . . . and the middle of the 13th century, with the appearance of the *Summa Contra Gentiles*."[19] (It was just then that the inner tradition went underground.) Thus:

3. From the time of Clement, the outer church had become increasingly closed to the inner tradition.
4. From the time of the establishment of the church under Constantine, what survived of the inner tradition had mostly gone into seclusion, so that practice of the Christian inner tradition was almost entirely limited to a few monastic locations, most of them in the eastern marches of Christendom, and the tradition became virtually invisible to most individuals.

The division between Eastern and Western churches became wider, until the inner tradition of the Royal Way barely survived except in the monasticism of the Eastern Church. There it survives today in certain special places and was restored by certain specific individuals. Saint Nilus of Sora, in thirteenth-century Russia, commented on monks of the time by quoting the earlier Philotheus of Sinai on the lack of experience of certain monks (quoted in chapter 9).[20]

This could have been said today, particularly because the Western Church, in which the inner tradition has had less influence on the prevalent culture, took a different form. In the thirteenth century, it faced an influx of Arab translations from, and commentaries on, the works of Aristotle, and in this form Greek philosophy reentered the mainstream of Western thought in a different way. This faced the Western church with the need once again to resolve problems with conflicting ideas. Because, this time, the inner tradition was distant or hidden from sight, the solution was different.

It was at this point that the debate between the hesychast Gregory Palamas and the Italian philosopher Barlaam, who proclaimed that intellect was the means for knowing God,[21] was resolved schismatically in a literal sense, by forming or reinforcing the rift between Eastern and Western churches. To this day, theologians of the Eastern Church believe that Palamas carried the day, while the Western churches believe that Barlaam proved the primacy of intellect as a basis for faith.

Thus the schism between the two churches was at root a schism between head and heart.

On Mount Athos today, considerably more than a thousand monks follow the Royal Way of the heart as practicing hesychasts. Before the First World War, there were many more. In earlier times, most monks joined in their teens. Now some come in their fifties and sixties, when the process known as "cutting off the will" (described later, chapter 10)—the basic form of obedience for the monk of the Royal Way—has become impossible for them: the way the mind of Western man normally develops with age makes it impossible. Today the modern world is beginning to reach out to those distant monks, as a flood of tourists and pilgrims disrupts monastic life and even creates traffic problems on the tracks of the Holy Mountain. At certain times of the year, large groups of young Greek men visit the mountain with the encouragement of their families, but often with little real interest in what they find there. For monks, as for lay people, for all people in the world, the question now is: How can the Way be found when it is impossible to isolate oneself for so many hours each day? Conditions change and, in the past, ways of seeking God have changed with them. Saint Nilus of Sora in his monastic rule wrote:

> In the past it was not only the holy fathers living as hermits in the solitude of the desert who kept themselves under spiritual restraints and attained grace and purity of soul: this discipline was likewise maintained by monks leading a community life, and even by those who had not removed from the world but lived in large cities, such as Symeon the New Theologian and his starets, Symeon the Studite, of the great Studion

monastery in so vast and populous a city as Constantinople, whose spiritual gifts shone like stars.

Blessed Hesychius of Jerusalem says: "Just as it is impossible to preserve life without eating and drinking, so it is impossible to achieve anything spiritual without that guarding of the mind which is called 'sobering,'[22] even for those who force themselves to avoid sin for fear of the pain of hell."

The technique of this exquisite, light-giving action, according to Symeon the New Theologian, is communicated to many souls through instruction; but there are some who are enabled by ardent faith to receive it directly from God.[23]

In the modern world, how many of us—even monks today, when many Western monks and nuns are forced to take jobs—can give sixteen hours a day to the quest? Yet the ordinary monk in community needs little special knowledge. He just does what he is told. But he must do it for long hours, and the abbot, the confessor, the elder who leads the monk, does need knowledge.

The Sources of My Investigation

Much of the knowledge of this Way belongs to a time when theology and psychology, philosophy and science, were all one discipline. This ancient *unity of knowledge* was one of the reasons why the modern individual cannot easily come to grips with older forms of the subject: we simply don't approach it in the same way. With the specialization of modern thought have come differences in the classification and expression of knowledge. These form rifts deeper than those caused by the need to translate from different languages, so that we can only bridge them through appropriate experience, and not in merely conceptual ways.

In this, the very types of knowledge are often named differently. Monastics in the Eastern Church today speak of *anthropology,* but to them this is a unitary form of knowledge, fundamentally different in structure from modern knowledge, and containing what were clearly psychological and theological statements. For example, there was a way of seeing theology that was essential to that early Christian psychological understanding. Rooted in the Bible, these teachings used the terminology of their time—including a psychological terminology which they had in common with the Greek and Roman philosophers of the Stoic school, a fact confirmed by a number of investigators.

Many differences make those ancient teachings hard to understand today: different terminology, the differences in the questions they asked then, the differences in texts over time and due to errors in copying and translation, and the shift of meaning that occurs when such ideas are not put into practice. Because of this, little of this early knowledge is understood today, and what is still understood has been so totally absorbed into modern thought—and so distorted and fragmented by attempting to "correct" it to fit the scientific views of our time—that we do not recognize its origins. Yet much of this ancient knowledge has survived in different forms. Some of them remain within the mainstream of the churches, often the Eastern. Some survive in the records of specific developments in the history of the church, and for historical reasons which will become clear, some have gone fully underground, so that when they emerged it was without the form and often without the approval of the church. Nevertheless, if one is willing to break free of the boundaries of specialization, there are a number of sources from which this ancient knowledge can be recovered, and not always in fragmentary form.

The Bible
plus the Apocrypha,
including the Dead Sea Scrolls

The Writings of
the Fathers of the Church

Eastern Monastic Practice

Church Liturgies

Special Teachings

Great Spiritual Texts

Alchemical and Mystery Teachings

Figure 1.1   Sources in which the forgotten teachings can be found today.

The Teachings of the Bible

It was said in the New Testament that Christianity will be complete when the gospel is preached throughout the world (Matthew 24:13–14). The Bible has now been readily available throughout the world for some decades, yet in another way the time is not yet come. We have described why the inner tradition which, in the first years of the Christian era, produced a different kind of person, has not yet reached the part of the world in which we live today. That form of Christianity has not been tried and failed, but has never yet been tried. In the first centuries of the church, at the time when Christianity produced its greatest results, men and women such as the Martyr Polycarp were able to withstand torture and fire and continue singing or praising God throughout. The modern individual finds this example unbelievable. Reports in texts such as the second-century *Ecclesiastical History* of Eusebius are convincing in their detail. The fact is that the Christianity of that time was tried, and it succeeded. But a second fact is that the form of Christianity that produced those results never reached us. It was the inner meaning of the gospel that worked those changes in people's hearts.

One effect of this situation is that if we admit that the Bible does have inner teachings—a conclusion that is inescapable if we are honest with ourselves—then, because the early inner interpretations have been forgotten, we often describe them as obscure, because narrow or purely invented modern interpretations have more and more become "common coinage." In general, meanings that could previously be discovered with a little effort can now be discovered in the Bible only after we have found clues in the early Fathers.

The Apocrypha

It has been suggested that the discovery of the so-called Dead Sea Scrolls, and particularly of the Gospel of Thomas, at this time of need is little short of a miracle. Indeed, there is little doubt of the value of some of the texts, particularly the *Gospel According to Thomas*, in filling in some of the gaps that remain in the record of early Christian teaching, nor of the fact that that gospel seems to be particularly comprehensible to the intellectual man of the modern era. Certain texts of the classical Apocrypha also repay investigation, but do not play any direct part in this particular study.

The Fathers of the Church

Immediately following the era of persecution, when many devout Christians moved away from the centers of civilization into the deserts and hard places, a great inner tradition grew up in the church concerning ways of achieving the inner states that form part of Christian possibility. That was the Christianity of the early Fathers. It was a small movement, which probably reached *and was understood by* a very small population.

To study the Fathers can provide us with a key that makes the Bible more accessible to us, and so invests it with greater meaning. The meanings assigned in this book to biblical texts are examples of this, and have been generated in the studies on which this book is based. The problem has been the enormous delay. At the time when they were written, these texts never reached the rest of the world at large, although they survived in three forms: in a great collection of texts of astonishing clarity and depth; in a feeble undercurrent that spread through Europe as a sometimes "secret" inner tradition; and in monastic form which preserved the experience better than either of the other two forms.

The fate of the written knowledge is one story. For far more than a thousand years after it was written down, printing did not exist. For an even longer time, modern book distribution and other forms of communications did not exist. Until now, the texts of this tradition have remained little known in and wholly unassimilated by the West. Much of that knowledge was preserved in writing only in the Alexandrian and Syrian churches. Some but not all of this reached the Greeks through Clement of Alexandria, Origen, and the saints known as the Cappadocian Fathers. More written knowledge from these Middle Eastern sources reached Russia about a century ago. Some reached the West from Russia and Greece in the first twenty years of this century, normally in obscure scholarly translations laden with Greek and Latin that made them wholly inaccessible to the majority of men and women.

But this—which forms a true discipline in the widest sense of the term—has never in two thousand years been generally available in complete form. The unwritten teachings have been even more inaccessible.

The written teachings of the early Fathers exist in two main forms: in the writings of the Fathers themselves, and in those of their successors, more recent teachers or authors in the same tradition, including a very few members of the Western churches who have obviously followed in the same line of work, and including monks and nuns and occasionally other clergy of the Eastern Church right down to the present time. Figure 1.2 shows the relation of a few key figures in this tradition. Now, by modern

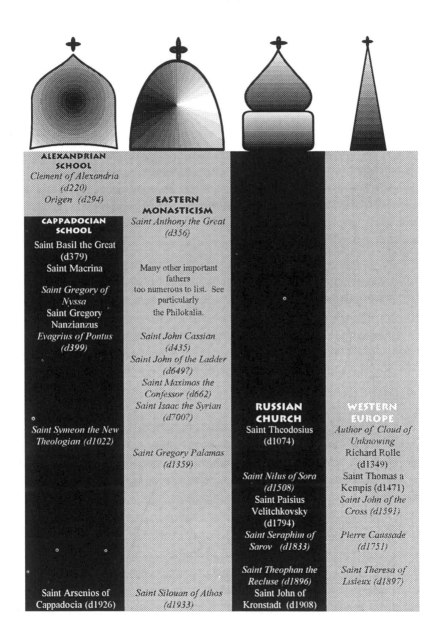

ALEXANDRIAN SCHOOL
Clement of Alexandria (d220)
Origen (d294)

CAPPADOCIAN SCHOOL
Saint Basil the Great (d379)
Saint Macrina
Saint Gregory of Nyssa
Saint Gregory Nanzianzus
Evagrius of Pontus (d399)

Saint Symeon the New Theologian (d1022)

Saint Arsenios of Cappadocia (d1926)

EASTERN MONASTICISM
Saint Anthony the Great (d356)

Many other important fathers too numerous to list. See particularly the Philokalia.

Saint John Cassian (d435)
Saint John of the Ladder (d649?)
Saint Maximos the Confessor (d662)
Saint Isaac the Syrian (d700?)

Saint Gregory Palamas (d1359)

Saint Silouan of Athos (d1933)

RUSSIAN CHURCH
Saint Theodosius (d1074)

Saint Nilus of Sora (d1508)
Saint Paisius Velitchkovsky (d1794)
Saint Seraphim of Sarov (d1833)

Saint Theophan the Recluse (d1896)
Saint John of Kronstadt (d1908)

WESTERN EUROPE
Author of Cloud of Unknowing
Richard Rolle (d1349)
Saint Thomas à Kempis (d1471)
Saint John of the Cross (d1591)

Pierre Caussade (d1751)

Saint Theresa of Lisieux (d1897)

Figure 1.2   Diagram of the history of the tradition. Names shown in italics are quoted or discussed in this book.

ways of publishing translation and explanation, this unique knowledge—some nearly two thousand years old—is becoming more readily accessible in its original form, but its assimilation to Western thought is only just beginning. Some texts that are only just being translated into English were available in French in the 1930s or the 1950s. But in the English-speaking world this is still an unknown teaching.

In view of the difficulties in reaching this knowledge today, what seems to be only an accident of history may be a greater miracle still. In this second half of the twentieth century, more than seventeen hundred years after many of them were written, much larger numbers of the works of the early Fathers of the church, until now inaccessible to the ordinary reader, are at last becoming available to us in English translation.

But why are these texts significant, and to whom are they significant? Their significance is that they give an unequivocal answer to an important question. They do not merely say, but clearly demonstrate, that a different quality was possessed by early Christianity. Because of this, they are significant to all Christians who have ever raised the question of Christian imperfection, have ever wondered whether Christianity was always flawed as it is now, who have ever asked the catch question: Why must Christian action so often differ from Christian intention?

These ancient texts are significant to every Christian who ever asked questions such as: How can I be more Christian? How can I free myself from my own bad habits? How can I learn to live the commandment; to feel growing in my own heart the qualities described in the Sermon on the Mount? How can I turn the other cheek? How can I love my enemies?

The early Fathers of the church continually asked questions like these; they gave their whole lives to them in a way we can hardly believe today, and in so doing, they began to find answers—answers that help us when we face the same questions today. It is the discoveries of those ancient men and women, answers that helped to shape our civilization, that have been forgotten and effectively missing from the English-speaking world for so long—and that are now again available. What all this means is that, now becoming available to the ordinary layperson for the first time is perhaps the greatest religious psychology in the world, much of it more than fifteen hundred years old but unsurpassed even today. For example, the texts of the Greek *Philokalia,* of which three of the five volumes are now available in English, are already proving valuable source material to professional psychologists. The studies of the Russian monastic teachings about what they name *provocation,*[24] an idea derived from the earlier Greek Fathers and described in recent books on the Russian Church, also have considerable significance in this field. Many other examples could be found. But this is hardly enough!

To help yourself be yourSelf—for Christianity this means to realize, not to distort human nature—you need to know what those words mean. But if ordinary mechanical skills are learned only by apprenticeship, how much more is this true for the skills of healing the soul?

We have rediscovered the instruction books, but we still need to know their meaning.

In the past century and a half, certain individuals, particularly in the Russian Church, have studied these texts, and some of them have written about them in terms easier for the modern reader to understand: these include Saint Theophan the Recluse and Boris Mouravieff. There has also been Fedotov, who introduced the second volume of his work *The Russian Religious Mind* with the words: "My intention is to describe the subjective side of religion, as opposed to its objective side; that is, opposed to the complex of organized dogmas, sacraments, rites, liturgy, Canon Law, and so on. I am interested in man, religious man, and his attitude towards God, the world, and his fellow men; his attitude is not only emotional, but also rational and volitional, the attitude of the whole man."[25]

Eastern Monastic Practice

In the Introduction I spoke of how so much time has passed since the early Fathers of the church wrote that the special meanings of the words have long been forgotten. There is an exception to that fact, and it makes it possible that the West might discover those lost meanings. The exception is that a large part of the inner tradition was preserved in unwritten but practical forms in Orthodox and Coptic monasteries and hermitages, particularly on Mount Athos and in other monasteries throughout the Orthodox world. This explains the wide knowledge of ancient Greek among the monks. Yet even this source is not perfect, as its history shows that it has periodically lost its inner meaning. Indeed several times it has had to be renewed over the centuries. Such a renewal is occurring now. These monasteries appear also to have been a major source of the highly practical teachings of Gurdjieff[26] and Ouspensky, although the linguistic problem of loss of meaning explains why such a small number were unable to convey to those limited to Western language all the key elements of the teaching as a method. The Orthodox Church, as it comes into the West, is facing the same difficulty.

Since the meaning of a text is found by linking the words to experience, the meanings of many of these ancient texts are stored—but stored *wordlessly*—in the memories of those who *practice* the monastic life, and particularly in that monasticism which uses the texts of the early Fathers as its guide. As mentioned earlier, the primary textbooks of Greek and Russian monasticism include the *Philokalia* and the *Gerontikon*. Some of the stories in the *Gerontikon* are probably true, others are clearly parables, whether or not they have foundation in fact.

But the important thing about this is that monastic texts relate to actual practice, and it is found that the effort to transmit to someone an actual practice eliminates many of the misunderstandings that occur in purely verbal communication. This means that today, after two thousand years of Christianity, the meanings of the Gospels and of all these later texts are more accurately preserved not simply in words but in the practices of the monastics, in the "life of the heart" lived in these monasteries—a life that can never be fully explained or intellectualized. These monks and nuns have generally been guided in their practice by those who have gone before, generation after generation, and such guidance means, more than anything else, a process of correcting mistakes. So those whose practices follow those of generations that have gone before them provide a unique resource by which the practical meaning of certain ideas can be checked. Even today, it is sometimes possible for the devout pilgrim to enter into these practices to the point of acquiring understanding, by processes that require much time. But that is another story, perhaps to be told later.

Monastic Rules

Some of these ideas survive in written form, too, in the great monastic *rules* of the Western Christian world, in the Rule of Saint Benedict, in the teachings of Saint Francis of Assisi, in the spiritual exercises of Saint Ignatius of Loyola—in their original form, not the later form shortened soon after his death. Many have survived or reemerged in Russia, from the fifteenth century on, in the teachings of Saint Nilus of Sora and others who created specific teachings for the needs of a particular time and place, as in the correspondence of Saint Theophan the Recluse or the instruction given by Saint John of Kronstadt.

It is sometimes difficult to distinguish between this classification and the next, but the distinction is generally valid. More to the point, although in written form they are not the equal of the unwritten teaching of a monastery, monastic rules are a compendium of practical instruction.

Church Liturgies

In certain parts of the Christian liturgy, and in the many other services of the Christian year, certain of the Fathers enshrined great truths in words, in images—statues, frescoes or icons—and others choreographed these truths into what we call the "ritualized" action of priest and deacon when the liturgy is properly performed. They were even built into the very architecture of some of the great churches.[27] Not all of these "objective" truths are disguised: many great truths are plainly stated in the words of the older liturgies, to be ignored by the modern worshiper who, too often of course, doubts them, perhaps because of the scientific prejudgment that "this is not real knowledge," or more often as a result of inattention.[28]

That "other Christianity," then, is still alive. The esoteric tradition is not a different form of Christianity, but an early strand in the tapestry of the Universal Church—a strand whose importance has long been forgotten, so that today it needs to be "lifted up," to draw an analogy from the weaver's craft, until it can once again be seen, be understood, and so be fitted back into its proper place in the fabric of the church. This is the thread of common experience that once stitched together the many churches into the One Church from which they sprang.

Once we learn to value it, much of this knowledge will be revealed. It can be obtained simply for the price of going to church and listening carefully, or by careful reading—but this is so only as long as we remember to ask ourselves: What does that actually mean?

But when we value something we learn, we come to understand it differently.

Great Spiritual Texts

Certain of these ideas survive sometimes in the great spiritual texts of the past few centuries: in *The Imitation of Christ* and in other books by those associated with the Society of the Common Lot in the "Low Countries" of Europe; in the English *Cloud of Unknowing;* in the teachings and poems of Saint John of the Cross; in Pierre Caussade's *Abandonment to Divine Providence*. Occasionally one can trace in these texts mentions of teachings that go back to the first centuries of the church. But in all these great texts, which are for many Western Christians their sole source of knowledge of this tradition, surprisingly little has survived of the vast resources of knowledge available to the early Church, resources that are now slowly being rediscovered and made available to those who can see their value.

Among these great texts are some that are certainly in line with the inner tradition known by the early Fathers, such as the teachings of Saint Theophan the Recluse, who from the depth of his spirituality and the richness of his scholarship was able to put the same ideas in the Russian of the nineteenth century, language which at least contains modern concepts lacking to the authors of the early centuries. Sources of this kind are still few and far between in the English language, so that I have had to contribute to their publication, as well as drawing the attention of those who are interested to the value of their content.

Alchemical and Mystery Teachings

Some of the ideas spread across Europe in disguised form in medieval times, particularly after the occupation of Greece by the Turks, and mixed with other streams to form European esotericism of the time. The Christian esoteric tradition also appears to have gone underground at certain times, but here it has in general been mixed with material from other sources, so that it is more often than not confusing to all but the best trained scholars, and we will not go into further detail about it at this time except to say that in alchemy were preserved certain items of Christian and pre-Christian psychological knowledge dealing with subjects so long ignored that today they would be regarded by the modern churches with considerable suspicion.

Chapter 2

The Burning Bush

There are two important differences about Christianity seen from the esoteric view, and these are exactly the reasons why the inner tradition can offer new hope in a troubled world. The first is the view that saints are not born holy, they are made holy. The second is that the process that produces holiness involves—and has always involved—a kind of psychological science which provides help for just those questions that neither modern psychology nor modern, moralistic religion know how to resolve. And the inner tradition is a science in just the sense that it depends on experiential confirmation, that is, on its own kind of experimental method. It says that specifically in the idea of *synergy*,[1] which means that although it is impossible without Christ's redemption, salvation also depends on our own inner efforts. In this view, the saints, the holiest Christians of all time, serve as examples of the basic principle that we are redeemed by Our Lord, but that this redemption becomes effective only through the efforts of the individual concerned. In other words, I cannot slander my neighbor, rob my employer, deny Christ, ignore God's requirements for me . . . and still claim to be saved by Christ's great sacrifice; by behaving in this way I make a mockery of Christianity itself, and it is directly because of this great gap between Christian claims and Christian performance that this great faith has fallen into disrepute in the modern world.

How is it, then, that a God who loved His creature created us imperfect? The traditional answer is found in the Book of Genesis; it is that man has *fallen*. Early tradition speaks about this; in the Canon of Saint Andrew of Crete (see p. 43) we are told about an inner, psychological fall as a result of an inner, psychological temptation. We will perhaps come to discover that this was itself, in the long term, not so much a tragedy as a stage in our growth to racial maturity.

This is no empty claim. The path of esotericism is marked by experiences, by glimpses of the different reality from which we once fell; glimpses that create certainty or at least restore hope as we pass through our uncertainties. They armor us against the greatest problem of modern religious thought, the tacit but entrenched rationalist definition of all inner experiences, including these visions which sometimes transform people's lives, as "subjective and therefore meaningless," a definition that resulted from the fundamental scientific redefinition[2] of the term *truth*. This self-imposed blindness has led to the existence of questions which from this viewpoint appear to be unanswerable. Often these questions arise directly from the inner experience of individuals and are of crucial importance to those individuals, but today they are treated as trivial not only by science, but even by many religious authorities. Yet these questions are unanswerable only because there has been a general turn away from inner experience, just as happened in the tenth century, when Saint Symeon the New Theologian (A.D. 949–1022) made great efforts to demonstrate the experiential element in Christian spirituality. Abbot of a Turkish Christian monastery, he was sent into exile for his pains, at the request of his own monks.

Yet although we generally see inner reality as illusion and the outer illusion as reality, inner experience is still with us, although often entirely forgotten. Indeed, although esoteric Christianity is seen in terms of inner experience, the experience of the esoteric path is not all inner for one specific reason, that at a certain point the boundaries between inner and outer dissolve in a new reality, a kingdom of which Jesus says, in the Gospel According to Thomas: "The kingdom is within you, and it is outside you."

Such teachings can only be understood if read in context, and the text given above hints, to those who know how to read it, that initially this kingdom, which is inside and outside us, can only be discovered within us, that is, through Self-knowledge. This is a basic tenet of inner knowledge, that we must first discover certain things within us, but once discovered within, they can also be recognized in other people. At a later stage the same applies to all the phenomena of the outside world. As I hope to show in this chapter, the mystical experiences at the peak of inner experience are often the point at which the inner breaks through into the outer, the subjective into the true objective.

A Hermit Speaks

One reason for the vagueness of modern Christianity about these points is the lack of examples. The scarcity of holiness in modern times has troubled me for a long time. It was already a persistent question when, on an early visit to Mount Athos in 1983, I spoke to a truly spiritual hermit, a *pneumaticos* in the terms they use there, and was given a "message to the West" . . . a message I was expressly told to pass on to the English-speaking world.

Put baldly, as it was given, this message has until now proved almost impossible to pass on, because as a message it only makes sense when we have the "meat" of it. So this book is the attempt to give the real meaning of that message and to expand on it as far as I am able, knowing that others will have to complete the task. The message is brief and simple, until one begins to ponder its implications.

"You English," said the hermit sitting in his simple cell, "have served man very well with your intellect, giving him many things he needs, the solutions of many problems that have made life easier for everyone."

He paused, to let the young Greek Australian serving as interpreter render his words to me, then continued, and as he did so I looked around the room. Benches made of simple planks lined two sides, an iron bed-stead was on a third, and an iron stove on the fourth. The interpreter began again: "Now you should do another work: to understand and to tell the world of the inner truth, the truth of the heart as well." The conversation continued for some time, but everything else that was said was overshadowed by the enormity of the message, the impossibility of ever fulfilling this charge.

Why is it so difficult to convey this message? The problem is that, to a greater degree even than was true of biblical man, and despite our belief in "progress," modern man is fallen man. We are psychologically fallen, that is, we are no longer in full possession of our faculties. The text known as the Canon of Saint Andrew of Crete, one of the most important of the early documents still in use today in the services of the Orthodox Church, provides an unexpected glimpse of what is unequivocally an inner, psychological interpretation of the Fall of Adam.

> My mind's Eve took the place of the bodily Eve
> for me—the passionate thought that was in my flesh.
> Showing me the sweets
> and gorging me ever on the poisonous food.
> Have mercy on me, O God, have mercy on me.

Worthily from Eden of old, Adam was exiled,
When he failed to keep, O Saviour,
Thy one commandment.
What shall I suffer, who am always rejecting
Thy lifegiving teachings.
Have mercy on me, O God, have mercy on me.[3]

The inner, psychological view that is revealed in this text was understood by men of the early centuries. But this kind of thinking has long been forgotten. Because of this, the hermit's message, as I understand it, is not so simple: before we can do what he has asked us to do, we must begin to remedy this *inner blindness*.

This is the task that the hermit has set us, disguised as a simple need to think about something different. The precision of this message is such that it clearly defines esoteric Christianity. This is exactly how esotericism understands the Fall of man: as a corruption of man's inner potential and of his basic goodness that depends on the full use of his faculties. The Fall describes a partial loss of faculties that echoes the insight of physician Hughlings Jackson, in the last century, who said that in any form of intoxication—by drugs, by drink (and of course by one's own emotions)—the higher faculties are lost first.

Each of these verses ends with the repetitive refrain of the Canon, the *Kyrie eleison,* "Lord have mercy," that sounds repeatedly in Orthodox services and is echoed time and again in all the texts of Christian esotericism. In this, esoteric Christianity differs from what most people in the West know of other esoteric teachings. In the Christian esoteric tradition, salvation from our state depends primarily on the mercy of God. For man unaided, says the tradition, salvation is impossible, although according to the same tradition, individual effort does play a most important part in this salvation, and this need to make individual effort is one of the major distinctions between inner Christianity and its purely outer forms.

Trial by Fire

"By Thy light we shall see light," says the Orthodox liturgy. If inner religion comes from inner experience,[4] then religion in our times has almost forgotten this key. The inner sense has been lost, or to be more exact, despite the fact that many people have glimpses of an inner life and of its great richness, these glimpses have not been understood, so they have not been put to use.

This loss of the inner sense has gone on a very long time. Yet to return to my experiences on Mount Athos, which so well illuminate this question, on one of my early visits there I glimpsed one of the less visible parts of the early tradition of the church, when I had a number of interesting and revealing conversations with my friend Father A. All of these talks touched on the question of what happens if the higher faculties are restored in full, even if briefly. One talk of particular importance was in the otherwise empty reception room of the monastery *archontariki* or guesthouse where, sitting on the cushioned seat running along the windows overhanging the blue-gray sea that Xerxes had once sailed his fleets over, he showed me an icon of the Virgin and child. Around the Virgin on this icon, he explained, the prophets[5] were shown, each so as to illustrate one aspect of their story in a way that helped to explain the "inner" meaning of the birth of Christ. There was Jacob with his ladder, Moses with the burning bush. . . .

Something about this burning bush analogy fell into place. A strange experience was lit up for me, a brief awakening that happened to me on a Christmas Eve many years before—a divine gift received at night, after I had tried to spend the whole day dedicated to Christ. As I drifted off to sleep a blow hit me in the solar plexus, energy rushed up my spine and out of the crown of my head. Immediately the world was different, on fire, the interior of objects around me suddenly visible in ceaseless motion. It was then that I first understood Moses' vision on Mount Sinai. Now, more than a decade later, in an ancient monastery three thousand miles further east, this icon enabled me to fit that experience into its biblical context. The link it established between the Old Testament image of the burning bush and the birth of Christ helped to explain this past experience. From this I began to understand how the forces existing in our unpurified minds—our fears and wishes, delusions and compulsions—prevent the birth of Christ within our consciousness. Without the purity of heart that is one of the elements of the wedding garment referred to in the Gospels, without being free from these compulsions, we are not invited to the wedding. The other gospel reference, in its inner sense, has to do with when the "Bridegroom" comes: "I indeed baptize you with water unto repentance: but he that cometh after me is mightier than I, whose shoes I am not worthy to bear: he shall baptize you with the Holy Ghost, and with fire" (Matthew 3:11). And one symbolic name for the Jewish inner tradition was derived from the chariot of fire that took the prophets to heaven. Come now, Lord, for Your servant awaits You.

But when this experience first happened to me, I was not ready for this coming: something in me, something that was present in me at least partly because of my lack of preparation for this event, became very fearful at what was occurring. The fear caused inner tensions, and with those tensions, the experience, the state of consciousness, came to an end.

Years later, seeing that icon in the guesthouse over the windblown Aegean, I began to formulate questions about this event, and this, of course, caused us to move on to the discussion of experiences. Stillness, the emotional stillness of *hesychia*—the word used by Fathers such as St. Gregory Palamas for the emotional stillness found in prayer—seems a very important factor in all the more significant experiences. But something else was also necessary, an abundance of energy of a certain kind that comes from such experiences: *dynamis,* Palamas' term for energy, then defined by change, almost exactly as it is in Newtonian physics, dynamis in potential, dynamis as change, dynamis come to rest again.

The fear of the unfamiliar that ended that experience is a commonplace on the inner path. Much esoteric work takes the form of a struggle against that fear. Our reaction to such an experience illuminates the fact that to enter a different form of life we ourselves must become different. We inhabit a fallen world, and we are trapped there because we ourselves are fallen. But who within us is it that is afraid to step out into the sunlight? We can learn to understand that this is not I. This is one route to *humility.*

But this understanding must include a remembrance that to say that we are fallen is also to say that our proper place in life is higher. This relates directly to the following gospel passage on the importance of humility:

> But when thou art bidden, go and sit down in the lowest room; that when he that bade thee cometh, he may say unto thee, Friend, go up higher: then shalt thou have worship in the presence of them that sit at meat with thee.
>
> For whosoever exalteth himself shall be abased; and he that humbleth himself shall be exalted (Luke 14:10–11).

Why did I suggest that what ended that experience was fear? Observation shows that something in us fears any glimpse of higher realities, even the faintest, which would be much less powerful than the one I am describing. Is this not the same thing that fears the uncertainties of the night, that fears anything we cannot control; the fear that drives men to become ever richer, to try to dominate others, to hide from the world, to pretend, to lie?

When we attempt to serve God, and attempt this realistically, realizing that to do so will bring to an end our partial or even purely imaginary control over what happens to us, then something in us resists mightily. I continually meet this problem in myself. The unpredictable, the uncontrollable, anything that I do not understand, all of this threatens the pretense of control that I present to the world, and all of this is to be avoided, if necessary violently. Observation of the inconsistencies in our nature, of the differences between our avowed aims and the moment-to-moment purposes for which we strive, shows us that something that has developed in us over the years has developed a life—and a sense of identity—all its own, and fears to lose this "life." Perhaps it sees the loss of its control over events as tantamount to loss of this identity: of this I am not sure, but I am very sure of the fear.

Symeon the New Theologian on Inner Experience

We have fallen from our proper state. Experiences of that state are now sometimes described as mystical. There are many kinds of mystical experience, and not all of them have the character of fire. In the Gospel of Saint John we read: "And the light shineth in darkness; and the darkness comprehended it not" (John 1:5). This famous passage has an inner as well as an outer meaning. It refers to the fact that in our normal state we cannot remember or understand the events that occur in higher states.[6] Saint Symeon the New Theologian wrote: "At the summit of the spiritual ascent, I saw a light, and in the light another, clearer light, and again in the midst of this light there shone a splendour as of the sun. From the sun there beamed forth a ray which filled all things, but whose nature remained incomprehensible."[7]

On another occasion he describes—as if it happened to somebody else—his first major experience of what is known as the *uncreated light,* an experience that supposedly happened when he was twenty years old:

> One day, as he stood and recited, "God have mercy upon me, a sinner,"[8] uttering it with his mind rather than with his mouth, suddenly a flood of divine radiance appeared from above and filled all the room. As this happened the young man lost all awareness of his surroundings and forgot that he was in a house or that he was under a roof. He saw nothing but light all around him and did not know whether he was standing on the ground. He was not afraid of falling; he was not concerned with the world, nor did anything pertaining to men and corporeal beings enter into his mind. Instead, he was wholly in the presence of immaterial light and seemed himself to have turned into light. Oblivious of all the world he was filled with tears and with ineffable joy and gladness. His mind then ascended to heaven and beheld yet another light, which was clearer than that which was close at hand.[9]

This light, and what precedes it, the "cleansing fire" of the Spirit, were not new with Symeon; they have had a long biblical history: "And now men see not the bright light which is in the clouds: but the wind passeth, and cleanseth them" (Job 37:21). This is the light that shines in the Darkness (John 1). It is the light of Christ, the joyful light at the heart of the universe, and it shines unseen, uncomprehended, in our own inmost heart. This is the Second Coming, its joyful advent the alchemical wedding itself. Saint Symeon also wrote: "The nous immersed in Your light becomes so bright that in the end it is light itself, in the likeness of Your glory. The nous of the man to whom this has been granted is called Your own: he is then deemed worthy to possess Your nous, and he is made one with You, never to be parted."[10]

This is the final stage in what is known as the illumination of the nous. It is told that eventually—if only rarely—this state may become permanent, a possibility that makes a great deal of sense of reports by pupils of Boris Mouravieff that he continually advised them to "work for permanence."

Saint Maximos on the Fall

These experiences tell us things we did not know about ourselves. Coming from the gospel tradition, the inner, psychological interpretation of the Fall is basically "good news" in a literal sense. It is news— confirmed by these experiences—of man's inherent goodness and the possibility of regaining it.

How did the early Fathers of the church interpret this story of the Fall of man told in Genesis? Normally they write of it not as a historical event but as a "psychological event," and then, generally, as an event applying to each individual. In this drama, each one of us is Adam, and each one of us possesses the possibility of ceasing to make the mistake that Adam made. Saint Maximos the Confessor, for example, is quoted in the Greek *Philokalia* as writing about it. He says first that the two trees represent two different ways of viewing the world:

> The tree of life, when understood as symbolizing wisdom, likewise differs greatly from the tree of knowledge of good and evil, in that the latter neither symbolizes wisdom nor is said to do so. Wisdom is characterized by intellect and intelligence [nous], the state which is opposite to wisdom by lack of intelligence and by sensation.
>
> Since man came into being composed of noetic soul and sentient body, one interpretation could be that the tree of life

is the soul's intellect, which is the seat of wisdom. The tree of
the knowledge of good and evil would then be the body's
power of sensation, which is clearly the seat of mindless impulses. Man received the Lord's commandment not to involve
himself actively and experientially with these impulses; but he
did not keep that commandment.[11]

Maximos then speaks further of this relation of the two trees to our
experience of life, suggesting that in some way we *choose* to experience
through one or other of these processes.

Both trees in scripture symbolize the intellect and the senses.[12]
Thus the intellect has the power to discriminate between the
spiritual and the sensible, between the eternal and the transitory. Or rather, as the soul's discriminatory power, the intellect
persuades the soul to cleave to the first and to transcend the
second. The senses have the power to discriminate between
pleasure and pain in the body. Or rather, as a power existing
in a body endowed with soul and sense perception, they persuade the body to embrace pleasure and reject pain.[13]

Next he fits all this together as a complete explanation of the key
points of the creation story in Genesis, and links this with a particular
conception of obedience to the divine commandment, and from this he
builds a detailed conception of good and bad in human behavior—all of
this founded on simple but exact psychology. In practice, confirmation of
this psychological doctrine is difficult to obtain through self-observation,
but with serious efforts of investigation the truth and practical usefulness
of it can be found. Here, in simple terms, is one statement of the Christian
answer to the questions asked on page 13, which add up to the single
question: How can I become truly Christian? In this book we will from
time to time meet other ways of conveying the same truths.

This is typical of the psychology of the early Fathers, making it
entirely amazing that this knowledge has been so thoroughly ignored. And
here is what Maximos said next:

If a man exercises only sensory discrimination between pain
and pleasure in the body, thus transgressing the divine commandment, he eats from the tree of the knowledge of good
and evil, that is to say, he succumbs to the mindless impulses
that pertain to the senses; for he possesses only the body's
power of discrimination, which makes him embrace pleasure
as something good and avoid pain as something evil. But if he
exercises only that noetic discrimination which distinguishes
between the eternal and the transitory, and so keeps the divine

commandment, he eats from the tree of life, that is to say, from the wisdom that appertains to his intellect; for he exercises only the power of discrimination associated with the soul, which makes him cleave to the glory of what is eternal as something good, and avoid the corruption of the transitory as something evil.[14]

There are, then, different levels of judgment. True goodness and true evil are something more than what appear to the fallen mind to be good and evil on the basis of sensory perception alone. This whole idea will be developed in a later chapter on discrimination, where we will find another early Father, Saint John Cassian, giving still more details about this ability, known as the power of discrimination of spirits.

Saint Maximos too had more to say, clearly defining the choice that faces us between the Spirit of God and the "spirit" of the sensory world: "Goodness as far as the intellect is concerned is a dispassionate predilection for the spirit; evil is an impassioned attachment to the senses. Goodness as far as the senses are concerned is the impassioned activity of the body under the stimulus of pleasure; evil is the state destitute of such activity."[15]

The Fall is also the reason why it is so difficult to convey the hermit's message, for it is a message containing a great deal of sense. A medieval book, a History of the Tree of Life, expresses elements of the esoteric teaching, telling how the wood of the cross on which Christ was crucified was taken from the dead trunk of the Tree of Life.

The fact is that today we have a fallen view of what constitutes knowledge. This view is different from that held by the early church, and it is actually a narrower view, as well as a more external view, as we will discover later in this book. And this narrow view limits what we consider to be knowledge and at the same time, according to the Fathers, traps our thinking into a narrow part of the nous, the "true intellect" which is so much greater than the discursive mind, so that either we totally ignore the spiritual, or narrow that too down to what "makes sense"—a revealing phrase, for the other characteristic of this limited idea of knowledge is that, as it is today, it is bound to the world revealed by the senses. Once understood and accepted, this difficult proposition suddenly seems easy. We wonder why we had so much difficulty with it. But in fact it can only be seen as a kind of fall—a further fall of already fallen man, a step further in the Fall of Adam, and, to overcome it, the original Fall must also be understood. Once the soul has fallen, it is difficult for it to return to that different world where is found the Tree of Life. A long search is required: this is normally an individual matter but, from time to time, a whole nation, even a whole civilization, has to perform that search in order to restore the inner paths that have been lost to it. We live in such a time, but caught up in our personal concerns, even our personal spiritual concerns, nobody perceives the need of the time.

Our Nature Is Fundamentally Good, but Has Been Distorted

Russia's Saint Theophan the Recluse wrote in the last century that man is good by nature, but his natural goodness has been overlaid by something artificial that must be in some way changed before his natural goodness is apparent. Among other things, this distorting overlay of artificiality limits what we can take in (or contain), and makes us slow to understand.

There is a clue in this: whenever we act unconsciously, our nature is invaded, the vacuum left by our lack of consciousness is filled by "borrowed" activity, is controlled from outside us. In simple form we can see this in the effects of indecision, in which events or the actions of others force us into incorrect decisions. This borrowed activity then keeps us "asleep." But, by combining memories of certain experiences with the habit of certain actions that arise from our inner nature, we can build within us a different kind of structure that, instead of obscuring consciousness, will awake the sleeping consciousness within. This was known by the early church as the illumination of the nous. It is hinted that this possibility, and what can happen in the enlightened nous, are what mankind was created for.

> Therefore let us not sleep, as do others; but let us watch and be sober.
>
> For they that sleep sleep in the night; and they that be drunken are drunken in the night.
>
> But let us, who are of the day, be sober, putting on the breastplate of faith and love; and for an helmet, the hope of salvation (1 Thessalonians 5:6–8).

Saint Theophan, "that mighty man of prayer," as he was once called, learned about these possibilities of man from a *starets*[16] or "elder" near Kiev, and found the key concept of the innate goodness of man expressed more clearly in his researches into ancient Syriac Christian sources—researches he made in the middle of the last century, during a seven-year sojourn in the Middle East on a mission to Jerusalem for the Russian Church. It was there that he discovered this idea, by then forgotten in the

West and even in the Orthodox East, that man is naturally good, but is now in an unnatural state. He discovered this in texts that went back to the days when the Syriac Church played a major part in the formation of early Christianity. The evil in man, he said, summarizing this discovery, arises outside him but, like a weed or tare[17] has taken root in him: so that ancient accident makes us vulnerable to accident today. As Saint Theophan puts it, then, man's nature is good. The evil arises, "by accident" in a quite technical sense, from outside him, but once it has taken root in him, it attracts his nous, his awareness, to further accidental forces.

Saint Isaac the Syrian, another great master of the esoteric church, who was one of the early sources rediscovered for the Russian Church by Theophan, had put this slightly differently, with the idea that sickness comes after health: "Sickness is posterior to health, and it is impossible that one and the same nature be both good and evil. Therefore of necessity, one must precede the other; and the one that is prior is also the natural, because anything which is accidental is not said to belong to a nature, but to intrude from without. And change follows upon every accident and intrusion. Nature, however, does not change or alter itself."[18]

From the psychological viewpoint, it is more important still that according to the gospel, these "weeds"—the term refers of course to the unnatural element in us—were sowed "while man slept." They occurred during that lowering of consciousness, that *Fall of man,* which caused Gurdjieff to teach that ordinary man is *asleep,* an idea that was developed by Ouspensky, who defined the normal state of consciousness of modern man as *waking sleep.*[19] Properly understood, this idea of *waking sleep* can help create the possibility of waking up again. The way it should be understood is that we are asleep to our full potential, and that during this partial sleep, *accident,* or chance, sows certain destructive tendencies in us which help to keep us asleep.

A more recent Christian psychiatrist and teacher, Karlfried von Durkheim, in his studies of an element called *hara,* a key factor in Japanese culture, in both its worldly and spiritual aspects, discovered this same need to overcome some unnatural element in us. He wrote about this that: "Hara, it is true, is part of man's original endowment, but, for that very reason, poses a task for him—for it is the task of man to become what he is. Man can fulfill his task of becoming a complete human being only if he overcomes again and again that within him which obstructs the way to this true becoming, and also if, at the same time, he apprehends and allows to grow within him that basic power which is always striving to carry him on to his fully human state."[20]

In esoteric Christianity, this knowledge is generally transmitted in unwritten form, but, because of the previous lack of a written expression for some part of this important concept, Durkheim's formulation adds meaning to the Orthodox interpretation of the biblical idea that we are made in the image and likeness of God. This links with the key idea that Christ Himself was the first and pure image of the Father. Origen, for example, calls Christ the Wisdom of God and describes this Wisdom as like a clean mirror that perfectly reflects the Father. This doctrine has widespread practical significance, the basic elements of which are developed by Origen in his *de Principiis,* which tells us how the Creator, being invisible to the eye, is manifested in the original and pure *image* or icon, Christ, who, as the Son, *knows* the Father: "no man knoweth the Son, but the Father; neither knoweth any man the Father, save the Son, and he to whomsoever the Son will reveal him" (Matthew 11:27).

So, in His words and actions, outwardly, as they are described in the events of the gospel, or inwardly as they occur as the image within us, as described by Palamas as the *energies* of God,[21] in either manner, Christ shows us the Father, whom we cannot otherwise see, and in this way we can know the Father.

George Capsanis, the hegoumen or abbot of the monastery of Osiou Grigoriou on Mount Athos, teaches today in the same tradition of the early Fathers. In what turns out to be an effective summary of the whole process of *theosis* or deification, he makes a series of points which, for convenience, we will separate out one by one:

— Man is made in the image of God, but in fallen man, "infected by sin,"[22] this image is obscured.
— As a result, the inmost man, made "according to the image," is incapable of fulfilling itself by becoming a likeness of God . . . of becoming Godlike.
— Christ, as an unchanged, uncorrupted icon of God, restores the image fallen in Adam to reveal the original beauty within us, at the same time teaching us and guiding us towards our divine archetype.
— Transfigured, Christ restored the radiance of a creation made dark by the Fall.
— Thus, when we become "conformed to the image of Christ" (Romans 8:29), we regain our own inmost nature.

He quotes the Orthodox *Vespers of the Transfiguration,* which says: "Transfigured, Thou hast made the nature which was darkened in Adam become radiant again, O Christ, transforming it into the glory and brilliance of the Godhead."

This summarizes the inner tradition of Christianity as followed by the Eastern Church. In the monastic form of this inner tradition, men even today seek by ascetic practices to redirect or transform their nature psychologically, so that the "latent divine image" appears in them, a process that is superficially akin to the development and "fixing" of a photographic image. Until it is fixed, or made permanent, we get a situation that has been familiar in monasticism for centuries, and is equally familiar with those who "work on themselves" in other ways, in which everyone falls every day—and falls many times each day and, to start with, many times each hour: "The monk falls and gets up again, falls and gets up again."[23]

But in this intermediate state, it is not our nature but our state that changes. In the Greek *Philokalia,* this is said in the following way: "The moon as it waxes and wanes illustrates the condition of man. Sometimes he does what is right: sometimes he sins and then through repentance [metanoia] returns to a holy life. The nous[24] of one who sins is not destroyed (as some of you think), just as the physical size of the moon does not diminish, but only its light."[25]

To understand this process requires a different way of looking at life and at ourselves; different, that is, from our modern, supposedly scientific, view of the world. To carry it out requires a different kind of effort from those efforts normal to our modern way of life.

The remainder of this book attempts to describe these differences, which together form that process known in the Eastern Church as *theosis:* deification.

Modern Man's Inability to Remember Inner Experience

A modern way of looking at the Fall is that of C. G. Jung, who described how the loss of contact with the inner life today has had very widespread effects on our outer life.[26] It also acts like a self-fulfilling prophecy, creating situations and attitudes which prevent the investigations that would recover this kind of knowledge and the natural human capabilities that give rise to it. In simple terms, it seems that our lack of persistence on the esoteric path, like our apparent lack of knowledge of the inner world, comes from the inability to *register* and remember inner experience. This is a direct result of what is known as the Fall, taken in its traditional psychological meaning.

This becomes an explanation of how we have become almost inextricably caught in external life, so that we have neither time nor attention for anything inward.

In this situation it is not our awareness of the inner life—the inner spirit—that is lost first. What goes first is our ability to *register* it and so remember it. But this leads to an external view of the inner teachings, and turns the morality of the inner tradition into the kind of external, legalistic code for which the Pharisees were famous.[27] But this loss of the inner sense has been developing for a very long time, and now our inner lives are not simply unnoticed or regarded as "subjective and thus unreal," but they have become largely unseen.

Saint Symeon today is regarded as one of the source theologians of the Orthodox Church. It sometimes seems as if few really understand what he was trying to convey[28] in this particular section of his writings, but those who have experienced this light will begin to understand.

A Theory of Knowledge Is a Barrier to Faith

The theory of knowledge expressed by these early Fathers is "explained" nonintellectually in a traditional icon of Saint Elizabeth, mother of John the Baptist (shown overleaf). It expresses the idea that intellectual knowledge is more limited than that of the heart, and is often (but not necessarily) limited to the sensory—an idea partially expressed by Socrates' discovery that he did not *know*: which means that ordinary, discursive intellect does not know God, nor can it ever know anything for certain.[29]

Considerably later, in the life of Saint Nilus of Sora (1433–1508), the same respect for a discriminatory form of intellect—the *nous,* in Greek terms—surfaced again in the Russian Church. Unlike many of his predecessors, he advised care in evaluating so-called spiritual writings: not all were equally valid. He wrote of the care taken in his own approach to such texts: "Most of all, I scrutinize the divine writings, first, the precepts of the Lord and their commentaries, and the traditions of the Apostles, also the doctrines of the Holy Fathers, and meditate on them. And what agrees with my reason I copy for myself and edify myself with it and hereon do I put my life and my breath."[30]

Nilus, says Fedotov after this quotation, used human reason as an instrument for exploring the scriptures. Like Paisious Velitchkovsky three centuries later, he was faced with mistranslated and corrupted texts and had to make great efforts to find the correct meaning, a process in which the early Fathers' respect for philosophical skills must have proved very helpful. "The concord between scripture and reason," writes Fedotov, still about Nilus, "is for him a necessary condition for behaviour." He quotes further: " 'When I have something to do I first examine the divine scriptures, and if I do not find what agrees with my reason in beginning the matter, I delay until I find it.' "[31]

People believe that reasoning and the whole question of knowledge are unimportant on the spiritual path. This is true in one sense, the sense developed by early Fathers such as Gregory Palamas, who

Figure 2.1   Icon of Saint Elizabeth

argued that intellect is only a path to ideas about God, not to the formation of an experiential relationship with God. Thus Saint Maximos wrote: "When you intend to know God do not seek the reasons about his being, for the human mind and that of any other being below God cannot discover this."[32]

But the idea of this specific limit of reason, of reason's inability to know God, must be understood exactly, as to turn it into a generalization and to say that reason cannot help to prepare us for such knowledge can, for people whose minds have formed in certain ways that are common today, be an effective and sometimes permanent obstacle to spiritual growth.

Contrary to what most people expect, it is experience—experience that results from the action of the Word—that transforms the mind and prepares it for the coming of its Lord. But simply to have experience is not enough; we must retain it, and for this, a good memory is also not enough. Before we can perceive and then *register* sufficient inner experience, so that it is retained and accessible in our memory, two things are necessary: first, relevant inner experiences must become more common and of longer duration in our lives, and second, we must value and accept these experiences as real and meaningful sources of knowledge.

In a monastic context, obedience to a *rule* and to an *elder* produces the experience necessary without the need to pass through a stage of theory or scholarship. For those without the support of rule and elder, additional knowledge, for instance of methods of extending our experience, is also necessary. Again there are problems here. Nothing we learn can directly show us God, and indeed knowledge of God is different from all other knowledge and cannot be reached intellectually, in the ordinary sense of intellect, but when this fact is understood, many people assume that to be given new knowledge of man is equally useless. This false attitude, based on a misunderstanding of a real truth, often becomes so entrenched that even commonsense perceptions of one's own nature are shut out by it.

Even for the monk, to retain and properly value the inner experience of his life—to accept and actually to value certain kinds of suffering,[33] for example—it is necessary that he change his whole concept of knowledge, and this, in effect, means that his whole worldview must change. Even more is this true of the layperson who works alone under the pressures of everyday life. For such people, other types of knowledge are equally important. Their conception of knowledge must become—and that in a significant sense—wider and more all-embracing than is normal in our times.

The problem is that before we can understand this theory of knowledge, we have to learn to perceive and register inner experience, and as we are we can do this only imperfectly.

More important still, experience gained casually is of little use: even if it is not incomplete, it is gained too slowly for our needs. Only the experience gained in putting things into practice reveals the knowledge we need and opens the doors of the recognition that makes knowledge usable. Before we can understand, we have to do, and so, as Saint Paul said, "renew our intelligence."

One of the things that emerges from this method, which I call "exegesis by practice," is that practical experience provides different data from that revealed by pure analysis unaided by praxis. One of several problems in normal exegetic methods is that information is formulated differently depending on how it is to be used, and there is little reason to imagine that this was not always so. In studying information provided by others, therefore, it is necessary to study it under the conditions in which it was intended to be understood. Since, in studying this tradition, we are studying knowledge intended to be conveyed through the medium of practice, to study it merely theoretically is to misunderstand. The intention has determined the form of the knowledge.

Among other things, this explains the method used in this book to study the doctrines of the Gospels and the early Fathers.

Gregory of Nyssa's View

I learned more about the burning bush image when I discovered a book by one of the ancient Fathers that is little read, but fairly readily available: Gregory of Nyssa's *Life of Moses*. When he speaks about the experience of higher knowledge, he uses the analogy of the burning bush. He writes:

> It is upon us who continue in this quiet and peaceful course of life that the truth will shine, illuminating the eyes of our soul with its own rays. This truth, which was then manifested by the ineffable and mysterious illumination which came to Moses, is God.
>
> And if the flame by which the soul of the prophet was illuminated was kindled from a thorny bush, even this fact will not be useless for our inquiry. For if truth is God and truth is light—the Gospel testifies by these sublime and divine names to the God who made himself visible to us in the flesh—such guidance of virtue leads us to know that light which has reached down even to human nature. Lest one think that the

radiance did not come from a material substance, this light did not shine from some luminary among the stars but came from an earthly bush and surpassed the heavenly luminaries in brilliance.

The light teaches us what we must do to stand within the rays of the true light: Sandaled feet cannot ascend that height where the light of truth is seen, but the dead and earthly covering of skins, which was placed around our nature at the beginning when we were found naked because of disobedience to the divine will, must be removed from the feet of the soul. When we do this, the knowledge of the truth will result and manifest itself. The full knowledge of being comes about by purifying our opinion concerning nonbeing.

In my view the definition of truth is this: not to have a mistaken apprehension of Being. Falsehood is a kind of impression which arises in the understanding about nonbeing: as though what does not exist does, in fact, exist. But truth is the sure apprehension of real Being. So, whoever applies himself in quietness to higher philosophical matters over a long period of time will barely apprehend what true Being is, and what nonbeing is, that is, what is existence only in appearance, with no self-subsisting nature.

It seems to me that at the time the great Moses was instructed in the theophany he came to know that none of those things which are apprehended by sense perception and contemplated by the understanding really subsists, but that the transcendent essence and cause of the universe, on which everything depends, alone subsists.[34]

Chapter 3

The Rediscovery of Spirit

On the individual scale, the task of overcoming the massive inertia of a fallen civilization seems impossible. Yet around thirty years ago, studies that began in the Himalayas in the 1930s led to the introduction to the West of what is now known as transcendental meditation, a phrase that translates the Sanskrit word *dhyana*. The new practice was entirely different from anything previously known in the West as meditation. The effects of this have been quite remarkable. From this practice, as long ago as the early sixties, many people obtained valuable inner experiences. Some of them experienced the inner light, the light that shines in the darkness, the light of what is called in Sanskrit *sat-chit-ananda*: being-bliss-consciousness, the *uncreated light*. In time these stimuli have helped re-awaken dormant possibilities within our own Christian civilization; for example, the experiences obtained in meditation have reawakened interest in Christian methods of inner prayer, in the Jesus Prayer or *prayer of the heart,* and in the centering prayer introduced by Father Thomas Keating. At the same time, within the Christian world, another important influence has survived to the present day. Reading about Mount Athos, I was struck by the comment by a previous visitor that "several monks now living are known to have had the experience of the uncreated light." Abbot George of Grigoriou expressed the priorities of such people when he said to me once that "the principle export of Athos is the Jesus Prayer." The inner experience that results from this kind of prayer has awakened many to inner Christianity, "for the salvation of the world,"[1] as the Eastern Church puts it. This is the exact Christian equivalent of the Indian *dhyana* meditation, although technically different in certain important ways. Practiced assiduously, both methods have many identical efforts, whose influence on the Christian faith is now substantial. People who have gained new understanding of their nature from using these methods are returning to the fold of a church they now understand more deeply. So large are the numbers now involved, that life in the West is beginning to take a new direction: new ways of thought are emerging, which are as yet immature, but which might be expected to lead in time to the development in our civilization of means to manage inner experience better, now that in this way Westerners are rediscovering their spiritual nature, previously hidden ever deeper by the Fall and its consequences. Ouspensky said, fifty years ago, that when talking of these things one should not speak of God. Already, virtually unnoticed, this civilization has become so different that today we can speak openly of things that not so long ago had to be spoken of in whispers. In a civilization that had for so long forgotten that man is spirit, spirit is now being remembered again. Because of this, to reveal these truths now may actually bring results. It may be that this is an evolutionary change in direction, a true *metanoia* of humanity turning toward the spiritual dimension of life.

This turnabout already exists, but the words for it, the statements that explain it and make it articulate are as yet lacking. When Spirit speaks to those who will listen, reminding them that their own inmost self is spirit, one result is the beginning of a restoration of the esoteric tradition. Another is a developing dialogue between the churches. Both are signs of a single living force acting within our human world. This growing awareness of spirit as Self—a growing awareness that "I am a spiritual being, more than just a body," is beginning to penetrate into the heart of our civilization. But the experience of *dhyana* or even the experience of the uncreated light is not the full Christian transformation. For this to occur, there must have been an actual shift within the individual of the center of awareness—a redirection of the *nous* from thought, imagination, and physical sensations to the heart.

In Western forms of the Christian esoteric tradition, we can as yet find few authors who touch on this important aspect with sufficient precision, so far have we lost our way. For some decades we have been forced to draw on the great Eastern thinkers to grasp this special way of understanding spirit as Self: an understanding of the fact that our real nature can be experienced as that of a spirit inhabiting, interpenetrating, and manifesting as a body, not merely as a physical body. And once this knowledge has been assimilated by a sufficient number of people, new forms of understanding will give new life to these ancient experiences.

What this all means is that a rekindling of religious experience—which is a form of direct knowledge—is actually occurring now not for hundreds but for millions of individuals who are now learning for themselves that they are spiritual beings. This knowledge, born of experience, contains in it the answers to many of our questions. It is the reason for this book, and for the studies that have led up to its writing. It is quite literally an immediate answer to the question of how we are again to open the doors of our Christian faith to consideration of those significant human experiences which at present are generally ignored; those rejected not only by science, but by the churches under the influence of science, and by many Christians. So, in answer to the question as to how we Christians are to recover confidence in our own religious experiences, we can only say that the task is in hand, that, through an unprecedented and generally unacknowledged cooperation of world faiths, the Christian world is rediscovering the realities of religious experience.

The Christian Overcomes the Fall

Recently a priest from Mount Athos echoed the hermit's instruction to me all those years ago, saying: "Mount Athos can help return to Europe an awareness of what its own, unique contribution among the great organizations of the world must be, that is, to comprehend the meaning of the human person and the idea of a personalist society."[2]

This would be to begin the restoration of that which was lost in the Fall. There is no more doubt that we are inwardly fallen, but the true Christian, the perfected Christian in the sense understood by the masters of the early church, is someone who has inwardly risen again from that Fall, and not only from the Fall that happened once, when our present "captivity," our *exile* from our own inner nature, began. The fully developed Christian,[3] who is Christian in being as well as in intention, has also risen from the Fall as a psychological event, a personal resurrection from a personal, psychological fall that happens every day, whenever we wake from sleep yet remain partially asleep. If once we begin to wake from that captivity, then each time we fall back into captivity it is the same *Fall of Adam.*

As certain of the early Fathers put it, in this inner sense, resurrection is the awakening of a new state—which can only mean a new state of consciousness—and the General Resurrection is the overdue awakening of humanity as a whole to a new and less corrupt psychological state. Indeed, on the evidence available it is not too fanciful to suppose that each civilization is an experiment, an attempt at that general awakening, and that each civilization that fails to attain this eventually dies. In evolutionary terms, in human beings, nature is still experimenting, and even now, at this time, and even in this book, the current experiment—which we know as Western civilization—continues, but we must recognize that right now the experiment, and with it the whole of the world we know, is, as Teilhard de Chardin, or more recently Boris Mouravieff, might have put it, at a crucial point.

How do these different threads relate? There is a question that arises when we try to define this civilization. Is it a Christian civilization in which, as Mouravieff points out, "The Gospel is now known through all the world"? Should we speak only of Western civilization, and if so, what is the significance of the fact that we no longer think of our civilization as Christian? For is it not true that our present civilization did indeed spring from the marriage of minds from the Greek and Semitic civilizations, a union that took shape in the early church? And if this is true, is it not strange that we feel apologetic today when called to profess our Christian roots?

The Life of Moses

With the rediscovery of spirit, a rediscovery of the spiritual dimensions of scripture is becoming a reality. A clue to this is found in the work of Gregory of Nyssa. Writing in his *Life of Moses* about his way of interpreting the events in the Book of Exodus, he once commented on the way historical passages of scripture should be read, and how we can draw a proper parallel between inner and outer realities in such an account. He wrote:

> If while trying to parallel completely the historical account to the sequence of such intellectual contemplation, someone should somehow discover something in the account which does not coincide with our understanding, he should not reject the whole enterprise. He should always keep in mind our discussion's goal, to which we are looking while we relate these details. We have already said in our prologue that the lives of honoured men would be set forth as a pattern of virtue for those who come after them.
>
> Those who emulate their lives, however, cannot experience the identical literal events. For how could one again find the people multiplying during their sojourn in Egypt? And how again find the tyrant who enslaves the people and bears

hostility to male offspring and allows the feminine and weaker to grow in numbers? And how again find all the other things which Scripture includes? Because therefore it has been shown to be impossible to imitate the marvels of these blessed men in these exact events, one might substitute a moral teaching for the literal sequence in those things which admit of such an approach. In this way those who have been striving toward virtue may find aid in living the virtuous life.

If the events require dropping from the literal account anything written which is foreign to the sequence of elevated understanding, we pass over this on the grounds that it is useless and unprofitable to our purpose, so as not to interrupt the guidance to virtue at such a point.[4]

This passage is quite clear in suggesting that the events of an exceptional man's life reflect the inner processes that made him exceptional, and so can be used to illustrate those inner processes in order to help others imitate him. The same principle was implied in a conversation with a remarkable hermit on Mount Athos who suggested that I should study the lives of individuals of great achievements of this kind.

In this way of using the text, Gregory seems to say, the reader must ignore some things as being merely historical events of no inner significance or, on the other hand, such events, perhaps reported elsewhere, may have been left out of a specific account as unnecessary to the inner purpose.

Philosophy in the Early Church

For a long time two meanings of subjectivity have been confused. The scientific world has correctly warned us against taking subjective opinion for evidence, but many people have taken this as a restriction against subjective *experience* as evidence, an entirely different thing. It has been widely assumed from this that nothing we experience within ourselves is knowledge, although in our hearts we know that inner experience tells us some things of which we need then have no doubts. Our heads have been trained to accept these statements as blindly as the medieval world accepted the statements of a then bigoted church. Like those churchmen, but on the other side of the debate, when we are faced with a consensus of our peers and the massed weight of the educated, even if we do feel doubts of these modern dogmas, we rarely take these doubts into account, such is the power of education. But it is these silenced doubts that give us one glimpse of the kind of theory

of knowledge that might have developed if the inner tradition had remained unhidden.

Underlying this is a clear distinction between two fundamental kinds
of knowledge, a distinction that will run like a central thread throughout
this book. Implied in this distinction between different kinds of knowledge
is the idea that there is a higher kind of knowledge which, until it is
complete, lacks its full power. When it reaches a certain stage of *completeness,* it stabilizes a change that gives us the strength to change our lives.

In modern terms, such as those used by Gurdjieff and Ouspensky,
these would be regarded as *exoteric* and *esoteric.* Between these two they
placed a third category, *mesoteric,* but according to Greek Orthodox author
Constantin Cavarnos, the original terminology used only the two terms.
He wrote:

> Greek Church writers appropriated the word "philosophy,"
> already in the early centuries, for denoting Christianity. In
> order to clarify and justify this appropriation, they drew a
> distinction between two kinds of philosophy: "External
> (exoterike, exothyraten) philosophy," and "internal (esoterike,
> eso) philosophy." The latter they also called "the true philoso-
> phy," "heavenly philosophy," "spiritual philosophy," "divine
> philosophy," "philosophy according to Christ," "sacred phi-
> losophy," "philosophy from Above," and "wisdom from Above."
>
> The first kind of philosophy, external philosophy, com-
> prises for them ancient Greek philosophy and the pagan phi-
> losophy of early Christian centuries. The second kind, "inter-
> nal philosophy," is identical with the Christian religion. This
> term is used to denote Orthodox Christian teaching in its
> totality; lived Christian teaching in general; some interior prac-
> tice, particularly inner attention and inner stillness and the
> monastic life.[5]

In fact, both the twofold and threefold divisions are valid in practice.
The twofold division distinguishes between two kinds of knowledge described by Saint Paul. Both exoteric and esoteric philosophy in this early
sense used the ordinary faculties of the human mind to their best, but the
two forms differ greatly in the meaning they give to their teachings, in the
way their statements are confirmed or verified, and in certain aspects of
the training necessary to produce a competent philosopher. Finally, they
differ in their overall outcome: exoteric philosophy generates *ideas,* esoteric philosophy brings ideas into being and changes *being;* the result at its
best is *sanctification,* so that the philosopher himself is the product and
demonstration of his philosophy.

Exoteric philosophy is thus part of the Knowledge of the World, to use Saint Paul's terminology. A product of individual human minds, it is by nature fragmentary, and the consensus it forms is subject to continual change. Because exoteric philosophy obtains its verification empirically, by Kantian intuition, it is subject to the limitations of that form of thinking, each meaning is circular and resting on some previous idea, a situation that leads to fragmentation so that philosophy, psychology, theology, and the physical sciences form separate disciplines.

Esoteric philosophy in this twofold sense is *gnosis*: it is Knowledge from God, although in those terms it also incorporates the fruits of human experience of how to live in alignment with that knowledge. A gift to the human mind from the Spirit, it is by nature unitive and hence coherent, and the consensus it forms is not subject to fundamental change, but evolves with time while remaining internally consistent. It is this fact, this coherence, this constancy, this unity of truth that reflects the truth of unity, which is the origin of the idea of the Perennial Philosophy. Esoteric philosophy is experiential in a mystical sense, not an everyday sense; it obtains its verification by direct intuition of the Spirit. This is how it presents a picture that is consistent and self-referential,[6] so that its meaning is obtained in the act of verification, not by comparison. Within it, philosophy, psychology, theology, and the physical sciences at one time formed a single discipline, their divisions dissolved in a divine simplicity.

The modern threefold terminology—exoteric, mesoteric, esoteric— distinguishes between different stages in the student's progress from one of these two kinds of knowledge to the other. In other words, it refers to his growth in understanding of the esoteric—so that the threefold terminology as used in this century is experientially correct.

Clement of Alexandria, Saint Basil the Great, and many others made this distinction between exoteric and esoteric because they believed that, to overcome problems of knowledge that existed in the Hellenic and Jewish worlds even in the earliest days of the church, philosophy had a practical use in the Christian life. Clement of Alexandria wrote nearly two thousand years ago that pre-Christian philosophers were often inspired by God, but that one had to be careful what one took from them. Not all that the early philosophers had written was inspired. Even after selective reading, what he called "pagan" philosophy was not to be taken in or put to use in a haphazard way. According to men such as Clement and Origen, the study of *external* philosophy was to be employed mainly as a preliminary training for the mind before this was transcended. True philosophy they saw as one with theology, and with the practice known as *ascesis*: it was the entry into a different kind of thinking and behavior, which led not to worldly success but to spiritual *salvation*. Yet the early Christian Fathers found uses for both the inner and external knowledge, reflected respectively in esoteric and exoteric philosophy. We need external knowledge even to obtain the necessities of life. But all true Christian philosophy is esoteric, in the sense that its aims and its worldview are rooted in inner experience, and in the actions dictated by that inner experience.

Clement said, for example: "But if the Hellenic philosophy comprehends not the whole extent of the truth, and besides is destitute of strength to perform the commandments of the Lord, yet it prepares the way for the truly royal teaching; training in some way or other, and moulding the character, and fitting him who believes in Providence for the reception of the truth."[7] This quotation contains important practical information. It distinguishes clearly the difference seen by many of the early Fathers in the effects of two teachings, and this view is confirmed in practical experience:

1. The Greek philosophical teachings are incomplete in the sense that they leave their student "destitute of strength to perform the commandments of the Lord."
2. The Christian inner teaching, if comprehended in full, is complete in the sense that once it has been fully assimilated or digested, it gives the student the strength to perform those commandments.

The student's ability to fulfill the commandments or rules of the path therefore forms a test either of a teaching or of a student's assimilation of that teaching. This is an important factor in esotericism. In terms of modern esotericism, it is this that distinguishes the rare real "schools" from their imitations. It often manifests as humility.

Gospel terms sometimes used for this kind of knowledge were *gnosis* and *epignosis*. We shall discuss later the distinction between this *Christian gnosis* and the teachings of the sects now known as the Gnostics; suffice it for the moment to say that the difference is the same as between the two forms of teaching described immediately above.

Gregory of Nyssa, his thinking descended from Clement and influenced by Saint Basil, distinguished these two kinds of knowledge with philosophical precision. Lacking the vocabulary of modern thought, he nevertheless managed to make himself clear by saying that one kind of knowledge was known by *measure,* and the other was associated with *virtue*. Gregory was one of the Cappadocian Fathers who did much to shape the Eastern Church, but whose works repeatedly touch on material more often restricted to the oral tradition. He managed to show clearly how a proper theory of knowledge expands upon our definition of knowledge and so finds a place for both kinds of knowledge, that which we meet in life and *gnosis*, when he wrote: "The perfection of everything which can be measured by the senses is marked off by certain definite boundaries. . . . The person who looks at a cubit or at the number ten knows that its perfection consists in the fact that it has both a beginning and an end. But in the case of virtue we have learned from the Apostle that its one limit of perfection is the fact that it has no limit."[8]

The same idea of the *immeasurable,* here expressed in terms of the nature of the gift of the Spirit to Christ, is found in the Gospel of Saint John:

> And what he hath seen and heard, that he testifieth; and no man receiveth his testimony.
>
> He that hath received his testimony hath set to his seal that God is true.
>
> For he whom God hath sent speaketh the words of God; for God giveth not the spirit by measure unto him (John 3:32–34).

Saint Isaac's Prayer for Gnosis

The Fathers say that our *nous,* the nonverbal intelligence which perceives direct experience and symbols as equally "real," will be free to function properly and objectively only when it is released from wrong thoughts and feelings. Today this means that it must be liberated from the narrow intellectualism of the Western world, and this can occur fully only when this *nous* is "informed" with gnosis, with noetic knowledge, equated, by Saint Paul and by the Fathers (including Clement, who quoted this passage by Paul in his *Stromata* or esoteric text), with knowledge given by God: "Which things also we speak, not in the words which man's wisdom teacheth, but which the Holy Ghost teacheth; comparing spiritual things with spiritual" (1 Corinthians 2:13).

The problem is that this kind of knowledge is not acceptable to the mind that still has not discovered the limits of its capabilities, that continues to believe that scientific theory is able to plumb the depths of reality. Saint Isaac the Syrian had a prayer that makes it clear that he understood that, because unaided or externally aided reason is unable to be sure of the divine, all true knowledge of God comes from God.

> O Lord, make me worthy to know you and love you,
> not in the knowledge arising from mental exercise
> and the dispersion of the mind,
> but make me worthy of that knowledge
> whereby the mind, in beholding you,

> glorifies your nature in this vision
> which steals from the mind the awareness of the world.

One of the practical implications of this is that the final stages of prayer are taught more by God than by man.

Two Very Different Kinds of Knowledge

In Saint Isaac's prayer, written in the seventh century, we will perhaps recognize the way it looks at the idea of the knowledge of God, linking this to inner instead of external experience, and to knowledge, revealed to us instead of deduced by us, that we are reading of the Tree of Life, instead of the Tree of Knowledge. In this different kind of knowledge, there are certain basics that will have been found in the ideas we have already been considering—specifically:

— This idea of two levels of knowledge: the worldly, based on observation and deduction, and the spiritual or esoteric, which is *gnosis*.
— The idea that everyday knowledge obscures higher knowledge. This was put succinctly by the Spanish Saint John of the Cross, who wrote: "We can only attain to God by stilling the faculties of understanding."
— There is also a third fact about this: the idea that true gnosis, an awareness of spirit, steals from the mind our awareness of the world.

According to one scholar, Morton Smith, Clement appears to have viewed the form of knowledge known as gnosis as an external form of knowledge, knowledge in the sense used by Karl Popper to define what he described as objective knowledge. Smith says: "Both Clement and this letter[9] conceive the gift of gnosis as a process of instruction in the elements of the Christian tradition, including the Lord's teaching—instruction given only to chosen candidates, and leading eventually to deification."[10]

However, for the written form of knowledge truly to possess the properties and have the effects defined above, it needs to be assimilated and linked to experience. As I understand it, there are in fact two forms of gnosis, related as are a human and his or her shadow: *true gnosis* is a truly spiritual form of knowledge that transforms those who experience it; the transmitted gnosis is an expression of that true gnosis, the divine word, *Logos ton Theon,* through the medium of the human *word,* through human communication, a representation of gnosis that draws the recipient toward the experience of the *true gnosis.*

This latter idea, this approach of considering the divine qualities, exists in the inner tradition of other faiths, and can be practiced by those whose weak faith prevents them considering the divine as unmanifest, when they can instead consider the important principles of life: love, truth, beauty, mercy, goodness, forbearance—and even principles that also seem to exist in the "inanimate" world, like infinity, eternity, perfection—and they can contemplate God by contemplating these qualities taken to their furthest possibilities.

The Inner World as a Window onto the Invisible World

This clear description of the difference in quality between inner knowledge and external knowledge gives us another glimpse of the kind of theory of knowledge that might have existed today if intellectual growth had not been so closely tied to sensory knowledge. By clearly distinguishing these kinds of knowledge, but at the same time accepting the validity of both, it seems clear that we would have become able to apply each where it is appropriate. In such a situation, we could have combined the progress of technology with individual and social self-knowledge, and this would have given us the ability to regulate that progress.

In fact, a scientific way has been developed of saying virtually the same thing: this is physicist David Bohm's criticism of the assumption that any scientific theory can be complete. His philosophically important criticism has been summarized thus: "Bohm criticized this assumption by pointing out that nature may be infinite."[11] This is *exactly* the same as saying, as did Gregory of Nyssa, that the limit of perfection has no limit. The summary continued: "Because it would not be possible for any theory to completely explain something that is infinite, Bohm suggested that open scientific enquiry might be better served if researchers refrained from making the assumption [of the completeness of an explanation]."[12] This is the same as saying that only measured or measurable dimensions can have measurable aggregates and hence only these can have definite limits. To make the parallel between Bohm's and Saint Gregory's ideas complete, we have to realize that Bohm is using the term *nature* to describe the totality described by Gregory's term *virtue,* and that this term is virtually equivalent to Plato's *One.*

Bohm continued to develop his ideas, so that Talbot could add on the next page that: "Classical science had always viewed the state of a system as a whole as merely the result of the interaction of its parts. However, the quantum potential stood this view on its ear and indicated that the behaviour of the parts was actually organized by the whole. This not only took Niels Bohr's suggestion that subatomic particles are not independent 'things,' but are part of an indivisible system one step further, but even suggested that wholeness was in some ways the more primary reality."[13]

Bohm's view of *nature,* seen in this light, if not derived from Plato's concept of the *One,* as it may be, is clearly approaching it very closely. This means that it also approaches the Christian view of reality, although it does not reach it. Certainly this view breaks the bounds of the physical or materialist view of life and shows with precision the direction in which a rapprochement between scientific and Christian worldviews is possible, a conclusion confirmed by the statement by 1973 Nobel physics laureate Brian Josephson, quoted in Talbot's summary, "Bohm's implicate order may someday even lead to the inclusion of God or Mind within the framework of science."[14]

This view is already adequate to define the philosophical boundaries of the physical sciences in Christian terms—although not at the same time setting boundaries for the higher Christian knowledge.[15] It also develops Whitehead's work on *assumptions,* opening the door to an understanding of scientific method as based on the challenging of assumptions, and, most important, it provides a tool by which the modern individual can comprehend the limits of intellect and of the "unholy alliance" of intellect and perception that have distorted the worldview of our civilization and "blinded the eyes of faith." To overcome this is a powerful act toward freeing oneself from the thrall of the fallen reasoning faculty, and one of the reasons why Clement of Alexandria could ask: "How will you love your neighbour if you do not philosophize?"

This question exactly defines the concept of philosophy as it was in the early days of the church. At first sight it looks quite different from the classical Greek philosophy that preceded the Christian era, but in fact Clement, a philosopher trained in Athens before he became Christian, said that it was a proper development and fulfillment of the same intention and inspiration which had already existed in the teachings of Socrates and Plato.

The invisible world, then, was visible before the Fall, either figuratively or actually. Yet for us today it is in an ordinary sense invisible, although it can be glimpsed in part within us, "through a glass darkly," as Saint Paul put it.[16] With the Fall, the inner reality became for us a hidden or secret inner world.

The nature of human perception is such that, as we are, we can see only the surfaces of things. We cannot see inside things, with rare exceptions such as water, and of course the flames of a fire. We can "see" inside people only as much as they are able to put into words. But when we still the surface noise and activity within us, we can see within ourselves. Then it is that we discover the truth of the often quoted words from Saint Isaac the Syrian, one of the great texts of the esoteric tradition, which says: "Enter eagerly into your inner treasure-house and you will see the treasure-house of heaven: for the two are the same, and one and the same entry reveals them both. The ladder leading to the Kingdom is within you, hidden in your soul. Plunge into yourself, washing yourself from sin, and you will see the rungs of the ladder by which you can ascend."[17]

In my experience, when we see in this way, then anything and everything can be seen in this way, as *fire,* even a humble thornbush. Christ promised just this: to bring *fire* in that cryptic saying: "I am come to send fire upon the earth, and what will I if it be already kindled" (Luke 12:49).

But many people have experiences they cannot interpret, just as I could not originally interpret this that I suppose must be called a mystical experience, a view of the world as if transformed into fire. Even Saint Gregory's explanation is not easy for us to understand today, so, in modern terms, what is the meaning of this moment of fire?

I think the answer to this is almost naively simple. To see a flame is to see *inside* matter while it is in a particularly active state. I think such experiences show that modern physics is accurate enough in its picture of matter to indicate that inside, beneath the surface our senses cannot penetrate, everything is like that, particles in ceaseless motion. I think the vision I experienced, as have so many before me, was simply that: seeing beneath the surface of life outside myself, when we ordinarily see beneath the surface only very incompletely, and only inside our minds.

But the greater lesson, the valuable self-knowledge I gained from this, perhaps, was the fear that I found in the moment of the fire. This fear arises naturally when we face the great unknowns of life, simply from our unfinished nature: what we are, what we know of ourselves, is so limited that we cannot face the fullness of our nature nor the fullness of the world around us. There is in this fear a doubt of our ability to cope, and sometimes a fear that we will lose the things that are precious to us, but which we know, somewhere inside us, are not really so important. Did Saint Paul know this same fear when he wrote: "It is a fearful thing to fall into the hands of the living God" (Hebrews 10:31)?

The senses, then, show a false or, to be more accurate, a purely external and thus incomplete reality. Reality is found within, but when we do begin to find it within, we discover, as the *Gospel According to Thomas* says: "The Kingdom is within you, *and* it is outside."

Esotericism, then, is about the inner world: that inner world which, when discovered, is also found to be outside us, that once was reality to our ancestors; the reality from which we have fallen and to which we seek a return: the reality of Being.

This too is the world of true prayer. It was about this inner world, dark for most of us most of the time, that the gospel teaching says: "Go into your closet and close yourself in, and your Father Who sees in secret will reward you openly" (Matthew 6:6). In this verse, the link between inner or esoteric experience, experience of the hidden, and the Christian doctrine of inner or noetic prayer, is established irrevocably.

So even in the story of the Fall itself, there is an outer and an inner interpretation. In the inner interpretation, both the garden and the earth outside the garden were part of what we now know through glimpses as the *inner world*. More than this, the description of the inner world that it gives us is part of a classical view of the inner world of the heart. In this classical view, the garden of the heart is a seedbed that can bring into being all kinds of plants.

With the loss of man's higher faculties comes a further change described in the story of the Fall. The world, now become simply an outer world, begins to produce "plants," which seem at first beautiful but which, as they become full grown, are found to have thorns and impenetrable tangles: to become briars of suffering.

What does the New Testament have to say about this? Unfortunately, the answer to this question depends on which version—which translation— you are reading. Some translations reveal a great deal more of the inner teaching than others. For example, one recent translation renders a passage in Romans in agreement with what has been written on the last few pages. This was written about the Jews by that once vehement Jew Paul; but it could as easily be written today about many people in all faiths. This version claims to be the most straightforward translation of the original Greek—and therefore closest to the version used by the early Fathers of the church. It says:

> There is not one innocent, not even one,
> No one who understands,
> No one seeking God.
> All declined into uselessness together
> With no one practicing kindness,
> Not a single one.[18]

When we go to the King James Version, the language, at least today, is not quite so specific. It loses its bite, but it still says a great deal.

> There is none righteous, no, not one;
> There is none that understandeth;

There is none that seeketh after God.
They are all gone out of the way,
They are together become unprofitable;
There is none that doeth good, no, not one
   (Romans 3:10–12).

Other versions have even less authority.

The Role of Knowledge in Spirituality

The part played by knowledge in spiritual development is never based purely on discursive intellect, so that it can only exist, in the container of a life that is in some sense religious, when it is founded on that clear perception that leads to spiritual adulthood, but is easily interrupted not only by adolescent fantasy, but by theory and overuse of language. The myth of the tower of Babel refers to this. Knowledge became fragmented after the Fall; it becomes fragmented today as long as we continue to feed from the Tree of the Knowledge of Good and Evil. Such knowledge is fragmented by the way we take it in: we regard single views or simple descriptions of some thing or object—taken from one point of view or based on a single idea—as being complete. Such knowledge has few connections with other objects, treating a single idea too narrowly and without its proper existential or contextual connections—a fragmentation that results when this kind of knowledge is *incomplete* but people yet consider that the knowledge they have of something presents a "complete" picture. This means that people who genuinely know part of something tend to see that part as being the whole, and draw misleading conclusions as a result.

With esoteric knowledge, because of this danger it is particularly important that we establish a view, of ourselves, and of the world, that is "complete" not in the finest detail—which is of course impossible—but in form and structure. Only esoteric doctrine that is "complete" in this way is effective in leading to inner change that is complete and unifying. This is one of the reasons why, in Clement's *Stromata,* a reverse process of reuniting fragmentary knowledge is suggested: he claimed that it is possible to *discover*[19] Christ by reconstructing the fragments of the truth, including genuine truths from sources other than the gospel; for God, he said, can reveal truth even to pagans, and this too will help us to discover for ourselves the *whole* Word, the living presence of Christ. This whole idea is difficult to understand as a reality, and becomes comprehensible not with study alone, but only as a result of struggling with our own illusions. "So, then, the barbarian and Hellenic philosophy has torn off a fragment of eternal truth not from the mythology of Dionysius, but from the theology of the ever-living Word. And He who brings again together the separate fragments, and makes them one, will without peril, be assured, contemplate the perfect Word, the truth."[20]

But how does one reunite the separated fragments? By *theoria,* the equivalent in the Greek Church of contemplation in Western Christianity: by studying the same thing from many angles, in its relationship to many other objects, so that all its *connections* are known, as well as the thing itself. It is then that "The truth shall set you free."

With our knowledge reunified and linked to true *gnosis,* and this gnosis acquired in full experience, we are free indeed.

And what must be reunified in this way? There is a phrase that recurs throughout the Bible, Old Testament and New; it is *Logos ton Theon,* the Word of God. To search through the Bible and read each occurrence of this phrase in its context gives a clear sense of something unique: some special communication first found in the prophets, later in the Apostles, and par excellence in Christ, who became directly identified with that Logos—with that form of communication, with the force that carried it, and with the power it possessed, under certain circumstances, to act within those who heard it. A power that it still possesses. "For the word of God is quick, and powerful, and sharper than any two-edged sword, piercing even to the dividing asunder of soul and spirit, and of the joints and marrow, and is a discerner of the thoughts and intents of the heart" (Hebrews 4:12).

Discernment is the product of a particular kind of knowledge, referred to earlier as *logos,* when that knowledge has been properly understood and remembered. This special kind of knowledge was once called *logos* because it was carried by *the word of God,* small *w,* and represented by Christ as the Word, large *W.*

This phrase, "the word of God," occurs many times in Old and New Testaments and always with the same significance. The knowledge it conveyed is also known in some Gospels and sometimes in Saint Paul as *gnosis.* This special knowledge has the power to create this special kind of discrimination.

Having the right knowledge, we become able to make the right choice. "For this cause also thank we God without ceasing, because, when ye received the word of God which ye heard of us, ye received it not as the word of men, but as it is in truth, the word of God, which effectually worketh also in you that believe" (1 Thessalonians 2:13). It is rather like taking a wisdom pill, although the medicine involves learning things about oneself that are often highly unpleasant in the learning.

This *gnosis* lights the way by which the animal or exterior man can become a spiritual or interior man, and the temporal can become eternal.

This is the meaning of one kind of discrimination, known as *the discernment of Spirits* (Greek *diakrisis*), discussed in more detail in chapter 13. The *Philokalia* says about this: "the power of discrimination, scrutinizing all the thoughts and actions of a man, distinguishes and sets aside everything that is base and not pleasing to God, and keeps him free from delusion."[21]

Saint Maximos on Contemplation

When you think of contemplation as pure reason, when you imagine, as you sometimes will for many years yet, that you can think about God, and perhaps even understand Him, with pure reason, remember that the Fathers did not believe this, and take up next in your studies the following passage from Saint Maximos the Confessor, who gave a good idea of what the early Fathers thought about it when he wrote: "When you intend to know God do not seek the reasons about His being, for the human mind and that of any other being below God cannot discover this. Rather, consider as you can the things about Him, for example, His eternity, immensity, infinity, His goodness, wisdom, and power which creates, governs, and judges creatures. For that person among others is a good theologian if he searches out the principles of these things, however much or little."[22]

The proper meaning of *theoria* survives today in the West in part of the extended meaning of the concept of "infused contemplation." In the Eastern Church this aspect is often ignored, and the practical elements implied in this term are brought—as they very well may be, as the concepts overlap—into descriptions of *prayer of the heart*.

Gnosis, gained in this way, is regarded as the only way that we can be united in love to higher worlds and eventually to the Lord. Evagrius said of this: "The food of the soul is said to be contemplative knowledge,[23] since it alone can unite us with the holy powers. This holds true since union between incorporeal beings follows quite naturally from their sharing the same deep attitudes."[24] Here we have taken the Greek word, sometimes rendered *bodiless,* in the sense better indicated here by the context as *incorporeal,* taking this to refer to those who are not ruled by the body. Most translations seem to suggest that it refers to those who are physically without a body, but we can see from the last sentence of the verse that Evagrius believed that when false emotional attitudes were removed, natural attitudes emerged—and that those natural attitudes were common to all "incorporeal" beings; that is, that these natural attitudes ruled all beings except those ruled by "corporeal" forces coming from outside them.

Before you claim for yourself that you are already free, that, at least, you already know the *Way* to God, that you already walk these paths and experience these realities, have a care, and carefully ponder the words of the Book of Job, where it says:

> Have the gates of death been opened unto thee? or has thou seen the doors of the shadow of death?
>
> Hast thou perceived the breadth of the earth? declare if thou knowest it all.
>
> Where is the way where light dwelleth? and as for darkness, where is the place thereof,
>
> That thou shouldest take it to the bound thereof, and that thou shouldest know the paths to the house thereof? (Job 38:17–20).

Chapter 4

The Wise and Foolish Virgins

The question of energy has been important to Christianity at least since the end of the twelfth century, when Saint Gregory Palamas, faced with the growth of what has since become known as rationalism, left his monastic life on Mount Athos to become a bishop in Thessalonika, where he entered the debate then raging with the philosopher Barlaam the Calabrian. In answer to Barlaam's claims that God was to be known by the intellect, Palamas made the point that God could not be known by thought, nor by observation, but that He could be known in the stillness of *hesychia:* by the presence of His energies within the still heart of the knower . . . a presence which could be known by "abstracting" the awareness from all the activities and images that normally fill the inner world and take all our attention, so that we become aware of activities that could be recognized as of divine origin by the fact that they had no earthly origin; that they did not act under our direct control or in response to anything directly perceivable. He wrote: " 'Such a union of the divinized with the light that comes from on high takes place by virtue of a cessation of all intellectual activity.' It is not the product of a cause or a relationship, for these are dependent upon the activity of the intellect, but it comes to be as a result of a process leading to total abstraction, without itself being that abstraction."[1]

When he was sure he had made the point, Saint Gregory resigned his bishopric and returned to the monastic life and to his fellow hesychasts.

Translations of the Bible actually seem to confuse *energy* with *virtue,* so important is this question, and so closely are the ideas connected on the esoteric path. The same confusion occurs in translations of the early

79

Fathers, if confusion it is. In fact, one of the great discoveries of this investigation has been the realization that virtue is the result of possessing specific energies.

One of the great problems of modern spirituality is that spiritual experience today is generally infrequent and unpredictable. This is in fact a question of energies, and these energies are a matter of what might be called "spiritual metabolism." Man, viewed merely as a body, metabolizes food (mixed in water) and air, and these are the fuels and combustive atmosphere that provide the energy, or in early Greek terms the *dynamis*, the force of movement, that gives movement and life to the body.

But Christian doctrine says that man is a *spirit*. Spirit too acts "on energy received," but normally the energy it receives is too little to sustain what we know as genuine spirituality. Without the necessary energies, the nous remains dark, the "eye of the soul" remains blind. The result is that after glimpses of the truth that they are spirit, individuals are thrust into the struggle to obtain sufficient energy to reopen the door that once opened so briefly. This is the beginning of the "unseen warfare." To succeed in this struggle we need special knowledge, knowledge that is only now reaching us and is as yet not generally accessible in our modern civilization, although it exists in the gospel and ways of understanding it exist in the esoteric tradition. Together, these tell us that the activity of our spiritual metabolism can be enhanced or augmented in certain ways. Certain keys to this process are encapsulated in the gospel parable of the wise and foolish virgins.

The Quest for Energies

Spiritual growth and practice require and develop certain subtle energies which tend to be in short supply in our normal ways of life. The importance of these higher energies is actually emphasized in the gospel, but in translation the connection is not obvious. One reference, which links with the idea of energies or actions in the Palamas sense, uses the idea of a supersubstantial bread (see chapter 11 for details). Another familiar passage says: "But he answered and said, It is written, Man shall not live by bread alone, but by every word that proceedeth out of the mouth of God" (Matthew 4:4). This is not about our normal food but about a change in our food, an improved metabolism producing new energies. When this becomes stable, it leads to visible changes in us that are evidence of other less obvious results of our *metanoia*. Evagrius made one meaning of this doctrine clearer when he wrote: "Just as bread is nourishment for the body and virtue for the soul, so is noetic prayer nourishment for the nous."[2]

This doctrine clearly links with a diagram that shows the three main levels of the human organism which must be changed in order to achieve a total and permanent transformation (see figure 4.1). Each requires appropriate energy. Recently, in the terminology introduced by Gurdjieff to fit in with modern thought, the foods for the psyche and the nous have been described as *energies*. Saint Gregory Palamas said that we cannot know God's essence, but we can know Him by His energies.

Nous	Noetic energy
Psyche	Psychic energy
Body	Physical energy of sugar metabolism

Figure 4.1   Basic division of energies.

In the quotation from Evagrius, the word translated *virtue* actually is the Greek word *dynamis*. In the Gospels, too, this word is also sometimes translated *virtue*. To understand what this means, how the same word can be translated as "activity," as "energy," or as "virtue," we can start from the experience many of you will have had from attending church services, or even from certain spiritual meetings. You may have realized that *some* of these events give you a strange kind of energy. People sometimes look different—sometimes *younger*—when they leave such events from how they looked when they came in through the door. This difference is the direct result of different energies—a different balance of energies within us. Certainly, these energies are little understood today, but although nothing is ever said about them, we experience their effects on us, and if we are honest we must sense that they are important, especially for those with true spiritual aims.

These energies connect directly with the following verse from the prayer of the Syrian Saint Joseph the Visionary, which spoke of what the tradition calls the "Glorification of the body." This said:

> May my body be sanctified by You,
> May my soul shine out for You,
> May my body be purified by You,
> of every image and form here on earth,
> and may my thoughts be cleansed by You

and my limbs be sanctified by You;
and my understanding shine out,
and may my mind be illumined by You.[3]

This change is a normal result of bringing our spiritual energies to the
highest pitch.

The Wedding Garment

M acarius the Great wrote at length about this question of change in
our substance and our energies, again linking virtue to energy
(dynamis), but also linking it to this glorification of the body:

> How, therefore, ought each of us to believe and strive and to
> be dedicated to live a full virtuous life? With much hope and
> endurance we should now desire the privilege of reviving that
> heavenly power and the glory of the Holy Spirit interiorly in
> the soul so that then, when our bodies will have been dis-
> solved, we may receive what shall clothe and vivify us. It says:
> "If so be that being clothed we shall not be found naked" (2
> Corinthians 5:3), and "He shall bring to life our mortal bodies
> by the Spirit that dwells in us" (Romans 8:11).
>
> For blessed Moses provided us with a certain type through
> the glory of the spirit which covered his countenance upon
> which no one could look with steadfast gaze. This type antici-
> pates how in the resurrection of the just the bodies of the
> saints will be glorified with a glory which even now the souls
> of the saintly and faithful people are deemed worthy to pos-
> sess within, in the indwelling of the inner man. It is written:
> "For we all with open face [that is to say, in the inward man],
> reflecting as in a mirror the glory of the Lord, are changed into
> the same image from glory to glory" (2 Corinthians 3:18).[4]

The Fathers intimated that we could experience the life to come in
the future, but that we could also experience that same life to come at any
moment in our lives—within ourselves. This is also clearly linked with the
idea that the human is the image of God, but in such a way that it also
connects to the modern idea of transparency, for a clear mirror is, in effect,
transparent; in apatheia the nous does not distort the image it reflects.
What is then reflected? Macarius, a little later than the paragraphs above,
added the passage quoted earlier in this book: "the blessed Moses shows
us what glory true Christians will receive in the resurrection: namely, the

glory of light and the spiritual delights of the Spirit which even now they are deemed worthy to possess interiorly."[5]

We will not now be surprised to learn that the gospel story of the wise and foolish virgins is a parable about higher energies.

> And when the king came in to see the guests, he saw there a man which had not on a wedding garment:
>
> And he saith unto him, Friend, how camest thou in hither not having a wedding garment? And he was speechless.
>
> Then said the king to the servants, Bind him hand and foot, and take him away, and cast him into outer darkness; there shall be weeping and gnashing of teeth.
>
> For many are called, but few are chosen (Matthew 22:11–14).

We should also bear in mind that it is immediately after Christ taught this, according to the gospel, that "Then went the Pharisees, and took counsel how they might entangle Him in his talk" (Matthew 22:15). Divided minds cause human conflict once again! But on the other hand, Evagrius wrote: "For the true wedding garment is the dispassion [apatheia] of the deiform soul which has renounced worldly desires."[6]

In the gospels, this combination of the "polished glass" of apatheia with the glorification that follows it is almost certainly one of the meanings of the "wedding" and its wonderful garment (Matthew 22:11). In such texts, the idea of an internal form of the glorification that can exist while we are still alive in this world defines the term Christian as a level to be achieved. This is of course part of the whole concept that also includes the idea of the bridegroom, and of the wedding feast to which came the wise and foolish virgins of the parable.

It is from passages like this that key Christian concepts are given an inner meaning, and that inner meaning is clearly linked to the possibility of experience in this life. This image is an important part of the esoteric tradition, and demonstrates one of the ways in which such stories convey far more than merely intellectual information. But to understand what they convey, they must be studied with care and attention, and linked to personal experience.

In the gospel imagery, the wedding garment represents the nous in its completed or purified and awakened form, the illuminated nous: the alchemical mirror prepared to reflect the truth. Recent commentaries, particularly of Theophan, opposing the Westernizing thought introduced into Russia by Peter the Great, are valuable for our attempts to understand this question, but we must realize that where these ideas have been presented out of their Christian context, there are certain dangers; in particular when out of context, and particularly when in written form, they seem to tell us to *do* something.[7] In the best hands, the practices of Christian ascesis are not seen quite like this: *synergy* is necessary. Synergy may include effort, but it also requires grace. Self-centered effort is not enough.

To reach full illumination of the nous is one of those things that is "impossible to man, but possible with God's help." Yet in the church, God's help is invited and intensified by certain efforts made to assist "Him who needs no assistance but values our intention."

Something else we must understand of what is implied in this image of the bridegroom: the *awakening* implied is, like a wedding, a change in our way of life; in this case it actually implies a change of being, a discontinuous change. It is fundamental that one cannot be in two states of being at the same time, so that to be in a *Christian condition*, one must have passed beyond the ordinary state—the being (or nonbeing) of fallen man. In the Jewish text of the *Zohar*, which has of course common roots to the Christian inner tradition, it is said that the path of knowledge has ten steps but the path of the heart has only one. What this means in practice is that change of being happens instantaneously, just as in the Zen doctrine of sudden illumination. One moment one is in one state of being, the next moment in another. There is no graduated scale.

Change of being is instantaneous, but sometimes there is a gradual change in the degree of access we have to the higher state of being. To start with, we normally experience very occasional and very brief moments of real being. When one of these lasts long enough for us to notice it, we often think, after one or a few such moments, that we have been "born again." But if this is so, then at one moment we were born, but the next moment we became again "unborn."

In the Greek, in the gospel sentence that is normally understood to read, "save a man be born again," the Greek word is *anothen*, which means "from above," and is linked with concepts of the descent of the Son and the Holy Spirit "from above," with baptismal regeneration "from above," and with the descent of divine gifts from above. The sentence therefore should read: "Verily, verily, I say unto thee, Except a man be born from above, he cannot see the kingdom of God" (John 3:3).

Truly to be born "from above" is something much greater. In essence, the esoteric tradition seems to suggest that such awakenings not only vary—in how often they happen, in how long they last, and in their intensity—but the range of this variation is very great. Tradition suggests that eventually such moments should change from rare and exciting events to something so common that it becomes the "mainspring" of our lives, *a true rebirth.*

But a permanent change of this kind is rare in modern times.

The necessity, in fact, is to regard such moments, taken singly, not as being born again, but as a beginning of repentance, a moment in which we have a brief and partial glimpse of what might be possible; this becomes the motivating factor for *metanoia.* Just as to believe that we already know something will prevent our seeking to learn, so to believe that because of a moment's glimpse of something we are already reborn prevents our seeking to improve ourselves, and so effectively cuts us off from putting into practice the esoteric teachings of the early church.

This is one reason why the Fathers taught the doctrine of *ascesis,* which says that to achieve these things we need to make great effort . . . for who will make such efforts when they think they have no need for them? "If ye know these things, happy are ye if ye do them" (John 13:17): This is so because all the other elements of the wedding garment depend on energies that are only made available, are only stable or permanent, in the degree to which we have achieved *apatheia* and so closed the doors through which those energies are normally wasted.

Here we have one definition of the difference that puzzles so many Christians and leads to so many false distinctions, that between the *called* and the *chosen.* Clement of Alexandria in his *Stromata* makes the relationship of this to *apatheia* even more clear: "For those who are the seed of Abraham, and besides servants of God, are 'the called'; and the sons of Jacob are the elect—those who have tripped up the energy of wickedness."[8]

The chosen have developed *apatheia.* The energy they have saved by this change shines out in them.

Shining Faces

These higher energies and their effect on human beings have been known for millennia. Homer in his *Argonauts* speaks of how the crew of the *Argos* attended the Eleusian mysteries during their voyage. They returned to the ship with shining faces; after a few weeks, says Homer, the shine faded, but "they remained changed men." The *Zohar*[9] speaks of a rabbi who went into a tent in the desert: in it he met the "masters of the Aggadah," and they all had shining faces.

But what does all of this mean to us? As with earlier traditions, the unwritten stream of the Christian esoteric tradition touches on such manifestations, but the shine comes rarely and fades quickly. To transmit it to others is relatively easy, yet it is only made permanent after many years of effort. Energy transformation mechanisms within people can begin to work more efficiently as a result of induction from others in whom they function better. But, after those involved go their different ways, old habits of their minds reassert themselves; the new energies, the new feelings, are replaced by the familiar. The old appearance returns to the face, the old posture to the body.

It has been said that it is sometimes easy to bring people to stillness, but the difficulty is to go beyond this: to acquire this power in oneself and so take a step toward making this state permanent.

Here is what the gospel says about this:

> Then shall the kingdom of heaven be likened unto ten virgins, which took their lamps, and went forth to meet the bridegroom.
>
> And five of them were wise, and five were foolish.
>
> They that were foolish took their lamps, and took no oil with them,
>
> But the wise took oil in their vessels with their lamps.
>
> While the bridegroom tarried, they all slumbered and slept.
>
> And at midnight there was a cry made, Behold, the bridegroom cometh; go ye out to meet him.
>
> Then all those virgins arose, and trimmed their lamps.
>
> And the foolish said unto the wise, Give us of your oil; for our lamps are gone out.
>
> But the wise answered, saying, Not so; lest there be not enough for us and you; but go ye rather to them that sell, and buy for yourselves.
>
> And while they went to buy, the bridegroom came; and they that were ready went in with him to the marriage; and the door was shut.
>
> Afterward came also the other virgins, saying, Lord, Lord, open to us.
>
> But he answered and said, Verily I say unto you, I know you not.
>
> Watch therefore, for ye know neither the day nor the hour when the Son of man cometh (Matthew 25:1–13).

Macarius the Great also explained this parable precisely in terms of a psychology of energy, which I shall try to describe briefly[10] in the form of a commentary. First of all, he defines the aims of the study and outlines its form thus: "Take for example the five prudent and vigilant virgins. They enthusiastically had taken in the supernatural vessels of their heart the oil of the supernatural grace of the Spirit—a thing not conformable to[11] their nature. For this reason they were able to enter together with the Bridegroom into the heavenly bridal chamber."[12]

Clearly the "oil of supernatural grace" defines a specific energy in the sense that Saint Dionysius the Areopagite and Saint Gregory Palamas speak of it.[13] It is more exactly defined by saying that this is not normal to their nature—the translator uses the term *conformable,* which is probably a more accurate translation, but less appropriate to the context—so that this "oil," this fuel, clearly was obtained from outside them, and from outside their ordinary life experience.

Why is this oil so important? Macarius makes the answer to this clear: translated in terms consistent to the Western model of causality, this "oil," which he later defines as "oil of gladness," was the "reason" why these virgins were able to enter the heavenly bridal chamber with the Bridegroom. This fits modern experience in the life of prayer, which confirms, time and again, that without this energy, experiences of the Spirit are fleeting and distant: the experience of something touches us from that "other world" but we cannot follow back to its "home."

Next, Macarius defines in more detail why the five foolish virgins were unable to follow the Bridegroom into his home. It is because they had not obtained this oil of gladness, but instead had "fallen asleep." And then he defines what he means by this term *sleep.* "The other foolish ones, however, content with their own nature, did not watch nor did they betake themselves to receive 'the oil of gladness' (Psalm 45:7) in their vessels. But still in the flesh, they fell into a deep sleep through negligence, inattentiveness, laziness, and ignorance, or even through considering themselves justified. Because of this they were excluded from the bridal chamber of the kingdom because they were unable to please the heavenly Bridegroom."

Extending the analogy of bride and groom, to read into the word *please* an analogy to the worldly concept that an *attraction* should exist between bride and groom, we learn that when the oil of gladness acts as an attraction between bride and groom, then the bride can enter the home of the Bridegroom, the kingdom of God. But why then does such a bride not possess this oil of gladness? Macarius has more to say. It is because: "Bound by ties of the world and by earthly love, they did not offer all their love and devotion to the heavenly Spouse, nor did they carry the oil with them."[14]

So two things are needed before we enter the spiritual world or "home of the spirit": the oil of gladness and the redirection of love. Macarius then attempts to describe such individuals more fully, and in so doing defines the condition that must be met before such *sanctification:* "But the souls who seek the sanctification of the Spirit, which is a thing that lies beyond the power of nature,[15] are completely bound with their whole love to the Lord. There they walk; there they pray; there they focus their thoughts, ignoring all other things."[16]

Clearly, one need described here is to be *wholehearted.* Sanctification involves the heart as a whole, and cannot be "halfhearted."

> For this reason they are considered worthy to receive the oil of divine grace and without any failure they succeed in passing to life, for they have been accepted by and found greatly pleasing to the spiritual Bridegroom.
>
> But other souls, who remain on the level of their own nature, crawl along the ground with their earthly thoughts. They think only in a human way. Their mind lives only on the earthly level. And still they are convinced in their own thoughts that they look to the Bridegroom and that they are adorned with the perfections of a carnal justification. But in reality they have not been born of the Spirit from above (John 3:3) and have not accepted[17] the oil of gladness.[18]

To make this state permanent, our whole psychological nature must change. It must change in the right way, and it must change at every level. More than this, the parable of the lamp can be extended in a modern image—and unlike some other parables it can be updated in this way without becoming untrue.

The classical lamp of the time of Christ was something like the Aladdin lamp of the fairy tales: a shallow teapot with a wick emerging from the spout. Typically, a modern oil lamp has the wick centrally above the oil reservoir, and the flame is sheltered from the wind by a glass chimney. This then becomes the perfect parable for the two main aspects of the esoteric path: the oil represents the energies that must already exist in us before new energies can be developed from them; the flame it feeds represents the production of the new and *visible* energies, which can occur only when another flame is touched to it to kindle it. The chimney protects the flame from the wind, so that it remains alight and burns steadily. But the chimney must also be kept clean, so that the light passes through it without being partially or wholly darkened.

A final note about this: in churches and in a few study groups that maintain a living inner connection with the tradition, people obtain clearly observable inner energies when they come together. Most of them quickly dissipate the new energies in gossip or excitement. A few maintain the disciplines of the Way and retain the energy. Much of this book is about ways of achieving this.

"Ask, and it shall be given you."

W hat does it mean to be wholehearted? The gospel teaching raises very different and seemingly unrelated questions. For example, it has told us to:

> Ask, and it shall be given you; seek, and ye shall find; knock, and it shall be opened unto you:
>
> For every one that asketh receiveth; and he that seeketh findeth; and to him that knocketh it shall be opened (Matthew 7:7–8).

When we come to this question, all that we have already said, almost all commentary on the teachings of Christ, suddenly seems almost meaningless. The gospel also asks: "Or what man is there of you, whom if his son ask bread, will he give him a stone?" (Matthew 7:9).

How then can we understand the teaching that we need but to ask in the same context with the idea that we need to *repent?* . . . that we need to turn around in ourselves before coming into real contact with God?

If all we have to do is to ask, what more could we need? Yet it is a fundamental principle of esotericism that the tradition is a coherent whole. A valuable test is that when we understand[19] the ideas of the esoteric tradition correctly, then the apparent disagreements between concepts will disappear. It is our misunderstandings that conflict, not our understandings, hence the idea, I think, expressed by P. D. Ouspensky that "you cannot understand and disagree."

An understanding that allows us to accept both these doctrines, the idea that we must repent and the idea that we have only to ask, is not far away from us as a possibility. The complexities of our nature complicate the whole thing, but basically the problem, as with all the key elements of esotericism, is not of what to do, but of what we are.

When the gospel tells us to ask and it will be given, too many people believe that this negates other instructions of Jesus. They imagine it means we need not repent nor seek the kingdom, that we can ignore the exacting requirements of Paul, and that the complex methods and instructions of the desert hermits that followed in later centuries were mere embroideries based on misunderstanding. This is not true. There is a good reason for everything in the tradition. Asking for help may be the perfect shortcut, but if this is possible for everyone, it is easy only for the just, only for the truly righteous, those who have no sense of guilt about themselves when faced with the divine, nor any reason to feel guilty. Who is able to ask with a whole heart? Only the one who is "right with God."

The righteous one, the one who is in true relation to God, needs no repentance; the corollary of this is that repentance produces righteousness, as we find in the following passage: "I say unto you, that likewise joy shall be in heaven over one sinner that repenteth, more than over ninety and nine just persons, which need no repentance" (Luke 15:7).

Christianity as a State of Being

When Macarius the Great described the difference in "being" between the "foolish virgins," which he regarded as a description of normal man—modern man—and the "wise virgins," he referred the latter term to those that elsewhere he described as "true Christians": those who had regained their divine birthright. He said of them: "they are greater and better than those of the world, because their intellect and thinking of the soul is permeated by the peace of Christ and the love of the Spirit, as the Lord had in mind when he said: 'They had passed from death to life' " (John 5:24). He then describes the normal Christian, someone who is Christian in intention but not in *being*. One who thinks he is a Christian, but *who does not act or perceive as a Christian does* . . . and this is a description that most of us, if we are honest, will recognize as applying to ourselves. This is the Christian who forgets to ask the Lord, who is unable to look the universe "straight in the eye" as he asks, who turns away in his guilt. (And if you begin to observe yourself more clearly, you will *recognize* the feeling of this turning away . . . unless you turn away from the observation.)

> It is, therefore, not in outward shape or form that the distinguishing characteristic of Christians consists. Many Christians believe that the difference does lie in some external sign. They are in mind and thought similar to those of the world. They undergo the same disturbing restlessness and instability of thoughts, lack of faith, confusion, agitation, and fear as all other people do. They really do differ somewhat in some external form and way of acting in a limited area, but in heart and mind they are shackled by earthly bonds. They do not have the divine rest and heavenly peace of the Spirit in their hearts because they never begged it of God nor did they ever believe that He would deign to grant these to them.[20]

The Startsi

B ut there is a different kind of Christian in the world of the Eastern Church, and among them some with a different consciousness.

In the monastic republic of Athos, for example, something of the quality of those early monks who shaped the church is reflected by today's monks, and especially by the rare "elder members" of the Eastern churches, the true *startsi* or *gerontes*. These elders are the "professors" of this other kind of knowledge, the researchers in this other science, whose results are shared more in present help than in written description, more in description than explanation.

These elders were the *startsi* of the Russian Church, their unique work in the church the practice of *starchestvo,* described here by émigré Russian and Oxford theologian Nicholas Zernov.

> Starchestvo was the practice of laymen appealing for spiritual counsel to certain monks known for their piety and wisdom, called Startzi. The center of the movement was at Optina Pustyn, a monastery near Tula in Central Russia. The tradition of Starchestvo was started there by Father Leonid (d. 1841), a disciple of the famous monk Paissy Velitchkovsky, who introduced it into Russian Church life at the end of the eighteenth Century. The full glory of that way of holiness was, however, revealed by a monk of another monastery, Saint Seraphim of Sarov (1750–1833), one of the greatest saints of the Russian church.[21]

Those who practice this science have little or no equivalent in the Western world, nor in Roman and Protestant churches, for the *starets* often has no outward status whatsoever, no rank, and instead may be totally wrapped in his humility. Yet he is the true theologian, and even those immediately around him would hesitate to claim such a high calling for themselves.

"Theology is such a high thing," said one of my friends on Athos recently, "that most of us here hesitate to call ourselves theologians." The *starets* it is who has what our modern Western world lacks, while the Western world hoards what the *starets* has rejected as trivial.

The truth of the heart, the truth of the *starets,* is not divisible as our truths are, idea from action, theory from practice: you cannot approach the knowledge learned by the *starets* without approaching the values held by the *starets.* You cannot take the knowledge of the *starets* without taking the values of the *starets.* You cannot justify such sweeping statements to modern man, yet even today you cannot know what the *starets* knows without becoming the *starets.* It is all beyond reason.

And when the *starets,* the elder, asks, then it is just as it was when the gospel said:

> Jesus answered and said unto them, Verily I say unto you, If ye have faith, and doubt not, ye shall not only do this which is done to the fig tree, but also if ye shall say unto this mountain, Be thou removed, and be thou cast into the sea; it shall be done.
>
> And all things, whatsoever ye shall ask in prayer, believing, ye shall receive (Matthew 21:21–22).

The problem is that, lacking purity of heart, we do not ask sincerely, or we forget to ask often enough, or we evade the issue from the sense of guilt that comes from our awareness of the gap between what we are and what we might be—between fallen man and our natural qualities, the qualities normal to the invisible, divine world to which we should belong.

If we can learn to accept ourselves, to face our imperfections consciously, without turning aside, then we can learn to ask consciously. When we ask "unconsciously," there is a question to ask. That question is: Who is it that asks?

With faith, the answer to this question changes: "If ye have faith as a grain of mustard seed, ye shall say unto this mountain, Remove hence to yonder place; and it shall remove; and nothing shall be impossible unto you" (Matthew 17:20).

The Prayer of Joseph the Visionary

Although the idea of the Royal Way has been attached to a number of different things, including the prayer of the heart that is so important to the Eastern Church, all these things are esoteric in the special sense that not only do they refer to inner processes, but they describe the action of unobservable and autonomous forces in our lives in a very special way that is clearly expressed in the Syriac prayer of Joseph the Visionary (part of which we quoted earlier), which talks about prayerful ways of changing the quality of the memory or "hidden mind," roughly equivalent to what we now call the *unconscious.* In the form given by Joseph this is an esoteric doctrine in the sense that it refers to *processes within the person praying* that cannot be observed externally, and it clearly describes the need to obtain help for this from a higher level. It is a good prayer for those who have reached a stage of dryness in their struggle with attention and with the overactive mind.

Cleanse my hidden mind
With the hyssop of Your grace,
for I draw near to the Holy of Holies
of your Mysteries.

Wash from me all understanding
that belongs to the flesh,
and may an understanding
which belongs to your Spirit
be mingled within my soul.

Cause to reside in me
a faith that perceives Your Mysteries,
so that I may perceive Your sacrifice
as You are, and not as I am.

Create eyes in me,
that I may see with Your eyes,
for I cannot see with my own eyes.

May every bodily image
be wiped away from my mind's eye,
and may You alone
be recognized before the eye of my mind.[22]

The Control of the Senses

On my first visit to Mount Athos, in 1982, I noticed that certain of the monks, particularly in public places away from their monasteries—on the boat, the jetty, in the little town of Karyes, the capital of their monastic republic—seemed not to look at one directly, not in a shifty sort of way, but because they were contained within themselves, their eyes not seeking contact nor their minds ranging round the world outside them

Later, when I was talking to Father D. of the Monastery of Simono-Petra about the Jesus Prayer, he suggested to me that I should turn my eyes down and away from the world when I was able. The two things were part of the same discipline.

The *rishis* of Raja Yoga in India teach that the mind should be treated like a young bride, and kept isolated from corrupting impressions from the outside world. This principle can be applied to Christian ascesis.

But there is more to it than this. Turning the eyes down both re-minds us and assists us to control and minimize our reactions to the events outside us. These reactions consume in mental and physical energy, in physical tensions and suchlike, the energies that should be transformed through prayer into higher energies. Our difficulty is that our minds—as they are—can be easily provoked into reacting to events outside us. But what reacts is inside us. Our reactions to events cause disturbance within us. The prevention of this disturbance is important in spiritual life, and observation shows that it can in fact be controlled in more than one way, although for various reasons certain individuals, and individuals in certain situations or at certain stages in their lives, may find one form of regulation easier or more possible than another.

The Blessed Callistus had more to say about this, using the image of *living water.* On the physical scale, water is the medium of life, and *living water* was the image that Jesus Himself had used to describe a certain "renewable inner resource" of energy which, he taught in John 4:14–18, was available to those who learn to seek a more than purely physical medium of life.

> If we do not bar our bodily senses, the fountain of water which the Lord promised to the woman of Samaria will not gush forth in us. This woman, seeking physical water, found the water of life flowing within her. As the earth by nature contains water which it pours forth as soon as the outlet is opened, so the earth of the heart by nature contains this spiritual water which gushes forth as soon as this becomes possible, like the light which our forefather Adam lost through transgression.
>
> As physical water flows continually from its source, so the living water, gushing forth from the soul as soon as it is opened, never ceases to flow. Flowing in the soul of the holy man Ignatius, it urged him to say: "There is in me no matter-loving fire, but water acts and speaks in me."[23]

The Five Virgins as the Senses

What then are these five virgins? Macarius defines them exactly and so clarifies the whole passage, writing of the virgins as the "five rational senses of the soul." The foolish virgins are the senses acting alone, when they are *irrational,* depending on their own nature. In that state, before we become aware of what is being perceived through those organs, other more subjective elements enter the process. The wise virgins perceive in simplicity, without subjective bias—the process described by Boris Mouravieff in his *Gnosis* as *constatation*—perception without prejudgment.

"The five rational senses of the soul, if they have received grace from above and the sanctification of the Spirit, truly are the prudent virgins. They have received from above the wisdom of grace. But if they continue depending solely on their own nature, they class themselves with the foolish virgins and show themselves to be children of this world. They have not put off the spirit of the world, even though, in their false thinking by some exterior word, opinion, or form, they believe themselves to be brides of the Bridegroom."[24] Here he shows clearly that he is speaking about the way in which we sense the world, and how this depends on whether we still remain *self-centered*,[25] subjective, still driven by our own impulses and reactions to the world and attentive to the same external things, or whether we have transcended this state and become "dependent" on the Lord "whose service is perfect freedom," which means, in effect, whether we are *God-centered*, which is to say, attentive to the Lord.

Then Macarius describes in more detail this state of dependence, this centering on God, and how different this is from our normal involvement in the life of the world.

Just as the souls who have completely given themselves to the Lord have their thoughts there, their prayers directed there, walk there, and are bound there by the desire of the love of God, so, on the contrary, the souls who have given themselves to the love of the world and wish to live completely on this earth walk there, have their thoughts there, and it is there where their minds live (Luke 12:34). For this reason they are unable to turn themselves over to the kind, prudential guidance of the Spirit. Something that is foreign to our basic nature, I mean heavenly grace, necessarily means being joined and drawn into our nature in order that we can enter the heavenly bridal chamber of the kingdom and obtain eternal salvation.

We have received into ourselves something that is foreign to our nature,[26] namely the corruption of our passions through the disobedience of the first man, which has strongly taken over in us, as though it were a certain part of our nature by custom and long habit.[27]

This must be expelled again by that which is also foreign to our nature, namely the heavenly gift of the Spirit, and so the original purity must be restored. And unless we will now receive the heavenly love of the Spirit through ardent petition and asking by faith and prayer and turning away from the world, and unless our nature will be joined to love, which is the Lord, and we are sanctified from the corrupting power of evil by means of that love of the Spirit, and unless we will persevere to the end unshaken, walking with diligence according to all of his commands, we will be unable to obtain the heavenly kingdom.[28]

We will note that Macarius's ideas about this contain several crucial concepts which will be developed later in the book.

1. In the first of the paragraphs above we learn that those who believe themselves to be "brides of the Bridegroom," to be united to Christ, before they have put aside their dependence on their own abilities, are simply deluding themselves. And from the next paragraph we learn that those whose minds and thoughts live in the world and are wholly concerned with the world are unable to turn themselves over to the "prudential guidance of the spirit."

2. On the other hand, those who correctly believe themselves to be united to Christ are united by the quite different direction taken by their own inner nature. Their thinking has completely changed, become more consistent and filled with higher thought: "souls who have completely given themselves to the Lord have their thoughts there, their prayers directed there, walk there, and are bound there by the desire of the love of God."

3. With this we have distinguished two different kinds of human: not born different, but in very different states that effectively make them different beings.

4. We learn that our habits are not natural to us, but have been learned from outside us, yet have come to seem so much a part of us that they now act as if they were part of our original nature.

5. We learn that these may be removed again through the active love of the Holy Spirit.

Koinonia *as Communion*

What is it like when there is enough oil for one's lamp? I got some kind of a glimpse of this on one of my visits to Mount Athos, where I had a unique experience of true emotion that began when Father A. took me to one of the tiny chapels in the main block of the monastery.

When we entered the chapel I saw around me several familiar faces, almost the same small group of monks as those who had invited me to join the few of them in a small liturgy to Saint Christopher in the gardener's cottage chapel at the end of my second visit to their monastery. I was aware of a great sense of love, of belonging, expressed by the Greek word *koinonia,* a sense that I had never experienced to the same degree in England, even among those with whom I have worked, studied, or served for years.

The celebrant, Father M., had also officiated at that earlier service. The old Father S., another friend, sat quietly at the back of the chapel, his head bowed much of the time in prayer. In the gloom, the few small candles shone on the icons and the simple furnishings. The service began and ended in stillness.

Early in the liturgy this sense of love and mystery overcame me, drove out my thoughts of self, and cleansing tears followed, what the early Fathers called "fire and tears." I began then to understand the theological significance of *koinonia.* In modern Greek theology it is said to represent the love that unites the Trinity and whose expression between members of the church expresses the loving nature of the Trinity in a true, emotional union within the church: a kingdom of love on earth.

Now, it was become real for me. It was hard to believe that only days before I had been playing my accustomed role in business meetings at which the whole thing would have been regarded as nonsense. It was not "sense," perhaps, in any literal way, but it was effective. After the service, I had a great sense of what I can only call "cleanness," of simplicity, and of sensitivity to things of which I am in my everyday life normally unaware. More even than on my previous visits I began to understand what was really possible for a human being, and began, just began, to rediscover the incentive to make that inner effort for myself. From the midst of those senseless tears had come equally "senseless" stillness.

In this strange moment I had become emptied of myself for a while, something very necessary for me. This, more clearly than ever before, and after six visits to the Holy Mountain, was exactly what I had been looking for.

This, the strange and practical significance of *koinonia,* explains why, in the Gospels and often reiterated by the Fathers, there is this need to be reconciled to one's brother, and why the whole idea of preceding communion with a reconciliation is so important to Orthodox thought even today. This idea is not only ethically valid, but is also important to real religious growth. The strength to pray comes from liturgy and love. The strength of the liturgical communion, as was later clearly demonstrated to me on Mount Athos, depends on one's unity with all those communicating. Clearly, an environment of love is an environment of prayer. A Syrian Father created a long prayer that included the following passages:

> At this moment
> when the wine is changed
> and becomes Your blood,
> may my thoughts be inebriated
> with the commixture of Your love.

And a little later in the same prayer:

> . . . stir up within me at this time, Lord,
> the sense of wonder at Your cross,
> fill me with fervour of faith at this moment,
> so that my thoughts may be inflamed
> with the fire of Your love,
> and may my eyes become for You
> rivulets of water to wash all my limbs.
> May Your hidden love
> be infused into my thoughts
> so that my hidden thoughts may flow for you
> with tears and groans.

And again:

> May I receive You
> not in the stomach that belongs to the body's limbs,
> but into the womb of my mind,
> so that You may be conceived there,
> as in the womb of the virgin.[29]

How can I describe my first communion on Mount Athos? I first began to draw conclusions some hours later that day. I was sitting beside the big pine tree overlooking the jetty, trying to sort out the many and fast-changing impressions of my visit. I would alternate between periods of questioning and periods repeating the Jesus Prayer. The stillness of the water reflected the stillness within. Somewhere across the little cove a muleteer shouted at his charges as they began their journey into the forested center of Athos. Birds sang. The novices practiced their chanting in the music school that occupied the top floor of the nearby old building, outside the monastery walls, a rickety-balconied building built against the cliff, and which also housed the carpenter's shop. Bees shopped lackadaisically at the broom on the cliff below me. A fishing boat moved slowly across the horizon. Behind all these sounds lay the stillness of Athos . . . an inward stillness. Within that stillness emerged a presence I can never describe. I was not then even sure how to put a name to the presence. I am still not sure.

Abbot Vasileios has words for the indescribable, for the event if not for that which gave it life:

> Thus the statement "For Thou art God ineffable, incomprehensible, invisible, inconceivable . . . " rises before us like a very mountain, steep and hard to approach, from which the uncreated breeze descends and swells the lungs of man, bringing life to his innermost parts with the joy of freedom, of something unqualified, dangerous and wholly alive. How often we want to make God conceivable, expressible, visible, perceptible to worldly senses. How much we want to worship idols. . . . The divine liturgy, however, does not allow us to do anything of the sort. It destroys our idols of God and raises up before us His saving Image, the Word "who is the image of the invisible God" (Colossians 1:15), the archetype of our true, hidden and Godmade being.[30]

In words, nothing had changed. Yet at heart, something had changed.

Something had touched me, and had left a memory of its passing . . . a "memory without image," which closed the eyes of the mind, gently upset all my preconceptions, destroyed all my idols, and took my idea of Christ and Christianity beyond the modern ideas that "He must have been a great teacher," and that Christianity is a great teaching, to something greater still. "God," said Evagrius of Pontus, "cannot be grasped by the mind. If He could be grasped, He would not be God."[31] Truly, I had "fallen through the hole" once again, had discovered the "reality" behind or beyond the "reality" I had discovered before.

In the Garden of *Panaghia*,[32] a seed began to grow.

Chapter 5

Gnosis Is Not Gnosticism

There was once a Christian conception of gnosis that was very different from what has recently become known as Gnosticism. Certain Greek words, rendered today in Anglicized form by the single word *gnosis,* occur both in the New Testament—in the Gospel of Saint Mark and in certain of Saint Paul's letters—and they are also found in the writings of many of the Fathers of the church, of whom Clement of Alexandria was most open, writing about the qualities of certain Christians who had become Gnostics, although simply in the Christian sense that they possessed certain inner knowledge. In the Christian psychology we are studying, the word *gnosis* and its derivatives are highly technical terms used with great precision, and this idea of gnosis was borrowed,[1] not originated, by the Gnostic sects. For this and other reasons, we are forced to say that the Christian form of gnosis is not in any sense Gnosticism, and that there is good reason for believing that it was not possessed by the Gnostic sects. The term refers to a specific form of inner knowledge—the roots of the word *gnosis* refer to knowledge by or through the *nous*—special knowledge that was sometimes given its special name in the effort to distinguish it from other, more common forms of knowledge.

But we have also learned that the inner knowledge of what was then one Church, not divided as it is now, was available, as Clement says, only to those who had been properly prepared. It was effectively and possibly intentionally hidden or hermetized around the time of Clement's banishment from Alexandria, some seventeen centuries ago. Certain forms of it then continued to be passed on through monasticism, where it could be relatively protected from church politics. The whole problem of evidence for inner truth is encapsulated in the continuing difficulties of proving that this Christian gnosis adheres closely to the original, inner form of Christ's teaching, and is therefore not simply another heretical sect claiming to be Christian. There is no "demonstrable" proof; the only convincing verification takes the form of experiences sometimes known as mystical, so is accessible only to those who are sensitized to this kind of experience. Inner truths thus depend for their survival on *confirmation* by the genuine spiritual experience of individuals, an experiential as opposed to a merely legalistic form of confirmation.

An Experiential Gnosis

In chapter 3 we described how today, after a long period in which spiritual experience was uncommon, or at least when few people were willing to speak about it and it occurred largely dissociated from earlier sources of knowledge about it, increasing numbers of individuals are now again beginning to become aware of their inner, spiritual nature. With new insight into the difference between inner and outer knowledge many people, rebuffed or confused when they seek inner knowledge from their churches, have turned to seek it elsewhere. Vast numbers have sought in the Eastern traditions whose inner knowledge has for a time been more accessible than that of our own tradition. A smaller but substantial number have been attracted to exciting doctrines that appear to be the inner knowledge, doctrines that were first offered in the early Christian centuries by the sects that today have become known as the Gnostics. However, one basic fact about this situation which is not so generally known is that there is a key difference between Christian doctrine and that of all of the so-called Gnostic sects. Each of these sects has a different answer to what C. S. Lewis called *The Problem of Pain,* and none of these widely varied and often fantastic answers agrees with the Christian answer, which is so hard to understand but which, in spite of this, when it is finally understood, has always been the same throughout two thousand years of Christian history. Thus, there appears to be one specific character to almost all Christian answers to this question, while the many and varied answers given to this same question in the teachings of the Gnostics all appear to the eye of self-knowledge to take the form of intellectual speculation, sometimes not falling very far short of modern science fiction, describing strange battles between strange beings with even more outlandish names.

Strangely enough, this Christian answer survives to comparatively recent times in Shakespeare's plays, where it is skillfully hermetized, so that it appears as cryptic statements, such as that in the passage from *As You Like It* that begins:

> Sweet are the uses of adversity;
> Which like a toad, ugly and venomous,
> Wears yet a gracious jewel in his head: a jeweled crown
> And this our life, exempt from public haunt,[2] upon its head
> Finds tongues in trees, books in the running brooks,
> Sermons in stones, and good in everything (Act 2, scene 1).

Christ taught that spiritual influences are known "by their fruits," and in these terms another difference between Christian and Gnostic teachings is shown by the characteristic moral laxity reported of certain Gnostic sects by early Christians, as in Clement's comments on the sect known as the Marcionites, whom he specifically referred to as "libertine Gnostics." It will be seen at least that there was a wide difference between such sects and the Christians of the time, with their emphasis on continence and even virginity as a spiritual method, while Clement himself described his "Gnostic" in terms that make it very clear he was far from being "libertine," writing that: "The Gnostic prays throughout his whole life, endeavouring by prayer to have fellowship with God. And, briefly, having reached to this, he leaves behind him all that is of no service, as having now received the perfection of the man that acts by love. But the distribution of the hours into a threefold division, honoured with as many prayers, those are acquainted with who know the blessed triad of the holy abodes."[3]

It would be possible to support this statement in a detailed study, but not in the space of this book. In the meantime we will try to define in this chapter the Christian concept of *gnosis* as a particular form of inner knowledge, while certain other parts of the book will give enough idea of the Christian answer to pain and suffering to allow comparison with the often outlandish and infinitely varied solutions to this same found in the teachings of the Gnostic sects.

Different Worldviews

For the modern individual, all this is very difficult. Most of the time, all we know as heart is changeable, appearing as excitements and sudden desires. Occasionally we may glimpse depths and richness that are mostly lacking from our lives, yet when we do, we have no "science of the heart" to help us get to know this other kind of emotion, for has not the heart been labled subjective and hence, by implication, "unscientific"? More than that, our very way of thought is based on circular definitions[4] that are convincing precisely because they are inescapable, so that they give no reason for listening to the heart. And how, without trusting in God, without confidence in a *hidden benevolence* in the universe, can we follow the teachings of Our Lord?

How, without waking the inmost heart to the divine reality, can we find the courage to "take no thought for the morrow"? To the eye attuned to an inner tradition, the circularity of contemporary reasoning, with its assumption of an identity between analyzed perception and knowledge, often seems to be closed against all ideas of the validity of nonsensory knowledge. Like a wagon train defended against Apaches, it guards us from the intuitions that reach us from a reality that is neither directly perceptible nor explainable in terms of the circular definitions of our time. Faith alone will break this circle: "Now faith is the substance of things hoped for, the evidence of things not seen" (Hebrews 11:1).

Because of its importance, this quotation occurs again later in this book in a quotation from St. Mark the Ascetic. On page xiv and elsewhere I described how the proper relationship of faith to knowledge has been generally misunderstood. To begin to understand what this means—that faith can become knowledge and knowledge become love—we must realize that this statement was never intended to speak of what can be seen, weighed, measured. Nor does it even hint toward something that can be *inferred* from sensory perception.

It is for this reason, because the data of the heart cannot be verified deterministically, predictably, on demand, that the modern individual ignores it. We, our minds, our thoughts, are permeated with a determinism that is actually only apparent, only a form of self-delusion. Because of this captivity of the intellect, we are unable to understand religious things. This incomprehension is, in part at least, because we have not accepted or even tried to understand the true religious view, the forgotten Christian "theory of continuous creation," in which God was Creator and is Creator still. Modern thought has made the world appear entirely constant instead of almost constant. It has worked this sleight of hand simply by this attitude of determinism, by describing repeating patterns as actual *laws*, which, by definition, are then binding in such a way that they effectively forbid the existence of any ultimate authority, any "supreme power" who can overrule his own laws. A small change in reasoning, but it takes away all hope. In this lies the difference between the deist views of thinkers such as Thomas Paine and the true Christian worldview. For the deist of the eighteenth century, God formed the universe and then left it to run by itself, like a clock once wound. Such a view leaves no place for the mystery of continuous creation, for the hidden authority of God, a power that makes the world we understand

and at the same time goes beyond understanding: the authority that explains the gospel saying "With men this is impossible; but with God all things are possible" (Matthew 19:26).

False Gnosis

B ecause it is so often used simply to describe ancient texts, whatever their source, we need to be extremely clear about the traditional meaning of this word *gnosis*. Saint Irenaeus of Lyons (died 202), was a dedicated opponent of the Gnostic sects, writing his most famous book against them: *Against Heresies: False Gnosis Unmasked and Refuted.* This title, if read with care, seems to imply that there also existed a "true gnosis," although on its own it cannot be taken as proof.

The essential difference between the Christian gnosis and that of the Gnostics is in the quality of the knowledge itself. In Christian esotericism, the true *faith* taught by the gospel and the Fathers forms the basis, the seed of a special kind of *inner knowledge;* it describes an inner reality, known first in words, but finally at the level of experience, as the Word, which cannot be entirely put into spoken words, and all of which, when put into words, is liable to be misunderstood. It also includes a psychological teaching which relates to ways to obtain the meaning of the teaching and put it into practice. The reality expressed by these teachings is at core *unchanging* and thus undifferentiated in the Platonic sense. The theological disagreements that have accumulated over two millennia are caused by misunderstandings of language, by the Babel of tongues.

Often it is possible to see that two sides in a disagreement of doctrine are both motivated by the desire to preserve the same inner truth.[5] It is to avoid such misunderstandings that esotericism took the form of an "unwritten tradition," and it was almost certainly to avoid the political disagreements that go with these misunderstandings—even today—that it has also sometimes been kept secret, at least since the time of Clement's exile from Alexandria as a result of such misunderstandings.

It may already have become clear that the reason for this lack of written form, and often for actual secrecy, is itself quite straightforward and does not normally stem from a desire to preserve an advantage or a sense of superiority over those who are excluded from the secret. Rather, it arises from a concern for the recipients. An honest analysis of the normal methods by which humans obtain knowledge will reveal that there is in fact an essential problem in obtaining knowledge of the unchanging (it is essential to our grasp of these ideas that we understand that what does not change cannot be registered by the mind in the way we register things that change), yet we have already briefly referred to *diakrisis* between the spirit or influence of the changing world and that of the undifferentiated divine reality—a subject dealt with in detail in chapter 13. In this situation, the difficulty of obtaining such knowledge on the one hand, and the difference between the two types of influence, lies both the question and its answer. This of course was the question around which developed the famous debate between Barlaam and Saint Gregory Palamas (p. 79). As mentioned earlier, the esoteric tradition says, in effect, that knowledge of the eternal can be obtained, but not by the normal human methods. God can be known as a different influence, a different spirit, in the sense used by Cassian: the *Spirit of God.*

This is the same as saying that to know God requires a different kind of knowledge. Almost all recent esoteric writers of substance have conveyed this idea by quoting the passage from Saint Paul that warns the student of manmade and hence changeable ideas: "Beware lest any man spoil you through philosophy and vain deceit, after the tradition of men, after the rudiments of the world, and not after Christ" (Colossians 2:8). In esotericism, this kind of knowledge is linked with the special knowledge called *gnosis*—which we described earlier as *noetic knowledge,* known by the nous—a knowledge that is entirely in keeping with the teaching of the Gospels, and is thus, as already suggested, essentially different from the teachings of the sects called the Gnostics.

The problem with this *Christian gnosis,* which is a kind of knowledge, not a select group of people, is that in this form, people misunderstand it: the average reader seems to imagine, when thinking of a form of knowledge called *gnosis,* that although this may consist of certain special ideas, those ideas will have the same form as what we ordinarily call knowledge—knowledge that can be fully expressed in words. We imagine that it can be understood and retained in memory in full—*in the form of words* and understood in relation to everyday experience. But this Christian gnosis, this *knowledge of the nous,* is something different from this. It can neither be fully expressed in words, nor can ordinary experience reveal its full depth, but, given to those who possess an inward stillness, it gives them access to certain kinds of nonsensory experience, and gives such experiences meaning.

What then is the *nous?* This is experienced as that single organ of consciousness which contains all our knowledge in itself, not verbal or diagrammatic knowledge, but direct knowledge, entirely different from the descriptions and definitions that with most people pass for knowledge.[6] This distinction is essentially of the unwritten tradition, as it is one of those things that really cannot be adequately conveyed in writing without the aid of inspiration or spiritual intuition.

As used in the Bible, the idea of *gnosis* appears to describe the special kind of knowledge behind the Gospels and certain other great spiritual works, books in which the same passage at different times can reveal what seem to ordinary minds to be different meanings, all of them valid. In the Old Testament it also appears in the Hebrew term *daath,* which in the Cabala is the knowledge that connects man to what that philosophy calls the "higher sephiroth," which appear to be identical with the *sat-chit-ananda*—the being-bliss-consciousness—of Indian thought. Eventually, true *gnosis,* the complete gnosis, has a specific quality: it seems as if, although gnosis as a type of knowledge is made up of different partial elements, when it becomes complete it becomes a unity, although not *The Unity.*

As mentioned already, the Greek word from which this word *gnosis* was obtained is certainly used in certain parts of the New Testament. The early Fathers whose works were recorded in books like the *Philokalia* also used the word *gnosis* to describe a particular form of knowledge. Although the idea of Gnosticism was derived from this word *gnosis,* it is clear that the early Christian use of the word has or had a simple and direct meaning far from the complexities of many of the sectarian Gnostic teachings. As a simple example, consider the direct way in which experiential knowledge liberates us from uncertainty. The essence of the Christian knowledge tradition was the familiar gospel idea that "the truth shall set you free," but even this most wonderful doctrine has to be understood before we can really benefit from it, although at the same time: "Through faith we understand that the worlds were framed by the word of God, so that things which are seen were not made of things which do appear" (Hebrews 11:3).

To be freed by truth, we must learn that truth, or to be more precise, since the Christian Truth is, in a particular sense, a *person,* we must learn of that Truth, and the learning of this spiritual truth is more than simply learning the words for it. The truth can set us free only when it is *understood.* That itself is one of the truths that brings freedom.

The Alexandrian Tradition

A modern rendering of extracts from the books of Clement of Alexandria translates *Gnostic* as *one who knows God.* This translation is correct, but it is not a full and complete translation, and does not include the full meaning of the word. The same translator comments:

> In his Miscellanies, Clement attacked their claims by describing the lifestyle and prayer life of one who truly knows God (i.e., a true "Gnostic"). He argued that those who deny or twist

the scriptures are not really "Gnostics," for they have not come to know God in truth.[7]

Clement wrote:

> And the gnosis itself is that which has descended by transmission to a few, having been imparted unwritten by the apostles. Hence, then, knowledge or wisdom ought to be exercised up to the eternal and unchangeable habit of contemplation.[8]

This confirms the existence of an unwritten Christian tradition, but why, in a time when literacy was expanding, should some of the knowledge be kept unwritten: what use is an unwritten or, to be more exact, partially written tradition? Saint Isaac the Syrian wrote about this in a way that gives clear indications as to how such incomplete texts may be put to practical use:

> As to the method of that other prayer, and its continuance without compulsion, it seems to me that it is not becoming for us to treat such things in detail, by describing their nature in speech or writings, lest the reader, being unable to understand anything of it, should judge it to be something useless; or if he should be acquainted with these things, should despise him who is not able to see the order of the things. From the one censure, from the other mockery would be the consequence. . . . But he who is desirous to know these things . . . may combine works with thought, by the grace of our Lord. And what in practice happens in these states he may experience personally.[9]

I most strongly recommend that the serious reader ponder this question at length before reading further in this book.

This aspect of Christianity, the "stream" that concerned itself so much with inner knowledge, existed and is sometimes supposed to have been developed in Alexandria,[10] and, as suggested already, it seems to have been suppressed in the second century, at the time of Clement, so that it had to go underground—along with the virtual disappearance of the methods of self-discipline with which it was associated. Yet really there is no secret about the continued existence of this unwritten tradition. But one will not be told things that one can as yet only distort, any more than a doctor will give you technical information which you will misunderstand because of lack of knowledge.

About thirty years ago evidence appeared, in fact, that strongly supports the idea that Clement himself was involved in a church that preserved information which was not made generally available but was kept for an "inner circle" of accomplished students. A large fragment of a letter, believed to be by Clement, was discovered by Harvard scholar Morton Smith. A lengthy investigation appears to confirm that this remarkably preserved fragment (it survived copied onto the flyleaf of another old book) is genuine, and part of it is also so relevant that it is worth quoting here. This letter talks about the writing, by Saint Mark himself, of an expanded version of Saint Mark's Gospel that was used in Clement's church, and certain quotations from otherwise unknown "additions" confirm that they are not part of the generally available version of that Gospel. We will also note that the following text hints at Mark himself having spent time in Alexandria.

> Mark, then, during Peter's stay in Rome, he wrote [an account of] the Lord's doings, not however, declaring all [of them], nor yet hinting at the secret [ones], but selecting those he thought most useful for increasing the faith of those being instructed. But when Peter died as a martyr, Mark came over to Alexandria, bringing both his own notes and those of Peter, from which he transferred to his former book the things suitable to whatever makes for progress toward knowledge (gnosis). [Thus] he composed a more spiritual Gospel for the use of those who were being perfected. Nevertheless, he yet did not divulge the things not to be uttered, nor did he write down the hierophantic teaching of the Lord, but to the stories already written he added yet others and, moreover, brought in certain ways of which he knew the interpretation would, as a mystagogue, lead his hearers into the innermost sanctuary of that truth hidden by seven [veils]. Thus, in sum, he prearranged matters, neither grudgingly nor incautiously, in my opinion, and, dying, he left his composition to the church in Alexandria, where it even yet is most carefully guarded, being read only to those who are being initiated into the great mysteries.[11]

A little later, the same text refers to Christ's giving teaching to an individual, a young man he had just miraculously raised from the dead.

> And they came into Bethany, and a certain woman, whose brother had died, was there. And coming, she prostrated herself before Jesus and says to him, "Son of David, have mercy on me." But the disciples rebuked her. And Jesus, being angered, went off with her into the garden where the tomb was, and straightway a great cry was heard from the tomb. And going near Jesus rolled away the stone from the door of the

tomb. And straightway, going in where the youth was, he stretched forward his hand and raised him, seizing his hand. But the youth, looking upon him, loved him and began to beseech him that he might be with him. And going out of the tomb they came into the house of the youth, for he was rich. And after six days Jesus told him what to do and in the evening the youth comes to him, wearing a linen cloth over [his] na-ked[12] [body]. And he remained with him that night, for Jesus taught him the mystery of the kingdom of god. And thence, arising, he returned to the other side of the Jordan.[13]

Writings that appear to reveal some of the doctrines of this version of Saint Mark appear in Origen—only a small percentage of whose writings survive to the present time, and those apparently extensively altered, also in the writings of Clement of Alexandria, the man often supposed to have been Origen's teacher[14] and certainly his predecessor as head of the Alexandrian school, and in other passages such as those now attributed to Evagrius, a pupil of Origen. In fact, this connection between these authors and the "knowledge tradition" seems to have been the common factor that has led to a general suspicion of these authors in Western and sometimes even in Eastern theology: what is ignored is of course not understood, and what is not understood is regarded as suspect.

Clement of Alexandria himself confirms the existence and special character of this Christian gnosis in texts such as the following: "This cannot be described as in other branches of study. But as the result of great intimacy with this subject, and living with it, a sudden light, like that kindled by a coruscating fire, arising in the soul, feeds itself."[15] The words are the representation of gnosis, and the experience, the intuition, the light is the *gnosis itself*. That *light of the nous* is itself gnosis, and sometimes the words that represent it may become the light itself. Yet even such knowledge may first be learned, or at least "learned of," from words, but it is understood, its meaning is known, only by direct if subtle intuition; so that the *true gnosis* is also that subtle, special intu-ition itself—but those who know of it in modern times also warn us to beware of assuming that guesswork or the vague intimations once known as "feminine intuition" are gnosis. The intuition of Christian gnosis is closer to *revelation*[16] than to either the "Kantian intuition" which every-one possesses, or the everyday forms of "Jungian intuition"—not surpris-ingly, considering Clement's Greek background, yet without departing from Christian experience or gospel teaching, where Christ says: "I am come to send fire on the earth; and what will I, if it be already kindled?" (Luke 12:49).

Clement's words powerfully and exactly echo Plato's statement in his seventh letter about unwritten knowledge. More important, as we have already shown, this kind of knowledge, this gnosis, is easily forgotten by many people even after they have experienced it, so that it is important in this context that the Greek word for truth in the Gospels is *alitheia* (truth). There is also an element of remembering, of course, where the Gospel of Saint John says: "We speak that we do know, and testify that we have seen; and ye receive not our witness" (John 3:11). We must of course be honest and admit that this is not intellectual proof of the validity of the esoteric tradition: but it does conform to inner experience.

Knowledge of God's Omnipotence

T he source of all hope, of all possibilities that are beyond us unaided, is the hidden power of God as manifest in the incarnation of Christ. To know of this, to be convinced of it without possibility of that conviction being overturned, this is something that can entirely change our lives. This and the ability of the Lord to meet every need were the subject of one of the sermons of Macarius the Great, in this remarkable passage:

> How could the infinite and ineffable ability "of the manifold wisdom of God" (Ephesians 3:10) create out of those things that did not exist bodies that are grosser and more subtle and more simple which subsist by His will? And how much more can He who is as He Himself wishes, through His ineffable compassion and incomprehensible goodness, not change and diminish and assimilate to Himself holy, worthy, and faithful souls by means of an assumed body? By such a body He, the invisible, is able to be seen by such souls, He, the untouchable one, may thus be felt according to the subtlety of the soul's nature. In this way also such souls may taste His sweetness and enjoy in actual experience the goodness of the light of inexpressible pleasure.
>
> When God wishes, He becomes fire, burning up every coarse passion that has taken root in the soul. "For our God is a consuming fire" (Hebrews 12:29). When He wishes, He becomes an inexpressible and mysterious rest so that the soul may find rest in God's rest. When He wishes He becomes joy and peace, cherishing and protecting the soul.
>
> If God also should wish to make Himself similar to one of His creatures for the exultation and happiness of his

intelligent creatures, as, for example, Jerusalem, the city, or the heavenly Mount Sion, He can do all things as He wishes, as it is said: "You come to Mount Sion and to the city of the living God, the heavenly Jerusalem" (Hebrews 12:22). All things are easy and possible for Him who can transform himself into any form that He wishes for the benefit of those souls who are worthy of and faithful to Him. Should anyone only strive to be pleasing to him and be acceptable, He certainly will see the heavenly good things in actual experience. He will have an experience of the unspeakable delights and truly immense riches of God which "eye has not seen nor ear heard nor has it entered into the mind of man to conceive" (1 Corinthians 2:9).

The Spirit of the Lord also becomes the rest of worthy souls and their joy and delight and eternal life. For the Lord transforms Himself into bread and drink as it is written in the Gospel: "whoever eats of this bread will live forever" (John 6:58). In this ineffable way He recreates the soul and fills it with spiritual happiness. For He says: "I am the bread of life" (John 6:35). Similarly He transforms himself into the drink of a heavenly fountain as He says: "Whoever will drink of the water which I shall give him, it shall be in him a fountain of water 'springing up to eternal life' " (John 4:14). And it is also said: "And we have all drunk of the same drink" (1 Corinthians 12:13, 10:4).

Thus He appeared to each of the holy fathers, exactly as He wished and as it seemed helpful to them.[17]

Our God, the God of the Christians, is a living God. An understanding of the authority and autonomy of God, described for example in the gospel story of the centurion, is important for its implications in our own lives. As we come to understand the hidden power and *providence* of God in our lives, we begin to change our attitude and to understand more of what is possible. To understand the power of God is important, because it can free us from the feeling that we are able to and must be able to solve the problems of our own lives, when: "Which of you by taking thought can add one cubit unto his stature?" (Matthew 6:27). But to understand this is problematical. As Saint Isaac the Syrian said, it is often only possible to perceive the providence of God when we possess no other support: when we have "no safety net" in our lives.

P. D. Ouspensky, the Russian philosopher who taught in England in the 1930s, told a story illustrating the way in which God might be limited: A seminarian is supposed to have answered this question by saying that God "Cannot take the ace of trumps with the deuce." The problem with this story is that although it contains a truth, or at least something that would be a problem for a God made in man's image, when this idea is used as a blunt tool, it attacks true faith: it is rightly understood as showing how, by creating time, God can maintain the fabric of a universe without capricious change, but this can then be wrongly taken as showing that God is Himself absolutely subject to or determined by the laws discovered by science. Thus does modern education and the scientific view of life weaken the understanding of people of faith, reinforcing our belief in a mechanical determinism and so, in showing a world with no escape from a predetermined future, creating fear. Theirs is a dead world, a blind machine that ennobles or ruins good or bad equally, with a blind lack of discrimination. Practicing Christians of the "old school," such as the monks on Athos, live instead in a living world, a world of miracles that are never predictable, never law conforming—and so do not allow the dependence, either on God or on the law, which is the panacea, the placebo, the false confidence that protects "sleeping man" from being awoken by the abrasive facts of his life.

Saint Therese of Lisieux describes in her autobiography how a letter of her mother tells how, while still a small child, she was able to answer this theological problem: "Celine asked the other day how God could be there in a tiny Host like that, and Baby [the child who was to become Saint Therese] said: 'There's nothing surprising about it. God is Almighty.' 'Almighty, what does that mean?' 'It means he can do anything he wants to.' "[18]

Breaking free of the view of the universe as a dead machine, seeing it as the creation of a God, of an omnipotent God, a God who is Love—warm, caring, responsive, ultimately conscious (or beyond even consciousness as we know it, but certainly not less than that), although entirely inexplicable—this is Christian life. Learning to live with and love that living universe, not of a God limited to law, but of laws subservient to a living God, this is awakening to Christianity as Christianity was once. But to ascribe to the living God of the Christian the determinism experienced or imagined by man is to make God in man's image: to limit Him by law as we imagine ourselves to be limited, and thus to make Him powerless to help us, so that to conceive of a God limited by law is to eliminate the hope of divine help in our lives.

In a West without Christian spirituality, there is not even a Christianity that has been tried and failed, but only a Christianity that has not been tried.

A World Without Gnosis

What is clearly true is that modern man lacks esoteric knowledge, and one of the reasons for this is the very great difficulty of learning enough about the unwritten tradition when it is so well hidden from us. The significance of this loss to us is twofold. It is important to the individual. It is equally important to society as a whole. It is important to the individual because of the proliferation of external concerns both in modern society and modern Christianity. Most people, including many clergy, have become almost willfully blind to certain human experiences—including certain religious experiences—and this because these experiences are classified according to our scientific worldview, our scientific mind-set, as *unreal* or *unscientific*. In effect, this means that, as it has been put, "Christianity has been the victim of a general cultural attack on the possibility of spirituality."[19] Today, spiritual experience is said to be "subjective," with the unfounded but generally accepted implication that what is subjective is unreal or illusory. What this means is that the Fall in consciousness has been followed by a second fall in our way of thinking, so that we are now influenced by fashionable ideas, of which the "unreality of the subjective" is one, an error in methods of thought that is a direct result of the limitations of the first Fall. As well as the initial limitation in our consciousness, therefore, we now have to correct a second limitation, the limitation created by *defined thought,* and that defined one-sidedly only from impressions obtained from the material world and confirmed by circular definition; so that there is now a belief almost universally accepted in our cultural milieu that anything not included in that circular definition is "unreal."[20] This leads to the conclusion that our experiences of the inner world, which are all that remains of the consciousness that preceded the Fall, are in fact delusions. The possibility of recovering that original consciousness depends on our increasing our awareness of this real world that is only supposedly a merely inner world, and this possibility is almost entirely blocked if we cling to any kind of *materialist* belief.

It is important to society because a world that ignores the inner life is a world without gnosis. To recover this gnosis is now extremely important to our civilization as a whole, for there is little doubt today that—even by earlier standards, albeit of "fallen" man—our Western civilization is now seriously out of balance; in fact, it has become increasingly obvious that although we are the most technically advanced civilization in recorded history, today's Westernized world is morally backward, if only in the specific sense that it is unable to cope with the human problems caused by its own technical achievements. This was confirmed early in 1992, when a joint report by the U.S. National Academy of Sciences and the British Royal Society stated: "If current predictions of population growth prove accurate and patterns of human activity on the planet remain unchanged, science and technology may not be able to prevent either irreversible degradation of the environment or continued poverty for much of the world."[21]

What is true but much more difficult to prove is that this imbalance is partially or wholly due to the imbalance in our knowledge. What is lacking today is self-control on a cultural scale: we cannot control ourselves, and as a result we cannot control the technology we use nor govern its social consequences. Prolonged reflection will show us that, just as control of the environment requires external or worldly knowledge, self-control, morality, and social stability require internal or esoteric knowledge. Another element of our present situation, then, is that humanity finds itself in an entirely new situation, requiring entirely new solutions. The problem with this is that nobody is any longer generating new solutions: there is no longer the deep knowledge that the early church called *gnosis* to act as a source for new solutions—or at least a medium not just of new phrasings, but of entirely new meanings.

And as man thinks, so he is: this is true for the individual and for a whole civilization.

The Question of Education

There is clear evidence[22] that the way the mind is formed when young predisposes it one way or another in its attitude toward religion and toward inner growth. The Hebrews appear to have been aware of this, and the Greeks, if not fully aware of this spiritual question, as well they may have been, were certainly aware of the social importance of education.

With their combined Hebrew and Greek heritage, for many centuries both Eastern and Western churches played a similar educational role in their societies; specifically, they helped to train behavior in certain ways and to introduce certain sensibilities and inculcate certain attitudes, some of which form the basis of modern morality and ethics. These attitudes and sensibilities were essential for those who wished to enter a life of prayer, but were also valuable for their effect on everyday life, in which they improved people's ability to live together in meaningful ways. Thus the religious life of the time placed its stamp on that society in a way similar to that in which certain branches of Greek monasticism today shape the behavior and attitudes of lay people who maintain contact with the monasteries. Seen objectively, this reveals the benefits possible to any society which shapes the minds of its members in this way.

Today, we live in a society in which one of the main problems is the number of people requiring treatment or hospitalization for what are called neuroses or mental illness. It is easy and probably correct to conclude that the almost epidemic growth of problems of this kind is directly traceable to the decline in what might be called "emotional education" in our society.

In our contemporary society, as the authority of the church has declined, the question of training the emotions has sometimes been taken over in part by schools originally formed by the church, among which the English so-called public schools, at least, were remarkably monastic in their character. As the form of education now becomes more and more career oriented, emotional education is more and more obviously left to the family, which often either neglects this role or is ignorant of how to perform it. The result in many cases is failure, often catastrophic.

It is certainly arguable in this case that to restore the emotional element of early educational methods would be highly beneficial both for individuals and for society as a whole.

Paideia *and Catechism*

To understand the way the early Fathers thought about this question, and how they tilled the soil that brought forth such "fruit unto repentance," such a crop of individuals of a spiritual power almost unimaginable in this time without saints, it is helpful to know that, even before their time, the Greece of Pericles, Plato, and Socrates possessed an established educational tradition. This was a program of character formation, and it seems to have been the idea of developing this further that inspired large parts of Plato's *Republic*. Werner Jaeger, a leading Harvard theologian of the 1960s, wrote about Greek philosophers of the slightly later time when Christianity began, that:

> They led their pupils to that spirituality which was the common link of all higher religion in late antiquity. They began to remember that it had been Plato who made the world of the soul visible for the first time to the inner eye of man, and they realized how radically that discovery had changed human life. . . . On their way upward, Plato became the guide who turned their eyes from material and sensual reality to the immaterial world in which the nobler-minded of the human race were to make their home.
>
> In this situation, Clement of Alexandria, the head of the Christian school of the Catechetes, and Origen became the founders of Christian philosophy.[23]

To prepare people by making them more sensitive to subtleties that include[24] spiritual feelings and intuitions, general aesthetic education is often recommended, especially under modern conditions, when aesthetics are largely ignored in education.

Greek *paideia* (the word originally meant and still means "children" in Greek, but is classically used as a general term for education)—specifically the *paideia* of Athens at the time of Plato and Pericles—included aesthetic elements as well as physical culture and intellectual concerns. The Stoic philosophy, which was a major force in Greece and Italy at the time that Clement taught in Alexandria, could be regarded as a specific form or an adult extension to *paideia,* and it is notable that it taught self-control. So, at the time of Christ, Greek education included elements that contributed to the formation of emotional sensibility and self-control. Plato, for instance, advocated teaching certain specific poetic and musical forms. Byzantine Christian society many centuries later taught a series of rules for music that defined precisely the way in which some combinations of sounds had a beneficial effect on the hearer while others were harmful. Those rules can still be studied.

In the early centuries of the church the aim not only of the education of children but of the training of Christian adults possessed a strong emphasis on emotional education: the proper preparation of the heart. Traces of this emphasis survive throughout the Western world. For instance, a Greek taxi driver, faced with impatient passengers, will counsel *hypomonie,* patience, and the word he uses is the same as that used by the Fathers of the Greek Church fifteen hundred years ago, when those who sought God were counseled to practice *hypomonie,* to endure with patience.

Today the training of the heart has almost disappeared from our educational system and is left to individuals to resolve as best they can through therapy, counseling, self-knowledge, or the substitutes—alcohol and drugs—adopted when no help seems to be available. The Western world is "reaping the whirlwind" as a result. A therapeutic expression of religious thought that took inner factors into account would quickly reverse this trend.

Chapter 6

The Work of God

Some people believe that inner growth and "working on oneself" are something we *do* of ourselves. Nothing much comes of it all until we learn that despite the great efforts we must make, this view is not wholly true. Others believe that spiritual change happens in an instant, as if by magic. Both these views are based on a lack of self-knowledge, on inadequate information about what actually happens. The inner change that matters is a work of God in synergy with man. This is a process, and a process "takes time."

The interpretation given earlier of John 3:3 as "born from above"[1] instead of the more usual phrasing of "born again" has a great significance for a proper understanding of the gospel message. Why is it important? This is partly because the idea of being born *from above* makes it clear that we do not "conceive ourselves," partly because it shows that a *process* is involved. Also, the idea of being "born from above" is analogous to physical birth, and the inner tradition makes it clear that this describes a long process of conception, gestation, and finally birth.

Look at the question in another way: if such a birth were instantaneous, then monks would be working for many, many years to attain what can be achieved in a second or two. The truth is that the working of God in the transformation of man does what is impossible for man to do unaided. But in this process or working not only does our Lord require man's cooperation, but, like all processes, it takes time. Saint Macarius the Great, a fourth-century associate of Gregory of Nyssa, once wrote: "Those who hear the word should give witness to the working of the Word in their own souls. The word of God is not an idle word, but it has its own work upon the soul. For this reason it is called a work, so that the work may be found in those who hear it. May the Lord therefore grant the work of truth in the hearers so that the Word may be found fruitful in us."[2]

Thus God works a transformation in man, often appearing to begin this process through knowledge—the good news that we can change.

> For though we walk in the flesh, we do not war after the flesh:
> (For the weapons of our warfare are not carnal, but mighty through God to the pulling down of strong holds;)
> Casting down imaginations, and every high thing that exalteth itself against the knowledge of God, and bringing into captivity every thought to the obedience of Christ; . . .
> Do ye look on things after the outward appearance? If any man trust to himself that he is Christ's, let him of himself think this again, that, as he is Christ's, even so are we Christ's" (2 Corinthians 10:3–5 & 7).

The Working of the Word

"Salvation belongeth unto the Lord, thy blessing is upon thy people."[3] So says the Orthodox vigil service. This expresses the fact that as esoteric psychology works a transformation in someone who makes appropriate efforts, then, in service, man brings God's work—inward and outward—to his particular place in the world. So that God's work is done *by* man, and also *on* man, in alliance with man's work upon himself. How can this happen, we might ask? Macarius the Great gives us part of the picture—but human language is incapable of giving it all!

> His very grace writes in their hearts the laws of the Spirit. They should not put all their trusting hopes solely in the scriptures written in ink. For divine grace writes on the "tables of the heart" (2 Corinthians 3:3) the laws of the spirit and the heavenly mysteries. For the heart directs and governs all the other organs of the body. And when grace pastures the heart, it rules over all the members and the thoughts. For there, in the heart, the mind abides, as well as the thoughts of the soul and all its hopes. This is how grace penetrates through all parts of the body.[4]

The process is a living one, a process that can occur in any one of us. I first began to understand this from a conversation with one of the monks of the monastery of SimonoPetra. "There are some places in this world," he told me as we sat on the balcony overlooking the sea far below, "where eternity has touched the earth, where things of eternal significance have happened, and some sense of this remains today. Athos is one of these places. By coming here, some people are able to reestablish contact with the eternal element within themselves." This memory of the living presence is both personal and communal, and is most important to the practice of religion in the Athonite sense: "For where two or three are gathered together in my name, there am I in the midst of them" (Matthew 18:20).

When they talk about the fact that in some places it is easier to reestablish contact with the eternal in us, however we understand it, it is on this eternal factor within us that the mind can rest and become still. Here, at the center of one's being, one finds Christ. Here lies truth, and here open the doors of that love that cannot betray.

This "place" is perhaps the least known and least understood key to Christian psychology. It seems to reflect the gospel image of the "strait gate," the eye of the needle, yet it also explains the parable of the talents. Understand this, and one understands so much else. Find this, and one finds how to put into practice so many ideas that otherwise remain mere theory. Carry out the instructions of the *geronte* or elder with sufficient care and persistence, and it is this "place" one comes to.

One becomes what one is, becomes for the first time not an imitation of someone else, but oneself . . . one becomes whole, for a moment, or for the rest of one's life—by becoming wholehearted; becomes complete by refusing to compromise one's best. One becomes whole by not compromising truth, becomes whole by not escaping from the sorrow of emptiness into continual distraction. Becomes whole by giving, not asking; by perceiving with care instead of jumping to conclusions; above all, one becomes whole by acting from the heart, by overcoming division in oneself, by acting from the real facts and not from one's illusions. by making *superefforts*.

But who is it that makes these superefforts?

Surrender into the Hands of God

Let me talk about my own experience again for a moment. I once faced a problem getting to Mount Athos. I had little time, since I must be off Athos again by the following Thursday, while the offices from which I had to obtain the documents needed to get into Athos would not open again to the public until 11 A.M. on Monday, and those offices were in bustling Thessalonika, still 140 kilometers from the Ouranopolis pierhead, from which the Athos ferry sails at 9:45 every morning.

Here was the real test of nearly thirty years of prayer and meditation. In spite of the uncertainties, it seemed important that I go. So I decided just that: to go anyway. If it was right that I should go to Athos, then something would resolve the difficulties, though I could not imagine what. I must leave myself in the hands of God, and by this must test my intention to place my well-being in God's hands. On my way, I met the abbot of the monastery to which I retreat, and he arranged for my brief visit, so that I traveled on to the mountain with him.

On our arrival he said to me that it was good that I had taken this course, had trusted in God and acted accordingly. From then on, his attitude toward me changed and he became willing to give more time to me.

It is now clear to me, from many similar events, that the monks recognize certain efforts and act to reinforce them. Here, then, superefforts are of many kinds, and are recognized not in terminology but in action.

This is important to understand: it is oneself, one's intentions, one's emotional condition, one's constancy which such situations test. They do not "test for truth," or discover for us whether God is real; they test us and our ability to live with the reality of a living God. Such a test is a question of attitude, of intention. If we are unwilling to see it as a test of ourselves, then it becomes, in intention at least, a challenge to God and, as the gospel puts it: "thou shalt not test the Lord thy God." (The word *tempt* in our English version translates the Greek *peirasmos:* the temptation that tries and tests us.)

True tests of our faith or lack of it exist, however, in all situations of uncertainty, and sometimes the test is to depend not on ourselves and our everyday methods of making sure, but, like Saint Paul as he sailed those coasts in much more difficult days, to do what we can but then leave the rest to God and His *synergia* to send what He will.

It is this, a true change of intent, a reversal in the direction of our will, that demonstrates true change of heart. I suspect also that this is not something that happens without effort, but something that happens only as long as we have in mind *mneme Theou,* remembrance of God.

Temptations test us at many stages on the journey to truth. Saint Maximos the Confessor wrote: "God searches the intention of everything that we do, [to discover] whether we do it for him or for any other motive."[5] A few paragraphs later he added: "The onslaughts or temptations are brought on sometimes to take away sins already committed, or those being committed in the present, or else to cut off those which could be committed. And this is apart from those which come upon one as a trial, as with Job."[6]

The Book of Job acquires an importance on the esoteric path once we really become aware of these trials or tests, since it represents what is probably the most complete description of the whole process in existence.

Doing the Will of God

M ore than to study the esoteric doctrine, to participate in any real way in the esoteric practice of Athos brings one face to face with a different world. In that world one discovers a more relaxed, more forgiving attitude to sin. A different attitude to life begins to surface within you in response, so that one begins to see this different world everywhere: around you; in the attitudes and actions of the monks; in the theology of their church; even in the behavior of nearby villagers. The big difference lies in the difference of the monk's attitude to things like authority and responsibility. Underlying this is a different way of understanding the concept of the "will of God," a difference which is perhaps crucial to the Orthodox view of life.

We tend to view the will of God legalistically, as something we should learn to obey as we learn to obey ordinary instructions from employers and others; that is, we regard it almost as a communication. The view on Athos is different, and links instead with the idea of the icon, with the idea of man made in God's image, the image made perfectly manifest by Christ. God's will according to this view is already existing within us.

This idea of Christ as the icon of the Father was long ago expressed in the following passage from the homilies of Saint Macarius the Great.

> And how much more can he who is as he himself wishes and is what he wishes, through his ineffable compassion and incomprehensible goodness, not change and diminish and assimilate to himself holy, worthy, and faithful souls by means of an assumed body? By such a body he, the invisible, is able to be seen by such souls, He, the untouchable one, may thus be felt according to the subtlety of the soul's nature. In this way also such souls may taste his sweetness and enjoy in actual experience the goodness of the light of inexpressible pleasure.[7]

This also links in some way with the gospel parable of the talents. God's will is within us, waiting to be discovered and expressed. It is not something to be learned or acquired. This inner image has to be "dug up." It must be "put to work," so that it becomes our real working idea of ourselves instead of the false view held by the Personality. It must not be left buried in our inmost hearts. Thus, to fulfill the will of God is not to go against one's real nature but to uncover one's real nature. "To be true to the Spirit" is to be true both to God and to oneself, something close to the Western idea of finding and expressing one's "real self." It is also closely related to the best meanings of our modern concept of *conscience*.

This is a big thing, and contains overtones of responsibility. Through my experiences on Athos I have come to see this as giving a wholly different view of virtue. This is a view based on observation, but on observation that is obtained only with difficulty. It is consistent with the idea, expanded elsewhere in this book, that if we are the icon, the image of God, this means that there is an innate goodness in the human being that, once uncovered, needs no outward enforcement. All we have to do is to become what we are: to be ourselves as God made us; to do what we see to be right according to our inherent sense of what is right and our best abilities. This view was clearly expressed by Theophan the Recluse (see p. 51). The full breadth of this idea that by being true to ourselves we are true to God, because we are then being true to something God-given within us, was made clearer to me in a conversation with the hermit Father J. on my sixth visit to Mount Athos. This visit to the hermit began one day when, after making the journey from Ouranopolis, outside Athos, to Karyes, the town at the center of the peninsula that is the capital of the monastic republic, and having obtained my *diamonitirion*,[8] I walked, already tired, to the Grigoriou *konachi*.[9]

"*Kali spera*,"[10] said Father T. as he answered the bell of the *konachi* and invited me in, ushering me through the wide hall with its great log chest and its glass doors into the chapel. He led me into the little living room with its icons, its iron stove, its long window, its long wide benches and hard cushions, just as I remembered it.

"*Katse.*"[11] He invited me to sit. But Father V. soon appeared with a full plate of a delicious soup with artichokes from the *konachi's* fertile garden. Then, among friends, we settled down to the serious business of trying to communicate. What did I need? Did I want to see Father J., the hermit in the forest, as they had heard I would? I think that was the gist of it. But the communication did not go well. Soon I was shown to a room to rest. I opened the windows as wide as I could for the air, and lay down gratefully for siesta. I was wakened two hours later by voices in the hall outside the guest room. As I emerged from my room I was introduced to a young man in a khaki sweatshirt: Andreas, a Canadian of Greek ancestry, who was staying with the monks at a nearby *kelli*.[12]

The coffee duly appeared, and we continued our conversation on the veranda with its magnificent view of the distant peak of Athos itself. Andreas briefly told me he was visiting the Holy Mountain for the second time, staying some two months in the summer before returning to Canada and college. He lived in the *kelli* with the monks, and while he was there, like a monk, he came under obedience to the *geronte* or elder monk who led that small community. Did I want to see Father J.? he asked. The best time would be the next morning. He would be happy to translate for me, but would need the permission of the father of his *kelli* first. He would telephone later if the *geronte* agreed. We arranged a time in the morning when he would come, and which would hopefully allow me to return to Karyes in time for my bus. Later, a telephone call confirmed that the trip was on.

Next morning I woke around six, and quickly made my way to the chapel to join Father V., who was saying matins on his own. He had just finished when Andreas arrived and began talking high-speed Greek to him. There followed the embarrassment of piled food, of which I could eat little since my stomach had not yet adapted either to Athos times nor Athos cooking. Finally, somewhat later than intended, we left, Father V. showing us the unmarked trail that cut straight from the *konachi*, through the thickly overgrown forest, to the mule track where the path to Father J.'s cell branched off. The journey was very much shorter than if we had gone through Karyes.

When we got to his *kelli*, Father J. was under the veranda splitting logs. "Who is it?" he called in Greek. My interpreter told him it was the Englishman who had been to see him twice before. "Wait!" came the reply. We waited. The gentle blows of the axe splitting wood merged into the silence of the forest. Big logging machines grumbled far away in the background without spoiling the stillness. A quarter of an hour passed. "Should I try again?" asked my companion. "No," I said, "he knows we are here. He will come when he is ready."

Two or three minutes later the old man emerged from the bushes near the gate and passed us the key. We followed him up the path, round the cottage, to the clearing on the far side where under a tree were some half dozen logs upended beside a larger one that served as a table. The old man greeted us, filled mugs with crystal clear water, left the *loukoumi* open beside them in traditional Athos hospitality, and disappeared into his home, saying that we had arrived so early that he still had chores to finish.

Ten minutes later he joined us again, and we began to talk. Again, as had happened on a previous visit I had made without an interpreter, I learned more from his manner than simply by his words. In essence, I discovered that it would be better if I had come to him better prepared, after my visit to the monasteries and not before, when my mind was still full of the world I had so recently left. I still regret that I did not think clearly enough at this time to follow up what he said as well as I might. I also regretted very much that I had not learned to speak Greek; the limitations of translation cause real problems when dealing with things both subtle and spiritual. Nevertheless, it was a conversation of great value to me and, I suspect, to others living in the West.

"Jesus tells us," I said at the beginning, "that we should not simply call on God but should do the will of God. If I wished to carry out this commandment, what should I be doing in my everyday life?" I think my young interpreter put it slightly differently, because the old man seemed slightly disappointed that this was all I was asking, and I remembered then that he had expected me to return at some future time and ask him one special question. That question was still unasked. However, he answered my current question very well, and in my eyes very much simplified the whole idea of doing the will of God.

It seems to me that Father J. does not talk theory. There is a quality in his advice that eliminates the distance and imprecision that normally come between us and important ideas. His words, as always, had seemed to directly link to experience.

He showed me quite precisely what was meant by the idea that we should be open to the best impulses that reach us, and dead to the temptations of our own weaknesses and of people's attempts to force us into different directions in our ordinary lives. There seems to be an element of "conscience" in this: of "saying what we feel and doing what we say." At the same time, it linked with the idea that to do the will of God we should "be ourselves," should learn to express ourselves not in a modern sense, but to express that Self which God had made of us "in the beginning."

To be true to our divine self-image, we need to be renewed in the way described by Saint Paul when he wrote: "be ye transformed by the renewing of your mind,[13] that ye may prove what is that good, and acceptable, and perfect will of God" (Romans 12:2).

Gregory of Nyssa and the Chariot Parable

One of the threads in Jewish thought that clearly appear in inner Christianity is found in the Merkabah tradition, the tradition of the *chariot of fire* by which certain of the prophets were taken up to heaven: a tradition that gives the chariot analogy its full emotional meaning, previously not revealed to us. The same basic elements are also found further east, and this whole structure appears not only to contain certain of the basic concepts of Christian thought, but to help to provide a formal framework for these doctrines. This framework fits experience with a high degree of accuracy, and forms a useful basis for practical working in a Christian Fourth Way.

In fact, this is still the subject of investigation. Although I already have experiential evidence for what is said, at this point it is the practical application that is important, and as it concerns unwritten tradition, this preliminary presentation cannot be fully documented but depends, in the traditional way, on the transmission of understanding.

> For who does not know that the Egyptian army—those horses, chariots and their drivers, archers, slingers, and the rest of the crowd in the enemies' line of battle—are the various passions of the soul by which man is enslaved? For the undisciplined intellectual drives and the sensual impulses to pleasure, sorrow, and covetousness are indistinguishable from the aforementioned army. Criticism is a stone straight from the sling, and the spirited rejoinder is a quivering spearpoint. The passion for pleasures is to be seen in the horses who themselves with irresistible drive pull the chariot.
>
> In the chariot there are three drivers whom the history calls "viziers." . . . you will perceive these three, who are completely carried along by the chariot, as the tripartite division of the soul, meaning the rational, the appetitive, and the spirited.[14]

In the story of the charioteer, the chariot of course represents the human body. When a single driver is described, this represents the Greek *nous*. The three viziers "who are completely carried along by the chariot" refers to what Gregory called "the tripartite division of the soul, meaning the rational, the appetitive, and the spirited," and this of course is the equivalent of the modern formulation of *three lower centers*. The horses represent the lower emotions, the reins the higher faculties of self-control that have to be formed or strengthened. The master or owner of the coach, the Lord himself, will not enter it until the driver is firmly in control. This is a particular state that is described in another work of Gregory of Nyssa, who wrote:

> if reason [Greek *dianoia*], which is the distinctive property of our nature, should gain dominion over those traits which are added to us from outside (the word of Scripture has revealed this as if in a riddle, bidding mankind to rule over the irrational creatures[15]), none of these impulses would work in us for servitude to evil, but fear would produce obedience in us, anger, courage, cowardice, caution, and the desiring impulse [eros] would[16] mediate to us the divine and immortal pleasure.[17]

This will not happen until the synergetic action of the Spirit acts, like the turning of the river through the Augean Stables in the mythical labors of Hercules, to clean out all the debris of the past, deposited within us by the action of the outside world. In the meantime, we are trapped in our past actions so that the horses we should command are instead able to drag us this way and that at whim, a process again described by Saint Gregory immediately after the previous passage:

> But if reason should let go of the reins and like some chari-oteer entangled in the chariot[18] should be dragged behind it, wherever the irrational motion of the yoke-animals carries it, then the impulses are turned into passions, as indeed we can see also in irrational animals. For when reason does not control the impulse which naturally lies in them, the fierce animals are destroyed by anger because they fight among themselves. . . . In these animals the energy of desire and pleasure is not occupied with anything higher, nor does any other of the faculties which appear in them lead in any way to a beneficial result. So also in us, if these faculties are not directed by reason towards what is right, but if instead the passions rule over the power of the mind, our humanity is changed from intelligence and godlike-ness to irrationality and mindlessness. We are turned into beasts by the force of these passions.[19]

The process of cleaning out the past is described, again by Gregory of Nyssa, but going back to his *Life of Moses,* in paragraphs immediately following those quoted earlier from that work.

> So all such things rush into the water with the Israelite who leads the way in the baleful passage. Then as the staff of faith leads on and the cloud provides light, the water gives life to those who find refuge in it but destroys their pursuers.
>
> Moreover, the history teaches us by this what kind of people they should be who come through the water. For if the enemy came up out of the water with them they would con-tinue in slavery even after the water since they would have brought up with them the tyrant, still alive, whom they did not drown in the deep.[20]

It is with the emotional flow that begins with water, with the tears of *compunction*, that this cleaning out begins to be effective. These tears, according to Theophan, are the smoke from the newly lit wood, still "wet" with *passions*. In time, the smoke becomes the flame of the spiritual fire in the heart.[21]

This process—which leads to *apatheia*, since the enemies described are the passions—is developed in progressively more detail as we go through the book. Experience will show you how if the *dianoia*—the discursive mind—responds to provocation (see chapter 14), so that it becomes sub-ordinate to the passions, we lose control of our minds, and also how the alternative, described as gaining dominion over external forces, stabilizes this to form an element in that *magnetization* which provides us with a basis for inner prayer that brings something new to our lives.

> Verily, verily, I say unto you, He that believeth on me hath everlasting life.
>
> I am that bread of life.
>
> Your fathers did eat manna in the wilderness, and are dead.
>
> This is the bread which cometh down from heaven, that a man may eat thereof, and not die.
>
> I am the living bread which came down from heaven: if any man eat of this bread, he shall live for ever: and the bread that I will give is my flesh, which I will give for the life of the world (John 6:47–51).

Then, the gospel tells us, the Jews around him misunderstood what he was saying, and took it *literally* and on a materialist level, asking a question that many of us have asked: "How can this man give us his flesh to eat?" (John 6:52). Christ at first explains to the Jews what can happen—but does so in a way that almost fits in with their literal view, but paradoxically creating even stronger conflict.

> Then Jesus said unto them, Verily, verily, I say unto you, Except ye eat the flesh of the Son of man, and drink his blood, ye have no life in you.
>
> Whoso eateth my flesh, and drinketh my blood, hath eternal life; and I will raise him up at the last day.
>
> For my flesh is meat indeed, and my blood is drink indeed.
>
> He that eateth my flesh, and drinketh my blood, dwelleth in me, and I in him.
>
> As the living Father hath sent me, and I live by the Father: so he that eateth me, even he shall live by me.
>
> This is that bread which came down from heaven: not as your fathers did eat manna, and are dead: he that eateth of this bread shall live for ever.
>
> These things said he in the synagogue, as he taught in Capernaum (John 6:53–59).

But afterwards, alone with his disciples, he gives one of the great keys to Christian mystery, explaining the inner truth, the doctrine of His inner tradition, that what He calls His flesh is in fact Spirit, not the substance of the physical body: "It is the spirit that quickeneth; the flesh profiteth nothing: the words that I speak unto you, they are spirit, and they are life" (John 6:63).

Work on Oneself

O utside monasticism, what we might call the path of repentance (metanoia) commonly begins with a search, the pursuit of answers to our deepest questions about the world and about ourselves. At a certain point, if we obtain good enough answers to our questions—normally these would be gospel answers—something begins to act in us: whether it is the power of the Word expressed in the gospel, or the guidance of specific individuals, we will, if we are sincere, become less concerned with the world outside us, and more with questioning ourselves . . . with looking into our inner world. It is at this point that the following quotation from Saint John—first quoted earlier—begins to apply: "If ye know these things, happy are ye if ye do them" (John 13:17).

Questioning ourselves leads to an awareness of the need for certain new knowledge, something that is perhaps the original concept behind the idea of the Good News or gospel. This is effective only to the degree that we understand it in its original meaning, or its multiplicity of meanings, instead of viewing it through the distorting glass of modern specialized thought.

This in turn can bring us into certain conditions of contact with others, koinonia in the Greek, a term which is more commonly used now for the communion service itself, but also means community. As our understanding deepens, the process then begins to follow a logical sequence, essentially Christian in character, yet in many ways similar to that known in the East as the method of cause and effect, or Karma Yoga. This process occurs unseen, although the results will be apparent.

> And he said, So is the kingdom of God, as if a man should cast seed into the ground;
> And should sleep, and rise night and day, and the seed should spring and grow up, he knoweth not how.
> For the earth bringeth forth fruit of herself; first the blade, then the ear, after that the full corn in the ear (Mark 4:26–28).

Since the spirit is unpredictable, the efforts we make will not produce results that are clearly a result of that effort, yet, say the Fathers in many places, including the passage by Macarius the Great near the end of chapter 5, without effort, there is no grace, and without grace, no growth. Yet if we persist in exposure to both these forces, then we will begin to recognize certain temporary changes in us; changes that occur when we are exposed to these forces but which run down between whiles. After a time, we become aware that the ideas and the teachings, however true they may be, are not making these needed changes permanent. The first outcome is usually a kind of addiction, in which we simply seek greater and greater exposure to the good influence that has begun to act on us.

In simple terms, a cult is something that imitates this spiritual process closely enough to have this initial addicting effect on some people, but which, because it does not convey the complete message, generates a form of reasoning which does not afterwards free them from their addiction and so cannot lead to genuine spiritual results. But with instruction that is sufficiently complete, with proper exposure to the gospel, we will quickly come to realize that it is up to us: that for those who know these things, "happy are ye if ye do them." That is, we may realize that some effort by ourselves is necessary if we are to become changed as we wish to be changed. This necessary effort is what many people in esoteric work describe as *work on oneself*.

Work on oneself is the effort of repentance, it is work for *permanence* of our spiritual states.

Modern Solutions

The monastic life is, or used to be, dedicated to this practice of purifying the heart by *metanoia*. Outside the special conditions of monasteries and hermitages, this particular form of *metanoia* may not always be possible. At different times in history, and for people in different situations in life, a different approach may be needed, so that nonmonastic *metanoia* differs from other forms of the religious life, in that not only is continual practice demanded of the student, but continual research is demanded of any community of such students and their leaders to adapt to changing needs as the circumstances of life change. This is less so of monasticism, but because of the time it demands—up to sixteen hours of daily prayer and liturgical life at the extremes—Boris Mouravieff said about this monastic way: "It is obvious that this method cannot operate in modern conditions of life and work. It would be useless and even stupid to attempt it for, if the searcher has the greatest will in the world, it cannot be applied the whole time, and, practiced for part of the time it can only lead to self-deception."[22]

In many people's everyday lives, to give sufficient time to the monastic forms of this practice is difficult, if not impossible. Other answers, other ways of working on oneself, are required. And today at least, and where they have received a modern education, even monks have been known to become too busy!

For these reasons, some mention of alternative methods by which laypeople can work on themselves under modern conditions will be made in the following chapters, but in practical terms this book is intended among other things to draw attention to the need for ongoing practical research in this field, as part of a program of restoration of the inner tradition to the full effectiveness it now lacks. As Livingstone said about the amount that must be done to rediscover darkest Africa, we must realize that to rediscover the Christian tradition much work has to be done.

But we must also realize something else, that a waking heart is a change of being.

Morton Smith, who was referred to earlier (pp. 108–9) as describing quite accurately the qualities of the Christian gnosis, in his book *The Secret Gospel*,[23] an attempt to simplify the complex thesis of his original book, describes the great difficulties he experienced attempting to understand what it was that Jesus had taught secretly. His *atheistic conclusion* is that Jesus transmitted to others a kind of possession by some spirit, that this was a kind of psychological process, and that, after Jesus' death, it could be transmitted from person to person by what he actually calls at one point *infection*.

If the atheistic preconception is removed from Smith's conclusions, they are fundamentally correct, although incomplete in detail to the point of distortion. But the addition of the atheistic viewpoint compounds this distortion or perhaps caused it. It seems an easy evasion, if time-honored, to say that this idea can only be understood from a position of faith, but this happens to be the fact.

It is in fact possible to identify in meaningful modern terms the greatest element missing from this whole view, an element that differentiates the processes described from any clinically pathological event. Symptomatic of schizophrenia and certain other psychoses is the generally recognized effect they have of creating an *incoherence*[24] of speech, reason, and behavior. It is possible to say, with Smith, that the characteristic of Christian experience, and a test of the truth in inner Christianity, since we are speaking of inner experience, is *coherence*: the tradition forms a coherent or internally consistent whole. It is worth remembering here that the classical medical test of *awakening* from anaesthesia is one of *coherence*. This should be understood in the sense that people often speak incoherently when emerging from anaesthesia, and they are not considered to have become *conscious* until they speak coherently.

I am not qualified to define the Holy Spirit, but it is clear from my own experience, as well as from my researches, that the great difference between pathological possession and the union of the Christian with Christ is that the pathological leads away from the conscious into the fragmented, whereas any true spiritual union leads in the opposite direction—away from the fragmented toward unity of consciousness.

This also links with our reference, on page 44, to Hughlings-Jackson's definition of intoxication as a state in which the higher faculties are lost first. Fallen humanity is thus in a kind of intoxication from which we have yet to emerge as a race. The parable of the *tares* (Matthew 13:27–30) refers to a *psychological intoxication*, an intoxication of ideas or sensations, entered in a state of partial sleep. "While men slept," an enemy sowed weeds among someone's wheat, so that the weeds grew up amongst the grain. The farmer refused to pull out the weeds, being afraid to damage the wheat. He then said that it would be easier to separate them at harvest time. Psychologically, this speaks of a state, not of physical sleep, but of absence (an opposite of *presence of mind*): an inattentive or distracted state, in which we take in ideas and sensations *indiscriminately*. What we take in in this state then influences our future thoughts and behavior, and can even reduce our future awareness.

In the parable, the solution is not to try to remove these unwanted memories immediately but to wait for the harvest and then "bind them into bundles." "Harvest," in this sense, is the time when we see what happens when our various thoughts and memories emerge and shape the events of our life. Then we should classify the harmful thoughts and memories in "bundles," and so we will learn to burn them in the fire of *compunction*.

As long as our minds are dominated by these images indiscriminately taken in in the past, people will be able to say of us that: ". . . these people have arrived at a certain concept of God, but not a conception truly worthy of Him and appropriate to His blessed nature. For their 'disordered heart was darkened by the machinations of the wicked demons who were instructing them.' "[25]

Most people believe that there is a great gulf between Eastern and Western thought. This fallacy is due to the Victorian idea that Indian philosophy regarded the world as unreal. This was a naive and quite incorrect interpretation: the doctrine in question actually claimed that the view of the world held by those who lacked a properly formulated conceptual system was inaccurate, that is, incorrect or illusory. In Indian thought, illusion (*maya*) arises through ignorance (*avidya*). We can see the action of this principle in ordinary thought, where we will discover that *ignorance leads to opinion*: it is our nature to form theories and opinions whenever we lack clear knowledge. Imperception in our perceptions, simple unawareness, lack of registering what we perceive, leave us open to imagination; that is, the same principle operates in our perceptions: we imagine (or dream) wherever we lack meaningful input, a fact clearly confirmed by sensory deprivation experiments. Where do these dreams and imaginings come from? Here is one of the great secrets of human psychology.

The essence of the Christian idea that "the truth shall set you free" is the same: that there is a kind of knowledge—the Fathers called it *gnosis*, the Indian *vidya* or *jnana*—which ends ignorance (Sanskrit *avidya*), and so overcomes illusion. The Christian insight that that truth is *personal*, is in fact a "person," does not change the way in which that truth acts. Theologically, at least, a "person" is much greater than a principle: Christ was "the Way, the Truth, and the Life."

According to the tradition, as we will have already understood, passions and desires are the tares that disturb or "intoxicate" the mind, and we will discover that they in fact make us blind to the more subtle actions of the spirit. A simple parable for this is the open sea. The rougher the waves, the more the depths of the ocean are hidden. With strong winds even the shallowest bottom is difficult to see. The early Fathers not only commented on this obscurity, but also wrote at different times about other things that disturb the mind or reveal it to be already disturbed.

One major problem of this kind was worldly concern or *anxiety*.

The Biblical Paradox of the Knowledge of God

What has the power to awaken us to a higher reality is the clear *recognition* that there is a higher reality. But Christian doctrine faces up squarely to the difficulty of recognizing this reality while we remain "asleep" to certain aspects of reality.

Evagrius speaks about gnosis as *theoria* or contemplation, but it must be understood that this concept is one whose meaning differs between Eastern and Western churches. The difference at root depends on the difference in the concepts of spirituality that crystallized at the great watershed of the debate in Thessalonika between Barlaam and Palamas (see p. 79); between the Western intellectual model, in the Platonic sense of intellectual, of a God inferred as if an ideal, and the hesychast model, established then on Mount Athos—where it survives to the present day.

The Orthodox liturgy refers to a God who cannot be known in essence, but whose actions on us can be known when we are sensitized so that we are able to register and retain them, in the phrase: "For with thee is the fountain of life: in thy light shall we see light" (Psalms 36:9).

In practice, His communications to us can then also be *known;* this knowledge is not from the senses and so is easily discounted. Saint Gregory Palamas put this by saying that God cannot be known in essence, but He can be known in His energies—the Greek word is *dynamis,* translated "energy," but known, as energy is known in physics, by the *actions* to which it gives rise, by the way God acts in us. Theophan, a master of this tradition in the last century, says the same: the Holy Spirit is known by its activity in the personality.

Constant frictions have arisen in theology because the Bible can be made to support two ideas that appear to be mutually exclusive: the idea that we cannot know God ("You cannot look on the face of God and live") and the idea reflected, for instance, in the theology of Athonite abbots such as George Capsanis of Grigoriou, who assumes the possibility of a form of knowledge, of knowing God through His transforming power, in saying that "a God who does not deify man can have no interest to man."[26]

In volume 1 of his book *Gnosis,* Boris Mouravieff wrote: "The affirmation: 'No man hath seen God at any time' seems a flagrant contradiction of the words of Jesus, quoted elsewhere by the same evangelist: 'If a man love Me, he will keep My word: and My Father will love him. And We will establish a dwelling in him.' "[27] This is one of the great problems of theology, going back to the earliest centuries of the church. Literal interpretation and imprecision have both frequently led to confusion. In this particular case we are considering, it is imprecise translation of these and other texts that leads to the idea that the Bible makes contradictory statements on this subject. Normal translations make it seem as if God both can be known and cannot be known, depending on which page you read! It was this that led to the controversy between Palamas and Barlaam. Philosophical training, such as that proposed by Clement and Origen, equips people to handle this kind of question. The conflict is resolved as soon as we recognize the different natures of the two kinds of knowledge. But the modern churches tend to turn away from intellectual training, so that the modern Christian is left face-to-face with this paradox with no means of resolving it. In everyday experience this exists in the persistent difficulty, now endemic in our society, in which people misinterpret this whole situation.

What was created in the early church as a means of resolving a problem has today become a source of confusion. As originally understood, these two paradoxical statements about the knowability of God deal with a Christian experience that is still common today. This is the experience that we cannot perceive God in the way in which we perceive the "things of the world." The idea that "no man hath seen God at any time" is simply a statement of this fact that God cannot be known in this way, that He cannot be seen. Eugraph Kovalevsky around 1970 put it like this, but he is describing the same situation: "Love for God is acquired in prayer, and it is prayer which provides the motive for loving God.[28] For it is almost impossible to love God. Let us be frank! Without grace we would see no reason to love God."[29]

This teaching is of great practical importance. A Christian who properly understands this statement will no longer be worried by the fact that he or she cannot *see* God, nor in any way know Him as we know things that fall in the field of the senses. The teaching thus reinforces our confidence in our own faculties in a situation where such reinforcement is necessary. Our attention and efforts can then be correctly focused on the realities of the situation, instead of pursuing the impossible or being hindered by attempts to resolve unanswerable questions. (A more detailed study of this idea is found early in Origen's *de Principiis*.)

The statement by Palamas, like others, shows how God can be *known* and defines the way in which we can begin to relate to Him, opening up to the inner life found in contemplative prayer and the prayer of the heart. A proper understanding of this changes the quality of the prayer life and makes its objectives clear, so that the individual finds his or her way more quickly into the subtleties of inner religion. This is why it is sometimes said that the way to knowledge of God is not direct, but is through knowledge of our own "real I."

Once this is clearly understood it becomes abundantly clear that the shift of interpretation of this biblical teaching shows that by the time of the debate in Thessalonika, this paradoxical doctrine of two ways of knowing God had declined from being a practical teaching to a question for philosophical debate. This division was the very essence of the schism in the church since, in those communities that had lost the use of this idea as an effective guide to prayer, the inner meaning of Christianity has gradually declined.

The link of this to the inner light, recognized as late as Saint Thomas à Kempis and Jan van Ruysbroeck as the light of Christ, confirms the inner meaning of the idea of Christ as the image or icon of the Father. According to the Fathers, the life and teachings of Christ, as expressed in the New Testament, are the *icon* that shows us the God we cannot see directly.

It is a common experience that we experience Jesus' words as having ever new meanings, so that in this sense their depth is infinite, just as the divine Himself is infinite. Yet this knowledge may and indeed must be interpreted with great precision. It is only then that it will exert its infinite power as the Word, its capacity to create the faculty of discrimination of spirits in us, and it is this that changes us, opens us to the Spirit of the Lord. This is the method of cause and effect, the method in which certain processes lead to certain results, implied by the Sufi philosopher Ibn Arabi, when he wrote:

> If the devil himself learned this knowledge,
> he would be transformed.[30]

The cause, the seed of this growth, is discrimination (Greek *diakrisis*), which germinates when it becomes strong enough to change our attitude to ourselves to the point where we do what is right instead of what we want to do. Only a special kind of knowledge, *gnosis*, has the power to create this kind of discrimination. It is this that works rather like taking a pill (see p. 76), which seems easy, although, like an unpalatable *medicine*, it is this that usually involves learning things about oneself that are highly unpleasant in the learning. Born beyond law, from the source of law, the effect of this *medicine* is lawful in the sense that it is predictable; as the cause is assimilated, the effect is produced by due process. The infinite and eternal acts "from above" on the finite, and makes that, in its turn, infinite and eternal. Thus this gnosis lights the way by which the animal or exterior man can become a spiritual or interior man, and the temporal become eternal.

At this point we face the question: What is this Spirit of God? Here theologians tremble, and rightly, for "he that shall blaspheme against the Holy Ghost hath never forgiveness, but is in danger of eternal damnation" (Mark 3:29). Yet great misunderstandings have arisen here, and great follies been made public, and it is time that something was said, if not about what this Spirit is, at least, about how it manifests in inner experience.

Ascesis as Work on Oneself

A scesis is work on oneself in order to overcome the effects of the past and so heal the soul, restoring our potential to the full. Ascesis is not taken seriously in modern times. This is partly due to a lack of understanding of the whole idea, and partly to the fact that so many monastic authors in the past have spoken of forms of ascesis too difficult for laypeople and even for many monastics. Today we have the idea that asceticism means to deny oneself pleasure, that it means "mortification of the body." Yet true ascesis is something very different from blind obedience to rules or from mechanical self-denial. The early Christian meaning of ascesis can be traced to Saint Paul's statement:

> I therefore so run, not as uncertainly; so fight I, not as one that beateth the air:

But I keep under my body, and bring it into subjection:
lest by any means, when I have preached to others, I myself
should be a castaway (1 Corinthians 9:26–27).

The early church, following Saint Paul, used the idea of ascesis to describe
the exercise necessary to become a different kind of being. Saint Anthony
the Great, in his *First Letter*, describes the different kinds of ascesis in a
passage that distinguishes three different motivating currents in human life.
In simple terms there can be three kinds of ascetic exercise. There can be
exercise of the body. Physical exercises practiced on their own tend to lead
to pride, and those in the past who have practiced this without knowledge
of the other forms of ascesis have led to the idea that asceticism is simply
senseless punishment of the body. But there can also be ascetic exercise of
the mind and, on all paths, too, there can be ascetic "exercise" of the nous
(see figure 6.1).

Physical ascesis is physical training with some emphasis on retention
of energy. It strengthens the body while keeping it controlled in order to
purify it. We can easily understand this physical ascesis, because it is like
ordinary physical training carried out by athletes before a contest: it consists of practices that will strengthen their performance and improve its
quality, and of accepting restrictions to deny themselves indulgences that
will weaken their performance. Working out like this benefits the body.
But in esoteric terms it is not valuable in itself, and practiced without the
higher forms it can indeed be a danger, as, taken alone, it feeds our
egotism. But it is valuable as a way to obtain enough strength and energy
for the higher forms of ascesis.

Psychological ascesis has the qualities of exercising the personality,
and of keeping it controlled in order to purify it. When it comes to
psychological ascesis, we have less experience, so we are less clear about
this idea. In a modern sense it means "to work on ourselves."

Noetic ascesis has the qualities of exercising the nous in such a way
as to illuminate and purify it. Thus it becomes the awakening of the nous.
When it comes to noetic ascesis, the closest we come to understanding
this idea today is the modern concern with meditation. Modern usage of
the word *meditation* changed in the early 1960s. Its meaning was extended
when it began to be used to translate the Sanskrit term *dhyana*.[31] *Dhyana*
comes very close to noetic ascesis. But most meditation practices are simply ascesis of the mind. They are not noetic ascesis, nor are they genuine
dhyana practice.

Yet certain forms of prayer, as well as some practices described as
meditation, are actually forms of noetic ascesis. These are the forms where
the two terms, *prayer* and *meditation*, seem to be interchangeable. It is
equally true that many practices now known as meditation and many

NOETIC ASCESIS
PSYCHOLOGICAL ASCESIS (or the Psychological Method)
PHYSICAL ASCESIS

Figure 6.1   Kinds of ascesis relate to the diferent energies.

specific prayer practices are merely psychological in nature, and that many of these do not even yield the slowing of mental activity necessary before noetic practice can begin.

True noetic ascesis is the "cure of the soul" taught by the early Fathers of the church. It leads to the wakening of consciousness as described in the teachings of Gurdjieff and Ouspensky. This noetic ascesis can be approached in two ways. One is through noetic prayer or meditation—a form of prayer that in time helps to lay the foundations of a different way of life. The other is a more generalized form that begins with learning to discern between worldly and spiritual influences and leads to the same transformed way of life. This generalized form is a primary process in Gurdjieff's Fourth Way, the way of understanding.

To absorb B influences, that is, the influences by which spirit is first recognized (called influences B in the Gurdjieff terminology, but see chapter 13), and to link them to our own inner experience increases our ability to discern or discriminate and absorb further such influences. This we must do with greater precision than we yet know. This precision is indicated in the idea of recognition. Recognition leads to effective discrimination: to diakrisis. In practice, better and more definite results are obtained when these two forms, prayer and more generalized work on oneself, are used in tandem. Then, with true spiritual experience throwing new light on our experience of the world, and the consequent awakening of the second stage of faith, noetic ascesis goes deeper.

But today even spiritual seekers do not understand ascesis. I myself searched for real spirituality for many years with only a fragmentary understanding of the need for ascesis. Father George, on Mount Athos, once remarked to me tentatively that I should think about the question of ascesis. At the time, I did not take the idea very seriously. I could not. Although in the Christian view of life, in the esoteric view, I came close to the views of the monks, in terms of practice we were still worlds apart. For me, the most I could possibly do was to give two half-hours to prayer or meditation each day, mental asceticism with little physical "cost." As life grew more difficult for me, even this became impossible. I could neither give time to ascetic exercises, nor did I see the need to overcome what seemed to me to be "normally human" appetites and comforts that since childhood had appeared to be the goals of human life and the normal standards of civilization. So I continued to live as I had lived, and nothing could really change in me.

The monastic idea of ascetism, when I first saw it, was very far from what I would have considered, before my visits to Mount Athos, to be a normal way of living. This is the real problem today: we cannot understand the value and purpose of ascesis. For ascesis has a purpose, but its real purpose is not physical, it is not simply psychological. The real goals even of physical asceticism are noetic. In esotericism, ascesis is practiced only with the aim of purifying and enlightening the nous, and it will only be successful if it is practiced from an understanding of that fact; if it emerges from the heart by assent—and that because, as a result of our seeing it to be necessary, we care enough to make the effort easy. True assent can be taken as a test: as evidence that our ascesis comes from the heart. Ascesis that does not come from the heart is false ascesis; it comes from pride, or it is a discipline imposed on us by others, and either of these leads to destruction. Another unknown thing about ascesis is that it is used as a means of testing oneself. For this, above all, it must be used intelligently and not destructively. If this is done, it will serve to help us to discover [32] the intentions of our hearts.

Chapter 7

Three Renunciations

One great problem is that our civilization is almost blind to true
emotion, which is unselfish love. This is a fact that we rarely notice,
even in ourselves and those closest to us. But occasionally people admit
that they do not really even know what love is.

To fill this gap, the early Fathers can offer real answers and usable—
if not easy—practical solutions that confirm and expand on modern knowledge. Brought up to date, their psychological teachings tell us that the
reason for this blindness to emotion is that modern thought has exces-
sively tilted toward an intellectual complexity that leaves little time for
emotion, while the level of intellectual activity and intellectually generated
physical activity obscures the true roots of emotional problems. It is in
describing these distortions of normal human nature that Freud's work
rings true, although this gives it a major difference from the early psychology of the Fathers, which was concerned with normal and with higher
states, not with the abnormal. To study the side effects of the third component that is present in such situations, which consists of distorted
emotions, or love gone sour, and doing so while love itself is masked by
the activity, leads to the misleading conclusion that emotion is merely
another form of mental activity.

In fact, because the roots of the emotional component are more
subtle than the ordinary activity of thought, the psychological tradition of
early Christianity, as well as many contemporary eastern forms, long ago
developed methods of resolving conflicts by separating out the emotional
element, and those methods, although not intended to deal with modern

pathologies, go deeper and produce more lasting results, confirming Jung's overall approach to psychotherapy. One example of how this emotional component was distinguished in a practical way was where Evagrius of Pontus wrote, well over a thousand years ago in his *Kephalia Gnostica*,[1] about three successive levels of what he called *renunciation*. These three renunciations are also described by Saint John Cassian, whose *Conferences*[2] give many valuable clues to their nature. He comments, on how he first heard of these three renunciations, that:

> We had believed that in giving ourselves wholeheartedly to the first renunciation we had come within sight of the summit of perfection. And here we were now with the beginnings of an awareness that even in our dreams we had not glimpsed the heights of monastic life. In the coenobitic communities we had heard something about the second renunciation. But as for the third, in which all perfection is gathered, and which surpasses the other two in every possible way, we know that until now we had never even heard tell of it.[3]

Cassian, who in the sixth century brought the tradition to the West from the desert communities of Sketis to found two monasteries in the South of France, says that we should "strive for these renunciations with the utmost zeal." But in fact, in studying what he writes about them it becomes clear that his text, said to be a record of a talk by Paphnutius (a Father under whom Cassian appears to have studied), is far from verbatim. It seems that the sources available to us suffer from the copyists' and/ or translators' errors so common in surviving writings of the early Fathers. As a result, when Cassian explains them more fully, the character of the second and third renunciations is far from entirely clear, although the basic differences are defined by him fairly precisely, thus: "The first renunciation has to do with the body. We come to despise all the riches and all goods of the world. With the second renunciation we repel our past, our vices, the passions governing spirit and flesh. And in the third renunciation, we draw our spirit away from the here and the visible and we do so in order solely to contemplate the things to come. Our passion is solely for the unseen."[4]

We must understand that these successive renunciations are needed on the esoteric path, because to recover our true—"God-given"—nature, or *essence*,[5] it is necessary to clarify and sensitize our minds at successively more subtle levels. Two of these levels are fairly generally understood today, but the third, of very subtle emotional disturbances, is almost unknown in our modern world, and it is its effects which manifest in the form of emotional *abreaction* in psychiatric treatment. It was in uncovering this that psychoanalysis has been such a formative force in modern thought, particularly in the work of C. G. Jung.

The problem is in part the existence of remembered feelings, known in this terminology as *passions,* which masquerade as true emotions but are in fact coarser. To eliminate disturbance only on the physical or mental levels will not correct disharmonies at the third or true emotional level, for which the psychology of the early Fathers provided specific and effective if often uncomfortable solutions.

Three Renunciations Defined

The classic parables of the treasure hid in the field and of the pearl of great price are parables of renunciation. They describe the need to give up something of less importance in order to obtain something of greater importance.

> Again, the kingdom of heaven is like unto treasure hid in a field; the which when a man hath found, he hideth, and for joy thereof goeth and selleth all that he hath, and buyeth that field (Matthew 13:44).

In fact, this same parable can be taken on more than one level. The first is the physical or *exoteric* level, where it implies the need to give up one way of life—for instance, the worldly—for another, for example the monastic. But according to Evagrius of Pontus there are, on the road to *theosis* or God-realization, three progressive renunciations. The text of the three paragraphs with which Evagrius introduces these three renunciations is so dense with meaning that it is difficult to understand without pondering it paragraph by paragraph, giving considerable time to each. The serious reader is advised to attempt this, but in the meantime we will try to give some idea of what it says, and link this to Cassian's descriptions and to experience.

The three renunciations can be related to the three kinds of ascesis (see figure 7.1).

The first renunciation is turning away from the body and from the "world." Evagrius wrote: "The first renunciation is the abandonment of the things of the world, which is produced by assenting to the science of God."[6]

The second renunciation is in fact a renunciation by the personality of its claim that the active content of mind is our true inner nature, the whole person. Evagrius says: "The second renunciation is the abandonment of evil, achieved by the grace of God combined with the effort of

THIRD RENUNCIATION	Of "knowingness."	NOETIC ASCESIS
SECOND RENUNCIATION	Of internal possessions: habits, habitual desires, and negative emotions.	PSYCHOLOGICAL ASCESIS
FIRST RENUNCIATION	Of external possessions.	PHYSICAL ASCESIS

Figure 7.1   Three renunciations related to three forms of ascesis.

man."[7] "So then the first renunciation is the giving up of goods that do not belong to us," says Cassian. "Hence it is not enough in itself for the achievement of perfection. One must pass on to the second renunciation, by which we give up what is really ours." And at another place in the same conference, he says: "With the second renunciation we repel our past, our vices, the passions governing spirit and flesh."[8]

The third renunciation lies beyond what we normally recognize as the activity of mind. Evagrius writes: "The third renunciation is the separation from ignorance, which is naturally made to appear to men according to the degree of their state."[9] In Cassian's version: "having driven out all sin, we will climb up to the high point of the third by which we come to despise, in heart and mind, not only all that is done in this world or possessed individually by men but the very superabundance of all the elements which are deemed everywhere so magnificent. . . . and as the apostle says, 'We look not at the things which are seen but at the unseen, for the things that are seen belong to time and the things that are unseen are forever' (2 Corinthians 4:18)." Cassian had further defined this third renunciation: "And in the third renunciation, we draw our spirit away from the here and the visible, and we do so in order solely to contemplate the things to come. Our passion is solely for the unseen."[10]

A fourth and final step: after the three renunciations, according to Cassian, one is able to take a fourth step. "We do this," he says, "so that we may earn the right to hear what was said to Abraham: 'Come into the land which I shall show you' (Genesis 12:1). And what this clearly means is that unless the three renunciations are achieved with all the fervour of the mind it will not be possible to reach this fourth, the return and reward for perfect renunciation. A land gained in this life when all passion is ousted and the heart is pure, a land which neither the virtue nor the effort of a toiling man will open up, but which the Lord himself promised to reveal."[11]

The First Renunciation: "Dying to the World"

> The first renunciation is the abandonment of the things of the world, which is produced by assenting to the science of God.[12]

The householder and the monk approach this first renunciation in different ways, but the underlying meaning of both approaches is the same.

This first renunciation, said to be "produced by assenting to[13] the science of God," is generally symbolized by the monk who "leaves the world" or by the Israelite who "comes out of Egypt." But this assent to the divine science really describes the first step on the inner, psychological path, the first step in attempting to follow this inner "science of God." This is essentially an intellectual assent, an intellectual commitment—a resolution to transcend all the expectations and all the imitation of the past that form the outermost level of our mind, our personality. The popular picture of the monastic life is of a peaceful escape from the world, but in fact the formation of this resolve signals the beginning of an inner struggle, and in many cases the monk is not permitted to return physically to the "outside world" until the worst of this interior warfare is over.

The monk assents to the science of God by following the instructions of that science in his whole way of life . . . by following a rule based on obedience to the word of God, Logos ton Theon. Thus he turns away from the world as he sees it. He begins this by assenting in immediate, physical form to the gospel teaching: "So therefore none of you can become My disciple if you do not give up all your possessions" (Luke 14:33).

As the next chapter makes clear, this idea of *possessions* has an inner meaning as well as the outer meaning that applies to the monk who renounces the world. The student of understanding renounces the world spiritually and in slow stages, as the result of a growing natural attraction for the events of the inner life.

The Turn Toward Reality

T he difference between the householder and the monk is in one sense purely conceptual. The point that becomes clear in studying the first renunciation is that, in his turn away from life, the monk, like the house-holder, actually turns toward reality—toward the essential. In thought the turnabout appears different, but inwardly, essentially, the actual experience is almost identical in both cases. The New Testament, its teachings formu-lated before the beginning of monasticism, deals with this in a sense that is common to both these views. As expressed by Saint Paul, it seems clear and factual enough, if difficult for some people to accept. To paraphrase from one of his epistles (1 Timothy 6:7–10): For as we brought nothing into the world, so we can take nothing out of it; but if we have food and clothing we should be content with these. But those who want to be rich fall into temptation, and they are trapped by many senseless and harmful desires that plunge people into ruin and destruction.

The problem lies in the desires, which lead to ruinous activity, but the solution lies in understanding the fact that the desires themselves come only from believing in the "world" as we see it. A further clue to what this means is the teaching of Karma Yoga about *discrimination*. This is arrived at, according to that tradition, by distinguishing between the unreal and the real. This is little different from Cassian's *diakrisis* between the spirit of the world and the Spirit of God (see chapter 13). But it does offer an alternative, that instead of renouncing the world externally, we can renounce the "influences" of the world that exist within us. But first the nature of this kind of renunciation must be exactly understood. The need to be exact about this is due to the danger of error: the result of any "act" of discrimination depends on the exact form of that discrimination, as described in chapter 13. The danger is to take some inner activity, some inner change, as the reality. The result then is not liberation but obsession. Thus we were warned by the Apostles: "Forasmuch then as we are the offspring of God, we ought not to think that the Godhead is like unto gold, or silver, or stone, graven by art and man's device" (Acts 17:29).

The phrase at the end of the quotation includes the Greek word *enthemysios,* a word of varying translations that might be rendered here as "graven by art and man's *meditation*," or perhaps "by man's conceptualiz-ing." Knowing that the authors almost certainly will have been familiar with the wax tablet image of memory used by Plato,[14] we can see that this passage can be taken in an inner sense, first as referring to different levels of inner substance, since in the language of the inner tradition gold, silver, and stone are often used to distinguish these levels, but also to refer to impressions graven in *memory*. The outer meaning is also true. Neither man-made statues nor man-made concepts and memories should be re-garded as the godhead, which is something else entirely from all reflec-tions or images.

The Two Nights

Afterrenunciation of the outside world, or its purely inner equivalent of *diakrisis*, come two further stages of *internal renunciation*. As these seem to have been beyond the experience of Saint John Cassian, so they are beyond almost all modern experience, so that all we can do is to outline a plan for study of the second and third renunciations, without claiming to give an exhaustive explanation. But we will certainly find some clues in the writings of Saint John of the Cross, the Spanish mystic, who spoke of these as *two nights* or stages in the purgation of the soul.

> In order to reach perfection, the soul has to pass, ordinarily, through two kinds of night, which spiritual writers call purgations, or purifications, of the soul, and which I have called night because in the one as in the other the soul travels, as it were, by night, in darkness.
>
> The first night is the night or purgation of the sensual part of the soul, which is the privation of all desire, wrought by God . . . the second night is the night of the spiritual part, which is for those who are more advanced, when God wishes to bring them into union with Himself.
>
> The soul cannot enter into the night of itself, because nobody is able of his own strength to empty his heart of all desires, so as to draw near unto God.
>
> The night is divided into three parts. The first may be likened to the commencement of night when material objects begin to be invisible. The second may be compared to midnight, which is utter darkness. The third resembles the close of night, which is God, when the dawn of day is at hand.
>
> There is no detachment if desire remains. Detachment consists in suppressing desire and avoiding pleasure; it is this that sets the soul free, even though possession may still be retained. It is not the things of the world that occupy or injure the soul, for they do not enter within, but rather the wish for and desire of them, which abide within it.[15]

This whole analogy can be looked at, from an inner or esoteric point of view, in terms of the way the world is experienced when our normal "defenses," the protective illusions behind which we hide, are missing.

But it is here that we meet one of the strangest properties common to all religions: the fact that religion can serve either to help us relate to life, to connect to life, or to cut us off from life.

This is the character of true faith, that, properly understood, it gives us an enhanced relationship to nature: to the nature of life and to our own nature. Improperly understood, it forms an additional *illusion* that comes between us and our perception of life: it is this misunderstanding that forms the opium of the people.

This is one of the reasons why the Indian tradition has been so revealing to a Western world that had lost touch with its own inner tradition.

In India the seeker after God passes through four stages of life. First he is student *brahmachari* (a young student who lives with his teacher for a while), then householder, then, when he has played his part in the world, he becomes forest dweller ("dweller in the garden"), then *sannyasi,* "renunciate." Here again we have progressive stages of renunciation. These stages represent the transformation of religion from delusion to true faith: the progressive removal of protection from the soul as it gains the strength to face life as it is.

The same removal of protection occurs in the earlier forms of monastic life. It can be discovered experimentally in *pilgrimage*—if that pilgrimage involves renunciation for a time of habitual forms of living—and it is for this reason that pilgrimage is very important in the Islamic faith.

For a moment, to look at the meaning of what I am describing, we will turn aside onto the path of *pilgrimage.* It is on pilgrimage that the layperson can experience the outer form of renunciation that forms the basis of monasticism, in order to better comprehend its inner nature. We think of Christianity as quite different from Islam with its hajj,[16] but in fact the same idea of pilgrimage exists in places like Lourdes, Rome, Jerusalem, and Athos. As we remarked earlier, Mount Athos is known by its monks as the Garden of *Panaghia* (see chapter 4 note 32), of Mary, "the All Holy One." This idea of the garden reveals in idea—and in experience—a strangely primitive world: on the one hand the natural world as it is, the most beautiful of all. It is unspoiled, and so it is beautiful. Because it is unspoiled it is also "unimproved"; this means that it is without protection for us, without the comforts, the entertainments, the distractions we desire, without the benefits of that human society—the Culture of Contentment again[17]—of human mutual support in the great art of distraction. It is a place of *exile,* of enforced independence, a bleak and empty place in which man finds himself whenever he is separated from all the distractions and protections of modern life.

Once one has experienced this garden in its fullness the world will never be quite the same. This is like the coldly beautiful world described by early exiles to the Russian labor camps: a world where a day is eighteen hours long, a day without distractions, without discussions, without entertainments, without comforts, a day face-to-face with simple reality. With the first renunciation, the lay seeker turns actively toward this reality; with the second, it becomes the ground of his life.

But today we have to learn even how to go on pilgrimage in this way instead of with all the accoutrements of the tourist, all the aids designed to help us keep to our accustomed way of life even when we are "exploring" other cultures.

It sounds fanciful, yet we are separated from such a world all the time, not only by thin cotton, by an eight-ounce glass pane, but by a much thicker wall of ideas and prejudices, attitudes and habits. Yet it is possible to find a doorway through this wall, and those who have been there will know of what I speak.

Through this doorway is the true *pardes* (Hebrew word for park or garden, one of the precursors of the English word *paradise*): not our contemporary garden of contentment, but the garden East of Eden in which human nature grows to the full, a true child of organic life. And all this imagery has very precise meaning.

Again, all this imagery and the ideas it expresses would appear fanciful if there were no support for it in fact. The fact is Mount Athos itself, a way of life—based on this idea and embodying in outer form this image of the garden. Here this image has sustained itself for more than a thousand years, and it is only now that it is under real threat for almost the first time since the Turkish conquest of Greece seven hundred years ago. Here, as a last relic of the forgotten Byzantine Empire, an earlier Christianity follows today the rules and precepts of the desert Fathers who began the monastic life more than fifteen hundred years ago. That beginning of monasticism was itself the attempt to protect and preserve the even earlier form of Christianity that began to decay from the time Constantine adopted Christianity as the established religion of the eastern Roman Empire, when the mixture of politics and religion began that continues to plague the Christian world up to the present time.

Inwardly, pilgrimage is a question of heart, not just of head nor simply of physical effort. It is, as Father I. of SimonoPetra once told me, a journey to a holy place, a place that can help one to discover the eternal *within oneself*. Pilgrimage is a journey to oneself. It is also willing devotion, and it is change enforced by circumstance, but by invited circumstance, and willingly accepted. On the one hand, one intensifies devotion by giving it expression in physical effort, so expressing the unity of spirit and body. On the other, by leaving behind all that is familiar and easy in one's life, one leaves behind too all that is habitual and repetitive. It is as if the pilgrim is able, in spirit, and for the duration of his pilgrimage, to obey Christ's injunction to "sell all that thou hast, and distribute unto the poor, and thou shalt have treasure in heaven: and come, follow me" (Luke 18:22).

This, of course, is a simple way of thinking about *metanoia*, of re-directing the heart: "For where your treasure is, there will your heart be also" (Matthew 6:21).

A modern way of looking at it is that on pilgrimage we sacrifice time. Time, the most precious commodity of modern life. When we lack it, we bemoan the fact. When it is "on our hands," we try to fill it. But on pilgrimage, by leaving behind all the things one uses to "fill the time," we find time within us for things that have for long been missing from our lives. By making the gift of time, we become free of the bonds of time . . . and so learn to regain control of time. By doing things we find difficult, we break free of the habit of choosing the "easy way" in everything. Once free of this, we discover that it is this habit of taking the easy way out that binds us to repeat the events of our lives with little change. So we overcome the imagined limitations that have too often become habitual boundaries to our lives. And so we discover that difficulties, far from limiting our freedom, can actually increase it.

By sacrificing time, we can gain freedom from ourselves.

But to discover this, we have to step outside the surprisingly narrow bounds of modern thought . . . and modern action, to step without hesitation onto the pilgrim's road, accepting the difficulties of unfamiliar conditions as well as accepting new ideas. The essence of pilgrimage, then, is giving up. We give up the ordinary for the extraordinary, the everyday for God, and not as a "bargain" from which one expects return. God, reported the early Fathers, makes no bargains of this kind.

So one gives up "oneself" simply in order to know a better self, or simply in order to prove, in one's own flesh, to one's own self, the reality of one's commitment to something higher than oneself. For example, habits are difficult to overcome. They are easily begun, but once they are begun it becomes difficult for us even to see them, and so they become almost impossible to remedy. So one idea of pilgrimage is the "friction struggle" against one's habits, begun by placing oneself in a position where one's habits do not provide solutions, are not acceptable, not appropriate. It is in such circumstances, I found, that these habits and attitudes become suddenly visible!

Bitter Waters

L et me digress a little to fill in some background. On Mount Athos is a bleak, exposed hillside known as Karoulia which in a book was once, I believe, called The Holy Planet Purgatory.[18] More often it is known as The Desert. This place on earth is named for a place in the human heart, and it might seem that it was so named because of its topography. It consists of steep rocky slopes at the storm-blasted tip of Mount Athos. Before the time of Alexander and Aristotle, it was at the foot of these cliffs that Xerxes' fleet was wrecked. He lost twenty thousand men.

Here is a place dedicated to the theological *exile* of monasticism. Now a dozen hermits live here, in strange houses that cling like swallows' nests to the inhospitable cliffs, while in summer tourists in motor boats lie off the inhospitable shore and attempt to understand the inexplicable at a distance with cameras and binoculars. There too an occasional pilgrim braves the steep paths, hauling himself up on chains to ask his question of those who have fled his importunate company and have not learned well enough the lessons of the *Gerontikon,* where stories of the early Fathers repeatedly tell of the tricks they used to avoid talking to worldly visitors, tricks sometimes still played in this inaccessible corner of the world.

This is the "desert" of Athos. Here the hermits go to be alone with themselves and their Creator—and specifically to "overcome the past," to purge their hearts of the final traces of their earlier selves, because this is the way in which they can be alone with God. One might believe this to be a fine, dramatic gesture, but one would be wrong. Here, nobody given to making such gestures would be permitted to remain. For a monk to live in Karoulia requires permission that traditionally is difficult to obtain. Even to live here, a man must already be much changed.

Sometimes, in the Fathers, and in the eremetic tradition of the Eastern Church up until the present time, the monk is advised to go into *exile* in this way, in order to purify the heart of the personal and the trivial.

A report on one of my visits to Mount Athos describes how I first came to understand this in more everyday terms: "I myself only began really to understand the reality that has come to flower on Athos on this second visit, when the strains of being thrust into an unfamiliar world 'came to a head' for me, and I first 'passed through' what Saint Gregory of Nyssa called the 'Red Sea' by escaping from my everyday 'Egypt' of concern for my own comfort and my need for continuous distraction. First, in terms of Saint Gregory's analogy, I meet that sensation of emptiness for which he uses the analogy of 'bitter waters,' but later I will emerge into what I have since learned to regard as an advanced stage of pilgrimage. It is here that real communication with the monks became possible. This happened because, by chance or by grace, I was now free to spend more time in one monastery. In these conditions I was able slowly to 'pass through' right into that different world of Byzantium preserved. I had time to attend all the day's services. Time for prayer. Time to learn from the monks their own way of viewing their life.

The experience began not in a monastery but in Mount Athos's one primitive hotel. Four iron beds, four rickety chairs, pillow, blanket, a small table, an oil lamp and several tacked-up postcards of icons made up the furnishings. "Like monastery," said the owner optimistically. I lay down, drew the blanket over my head, and attempted to take my siesta. It was around three in the afternoon, and the day stretched interminably before me.

It was during this long day, with no monastic spirituality to compensate for the barren environment, that I met in full strength Saint Gregory's "bitter waters" of separation from the outside world, and so learned something about how, in our Western world, we use our comforts and our distractions to hide from ourselves and our own emptiness. (These are what the monk leaves behind him when he is said to leave the "world.") At the same time I learned to value more fully the unique riches of the monastic world that had been so kindly opened to me.

At times like this, no matter what the external circumstance, the pattern is always the same. I would first face the freewheeling thoughts of my own mind and then, when I managed to step back from these thoughts that continued to run through my head, I would meet this emptiness, this bitterness that emerges when one faces an immediate future that is not only without pleasures and without distractions, but also offers no certainty of something to replace those distractions.

Then, if I would persist too long, would come anger.

The actual experience of this renunciation is described in different ways by different Fathers. One valuable description is given in Gregory of Nyssa's book *The Life of Moses,* where he speaks of the bitter waters found by the Israelites in the desert—described in Exodus 15:22–25—as being sweetened by wood, "the wood of the cross." This wood is symbolic of a higher form of love: a higher emotional love which combines with itself a special kind of knowledge that is *gnosis*.

On the monastic path, the monk must die to the world.

> The monk promises—throughout his life—to follow the narrow and hard way of repentance. He breaks away from the things of the world in order to achieve the one thing which he desires. He dies in relation to the old life, that he may live the new one which Christ offers him in the Church. The monk pursues perfect repentance by means of continual asceticism: vigils; fasting; prayer; the cutting away of his will, and unquestioning obedience to his elder. In the practice of these he forces himself to deny his private and selfish will, and to love God's will. A monk is "a perpetual forcing of nature." The word of the

Lord is thus fulfilled: "The kingdom of heaven is taken by violence, and the violent take it by force" (Matthew 11:12).[19]

It is in this tilled ground, in this heart *naked* to the inner world, that
the sweetness of God's grace can be felt more often, more fully, and can
finally take root.

The problem is that if this method fails, as it usually does when
transplanted into the very different conditions of Western life today, with
all its distractions—and sadly this appears to be generally true even for
Westerners if they become monks on Athos but bring Western civilization
with them in their minds—there is great disappointment, making it difficult for them to prolong the effort. This, and the need, for all but those
who begin very young, to solve this in a different way, is the primary
spiritual question of our age. The problem is that with this failure the
mind becomes restless, so that persistent practice then becomes difficult:
although we now know the ways of the past, for those who have been
many years on the Way, a new answer—new hope—is needed.

In his *Life of Moses*, Saint Gregory writes about this nakedness of
heart in these words:

> . . . after crossing the day's march, and during this time they
> encamped in a place where they found water which they could
> not at first drink because of its bitter taste. But the wood that
> Moses cast into the water made it a pleasant drink for them in
> their thirst.
>
> The text corresponds to what actually happens; when a
> man has given up the Egyptian pleasures to which he had
> been enslaved before crossing the water, his life seems at first
> bitter and disagreeable now his pleasures have been taken
> away. But once the wood is cast into the waters, that is, once
> he unites himself to the mystery of the resurrection, which had
> its beginning in the wood (and by the wood here you surely
> understand the Cross), then the life of virtue becomes sweeter
> and more refreshing than all the sweetness that makes the
> sense tingle with pleasure, because it has been seasoned by
> our hope in the things to come.[20]

On every visit to Athos, I have at some time rediscovered this
"well of bitter waters" that was first described by a Father of the church
so long ago. In the monasteries, I have also discovered the palliative for
this unease. There, as Saint Gregory of Nyssa put it, they possess the
wood of the cross, symbolic of the living liturgy, of the *Resurrection*
itself, to sweeten the bitterness. Here, I am now convinced, is an *elixir,*

a medicine for this bitterness. This was why the early Fathers could recommend exile, could recommend the solitary life. But we cannot easily retain this state in our ordinary lives, and so when I go there again it is only after withstanding this inner desert, this sense of emptiness, for a day, sometimes for several days, that I discover once again the inner well of peace and happiness that makes it possible for the monk to live his hard and outwardly unrewarding life. So much does the effect of our ordinary life cling to us—or to be more exact, so much do we cling to our ordinary life—that this benefit has often emerged only toward the end of my visits. This is why the Gospel According to Thomas says: "The fox has his lair, the bird has his nest, but the Son of Man has no place to lay his head."

The Second Renunciation

The second renunciation is the abandonment of evil, achieved by the grace of God combined with the effort of man.[21]

Monastic or nonmonastic, the inner meaning is essentially the same. But the second and third renunciations seem to be the same for every seeker of God, since they are entirely internal. Seen in mesoteric terms the second renunciation could be described by taking the same parable of the treasure in the field to describe a particular psychological process, in which we discover the power of the transcendent to renew the mind and subsequently renounce those contents of the active mind or personality absorbed from the outside world. In particular, the second renunciation is to renounce those desires and dislikes that disturb the emotions.

The outer meaning of the passage in Luke, quoted earlier in this chapter, where Christ speaks of his disciples "giving up possessions," is, of course, one of the origins of coenobitic or common-life monasticism. But the original Greek of this passage contrasts the self-centered disciple's need to surrender his inner possessions with Christ's reference to his becoming a disciple *of myself,* and this emphasis reveals more clearly the inner meaning that is partially hidden in English translation. It must be remembered that the word *disciple* refers to someone following a *discipline.* The passage therefore refers to the need to move from a self-centered life to what Eastern monastics call a *theocentric* life: in modern terms, to replace a false self with a true Self or "real I."

This is supported by the fact that in the early days of Christianity, for instance in the Egyptian desert at the time of Saint Anthony the

Great, the ideas of monasticism and of the common life had broader meanings than those now set by contemporary usage, so that it is difficult not to assume that it was because monks, nuns, and hermits were the only ones to have time to write about these subjects that these ideas eventually narrowed to interpretations which essentially reflect the monastic methodology.

So strong is the hold of life over us that students of this work who begin to achieve *diakrisis* discover that they still want certain things, even though they are no longer convinced of the reality of those things. Thus, monk or householder, after a much longer time, every student on this Way will come to face the *second renunciation*. The external renunciation of the world must be followed by an inner renunciation of our desire for the world, a renunciation whose nature must be exactly understood and achieved. In Fr. George Maloney's introduction to his translation of Saint Macarius the Great, he said:

> One chief emphasis throughout the writings of Macarius is the call not only to serve God absolutely by renouncing through spiritual and actual poverty all attachments to persons and things, but also to enter into the depths of one's soul and do the inner spiritual battle—to renounce even one's false self. He explains in his Great Letter what renouncing oneself means:
>
> "What does it mean to renounce one's own self except to give oneself completely to the fraternity and never to accomplish absolutely one's own desires, but to be totally available to the Word of God."[22]

In the Christian gospel, what is perhaps the most important test, the test of the second renunciation, is precisely defined and set up in advance for us in the famous passage about the lilies of the field.

> Wherefore, if God so clothe the grass of the field, which today is, and tomorrow is cast into the oven, shall he not much more clothe you, O ye of little faith?
>
> Therefore take no thought, saying, What shall we eat? or, What shall we drink? or, Wherewithal shall we be clothed?
>
> (For after all these things do the Gentiles seek:) for your heavenly Father knoweth that ye have need of all these things.
>
> But seek ye first the kingdom of God, and his righteousness; and all these things shall be added unto you.

Take therefore no thought for the morrow: for the morrow shall take thought for the things of itself. Sufficient unto the day is the evil thereof (Matthew 6:30–34).

Can we see how important this is? Can we see how it applies to us, personally? No! Then we have not yet understood the nature of the second renunciation. Can we actually believe this doctrine? Can we accept it and base our lives upon it? No! Then, even if we have understood it, we have not yet passed the test of the second renunciation. If the nature of this renunciation is understood, it will seem to go so counter to modern thought, and will seem so restrictive and so difficult to those accustomed to a life of comfort and distraction, that modern man has become almost incapable of accepting the necessity for this second renunciation.

The same is true of the passage from Saint Matthew. It makes little sense to modern mind and modern ways of life, for it defines a major blind spot in modern man, a blind spot or buffer[23] that, above all others, is responsible for the injustices and suffering occurring in our society today.

At the same time, this renunciation is not limited to Christian tradition. In a practical sense, it is identical with the "second qualification," vairyagya, or emotional discrimination, in Shankara's Vivekachudamani, or Crest Jewel of Discrimination, which is one of the keys to the Yoga of the Bhagavad Gita. It is through this faculty of emotional discrimination that we recognize, somewhere inside us, that Christ, in his actions and in his words, shows us something unworldly in a literal sense, something coming from beyond the world we know, so that it was perfectly consistent that he taught us

Love not the world, neither the things that are in the world. If any man love the world, the love of the Father is not in him.

For all that is in the world—the lust of the flesh, and the lust of the eyes, and the pride of life—is not of the Father, but is of the world.

And the world passeth away, and the lust thereof: but he that doeth the will of God abideth forever (1 John 2:15–17).

But Evagrius perhaps most precisely defined the second renunciation when he wrote: "For the true wedding garment is the dispassion [apatheia] of the deiform soul which has renounced worldly desires."[24]

What does all this mean in practice?

"Transcending Knowledge with My Thought"

S aint John of the Cross introduced the second renunciation in his well-known poem:

> I entered in, I know not where,
> And I remained, though knowing naught,
> Transcending knowledge[25] with my thought.

This clearly refers to those moments when we go beyond discursive thought and all the activity of the mind to that still place that the early Fathers called the heart—not the physical heart but the psychological heart which is associated with the "closet" to which Christ said we should retire in order to pray. The next verse of the poem describes a further stage associated with the "third renunciation," which will be described a few pages further on.

The early English text of the *Cloud of Unknowing*—written in the medieval Saint Denys tradition—recommends a certain practice intended to assist the mind in transcending discursive thought:

> Lift up thine heart unto God with a meek stirring of love; and mean himself and none of his goods. And therefore look you that thou loathe to think on aught but himself, so that naught work in thy mind nor in thy will but only himself. And do that in thee is to forget all the creatures that ever God made and the works of them, so that thy thought or thy desire be not directed or stretched to any of them, neither in general nor in special. But let them be, and take no heed of them.
>
> This is the work of the soul that most pleaseth God. All saints and angels have joy of this work and hasten them to help it with all their might. All fiends be mad when thou dost thus, and try for to defeat it in all that they can. All men living on earth be wonderfully helped by this work, thou knowest not how. Yea, the souls in purgatory are eased of their pains by virtue of this work. Thou thyself are cleansed and made virtuous by no work so much. And yet it is the lightest work of all, when a soul is helped by grace in a sensible list; and soonest done. But else it is hard and wonderful for thee to do.
>
> Cease not, therefore, but travail therein till thou feel list. For at the first time when thou dost it, thou findest but a darkness, and as it were a cloud of unknowing, thou knowest not what, saving that thou feelest in thy will a naked intent unto God. This darkness and this cloud, however thou dost,

is betwixt thee and thy God, and hindereth thee, so that thou mayest neither see him clearly by light of understanding in thy reason, nor feel him in sweetness of love in thine affection. And therefore shape thee to bide in this darkness as long as thou mayest, evermore crying after him whom thou lovest. For if ever thou shalt see him or feel him, as it may be here, it must always be in this cloud and in this darkness. And if thou wilt busily travail as I bid thee, I trust in his mercy that thou shalt come thereto.[26]

The Third Renunciation

Evagrius wrote of this:

The third renunciation is the separation from ignorance, which is naturally made to appear to men according to the degree of their state.[27]

This third renunciation is also the subject of the verse of the poem by Saint John of the Cross immediately following the verse quoted on the previous page:

Of when I entered I know naught,
But when I saw that I was there
(Though where it was I did not care)
Strange things I learned, with greatness fraught.
Yet what I heard I'll not declare.
But there I stayed, though knowing naught,
Transcending knowledge with my thought.[28]

Paradoxically, Evagrius's separation from ignorance is the result of "transcending knowledge" with our thought. The knowledge gained in this state—sometimes today known as *contemplative knowledge*—is such that all previous knowledge appears as ignorance.

By renunciation of one form of knowledge we obtain another—knowledge that is more than knowledge:

Again, the kingdom of heaven is like unto treasure hid in a field; the which when a man hath found, he hideth, and for joy thereof goeth and selleth all that he hath, and buyeth that field (Matthew 13:44).

The third and deepest interpretation of this parable describes noetic prayer, in which we sacrifice or sell all our mental possessions, leaving the field of our *nous* clear and without image, and in this empty field we then discover the joy of the Lord, the bliss that is the food of the Spirit. When we discover this bliss, all other pleasures pale by comparison, so that from this moment we will begin to set aside every other desire until only one desire remains to us. At this point we will understand the idea of the one thing needful not only with the head, but with the heart. More to the point, as this process continues and we have further glimpses of this treasure, we will perhaps find that at its most intense it becomes a light like an inner sun, the light described by the monks of Athos, in the words of certain early Fathers, as the uncreated light.

At this moment we will understand why another, similar parable uses the image of the pearl of great price (Matthew 13:46).

Cassian also has something to say about this step:

All this happens when [we are] dead with Christ to all that is in this world, our gaze, as the apostle proclaims, is "not upon those things which are seen but on the unseen; for the things which are seen belong to time and the things which are not seen are everlasting"[29] (2 Corinthians 4:18). In our hearts we leave this time-ridden, visible house and we firmly turn our eyes and mind to where we will remain forever. And we will achieve this when, still in the flesh, we begin to soldier in the Lord, not as flesh would have it, but when our deeds and our virtues join the apostle in crying out, "Our homeland is in heaven" (Philippians 3:20).[30]

For most of us, including many monastics, this is not an instant renunciation, but a great struggle with our parochial nature; not self-centered thought but the narrow personal self itself, our obstacle in the struggle to do the Lord's will: "Not every one that saith unto me, Lord, Lord, shall enter into the kingdom of heaven; but he that doeth the will of my Father which is in heaven" (Matthew 7:21). And again: "For I came down from heaven, not to do mine own will, but the will of him that sent me" (John 6:38).

Saint Cyprien of Carthage said of this:

The will of God is what Christ did and taught. Humility in conduct; firmness in faith; modesty in speech; justice in judgments; kindness in almsgiving; discipline in human morality; acting without prejudice and [showing] dignity and understanding when we are its victims; keeping the peace with our brothers; loving God with all our heart; to love Him because He is Father and to fear Him because He is God; to prefer nothing above Christ, as He has preferred us above all; to bind ourselves unconditionally to His spirit of charity, but to take up our cross with courage and confidence; when the time comes to enter the battle in His name or in His honour; to demonstrate confidence in difficulties so as to remain strong in the struggle; patience in death in order to earn our crown. All of this is a clear sign of our will to be co-heirs of Christ, to act according to the law of God, to do the will of God.[31]

It has been said that before we can be *born from above,* we must first die. Until we have walked in the "light" of *diakrisis,* and by this light have struggled on the way of *metanoia* for many years, most of us find that it is difficult to perceive and distinguish real from unreal, what is self from what is not-self, eternal self from what is to die by death dividing self from Self. One day we will discover that it was at least in part for this reason, to make this perception possible and so give us the saving power of *diakrisis,* that our Lord came into the world. What is to die in us is false self: and it is to this, I believe, that the third renunciation refers. This is the true and final meaning of the *strait gate* . . . through which we can carry no excess baggage.

> Now we shall be worthy of the true perfection of this third renunciation when the mind is no longer dulled by fleshly contagion, when every worldly wish and character has been expertly polished away, when unfaltering meditation on the things of God and the practice of contemplation has so passed over to the unseen that there the surrounding frailty and domain of the flesh are felt no longer and there is rapture amongst the bodiless realms above. The mind is so caught up in this way that the hearing no longer takes in the voices of outside and images of passers-by no longer come to sight and the eye no longer sees the mounds confronting it or the gigantic objects rising up against it.
>
> No one will possess the truth and power of all this unless he has direct experience to teach him.[32]

The narrow way, the way of *diakrisis* and *metanoia,* leads to this. It leads to the emergence of *a different self* whose steward is this change of heart that turns our wanting in the opposite direction. What exactly must be discriminated within us in order to become a different self? To answer this, we must ask ourselves an apparently simple question: Who am I?

You will discover first of all that you have different answers to this question at different times, and in different circumstances. We *identify* ourselves differently from moment to moment. But through compassion with our fellow humans, we may experience an "I" that is greater than all others. It is this that transcends our little local self.

Saint John of the Cross wrote about this third renunciation:

> Few there are that find the narrow gate. Mark here the reason for this saying, which is that there are but few who understand how, and desire, to enter into this supreme detachment and emptiness of spirit.
>
> To follow Christ is to deny self, this is not that other course which is nothing but to seek oneself in God, which is the very opposite of love. For to seek self in God is to seek for comfort and refreshment in God. But to seek God in Himself is not only to be willingly deprived of this thing and of that for God, but to incline ourselves to will and choose for Christ's sake whatever is most disagreeable, whether proceeding from God or from the world; this is to love God.[33]

The question of why so few find salvation can be taken at many different levels; the mildest echoes what Ouspensky said when, asked why everyone could not be changed, he said that not everybody wants to change. In simple terms, this is why the self-seeking person normally takes the path of "self-seeking into God," of seeking satisfactions from God, in preference to the Royal Road of self-denial which is the path of *metanoia* and of the true service of God. In modern times, for those who have some sense of the latter path, a long and painful purgation is normally necessary.

But this also explains many sayings of Gurdjieff about the whole question of doing what is difficult: why we should "do what it does not like,"[34] as he put it, along with his idea of *intentional suffering*.

Saint Theophan the Recluse writes about the same thing in his commentary on Psalm 118: "the word 'undefiled' in the original is the same as that used to describe lambs made ready for the Easter sacrifice. This points to the fact that those entering the road of the commandments in order to achieve the undefiled state must doom themselves as if for immolation. Only one who considers himself dead shall be able to withstand all temptations and difficulties; for what can be unbearable to one already dead?"[35]

As we are, we cannot live as Theophan suggests. Only a different "I" can live in this way. As some of the stories from the Russian labor camps make clear, to face life in this way withers the everyday ego, and the only salvation then is to wake the different and authentic "I" that sleeps in our "inmost heart." There is a story of the early Fathers about how, in order to explain the nature of *detachment,* one of them took two pupils to contemplate a corpse: "That is how you should be," he told them, "praise him or criticize him, he does not react." Maurice Nicoll once used the Chinese parable of the fighting cock to illustrate this idea. This story goes:

> Chisengtse used to raise fighting cocks for the king. After ten days had passed, the king asked if his cock was ready for a fight. "Not yet," he replied. "The cock is still very impulsive and haughty."
>
> After another ten days, the king asked again, and he replied: "Not yet, his eyes still have an angry look and he is full of fight."
>
> Another ten days passed and he said, "He is about ready. When he hears other cocks crow, he does not even react. You look at him, and he appears like a wooden cock. No other cock will dare to fight him, but will run away at first sight."[36]

We do not yet possess constancy like this. Our changeable nature is revealed by our changing moods, by the way our wishes are different and often conflicting, and by the fact that we believe things that conflict.

This describes the emergence of that inner autonomy of spirit that is the goal of esotericism.

The most obvious answer to the question of freeing ourselves from outside disturbances simply increases our sensitivity to the disturbances in our minds. For the layperson, without benefit of monastic enclosure from the world, this opens the door to all kinds of anxiety. But, more surprisingly, it opens the door of the monk's or hermit's cell to *demons,* in the sense that Evagrius used this term: persistent and autonomous activities arising from the active contents of his own mind. These *demons,* says Saint Maximos, act on us directly from within, or indirectly through their effect on other people, that is: "Either the demons tempt us themselves, or they equip those who do not fear the Lord against us: themselves, when we are alone, away from others, just as they tempted the Lord in the desert; through others, when we associate with them, as they tempted the Lord through the Pharisees. It is for us to look to our model and beat them back on both fronts."[37]

Monk or lay, we need a way of dealing with one or other of these and sometimes with both; with outside *and* inside disturbance. Sometimes, of course, but not always, the answers the layperson obtains will be different from those obtained by the monk. But there is one additional clue, one reason why the answers are not different as often as we would expect, and it is this: externals can only disturb us by acting on something in the contents of our psyche. This means that if we work against the inner, psychological causes of these disturbances, we will also be working to neutralize disturbances that originate outside us. Again there is a clue in Maximos's text: we are to learn from the methods taught and used by our Lord, the method taught by Him in beating back the inner demons by learning the love of the Lord, while dealing with the outer demons by answering them as He answered the Pharisees.

> Then went the Pharisees, and took counsel how they might entangle him in his talk.
>
> And they sent out unto him their disciples with the Herodians, saying, Master, we know that thou art true, and teachest the way of God in truth, neither carest thou for any man: for thou regardest not the person of men.
>
> Tell us therefore, What thinkest thou? Is it lawful to give tribute unto Caesar, or not?
>
> But Jesus perceived their wickedness, and said, Why tempt ye me, ye hypocrites?
>
> Show me the tribute money. And they brought unto him a penny.
>
> And he saith unto them, Whose is this image and superscription?
>
> They say unto him, Caesar's. Then saith he unto them, Render therefore unto Caesar the things which are Caesar's; and unto God the things that are God's (Matthew 22:15–21).

In psychological terms, to render unto Caesar the things that are Caesar's and unto God the things that are God's is to act appropriately: to deal with inner and outer, spiritual and worldly, each in their own terms. In medieval times, special disciplines were created for the few laypeople who were so financially well off that they were able to use their wealth to insulate themselves from the world.[38] But now few people can take such a path. For those who cannot afford to insulate themselves from the world, and whose character or responsibilities prevent their becoming monks or setting aside very long periods each day for prayer and contemplation, the only alternative is to eliminate the inner element of each disturbance, so eliminating all reaction or response to that cause. But in the end, persistence in prayer only succeeds after a long struggle. One way or another, everyone must work against those elements in their character which disturb them directly or allow the external elements to disturb them.

One who, without leaving the world, roots out the inner elements that tie him to the world, has entered the path.

In a traditional phrase, the result of this is that he acts as if he were in the world but not of it: he no longer *assents* to the influence of the world.

The Parting of the Ways

This is the point where the disciples of Jesus left him, as described in chapter 6 of the Gospel of Saint John:

> Many therefore of his disciples, when they had heard this, said, This is an hard saying; who can hear it?
>
> When Jesus knew in himself that his disciples murmured at it, he said unto them, Doth this offend you?
>
> What and if ye shall see the Son of man ascend up where he was before?
>
> It is the spirit that quickeneth; the flesh profiteth nothing: the words that I speak unto you, they are spirit, and they are life.
>
> But there are some of you that believe not. For Jesus knew from the beginning who they were that believed not, and who should betray him.
>
> And he said, Therefore said I unto you, that no man can come unto me, except it were given unto him of my Father.
>
> From that time many of his disciples went back, and walked no more with him (John 6:60–66).

Gospel teachings about the *strait gate* and the *narrow way* refer in their simplest sense to the difficult choice that must be taken at this point, where we must go beyond the point which we can see; beyond what we can control.

The ambiguity of the description used here is normal. These choices are so difficult to define directly that, on the Christian path, they are normally defined indirectly; for instance, they may describe the choice that must be made in terms of *indicators* or *signs* whose presence will tell us when we have made the right decision. Some of these *signs* serve as *analogies* for what we must observe, but first we must learn to interpret such analogies. Others are simply *indicators*, but when we observe them this tells us that we are making the right choice. One method is that of negative definition, when we are advised what not to do: *not* to take the line of least resistance, for example, or *not* to choose the comfortable or the easy in preference to what we see to be necessary. This method is linked to what is called apophatic theology, which defines God by speaking of what He is not. As a method it can leave us intentionally exposed to circumstances beyond our control, forced to live out in reality the situation described in the gospel passage about the lilies of the field. The inner anxiety that results is one of the meanings of the monastic term *exile*.

A Fourth Stage

Cassian wrote, as quoted on page 161, about our need to come out of this "time-ridden, visible house, and firmly turn our minds to where we will remain forever." This is clearly a parable similar to that sometimes used in India by one Yoga teacher,[39] who describes this by saying that man has two homes. One is a mean, dark, uncomfortable house, where man ordinarily lives. The other is a magnificent house full of good things and magnificent impressions. By prayer or meditation one comes out of the old house but then, for a long time, one finds oneself between the two houses. Eventually one comes to the great house.

The three renunciations refer to the need to come out of the small, mean house.

But in Yoga the final stage of consciousness possible to man is called *turiya,* which simply means *fourth.* Cassian also wrote about a fourth stage, "the return and reward for perfect renunciation." This is where we move into the great house that has everything we need. But Cassian calls it a land, as the gospel called it a *kingdom:* "a land gained in this life when all passion is ousted and the heart is pure, a land which neither the virtue nor the effort of a toiling man will open up, but which the Lord himself promised to reveal. 'Come,' He said, 'into the land which I shall show you' (Genesis 12:1)."[40]

It is at that moment that one has become—finally, and for all time— a different Self.

This is to become one with that which one has glimpsed afar throughout one's life, with that which has been calling one.

Theosis: *Deification*

Why do I not accept with equanimity that we do not meet saints in our lives? Why do I not simply accept that the very idea of saints is an empty one? Investigating this question, I have become increasingly aware that beyond the detailed differences between Eastern and Western churches, and between people of faith and the atheists and humanists who have become so universal in a scientifically oriented world, there is another great difference that singles out certain of those who approach the inner interpretation of faith. Most of the time little different from their peers, they occasionally touch on something different, something transforming that changes their behavior, their appearance . . . everything. Each time, talking to them soon after this has happened, you discover that they have touched on something deep within themselves, deep in the silence, and as powerful as it is deep within.

Do I expect you to take my word for this? Certainly not. But one of my aims in writing this book has been that, here and there throughout its pages, I hope to give you a small glimpse of some of these men and women as I have seen them, a glimpse of them in the only way one can ever see them, living in their own world, a different world for people who are different.

The interesting thing is that the inner wellspring of this difference is something almost *impersonal,* which yet transcends the personal, just as, theologically, the Lord transcends all human attempts to define or describe Him. He is not accessible to us as long as we remain *personal people,* defined by the chance events—the weeds or tares of the gospel—that have taken root in us. Yet He is *personal,* in the quite different sense in which a human person is too deep, too rich, too complete and complex ever to be described in every detail.

We can only be known in the composite ways in which we are *recognized.* As a human is not known in detail, so the Lord cannot be thought of, and certainly not known, in detail, but we can learn to *recognize* Him by His presence in our lives, His actions (in Greek, *dynamis,* "energies" again). He is "less than a person" only in the sense that He is less obvious, that He does not appear directly to the senses or even the inner sense, but He remains infinitely more than a person in the breadth of His presence as normally hidden in but eventually discovered in our lives. But words fail me here, even conceptualizing fails here, so that whatever I write will be imperfect. Yet, to put ancient conceptions in simple, modern terms, it is true that, although not bound as personal people are bound, He possesses all the possibilities that might lead to our definition of a person as more than a thing . . . and more than this, more than anyone can conceive of.

But my words are not enough. We can perhaps come close by pondering this prayer by Saint Symeon the New Theologian: in this way, by slow examination, you may learn to pray in this way and mean it. Then you will understand.

> Come, my breath and my life,
> Come, the consolation of my soul.

Come, my joy, my glory, my endless delight.
I give thanks,
For you have become one spirit with me,
in a union without confusion.
Unchanging and unaltered,
God over all,
You have yet become all in all to me:
Food inexplicable, freely bestowed,
Ever nourishing my soul;
a fountain springing up within my heart,
a garment of light consuming the demons,
purification that washes me clean
through the immortal and holy tears.[41]

A Modern Understanding of the Three Renunciations

It is possible that we may begin to understand this in modern terms, beginning with Cassian who, to show how they related together, linked the three renunciations to the three books of Solomon: "The three books of Solomon accord with these three renunciations. Corresponding to the first renunciation is Proverbs, in which the desire for the things of the flesh and for earthly sin are excoriated. Corresponding to the second renunciation is Ecclesiasticus, where the vanity of everything under the sun is proclaimed. And applicable to the third is the Song of Songs, in which the mind, rising beyond all things visible, contemplates all that is of heaven and is brought into union with the Word of God."[42]

In modern esoteric science, these three renunciations and the step that follows them could be named

1. Discrimination—change of mind—a renunciation of belief in ordinary worldly goals
2. Detachment—change of heart—a loss of conviction in our view of the world
3. Awakening—renewal of intelligence (nous)—a new kind of knowledge
4. Union—complete absorption in the divine.

Let me try to explain how I currently understand this process. At the same time I must ask you to accept that my understanding is still growing, for it is by the growth of this kind of understanding that we finally find ourselves on the Way itself, in terms of the idea that the Way has first to be reached before we can travel it.

By long persistence in the effort to discriminate between the transient and the permanent, the worldly and the divine, in Christian terms, based on our own glimpses of a different way of being and experiencing, when that experience is supported by knowledge coming from those with deeper experience of the same thing . . . "We come to despise all the riches and all goods of the world."[43]

It must be understood that this is not a sudden discovery; that single experiences of this seem to transform us, but after a short while other memories assert themselves, and we revert to what we were. The first renunciation, for those who must live in the world, consists of a slow process of repeated "dipping," like dipping cloth to dye it, leading to cumulative small changes. The result is a change not of our color but of the aim or direction in our lives, a change in our *wanting*. This change in our wanting forms a *track* that in time leads us to the beginning of the second stage, what Boris Mouravieff calls the *ladder* or the staircase.

This complete change of aim leads to the possibility of the second renunciation. Now we begin to lose our automatic and indiscriminate belief in the contents of our own minds and memories. With growing self-knowledge, we *recognize* these for what they are, *recognizing* that they are not our own, are not true to our real nature, and so on, and by this recognition "we *repel* our past, our vices, the passions governing spirit and flesh."[44] This is the staircase that leads us up to the Way itself, regarded as beginning above the level of ordinary life.

From this change, our hearts begin to become pure. With this, we begin more often and more fully to glimpse the different reality. Our memory slowly filled by these glimpses, we become able to "draw our spirit away from the here and the visible, and we do so in order solely to contemplate the things to come. Our passion is solely for the unseen."[45]

When this process becomes cumulative rather than occasional, we are on the Way. So, by three steps of renunciation, we enter into a different experience of the world. But is it as simple as this?

Of course not. This is the journey, but on that journey, there are many adventures that are not shown on the simple map I have just given you. With the awakening of a different reality within us, what we do and what we say begins to change.

> Nor do men light a lamp and put it under a bushel, but on
> a stand, and it gives light to all in the house.
>   Let your light so shine before men, that they may see
> your good works and give glory to your Father who is in
> heaven (Matthew 5:15–16).

After we have acquired some control over the passions, and have discovered that our *apatheia*, our dispassion, is still only temporary, we can discover the root of the problem, which lies in the fact that passions are reawakened as long as our hearts are still turned toward the perceptible world, believing in its reality. This is an emotional delusion, and it is this which leads to ruinous activity.

To free ourselves from these emotional delusions, we must first recognize that to think of the world as transient is not enough. We must be totally convinced of this fact, and continually aware of it.

Saint Silouan of Mount Athos

S aint Silouan was one man in whom this process became visible in the early part of the present century. Miracles do happen in association with this man, or are supposed to, and I am sure of this for personal reasons. Silouan was a recent saint, canonized in 1988. At least two of his pupils died only recently in England, both I think in their nineties, and one of them, the devout Father Sophrony, founded a monastery on the Athonite style in England, in Essex, that is still running. Silouan himself died in the 1930s on Mount Athos. But even more important, he said one thing that is of great interest to people who study other forms of the tradition—particularly to those who study the work of Gurdjieff and the idea of "intentional suffering," which Gurdjieff brought forward but did not originate.[46] Earlier, we referred to a statement which Silouan says was dictated to him at one time, during his long years of work on himself, a statement that came "from the Spirit": "Keep your soul in hell, but do not despair."

This phrase, which I found memorable but puzzling when I first read it, is now used as the basis of a discipline by monks who describe it specifically as a means of gaining humility, something confirmed by Saint Therese's example given earlier. It was spoken of as a method, not simply as an idea, and it was also described as a specific antidote to pride.

Of course, it is not normally necessary to create suffering for ourselves, simply not to avoid it when it comes . . . in other words, not to indulge in what Gurdjieff called "self-calming."

Gregory of Nyssa wrote, about self-calming, that "we must surely think that man pathetic who allows himself to sink into the pleasures of this world."[47]

Allied in this way, this discipline is an exact continuation of the traditional doctrine of "intentional suffering," but we should take into account that I was specifically told by one of the monks of that monastery founded by Silouan's pupil Sophrony,[48] that this must be carried out within measure, as it can otherwise be dangerous, so that one should be very careful when following this instruction not to take it too far—it can in fact keep your soul in hell for so long that you haven't got the strength to do anything about it anymore. Now this is something that touches on very deep questions indeed. It is without meaning until you have begun to have an interaction between yourself and the divine within your heart— between what is "external" although inside you and what is really "you."

Until that interaction has begun, this statement can never be more than a theory to you. As we quoted Cassian earlier, "No one will possess the truth and power of all this unless he has direct experience to teach him."

First it must become real to you. Then it must become a *struggle*. After the struggle comes the stillness of *hesychia*.

Chapter 8

Faith and Assent

A *ssent* is the choice by the nous that, from moment to moment, determines how we act, how we think, and which sensations and
feelings we attend to and which we ignore. Christian obedience to the
Commandments depends on our *assent* to those Commandments. "Thy
will be done," says the Lord's Prayer. To succumb to temptation is a matter
of assenting to temptations or *provocations*.[1] "Lead us not into temptation,"
says the prayer. Well understood by people such as Clement of Alexandria,
this concept is strange to most modern religious thought. Although its
relation to faith is sometimes partially understood,[2] the important psychological implications of assent are now almost totally ignored, since they do
not agree with our modern ideas of *free will*. Today, what was once generally known—that faith in some way links with assent, and that through
that assent, our belief may shape our action—is generally forgotten. More
important, an extension of this idea is totally unknown. Our idea of faith
has changed from that held in the early church, and is now based on
Aquinas's differentiation of knowledge from blind belief.[3] Valid as this is,
in esoteric terms it is also necessary to perceive that faith can become
knowledge. By leaving out that factor, Aquinas helped shape our society's
devaluing of inner knowledge. Much earlier, Maximos the Confessor confirmed the esoteric idea of faith as leading to knowledge and then to love.

This is best understood by seeing that certain actions must result
from our assenting to the Word. A completely different set of actions result
if, instead, we assent to "worldly" ideas. The experience these actions give
rise to gives certain knowledge about the meaning of the Word, and this

knowledge, being experiential, cannot then be lost. Equally unknown is the corollary of this, that to believe something that cannot be confirmed in practice will increase our uncertainty. A weak attitude of assent to Christian (or any other) doctrine has the effect of changing our ideas without changing our actions. Because a strong and confirmed faith leads us to assent to *actions* supported by that belief as we understand it, and to avoid actions which appear to us to conflict with that belief, it can lead to a transformation of our nature. It is entirely up to us, says Clement: "to free ourselves from ignorance, and from evil and voluptuous choice, and above all, to withhold our assent from those delusive phantasies, depends on ourselves."[4] Assent is an act of free will and involved in the mysterious process by which free will aligns itself with the Will of God: "Not every one that saith unto me, Lord, Lord, shall enter into the kingdom of heaven; but he that doeth the will of my Father which is in heaven" (Matthew 7:21).

The Philosophy of Assent

The idea of assent has two aspects, which could be called philosophical and psychological.

— *Philosophical assent* is the need to assent to the Word of God. This is the assent of faith as understood today. It links with what the early Fathers recognized as a first stage of faith.
— *Psychological assent* is the moment-to-moment assent we make to the possibilities of our lives. Either we assent to what we understand as coming from God, or we assent to what we chose for personal motives. This was the assent referred to by the early Fathers and described in certain parts of the previous chapters. Assent to the divine links with what the early Fathers recognized as the second stage of faith.

To what we give assent, that determines our lives. To give assent to some view or action based on Christian teaching is not only *assent to faith*: it has then become obedience to the Word. It is this which leads to a real, positive change in us and in our lives. Without some kind of philosophical assent, without adopting some definite belief about ourselves and about life, we will assent in a random manner to the actions "suggested" by our minds. In this situation, our lives will be shaped by constant reaction to outside or inside events. But eventually we may rebel against this situation. Theophan the Recluse describes this moment in a way that shows the part played by the Word of God in the process: "There will come a moment when the mental student of the word of God will be overcome by a desire to turn to its instructions, and will decide to follow them unswervingly. Then all the previously accumulated information from God's word will serve as ready material for the formation of the inner man, just as the seed is fed by the elements surrounding that seed."[5]

In our investigation we are discovering that there are definite reasons why today it is difficult to assent to these doctrines. The most important of these reasons is because in recent centuries these rules and doctrines have too often diverged from the early teachings, so that we forget that the early teachings kept the faith, that they remained consistent not only to inner experience but both to the Word of God and to the intuitions of faith.

This, properly understood, gives us a different definition of knowledge from the ordinary scientific view; it is almost an "engineering" definition: If it works, build it! This test of Clement's was not to ask, Does it make sense? nor to ask, Does one idea agree with other ideas? but to ask, Does it work? This hints at a principle that recurs in esoteric Christianity. The acceptance of this principle—or the understanding of and assent to it—turns many contemporary ideas of Christianity on their heads and opens the door to a rapid transition to that earlier Christianity described in this book. The roots of this principle lie in everyday life, in what we called engineering knowledge—knowledge tested against the criterion of practicality instead of against intellectual criteria. This is the idea that practical experience is not only more certain but also more complete and detailed than theory.

In esotericism something else is added to this, the idea that we can experience the acquisition of a kind of knowledge—*gnosis*—not based on sensory experience nor purely on intellectual apprehension. To summarize, the principle is that:

> Faith leads through assent to practice,
> and through practice confirms its object,
> leading to noetic knowledge (gnosis),
> and this noetic knowledge, founded on experience,
> and completed by inspiration,
> cannot be overthrown by reasoned argument.

This principle not only provides a major tool in Christian spirituality, but it also forms the basis of a Christian epistemology different in a small but significant way from that promoted by Aquinas.

It was French scholar Etienne Gilson who drew attention to the importance of a distinction made by Aquinas in the face of the conflicting ideas raised in medieval thought, said to be in response to the sudden discovery of the almost forgotten works of Aristotle in Arabic translation, when these powerful writings were thrown into an almost purely religious intellectual world.

Despite his definition of *revelation* in terms of the inner light, a definition entirely in keeping with the inner tradition, the exact form of Aquinas's distinction of belief and knowledge is crucial to the shaping of our modern world, and has contributed to the relegation of inner knowledge to what Michael Polanyi would have called "the tacit dimension," in which it is either forgotten or "taken for granted." There is little doubt, then, that Aquinas clarified for centuries to come—until the present time—the difference between belief and knowledge, and so shaped our age.

And it is clear that the way in which he did so was in part conceived in purely outer terms. Aquinas had correctly differentiated knowledge from blind belief. Pieper summarizes the classical consensus on this point thus: "The Great theologians, too, attest to the same thing. Credentur absentia, Augustine says. That means that the formal subject of belief is what is not apparent to the eye, what is not obvious of its own accord, what is not attainable either by direct perception or logical inference. Thomas Aquinas formulates the same idea as follows: 'Belief cannot refer to something that one sees . . . and what can be proved likewise does not pertain to belief.' "[6] But, he adds at this point—and the addition is important: "Naturally, this cannot mean that in the act of belief the believer simply takes leave of his own perceptions . . . naturally it would not make sense to talk about belief if the subject for belief could be proved. Nevertheless the believer must, for example, know enough about the matter to understand 'what it is all about.' An altogether incomprehensible communication is no communication at all. . . . For belief to be possible at all, it is assumed that the communication has in some way been understood."[7]

Although Etienne Gilson again drew attention to the distinction by Aquinas of knowledge from blind belief, he does not mention that Aquinas did not take into account the two stages of faith known by the Fathers, nor distinguish between both kinds of faith and blind belief. Missing these factors, Aquinas did not perceive—or at least did not include in his conceptualization—the possibility that faith can become knowledge: the fact, affirmed by the Fathers, that faith in a truth can be *confirmed,* and that in so doing it can blossom into a special kind of knowledge. By ignoring this possibility Aquinas helped shape the West as it is today, in a way that has released the full force of greed and ignorance into our society.

Saint Maximos the Confessor put it: "The reward of self-mastery is detachment, and that of faith is knowledge. And detachment gives rise to discernment, while knowledge gives rise to love for God."[8]

In fact, if the small seed of real faith can grow into the great tree of real knowledge, it is equally easy to see that blind and misconceived belief is not real faith, and that it is not real faith precisely *because* it cannot blossom into knowledge that is consistent. Among other things, real faith has a real power of transformation, and this power is lacking in blind belief. It was because of this power that Saint Paul could write: "and the life which I now live in the flesh I live by the faith of the Son of God, who loved me, and gave himself for me" (Galatians 2:20).

The Psychology of Assent

But although our assent is freely given, it depends at any moment on what we think just then about the world, about ourselves, and about God. Thus we will not free ourselves from assenting to delusion unless we make the effort intentionally to assent *to* something. In the past, in the Christian church, including the esoteric tradition, what had the power to liberate us first from misconception and then from erroneous action was seen as assent to the rules and doctrines of the church, or to a specific *rule* or code within that church. If we lacked some form of this assent of faith, then, as described earlier, for lack of any definite *intention* we would find ourselves assenting to *provocations,* as described in a passage from Kontzevitch (quoted in full in chapter 14), "which is a declaration of agreement with the passion whispered by the thought (Saint Ephraim the Syrian), or consent [assent] of the soul to what has been presented to it by the thought, accompanied by delight (Saint John Climacus)."[9]

Kontzevitch later wrote about assent to faith as assenting to what is useful. Clement of Alexandria suggested a "test" in which practice leads to understanding: "Voluntarily to follow what is useful is the first principle of understanding. Unswerving choice, then, gives considerable momentum in the direction of knowledge. The exercise of faith directly becomes knowledge, reposing on a sure foundation."[10]

Our idea of faith has changed from that held in the early church, perhaps because the narrowness of Aquinas's definition suited the tenor of his times, but left us without an answer to modern empiricism. I remarked earlier that faith can become confirmed, in esoteric terms can become knowledge.

In the esoteric view, only when the glimpses of truth that every seeker has experienced are followed by some kind of effort toward purification will these brief moments form the seed and foundation of a permanently changed state. (See chapter 10 on the true meaning of *metanoia* and the paths of the heart and of knowledge.)

Two Stages of Faith

But what then of the question of real faith? We said earlier (chapter 3) that a new belief in our spiritual nature is now being attained by many people, for millions of whom this now takes the form of knowledge gained by experience. We also wrote of the two stages of faith discovered in the Bible by the early Fathers. In fact, the new belief in our spiritual nature that is now arising is a beginning of the second kind of faith. The first kind is a natural faith, innate and present in the child, and it is important to understand *that this innate faith precedes doctrine and is common to all faiths.*

It is this universal kind of faith, not an exclusive belief, that was taught by Christ. Unfortunately, this innate faith is generally masked in the adult, often by doubts or by what Boris Mouravieff called errors of conception: by a belief in ideas which so often masquerade as faith. When innate faith does survive into adulthood, it is generally regarded as identical with blind belief, that is, with belief that is unsupportable.

But what is this innate faith? Jacob Needleman, in his book *The Heart of Philosophy*, suggests that in its true, inner sense, the term *faith* refers to something that begins in the human being's natural tendency to self-enquiry. This is the often suppressed inclination, when enquiring beyond the boundaries of the visible and the measurable, to do so within oneself: to respond to the lack of an external and visible explanation for things by seeking an internal and thus—in conventional terms—an invisible explanation. Taken in Christian context, it clothes its discoveries in Christian doctrine, but gives that an inner, experiential meaning and a moral value lacking in external interpretations of the Gospel. Thus, experience confirms doctrine, and the church is freed from the need to continually revise its teachings to respond to purely outer change.

But this is different from the kind of faith that changes our character. The enquiry of faith, pursued energetically and self-critically, leads in time to the confirmation of faith: the stage where faith becomes certain, and it is this certainty that transforms the human heart. To assent to faith is to agree with or consent to those ideas or actions, which present themselves to us and which appear to be *consistent* with our faith whether we turn our enquiry inward in response to innate faith, or transform our whole way of life as a natural response to the new certainty of confirmed faith. It was Clement again who wrote: " 'Except ye believe, neither shall ye understand.' "[11] . . . But faith, which the Greeks disparage, deeming it futile and barbarous, is a voluntary preconception, the assent of piety—'the subject of things hoped for, the evidence of things not seen.' 'But without faith it is impossible to please God.' Others have defined faith to be a uniting assent to an unseen object, as certainly the proof of an unknown thing is an evident assent."[12]

Thus even the idea that faith can become knowledge is an incomplete expression of the truth understood by the early Fathers, for we have already seen how they believed that the expression of faith in life has two stages, which seem so different that they have given rise to two quite different ideas of what faith is.

More often than not, people know only about one of these two kinds of faith. The first is in the head, where faith becomes knowledge, and the second in the heart. Taken on its own, the first stage, faith that becomes knowledge, can conceivably be seen as the same as Aquinas's idea of faith as mutually exclusive from knowledge. It was about this kind of faith that James, the brother of Jesus, wrote: "Exhort you that ye should earnestly contend for the faith which was once delivered to the saints" (Jude 1:3). This kind of faith works through the law, not by ignoring it. Many confusions arise from statements, in the Bible and in the Fathers, speaking of the expression of faith through works of service and purification, with the doctrine of Saint Paul known as justification by faith.

But in the early centuries of the church the word *faith* had already acquired two different meanings, and these represent these two different stages in its growth in the individual. The first of these, the faith that can become knowledge, is more than purely intellectual conviction. The Fathers said that this first form of faith was gained by *hearing,* which could support the idea that faith of conviction is very little different from blind belief. But experience shows that it is gained not by hearing unsupported doctrine but by the *recognition* that occurs when a clear statement evokes a particular kind of memory that we were previously unable to articulate adequately. The memories that give rise to this first faith are recollections based on one or more glimpses that were not long enough or not intense enough that we can clearly describe them, even to ourselves. When the nous recognizes that about which it is hearing, engagement of the heart occurs, and at this exact moment the character of belief changes and faith of conviction comes into being. Since this conviction comes not from any argument but from a memory that is often subconscious,[13] this faith is not blind, yet, as Saint Paul puts it, it still sees as if "through a glass, darkly."

The process begins to take this form when—once and for all—we put this pursuit, and our own inner transformation, above everything else. "Now, as regards those who have entered with all their heart," wrote Saint Anthony, "and have made themselves despise all afflictions of the flesh, valiantly resisting all the warfare that rises against them, until they conquered, think that, first of all, the Spirit calls them, and makes the warfare light for them, and sweetens for them the works of repentance, showing them how they ought to repent in body and soul, until He has taught them how to be converted to God who created them. And He delivers to them works whereby they may constrain their soul and their body, that both may be purified and enter together into their inheritance."[14]

But before this, we have had to reach this point. The first kind of faith leads to purification. Purification leads to the second stage of faith. Saint Anthony describes the form this takes in the monastic method as understood by the early monks of the desert: "First the body is purified by much fasting, by many vigils and prayers, and by the service which makes a man to be straitened in body, cutting off from himself all the lusts of the flesh. And the Spirit of Repentance is made his guide in these things, and tests him by means of them, lest the enemy should turn him back again."[15] This purification occurs while our faith is still the first kind of faith, the combination of verbal teaching whose truth is confirmed to us by memories: memories of a higher state, but memories that are themselves as yet unclear. At this stage these memories are difficult to remember. They are incomplete, and do not convey as much to us as they might.

But with the reinforcement of good teaching from those whose memories are clear, they can take us to the point of richer experience which, in its turn, as described earlier, leads to the second stage of faith. This second kind of faith leads to illumination, so that the faith that justifies without further effort is the second form of faith, faith of consciousness.

Faith Without Works

There appears to be a contradiction in this title. How do we reconcile this idea of faith without works with the paradoxical fact that the same Bible also tells us that:

> Every good gift and every perfect gift is from above, and cometh down from the Father of lights, with whom is no variableness, neither shadow or turning.
>
> Of his own will begat he us with the word of truth, that we should be a kind of firstfruits of his creatures. . . .
>
> But be ye doers of the word, and not hearers only, deceiving your own selves.
>
> For if any be a hearer of the word, and not a doer, he is like unto a man beholding his natural face in a glass:
>
> For he beholdeth himself, and goeth his way, and straightway forgetteth what manner of man he was.

But whoso looketh into the perfect law of liberty, and continueth therein, he being not a forgetful hearer, but a doer of the work, this man shall be blessed in his deed.

If any man among you seem to be religious, and bridleth not his tongue, but deceiveth his own heart, this man's religion is vain. . . .

So speak ye, and so do, as they that shall be judged by the law of liberty.

For he shall have judgment without mercy, that hath showed no mercy; and mercy rejoiceth against judgment.

What doth it profit, my brethren, though a man say he hath faith, and have not works? can faith save him?

If a brother or sister be naked, and destitute of daily food,

And one of you say unto them, Depart in peace, be ye warmed and filled; notwithstanding ye give them not those things which are needful to the body; what doth it profit?

Even so faith, if it hath not works, is dead, being alone.

Yea, a man may say, Thou hast faith, and I have works: show me thy faith without thy works, and I will show thee my faith by my works.

Thou believest that there is one God; thou doest well: the devils also believe, and tremble.

But wilt thou know, O vain man, that faith without works is dead? (James 1:17–18, 22–26; 2:12–20).

This doctrine in the Epistle of James appears so legalistic, and seems so contradictory to Saint Paul's teaching of justification by faith, not by works, that thought alone cannot easily reconcile this disagreement. Understood in external terms, it is often taken as evidence of a political change in the "control" of the church. Yet to the inner tradition, to the understanding of the heart, it loses its legalistic appearance, and when this happens, no conflict exists: instead, both doctrines are true.[16] Faith does not demand works, but is demonstrated by works done spontaneously by the person who has faith. Works are not an obligation but simply an occurrence with such a person.

Faith of Consciousness

The relation of watchfulness to change of heart is reflected by the existence of these two very different phases of faith. The higher becomes apparent when the cure of the soul leads to greater intensity of faith. When this has grown until it is clear and readily accessible in the memory, it becomes the second stage of faith. It is this which, according to Saint Paul, is "the certainty of things unseen" (Hebrews 1:11).

As a "steady state" experience, this direct revelation of the spiritual reality lies beyond the first faith, yet the first brief glimpse of this, like a grain of mustard seed buried in the memory, causes that first faith, which, when brought into consciousness and kept in mind, is the faith that moves mountains.

This is the faith that redeems. It is the cure of the soul as the permanent establishment of a major change in the levels of being and consciousness, a change of the same degree as the change we experience every morning between sleep and waking, a true rebirth. It wakes us, after purification, to the experiential knowledge known as divine vision or *theoria*—which means "vision" in this sense defined by Saint Denys[17] as *epistemi*, science, or certain knowledge.

Spiritual vision is a gift from God, although usually given in response to prayer, or in some form of obedience to therapeutic interpretation of the gospel. It is this that justifies, for only this higher faith surpasses the works of the law (Romans 3:28). It is this that

1. changes the heart
2. leads to substantial changes in being
3. "moves mountains"
4. leads to salvation

This vision is sometimes called "theology," but in this sense this word theology has a different meaning from that usually given it today. Saint Gregory Palamas says that the Fathers of the church did not theologize like Aristotle, but like the Apostles.[18] The theology of the Fathers is like the light of the sun compared against the ordinary modern meaning of theology, which is that given to it by Aristotle; to him it was an intellectual study. But in its therapeutic meaning, theology is a verbal description of experiential knowledge.

All this means that although Aquinas's formulation is correct so far as it goes, it is not possible to learn from it that real faith has a real power of transformation that is entirely lacking in blind belief. Aquinas's words appear to lead people to the opposite conclusion. Yet even then it is one thing to believe—on the evidence of experience—that we are spiritual beings. It is quite another thing to believe in the spiritual roots of everything, and to form a relationship in faith with Being[19] itself, the Being that forms that living, spiritual universe. Blind belief is easily come by. Faith in one's inner self and the knowledge that comes from this requires certain efforts on our part. Faith in the Word is confirmed by realization: by the fact that what is revealed by Scripture is understood when we observe that what it describes is actually happening in our lives. Then teaching in words becomes the teaching of the Word, and so becomes a part of our very being.

But real faith in the power of the living God goes deep and is less than common in the modern world.

Also, Saint Isaac the Syrian suggests that there is another reason why people choose knowledge over faith, even though in this way they choose knowledge which does not accord with faith: "When lack of grace dominates a man then . . . for him, knowledge is greater than faith, for he relies on investigation; trust in God is not present in everything he does, and divine providence for man is understood differently. Such a man is continually waylaid in these matters by those who 'in a moonless night lie in ambush to shoot down a man with their arrows.' "[20] The complexity of this relation between faith and knowledge needs to be pondered at considerable length.

What is the significance of choosing knowledge that does not accord with faith? Is the nature of knowledge, thus chosen, the same as the nature of knowledge learned as a product of faith? If not, is it not fragmentary knowledge that will remain forever incomplete? And does not this explain the paradox of science, where something can be regarded as proved, and then a new discovery can be made which is not included in the original description?

The Common Ground of Faith

This directly answers what was to have been our third question: How are we to restore to Christianity that ground that is common to all great faiths . . . without simply "borrowing" from other faiths? First we must remember that faith itself is a common ground, a common experience to mankind, that different faiths have faith in common: that although that faith takes different forms in different faiths, faith itself, underlying all its forms, has at root a single nature and a common strength and is itself the common experience of the "faithful" of all faiths. More than this, my own observations show that those who possess a clear faith can recognize and respect this in others, even if those others belong to a *different "true faith."* It is those who have no faith, but only blind belief, who become blind and bigoted against any form of faith that does not fit the outer form of their belief.

But words are second to the fact itself, even to the fact of faith, and the thing is happening, the miracle is taking place. The common ground of faith is being rebuilt before our eyes. As once the wave of intellectual-ization blinded first a few people, then many, to their own spiritual reality, limiting their abilities by making them ignorant of their possibilities, so now a new wave travels through the West, and this wave is made up of millions who are already discovering the fact that they are spirit. But so young, so unformed is this renewal of intelligence that we do not yet see it in others, but only in ourselves.

It is when we begin to see this in others that we may have our own part to play in the miracle.

Chapter 9

The Eye of the Soul

The Fathers made it clear in many passages that the part of mind which discriminates was the *nous*, described by them as "the eye of the soul," which may at one time be filled with thoughts and images but at another time may be free from all this, or separated from it all. "When there are no fantasies or mental images in the heart, the nous is established in its true nature, ready to contemplate whatever is full of delight, spiritual and close to God."[1] More than this, masters of the inner tradition such as Saint Hesychius equate the nous with the inner self or, in modern terms, the "real I." Saint Hesychius wrote: "Only he who has renounced the impassioned thoughts of his inner self, which is the nous, is a true monk. It is easy to be a monk in one's outer self if one wants to be; but no small struggle is required to be a monk in one's inner self."[2] Thus the nous is the true self, the cognitive power at the center of our being, the unitive power of knowing that brings together awareness of every form of perception, thought, memory and all other sensations.

Before we can know God, this "inner eye" must be transformed or enlightened by directing it to God, and not to Mammon. "The body sees by means of the eyes, and the soul by means of the *nous*. A body without eyes is blind, and cannot see the sun shining on earth and ocean or enjoy its light. Likewise the soul without a pure intellect and a holy way of life is blind: it does not apprehend God."[3] The English words commonly used to translate the Greek word *nous*—words like "mind" or "intellect"—are so misleading. They can easily be taken as referring to verbal thought. If we understand this correctly, we can understand the idea in the Gospel According to Thomas, that we should "Be passers by. . . . "[4]

This describes the proper state of the "eye of the soul," as well as describing how we can act from a different center of gravity, one that can form a new foundation for life. This is different from the self-centered life, the ordinary life in the world. Most people's lives gravitate around their reactions to, thoughts about, and feelings resulting from the events of one's life, while the theocentric life, whose center of gravity is the presence, the subtle but real action of Christ within one, is actually centered in our organism in a different way, in the nous. In this state, we no longer react to life, and it is only then that we can become a channel for the Lord.

Saint Anthony the Great described a process of purifying the nous by eliminating the disturbances aroused in it by thoughts, feelings, images, imitative movements—all the things that have been unconsciously taken in and remembered by the personality. This must be understood as a withdrawal from the normal waking state with its images and activities. In the early stages, this leaves the nous in darkness. With time this darkness is "enlightened," and when this occurs it is possible to withdraw from the images without their being removed: this is the true *inner separation,* a key point on the Way, referred to many times in this book, at which one begins inwardly to choose, instead of reacting to events.

To achieve this illumination and separation requires a special kind of effort, and this is the real nature of ascesis, noetic ascesis for the enlightening of the nous. This ascetic effort often begins with external methods or exercises, as in the preliminary steps of the Eightfold Yoga of Patanjali. In the Christian esoteric tradition, monasticism begins with similar external processes, although in a later chapter (chapter 12) we will show how lay forms generally begin with a psychological ascesis.

Saint Nilus of Sora, in thirteenth-century Russia, commented on monks of the time by quoting the earlier Philotheus of Sinai as having described "certain monks who, owing to their lack of experience, are content with performing good works, but know nothing of spiritual contests, victories and defeats, and who therefore neglect the mind; and he counsels us to pray for these monks and to teach them, while they guard themselves against evil actions, to purify the mind,[5] which is the eye of the soul."[6] The conclusion from this is that monastics, too, need not only physical and noetic ascesis but also psychological ascesis, and indeed the teachings of early monastics given in the *Philokalia* confirm this conclusion.

Transformation of the Heart

It is fundamental to the esoteric tradition, as to all Orthodox teachings today, that grace and effort are both almost equally necessary to salvation or, in inner terms, to the inner transformation of man, and although what we do cannot determine what God will do, unless we have real faith in His existence the likelihood of grace is considerably diminished for us. Equally important, it is our *assent to faith* that works those repeated small changes in us whose cumulative effect transforms our whole psychology. In Saint John, in the Gauss translation, it says of those who do really believe, not just in their own inner depths, but in the invisible Kingdom and its King, that: "whoever accepts his [Christ's] testimony has signed his name to the reality of God. Because the one whom God sent tells what God said: there's no limit to the spirit he gives forth. The Father loves the son and has put everything in his hands. Whoever believes in the son has everlasting life, but whoever is not convinced by the son will never see Life; no, the wrath of God rests upon him."[7]

At first sight this seems different from the teachings of the Fathers, who often looked at the transformation of the heart as a hard struggle with the passions. For much of the monk's life—as for everyone who really sets out on the esoteric path—this struggle is a major factor. But despite the significance of this and the need to give guidance about it, many of the Fathers—and their spiritual descendants today—have also looked at the same question in a quite different and positive way, saying that it is the way in which love itself is transformed and redirected into *a higher eroticism* that leads and binds the heart in a two-way relationship to the Lord. This process is in some ways analogous to modern concepts of psychological transformation, yet contains an element of mystery and true mysticism that goes beyond modern thought. The same was said by Bishop Kallistos Ware in a 1992 issue of *Sobornost*, where he wrote of prayer something that applies to all forms of the ascetic struggle, of which prayer is the chief but not the only form: "Techniques are subsidiary; it is our encounter face to face, through the prayer, with the living person of Jesus that alone has a primary value."[8]

There is an ancient Syrian prayer that brings to life this idea of the synergetic link between grace and effort in the verse: "Cause to reside in me a faith that perceives Your Mysteries, so that I may perceive Your sacrifice as You are, and not as I am."[9] This prayer echoes the sense of the familiar line in the Lord's Prayer, "Thy Kingdom come." This whole idea of a kingdom of God, of a different world that can be known in a different way, is not trivial. To accept and understand this is crucial: without it, one's faith is not faith, it is "belief tailored to modern thought," and tailored faith bears fruit not in spirituality but in hypocrisy. The same idea seems to have existed in the teachings of Gurdjieff and Ouspensky, for example in Ouspensky's idea that "man cannot do," but because, in deference to the prejudices of their times and their mission to speak to the agnostic, they would not speak of God, neither the meaning of this nor the crucial importance of understanding it correctly was ever clear to anyone.

In simple terms, until we begin to understand that God does what He wishes, we cannot understand how He can overcome the so-called deterministic laws which our modern picture of the world shows as shaping our lives.

Thus the scientific views of the absolute determinism of "natural law" is at variance with Christian faith . . . and that not only in its inner forms but in all its early forms. And that early *theocentric* view of reality offers the only escape from "the world," that is, from the contemporary form of the illusion that binds our lives. This is an expression of the fact that, because only God really *does,* man can *do* only by uniting his will with the will of God. But this means much more than we might first understand of it, something described in the old idea that you should "Confess your faults one to another, and pray one for another, that ye may be healed. The effectual fervent prayer of a righteous man availeth much" (James 5:16). We cannot have two centers to our lives. We become spiritual only when we become, in the words of the Athonite Father George Capsanis, *theocentric* instead of being self-centered. This is the same as saying: "But seek ye first the kingdom of God, and his righteousness; and all these things shall be added unto you" (Matthew 6:33).

The New Man as the Prodigal Son

Metanoia is both temporary and, in its final stage, permanent. Temporarily, it can happen at any moment of the day or night, when we correctly discriminate in that moment between the back-to-front truth of the world, which sees us as being and doing, and the gospel truth, which recognizes that Being and Doing belong to God.

But the point is that *metanoia* signifies a return to the source: a turning back, and the journey of return. In the Orthodox Church it is symbolized most often by the parable of the prodigal son. This view is entirely appropriate to the inner tradition.

> And he said, A certain man had two sons:
>
> And the younger of them said to his father, Father, give me the portion of goods that falleth to me. And he divided unto them his living.
>
> And not many days after the younger son gathered all together, and took his journey into a far country, and there wasted his substance with riotous living.
>
> And when he had spent all, there arose a mighty famine in that land; and he began to be in want.

And he went and joined himself to a citizen of that country; and he sent him into his fields to feed swine.

And he would fain have filled his belly with the husks that the swine did eat: and no man gave unto him.

And when he came to himself, he said, How many hired servants of my father's have bread enough and to spare, and I perish with hunger! (Luke 15:11–17).

The phrase *when he came to himself* is clearly a reference to an early stage of Self-remembering and the result of this *metanoia,* a change in direction in life, leading to complete transformation.

I will arise and go to my father, and will say unto him, Father, I have sinned against heaven, and before thee,

And am no more worthy to be called thy son: make me as one of thy hired servants.

And he arose, and came to his father. But when he was yet a great way off, his father saw him, and had compassion, and ran, and fell on his neck, and kissed him.

And the son said unto him, Father, I have sinned against heaven, and in thy sight, and am no more worthy to be called thy son.

But the father said to his servants, Bring forth the best robe, and put it on him; and put a ring on his hand, and shoes on his feet:

And bring hither the fatted calf, and kill it; and let us eat, and be merry:

For this my son was dead, and is alive again; he was lost, and is found. And they began to be merry (Luke 15:18–24).

We will recognize in this parable certain *stages,* briefly and inadequately summarized as follows:

1. *A fall:* The son loses his *birthright* in self-indulgence in a "far country"—our world.
2. *The result of the fall:* In time, he feels a lack, and so takes employment with a citizen of that country, wanting even the coarsest food of that country, but nobody gives it to him.
3. *An awakening:* He *comes to himself,* recognizes his situation, and *remembers* the alternative of his father's household.
4. *A decision:* He then *forms a resolution* to return "home," accepting his humiliation, and begins the return journey.
5. *A confirmation:* His father comes out to meet him.

6. *A new attitude:* He confesses his fault to the father.
7. *A new life:* The father does not punish him, but instead immediately gives him the "good things" he has been lacking. The errant son has *come back to life.*

Yet in fact *metanoia*, repentance, except in a few exceptional cases, does not begin in a single moment of conversion, a flash of insight that immediately and forever transforms our lives; nor is it no more than an occasional impulse, an occasional change of direction; nor is it change of thought without a change in feelings and impulses that also form our minds. Instead it is a continual—and almost impossible—struggle to perceive the truth about ourselves and, in response, to turn away from the past and so keep ourselves turned toward God.

"The whole life of the monk becomes a study of repentance, his way of life a way of repentance,"[10] writes Abbot George Capsanis of the Athos Monastery of Grigoriou. He too is familiar with the idea of the new man, but he speaks of a more difficult birth, not an easy *metanoia* but a *metanoia* of impossible effort: "In the midst of the birth pangs of repentance, the new man according to God is slowly begotten. Belonging to the struggle for repentance is the effort of continually guarding one's thoughts: it is by putting away from oneself all the evil and demonic temptations that act to soil the mind that one is able to keep the heart pure, and it is such a heart that reflects God."[11] Then he refers to the familiar beatitude: "Blessed are the pure in heart: for they shall see God" (Matthew 5:8).

The struggle is a struggle for purity of heart, for *apatheia,* in the words of the early Fathers such as Evagrius. Consider the meaning, the significance of this idea of a struggle. It occurs when we believe that, having seen the emptiness of everyday life, we have chosen the "better part," like Mary in the famous gospel story of Martha and Mary. (Described at the beginning of chapter 11.)

But many of us have yet to learn that it is not enough to choose once, nor even once a day, nor even enough to practice the efforts of the Royal Way as we know it: that the struggle is one that will eventually demand of us continual choices, repeated choices of the "better part" of ourselves.

Those who have even begun to do this will recognize this description, recognize the constant failures that erode our confidence and at the same time attack our pride, and understand not only why Saint Silouan reported that the Spirit had told him to "Keep your soul in hell, but do not despair," but also why monks guided by a pupil of Silouan say that the point of this instruction is a means of working toward humility.

This is a connection that will only be believable to those who have made prolonged efforts of this kind.

This *humility* comes about as a result of self-knowledge, and indeed it is a test of true self-knowledge. No effort—and no teaching—is true and transformative that does not lead to humility, that does not turn us around and, closing us off from the pressures of the world, begin to open us to the constant pressure of the Love of God, about which the gospel says: "Behold, I stand at the door and knock" (Revelation 3:20).

This is the true form of *metanoia*, complete *metanoia*, which normally comes after this struggle has become part of our being, when the change of heart becomes permanent. When this happens, this is where, in the life of prayer, we become aware that it is not we who are praying, but the Lord is praying in us.

At this stage, in the effort to choose the divine against the personal in each of the little decisions that precede every action of our lives, we discover that we are working not for a different idea of life, but for a different consciousness of life: it is then that I discover that I am working not for some idea, but for the emergence of a different "I," a different self.

Mneme Theou

We have said that in the present time many people are rediscovering their spiritual nature. But to know that one is a spiritual being is not enough. For this to transform us wholly, it must not only be an article of faith; it must be more even than certain knowledge: to transform us at every moment, it must be remembered at every moment. This is what it means to choose the divine.

The monasticism of the Eastern church is famed for its hesychastic methods of inner prayer and the stillness this brings. But on Athos some monks instead work on the path of *philoxenia*[12] (love of strangers or hospitality), attempting to make their actions revolve about the Spirit of God as they see this in other human beings. Both of these paths, of *hesychia* and of *philoxenia*, are monastic forms of repentance, based on remembering. In practice, like most other elements of spiritual practice, both these forms develop as the sometimes formalized outward element of persistent attempts to keep alive inner efforts that are too easily forgotten without some mnemonic aid. There are other versions, at least in their external form: I have seen a monk on Mount Athos prostrating himself to everyone who leaves the *katholikon*, seeking forgiveness from one after another.

On Athos the exercise of turning the heart to God is called by the name *mneme Theou*, which is both an exercise in its own right and something that occurs almost spontaneously whenever prayer goes into the heart. Prayer is still incomplete as long as it lacks this element of remembrance of God. *Mneme Theou* is thus an essential element in a life of *metanoia,* and an essential part of the fullest experience of *metanoia* itself. The heart turned fully to God wishes to think of nothing else. It turns for the solution of its problems not to the world but to God. This is what Theophan called "magnetization to God." It was also Theophan who wrote about this in a letter: "Inner disorder you know from experience. You have decided to destroy it, so get busy at once to remove the cause. The spirit has lost its natural support, which is God. The spirit recovers this through remembrance of God. Always be with the Lord whatever you are doing; always turn your mind to Him. Try to behave as one would before a King. You will quickly acquire the habit, but do not let it slip or interrupt it. If you carry out this small rule conscientiously, then as long as this reverent attention to God is maintained, the inner confusion will be removed from within."[13]

This, and no intellectual conception of reality, is why Father George Capsanis of Grigoriou said that when a monk's repentance is real, his idea of God is real. This is why the idea that we must remember God is central to Athonite Christianity. More intellectually, to paraphrase what one writer said about this some years back, remembering means re-membering: re-connecting oneself inside. But more than this, in some strange way what I obtain for myself in moments of remembering becomes the spring, the source of all my unselfish actions. When we are able to see ourselves without the normal pride, the normal conceit in our own superiority, we will understand that without the "Mary" of *metanoia,* the "Martha" of our charity retains a taint of selfishness that spoils the whole. All my charity, ultimately all charity, is founded on or inspired by this remembering; but, whenever we "forget," we forget also the importance of remembering. Then, as Saint Paul said: "And even as they did not like to retain God in their knowledge, God gave them over to a reprobate mind, to do those things which are not convenient" (Romans 1:28).

On Athos, then, *mneme Theou,* remembering God, means something that is more than merely a "subjective" recollection. "Objectively," if one can say that, it means reconnecting oneself to God and His grace. The effort, the process involved, is very like that needed to remember a forgotten fact. It too sometimes succeeds and sometimes fails. It succeeds, paradoxically, when we "forget ourselves," forget our ordinary thoughts, our ordinary motives, our insistent but very personal hopes and fears. Then, when it fully succeeds, it connects us not only to something past, to some memory of something that once happened, but connects us to something, to someone existing now. As described in the parable of the prodigal son, this remembering is all that God asks of us. We must "Seek first God's kingdom," and if we do this, He will do everything else that we need. What is involved, to put it another way, is "to remember with the heart."

But for most of us, remembering with the heart is not as easy as it should be. It depends on recognition, and for a busy modern mind we first have to learn to recognize that something is missing, to perceive an absence of Spirit. Yet the benefit it produces can be progressive. When we remember this, something very important changes within us. When we remember, then we no longer act out of habit, out of our *prolipsis* (our predispositions built up over a lifetime and, according to the Fathers, some of them from before this life). When we remember, we act from a different will, but until we experience this strongly enough to begin to recognize it, we will not understand this statement nor value the fact as we should. The problem is that where we wish more often, we remember more often; and usually our wishing, shaped by our past experience and fed and bounded by the content of our memories, is based on what the monk would call "worldly pleasures," for we think most of what we love most, and, to begin with, we love ourselves most. So to help us overcome our own past, the inner tradition provides tools to help us to remember God . . . in ourselves, in the universe, in other people . . . tools to help us love.

The Struggle for Metanoia

When Jesus was baptized in Jordan: "From that time Jesus began to preach, and to say, Repent: for the kingdom of heaven is at hand" (Matthew 4:17). Translated "repentance," according to its roots, the Greek word *metanoia* means a transformation of the nous. What this means is described in the following passage by Saint John of Karpathos, part of which was quoted in chapter 2, in which, as commonly used by the early Fathers, the word *metanoia* was referred to the most important esoteric concept of illumination of the nous. "The moon as it waxes and wanes illustrates the condition of man. Sometimes he does what is right: sometimes he sins and then through *metanoia* returns to a holy life. The nous[14] of one who sins is not destroyed, (as some of you think), just as the physical size of the moon does not diminish, but only its light. Through *metanoia* a man regains his true splendour, just as the moon after a period of waning clothes itself once more in its full light. If a man believes in Christ, 'even though he dies, he shall live' (John 11:25), he shall know that 'I the Lord have spoken and will do it' (Ezekiel 17:24)."[15]

In most English translations of the Bible, *metanoia* is translated "repentance." Whatever it meant when the King James translation was originally produced, today the English word has acquired moralistic overtones that have obscured and confused the early meaning. It is not generally understood that the word *metanoia* (meta-noia) actually refers to the renewal of the nous described by Saint Paul in Romans: "And be not conformed to this world: but be ye transformed by the renewing of your nous,[16] that ye may prove what is that good, and acceptable, and perfect, will of God" (Romans 12:2). Of course, in most translations of this passage the word *nous* is translated "mind" or "intelligence," the latter coming closest to the Greek meaning but not close enough.

This need for inner healing or renewal of the nous, and the cleansing of the psyche that is necessary before this nous can be illuminated, is described in the following passage of the gospel:

> Woe unto you, scribes and Pharisees, hypocrites! for ye make clean the outside of the cup and of the platter, but within they are full of extortion and excess.
>
> Thou blind Pharisee, cleanse first that which is within the cup and platter, that the outside of them may be clean also.
>
> Woe unto you, scribes and Pharisees, hypocrites! for ye are like unto whited sepulchers, which indeed appear beautiful outward, but are within full of dead men's bones, and of all uncleanness (Matthew 23:25–27).

This renewal of the nous, the healing of the soul, is the precise goal of the therapeutic interpretation of Orthodox Christian methods—described earlier—that is now reemerging in the Greek Church. Complete renewal requires true or complete *metanoia,* and this in turn depends on complete *diakrisis . . .* which must be understood as a true discrimination of spirits. This may appear simple but goes very deep, so that this chapter will only be able to begin an explanation of what it means. But nothing else will go deep enough into the heart. Proper discrimination between spirits or influences will renew the mind, and this will intensify our yearning for the higher spiritual levels. This yearning or zeal will then work widespread changes in our psyche. The process is equivalent to that described in the Sanskrit word *vairyagya.* To the degree that we *repent,* or to the degree that we achieve the lesser liberation of *vairyagya,* we will "close the taps" through which we normally waste our inner energies, and as we do this, the "cup" of our heart begins to be "filled."

This chapter therefore introduces a psychological way of understanding how the key concept described by *metanoia* can be linked spiritually with the sacrament of confession—but from a psychological viewpoint this should be regarded as a sacrament of self-knowledge. In esoteric terms, this is probably the most important sacrament, and, with a true *pneumaticos* or spirit-bearing elder, can become a remarkable tool for development, intensifying the approach to *metanoia.*

This means that *metanoia* is not possible without an intense struggle, a struggle with old attitudes and habits of mind that can lead, if successful, to a change first, transiently, in the state and finally in the *content* of the heart—a change demonstrated by the condition known as *apatheia,* dispassion. When *apatheia* is established in us, what we want will change, and then the form of awareness called *diakrisis* begins to become a normal element in our consciousness.

The problem is that as the esoteric meaning of the Christian tradition has been progressively forgotten, this idea of repentance has also been misunderstood. Today, it is believed that to repent is something we are supposed to do. In this case we are so unsure of what it is that we are supposed to do that nobody, of course, does anything. Let us be grateful for this small mercy, for *metanoia* is not something you are supposed to be able to do. It is a change of heart that comes about as a result of your becoming aware of the dangers in continuing to want what you have always wanted; it occurs in that moment when we realize that we actually want God more than we want our ordinary satisfactions.

In changing the way we perceive the world, *diakrisis* changes the way we perceive ourselves. It is this change, when it becomes absolute, that is described as *renewal* of the mind. Thus, *diakrisis,* if it goes into the heart, which is rare these days for a number of reasons, and if it is sustained, will *automatically*[17] lead to a changed attitude to ourselves. When this change in our attitude to ourselves reaches "critical mass," there begins what is normally a long and difficult *struggle* with the attitudes and habits of mind that have ruled us until now.

"The love of the soul is its salvation"

Outside monasticism, the *forms* of repentance and of transformation of eros are even more varied—although all must pass through the same final constriction. Mouravieff's concept of the polar being[18] is a teaching of repentance. It contains, among other meanings, the idea of a path of repentance in the marriage relationship, and also in the family, a form that is extensible to a form of repentance in society at large. It expresses in modern form the idea of *virginity* that existed in the very early church, when couples would occasionally marry and then avoid any physical relationship, instead devoting their lives to God.

Why was this done? What reason could there be for doing it today? Consider the psychological power of love. Individuals, when they fall in love, act in flagrant disregard of their own previous character; their priorities are changed, their values transformed, their ability to make effort increased and at the same time narrowed, so that only one aim exists for them, and activities into which they had put years of effort are forgotten overnight. It is clear that these powerful if purely natural energies are able to redirect the heart.

Yet in the Fathers and before them, in Plato, there is a higher, divine eros and a lower, physical eros. Boris Mouravieff repeats a text of the esoteric tradition called *The Golden Book*, from which he quotes several times, and from which Gurdjieff's aphorisms are supposed to have been obtained, a text which—not surprisingly if it is secret—I have not so far managed to locate, and which said:

> Our Lord is great and glorious,
> He fills the Universe with His Love!
> Thy love belongs to him;
> The love of the soul is its salvation.[19]

The transformation of the eros turns this powerful force into a new direction, into the search for God. Then the successful seekers will act in flagrant disregard of their own previous character; their priorities will become spiritual priorities, their values be transformed to Christian values, their ability to make effort increased and at the same time narrowed, so that the only aim that exists for them is to serve the Lord.

The real meaning of the transformation of eros, then, is not a negation of sex, something that is in itself God-given, but the need—at a certain point in the growth of the individual—to redirect emotions that have become subordinated to sex; to narrow down to that one desire which is love itself as a single thing: that love which, being a love for the source of love, does not immolate itself in its success. So the difficult question is not whether this should be done, but how to achieve this sublimation.

This question is further modified by the nature of the eros itself. To the inner tradition, eros is not simply physical love, but the love of the soul for its lost beloved—the spirit: in this form the divine eros is actually natural to the human being. It manifests early in life as an innate curiosity that as we mature turns inward and in doing so must entrain the lower eroticism and attract it toward a different reality. This however is a high stage and for most people the divine eros is seen in the pursuit of self-knowledge. The seeking of truth within us, however feeble it is in its beginning, is the first small shoot of the divine eros.

The whole point seems to be that we should change the direction as well as the intensity of our love, should turn self-love into love of our Lord, and should *magnetize* ourselves through and through with this higher form of love so that we do not again turn back to the demands of the world.

To describe these methods in detail is beyond the range of this generalized book, and indeed little detailed information exists in writing in this line, beyond hints comprehensible only to those qualified to put them to practical use.

Mouravieff, however, gives certain clues: some specific, which I will not reproduce, some more general. For example, immediately after the passage from *The Golden Book* he wrote:

> Unfortunately, man does not know how to distinguish Love from passion, so he often takes the reflection for its source. One definition, not of Love, which is indefinable, but of its attributes,[20] has been given by Saint Paul in terms which are as precise as they are meaningful.
>
> "Love suffereth long, and is kind; Love envieth not; Love vaunteth not itself, is not puffed up, doth not behave itself unseemly, seeketh not her own, is not easily provoked, thinketh no evil: Rejoiceth not in iniquity, but rejoiceth in the truth; Beareth all things, believeth all things; hopeth all things; endureth all things. Love never faileth; but whether there be prophecies, they shall fail; whether there be tongues they shall cease; whether there be knowledge, it shall vanish away" (1 Corinthians 13:4–8).
>
> If we meditate on this text, we will understand that a true abyss separates love from a "loving" passion, yet we so often take the latter for love!
>
> But passion's motivation is to possess, and this produces effects diametrically opposed to those described in Saint Paul's text. The spirit of Love is to give with no return.[21]

Once again we are speaking of seeing through illusion, but this time it is entirely clear that the illusions we must overcome are emotional delusions. Gifted with the Spirit of repentance, we must see through these passions, must see them for what they are—as "second-hand emotions," memories of past emotion—in order to become free of them.

In the resulting freedom from distraction by emotional delusion, we have again found the *apatheia* of Evagrius and other Fathers. Here too we find something else. Intellectual discrimination leads to what might be called a "change of mind." This is often regarded as being genuine *metanoia;* the true inner change of repentance. But the *nous* is the knowing power of the inmost heart, known, as said earlier, as the eye of the soul; and *metanoia,* the change of nous, is a change of heart. It is this that is demonstrated by *apatheia,* by lack of passionate delusion.

The Spirit of repentance brings *emotional discrimination,* and this emotional discrimination is the secret of the transformation of the sex force, as well as of the transformation of the negative emotions of anger and despair.

We have to know real emotions from unreal. To remember the real. To ponder the passage from Saint Paul given above is perhaps the most effective way of taking to heart the difference between the two.

This sensitivity to the difference between true and false emotions takes the power from the false emotions.

It is at this point that a change occurs; now the God-given natural goodness within us, to which Saint Theophan referred, emerges naturally as our real character. The *image* becomes a *likeness:* the image of the divine within us emerges as we become "like unto our Lord."

This is *sanctification.* Saint Maximos had this to say about what might be called the sanctification of Love: "The one who is perfect in love and has reached the summit of detachment knows no distinction between his own and another's, between faithful and unfaithful, between slave and freeman, or indeed between male and female. But having risen above the tyranny of the passions and looking to the one nature of men, he regards all equally and is equally disposed toward all. For in him there is neither Greek nor Jew, neither male nor female, neither slave nor freeman, but Christ is everything and in everything."[22] This describes a state of being which may be experienced, a place in the universe that may be reached by us. Far greater than this, it describes a permanent state of being which, it has been said, may be accomplished, may be reached in this life. "And from the days of John the Baptist until now the kingdom of heaven suffereth violence, and the violent take it by force" (Matthew 11:12).

I wrote earlier that prayer is a form of asceticism and involves a struggle. For many years, true prayer becomes a continual struggle with oneself.

At the same time, for those who are not free either to be monastics or to live like monastics, for those who are not free to give the same amount of time to the ascetic exercises described above, this list can be varied in detail, as long as the basic principle is followed. Here those who are not monastic meet the question of what forms of ascesis are possible to them. This is a real question and requires more exact guidance than can be given in this or any book. In actuality it requires the guidance of what the Eastern Church calls an *elder* (*geronte* or *starets*), an experienced guide who is inspired by the Spirit.

But even with such guidance, this question turns into two separate questions: one is the question of what forms of ascesis can be practiced in everyday life, a question developed in the next chapter. The other is the question of the false choices that we continually make: of overcoming the illusion of difficulty that makes us give up. The nature of this delusion is such that any kind of ascesis can appear to us to be impossible. This is exactly where the gospel teaching is relevant that describes the Royal

Road thus: "Narrow is the gate and hard is the way that leads to life" (Matthew 7:14).

The problem is that, when first the struggle becomes wholly real, it becomes much more difficult, and when one first meets this degree of difficulty, the whole thing appears totally impossible.

Yet this is where the *Royal Road* begins.

To walk on this road, to make the step to different being, demands a different level of exertion, or to be more exact, exertion of a different kind, originating from what we today might call "a different place in us."

This kind of effort is one of the characteristics of passing through the change of state signified by the image of the "strait gate." It is at this point that one can first truly begin to say with Saint Paul: "I am crucified with Christ: nevertheless I live; yet not I, but Christ liveth in me" (Galatians 2:20).

It is at this point that many people give up, surrender the struggle, seek easier ways . . . even if those easier ways mean reaching lesser goals. But this difficulty is itself an illusion: an illusion with which we must struggle.

Vigils require what might be called superefforts. But those superefforts are efforts against illusion. For some people, fasting requires superefforts. But again, those superefforts are efforts against illusion . . . efforts to transcend the imaginary limits on our capacities we have habitually accepted. For others with their busy lives, prayer requires superefforts. But those superefforts too—like all the superefforts of ascesis—are in large part efforts against illusion. Superefforts are a struggle with expectations, the effort to do what we are really capable of, instead of that to which we have habitually believed ourselves to be limited.

With these superefforts (although they have been given many different names), we first enter the ascetic path that is the narrow way of Christ. As part of the *unwritten tradition,* the monks of Athos recognize and even reward superefforts, although I have never heard them speak directly about them.

In the smaller communities in places like Athos, monks make superefforts of self-denial, but such efforts cannot be made simply by telling people to make them. An example exists in a recent book about Mount Athos, which describes a certain Father Gregory: "He wouldn't permit himself even one sip of water more than was necessary. During the periods of fast he ate once a day. . . from the time he came to our group, and as long as I remember him, he never put sweets in his mouth. He slept, like Father Joachim, seated down on the ground in a corner of his cell covered with blankets without removing any of his clothing."[23] Not surprisingly, even to the fellow monks of his *kalyvia* or community house,

Father Gregory was a remarkable man. But similar individuals exist in the same communities today.

Why do they make such efforts? Boris Mouravieff, for example, spoke of the awakening of a "real I" within us whose authority was different from the capricious authority of the ordinary content of the psyche. People attempt to awaken this "I" by means of superefforts.

Recognition

Talking about discrimination, Evagrius wrote of the need to recognize the different kinds of being within us. This idea of recognition, as well as the relation of the idea of beings to being, needs to be expanded in order to understand these ideas in modern terms.

Noetic ascesis, the awakening of the nous, begins with learning to discern between worldly and spiritual influences, influences that come from the perception of the spirit, and increase our ability to discern or discriminate. This we must do with greater precision than we yet know. This precision is indicated in the idea of recognition. Recognition leads to effective discrimination: to *diakrisis*. With this precision we will begin to recognize the "beings" that act within us. Recognizing them, we can become free of them, just as a thief, once recognized, becomes unable to steal from us.

Evagrius describes the many fragmented beings or partial "I"s as demons in the following passage:

> We must take care to recognize the different types of demons and take note of the circumstances of their coming. We shall know these from our thoughts—which we shall know from the objects—we ought to consider which of the demons are less frequent in their assaults, which are the more vexatious, which are the ones which yield the field more readily and which the more resistant. Finally, we should note which are the ones which make sudden raids and snatch off the spirit to blasphemy. Now it is essential to understand these matters so that when these various evil thoughts set their own proper forces to work we are in a position to address effective words against them, that is to say, those words which correctly characterize the one present. And we must do this before they drive us out of our own state of mind. In this manner we shall make ready progress by the grace of God. We shall pack them off chafing with chagrin and marveling at our perspicacity.

When the demons achieve nothing in their struggles against a monk they withdraw a bit and observe to see which of the virtues he neglects in the meantime. Then all of a sudden they attack him from this point and ravage the poor fellow.[24]

To recognize types of demons comes from having seen—constated[25]—them many times before. Recognition is not formed from a single glimpse, nor does theory become recognition until we experience what it describes on a number of different occasions. When we begin to recognize the demons we can see why they are called demons: the name must have been given originally much as pilots in aerial warfare refer to hostile planes as "bandits."

In practice, demons are recognizable, recurrent forms of influence that have become embodied in our thoughts. They are familiar and too often welcome faces.

In other sources they are said to possess a person, but can be dealt with by appropriate words. It is easy from this to view them, in an external way, as hostile beings having their own body, whether visible or not. But this is misleading; in fact everything about demons that is recorded by reliable sources—such as Evagrius—defines them in purely psychological terms, and this is the inner tradition. There is another factor about demons: they are "psychological" in character, being part of our inner experience, and there is nothing in passages like this from Evagrius to suggest that they have any existence external to the person who experiences them. We speak of people being possessed or obsessed by a demon, who "can drive them out of their own state of mind." We also speak of being possessed or obsessed by an idea, by a belief, by an emotion. . . . Finally, Evagrius makes it clear that the words that can be used to deal with them are no magical incantation, but "words which correctly characterize the one present."

In modern terms we see our inner life in such a different way that it is difficult—to be exact, it is emotionally difficult, touching on and threatening our wants, our desires—to recognize modern descriptions of certain of these demons as being the same thing that Evagrius and others wrote about so long ago. Yet Allan Bloom, an American political philosopher, described them clearly and even referred to the fact that they can be known by recognition.

> Yet if a student can—and this is most difficult and unusual—draw back, get a critical distance on what he clings to, come to doubt the ultimate value of what he loves, he has taken the first and most difficult step toward the philosophic conversion. Indignation is the soul's defence against the wound of

doubt about its own; it reorders the cosmos to support the justice of its cause. It justifies putting Socrates to death. Recognizing indignation for what it is constitutes knowledge of the soul, and is thus an experience more philosophic than the study of mathematics. It is Plato's teaching that music, by its nature, encompasses all that is today most resistant to philosophy. So it may well be that through the thicket of our greatest corruption runs the path to awareness of the oldest truths.[26]

It is easy to see how this links with the provocations described by Evagrius (see chapter 14), and from this, if we study it in depth, we will begin to see how these "demons" provoke the mind in ways that change its character and make it behave unnaturally. In spite of the fact that occasional insights of this kind still occur, it is easy to see how people assume that these demons were once regarded as some kind of creature. In one sense, indeed, this view is correct. As Allan Bloom indicates, the whole picture forms part of the structure that sustains our intentional self-delusions, the lies we tell to ourselves to avoid the need to change ourselves. On one visit to Mount Athos, a few years after the troubles in Cyprus, I was disturbed on two successive nights by the great howling noises that came from the next-door guest room. On Athos, where the first services begin at 2:30 A.M., sleep is valuable, so the next day, I asked one of the monks, my friend Father A., what was happening: "It is a man from Cyprus," he told me. "He is troubled with demons, and is here for us to help him." My friend paused, looked me straight in the eye, and added: "But you need not worry, it will never happen to an Englishman."

Despite the ambiguity of the translation of Evagrius, we can see that this passage tells us that they are driven off by correctly recognizing or in other words identifying the demon, or the person for whom they are present. So we can list certain characteristics shared by these demons.

1. They are psychological, not physical, in their nature, having no external existence.
2. But their coming is explained or linked to specific kinds of outside circumstance.
3. They are recurrent; each has a different character, but we can recognize them by their characteristics.
4. They can possess or obsess us.
5. But they can be overcome by correctly identifying them; that is, by *recognition*.

Recognition as such is not mentioned by the early Fathers, although like Evagrius they sometimes write about recognizing something. It is just beginning to be distinguished by modern thought. Neurophysiologist Sir John Eccles, in his interesting studies of memory and knowledge, speaks of a recognition memory. In our own studies we will find that recognition and discrimination are inextricably linked, but we also have to realize that we recognize something only through experience of that thing. We can clearly differentiate one thing from others only where we have experience. Knowing the names of things does not in itself give us the ability to recognize and discriminate among them. Thus the idea of recognition provides a way for people in normal contemporary states of mind to approach the higher kinds of discrimination. On the horizontal level, you cannot discriminate between two things without recognizing them both, cannot recognize them without being able to distinguish them exactly, without knowing clearly what belongs to them and what does not.

In terms of inner practice, recognition of B influences, of the truly spiritual presence in our lives—but only a complete recognition, that recognizes the influence and its effects—will give us the strength to turn away from the harmful A influences. Then we can become free of them by inviting God's help. This form of discrimination (diakrisis) is described in detail in chapter 13.

Remember that Evagrius wrote: "we shall make ready progress by the grace of God."

But here is a key: if recognition is an element in discrimination, then it is an element in the discernment of spirits, and this poses the question of how we are to recognize the different kinds of spirit. Here those involved in the unwritten tradition today sometimes repeat the term used in early written texts, in which these influences are recognized by a sense normally named "taste," but which is certainly not the ordinary physical sense of taste, although it is analogous to it.

Here it is helpful to know that the esoteric path is seen as divided into three or sometimes four stages. The division of the esoteric path into three stages goes back at least as far as Clement of Alexandria, head of the great catechetical school in that city in the second century, when he wrote of three stages on the Way, summarized by Morton Smith as: "protreptic, for complete 'outsiders,' pedagogic (paraenetic), for catechumens and ordinary Christians; the didascalic, for the advanced students, the gnostics."[27]

Smith also quotes another commentator, Méhat, as saying: "the distinction between the neophytes, still subject to elementary instruction, and the more advanced Christians who are initiated into the true doctrine, ought to be given more attention than it has hitherto received. For my part, I think the origin of this distinction lies in a common practice of the Church, established long before Clement's time, and going much further back than is generally supposed."[28] Supporting this statement, Clement himself wrote three major works at different "levels," that is, intended to be understood at three different levels of understanding and experience: the first of these works was an "exoteric" text, the second a "mesoteric" text, known as the Pedagogue or Instructor, and the third an "esoteric" text, presumably dealing with the "greater mysteries," the *Stromata* or Miscellanies.

Chapter 10

Metanoia and Ascesis

M*etanoia* is two things: a slow transformation of the nous and a sudden reversal. The first is an inner healing process by which we lengthen and deepen the stillness of the nous until it begins to become enlightened, and so begins to overcome the effects of the Fall. But the final change is discontinuous: in this context a partial reversal of direction is a meaningless concept, so that we will discover that *metanoia* can be instantaneous and in some sense is always instantaneous, yet to those who work at it, *metanoia* is a slow and difficult process; only when we face and work against this difficulty does the Christian religion pass for us from being an idea to being a reality. Only then can we behave as Christians, as well as thinking that we are Christians.

But although *metanoia* is the result of a gradual preparation, it cannot be half-hearted or partial: if it is not complete it is not true *metanoia*. It is Saint Neilos the Ascetic, in the *Philokalia* again, who expresses this difficulty, and in doing so introduces the parable of the headless axe. Among other things, this passage is a splendid example of the way the Fathers understood the language of parable.

> Remember how one of Elisha's followers was cutting wood by the Jordan, and the head of the axe flew off and fell into the river. Realizing that he was in trouble—for the axe had been borrowed—he cried out to his teacher: "Alas, master!" (2 Kings 6:5). The same thing happens to those who try to teach on the basis of what they have wrongly understood from others, and who cannot complete the task because they do not speak from

personal experience. Half way through, they are discovered to be contradicting themselves; and then they admit their ignorance, finding themselves in trouble because their teaching is merely borrowed.

In the Biblical story Elisha then threw the stick into the Jordan and brought to the surface the axe-head his disciple had lost (cf. 2 Kings 6:6); that is to say, he revealed a thought which his disciple believed to be hidden deep within him and he exposed it to the view of those present. Here the Jordan signifies speaking about repentance, for it was in the Jordan that John performed the baptism of repentance. Now if someone does not speak accurately about repentance, but makes his listeners despise it by failing to communicate its hidden power, he lets the axe-head fall into the Jordan. But then a stick—and this signifies the cross—brings the axe-head up from the depths to the surface. For prior to the cross the full meaning of repentance was hidden, and anyone who tried to say something about it could easily be convicted of speaking rashly and inadequately. After the Crucifixion, however, the meaning of repentance became clear to all, for it had been revealed at the appointed time through the wood of the cross."[1]

To me, one reason why all this is so important on the esoteric path is reasonably clear: it is only when I remember in the right way, with the heart, and not simply with the head, that something important and very desirable happens to me. Then, all that is personal and trivial falls away. Then, I am all too briefly drawn toward a new clarity, a new breadth, a new peace. This shift of our awareness from being head-centered to being heart-centered is one factor in *metanoia*. But it is always so difficult to explain this difference, or even to remember it. This is why the idea of *repentance* loses its power. At the same time, true repentance depends on grace: on the Spirit of Repentance, as Saint Anthony named it right back at the beginning of Christian monasticism.

Modern Views of Metanoia

P sychological methods of working toward *metanoia* survive today in the Eastern Church, and particularly in its monasteries these methods are little changed over nearly two thousand years. But how is *repentance* understood on the Royal Road?

One key to both these questions also defines the Christian conception of psychological development, which is ontological, a concept of development of being. The characteristic of this view is that both the cause and the result of *metanoia* is a living awareness of the Spirit of God. This key can be found in the famous passage in which Saint Seraphim of Sarov is reported to have answered an unspoken question of N. A. Motilov as follows:

> "The Lord has revealed to me," said Saint Seraphim, "that in your childhood you had a great desire to know the aim of our Christian life. . . . But no-one has given you a precise answer. They have said to you: 'Go to church, pray to God, do the commandments of God, do good—that is the aim of the Christian life . . . do not seek things which are beyond you. . . . But they did not speak as they should.
>
> " . . . Prayer, fasting, vigil and all other Christian practices, however good they may be in themselves, do not constitute the aim of our Christian life, although they serve as the indispensable means of reaching this end. The true aim of the Christian life consists in the acquisition of the holy Spirit of God."[2]

In the last chapter, we began to define what it means to acquire the Holy Spirit. It begins with *diakrisis*, with *discrimination of spirits*. This leads to a shift from a self-centered, anthropocentric life, driven by the spirit of the world, to a God-centered, theocentric life, focused upon the Spirit of God: a life in which the living presence, the "influence from outside ordinary life," has become the core and goal of our being. A more recent Russian author in the esoteric tradition summarized the situation, writing about "Westernized" man that his present state is so unnatural that he is spiritually starved until he learns to return to his natural condition. This idea links with the description given by Maurice Nicoll (see p. 210 below), but takes the idea of turning the mind around out of a purely intellectual context, and gives it greater depth. This commentator, the émigré founder of the French Orthodox Church, wrote: "The tragedy of original sin is that the world is turned upside-down. The spirit should be nourished by God and breathe Him. The soul should be nourished by the spirit and breathe it. The body should be nourished by the soul and breathe it. And the world should be nourished by the human body and breathe it. Having turned away from God, having reversed the values, cut off the contact between him and the Creator— which is the first death—the human spirit lost its true nourishment and breathing. I said nourishment and breathing, and you have already guessed that it is because Christ said 'I am your food,'[3] and the Holy Spirit is called by that name: Spirit, Breath, Air, Wind."[4] This accurately describes the problem resolved by *apatheia*, the end result of the second of the three renunciations (see chapter 7). The second renunciation is to renounce those desires that disturb the emotions.

Theophan the Recluse also said about this, referring to what he described as the final result of the Fall: "The spiritual self had power over the soul and body while it was in living communion with God. Then it received divine power from Him. When living communion with God was cut off, so was the flow of divine power. Left to itself, the spirit could no longer master the soul or body, but was taken captive by them. Then the soul—and through it the body—assumed control over man, so that his life revolved around them. The spirit remained in him but no longer had any power. It still made its presence felt, sometimes through fear of God, sometimes through remorse from the conscience."[5] It is clear that to reverse or overcome this Fall and so reconnect us to the divine Spirit, a radical change of direction in our psyche, a total *metanoia*, is required . . . and that it is this that demands a complete change in our being and our consciousness.

Saint Gregory of Sinai, another early Father, here describes the inner mechanism by which grace leads to inner clarity and sows the seed of a different consciousness: "The Holy Spirit attracts the nous to itself, drawing it into the depth of the heart and preventing its usual wandering about."[6] This condition stabilizes the mind and gives it authority. In practical terms, however, the necessity is to reach this state, to achieve *metanoia*.

Metanoia *as Change of Being*

This whole book is about *metanoia*, about the whole process of psychological change that forms the main subject of the esoteric tradition. Yet if *metanoia* is understood at all today, it is not sufficiently understood. Psychologically, *metanoia* is now seen mainly on an intellectual level. This is a result of our loss of understanding of how the old psychology of the Fathers viewed things. Attempted without this understanding, the idea of *metanoia* almost always becomes, as it has been said, like a "headless axe"; it turns what should be an intense psychological struggle into a feeble complacency. *Metanoia*, in its classical sense, is the result of the very difficult struggle needed to achieve a true change of heart. Taken merely as an intellectual change, it fails in this aim. And, as I have already suggested, in the gospel *metanoia* forms one of the key definitions of the Christian message: "I am not come to call the righteous, but sinners to repentance" (Matthew 9:13). Thus says the gospel. But to find the full meaning of this word *metanoia*, and to learn why it is offered not to the righteous, but to sinners, we must come at an answer to this question slowly.

First we must understand the nature of the change in our being that is possible on the inner path. This transformation depends on the liberation of the nous from the personal, the trivial, and the transient. Full change of being requires complete *metanoia*: total transformation of the nous. Western theology does not see how this experience fits into everyday life, although momentary changes of being are described in researches such as those of Alister Hardy[7] and were called peak experiences by Abram Maslow.[8] In fact, since change of being is sudden, the experience of *metanoia* is the moment of truth, the moment of real being, a transparency of the soul. We will remember such moments in our lives, and careful investigation suggests that serious seekers are driven by such memories and the desire to recapture them. But reality is now: to be is to be in the moment, and any pursuit of it in past or future is doomed to fail.

Diakrisis is only true if it leads toward this true change of the noetic heart. This has to be understood quite precisely. Any imprecision and there is no result, and then the statement appears untrue. Only one state has this effect on us. But at first thought it does not seem as if the process is entirely mysterious: very much the opposite. Effective *diakrisis* is nothing more than clear psychological perception, a perception of ourselves in the "light"[9] of the Spirit of repentance, and given form by real knowledge of our human nature. This perception may show us how we are obtaining and using spiritual energies; for example, it may show us that by using them in a selfish way we are wasting them and limiting our real possibilities. We may be using them to "top up" our energies, going to church or to some group meeting simply so that we will feel better, for example. And afterwards, in the next two or three days, we may lose everything again by using whatever energies we have gained simply to enjoy ordinary life. The discovery of this fact, if properly understood, and if we fully understand the alternative we are losing by this, will lead to our seeking ways of retaining and even increasing these energies every day. This search, if serious, will lead us to some form of psychological *metanoia*: some inner effort to free ourselves from these distortions. These may be removed through the active love of the Holy Spirit, but before this can act in us in this way, two conditions must normally[10] be met.

In his book *The New Man*, written in the late 1930s, psychologist Maurice Nicoll—a pupil of Jung, at one time named to succeed him, and then the only one of his students regarded by P. D. Ouspensky as able to teach in his own right—introduced the idea of repentance as a massive change in the psychology of the individual, first quoting the gospel saying that: "Except your righteousness shall exceed the righteousness of the scribes and Pharisees, ye shall in no wise enter the kingdom of heaven"

(Matthew 5:20). A few pages later in his book he described in some detail the kind of change necessary:

> no one can continue to justify himself in the way he has always done and expect to become another and a New Man . . . a man must come to realize that he is almost nothing as he is, and that all his vanity, merit, conceit, self-esteem, self-liking, self-satisfaction and self-love, and all his imagination of himself, is practically an illusion.
>
> It is indeed only possible to understand that harsh teaching of Christ[11] in view of its aim, which is to break up a man's whole psychology, the man as life has made him, the man he regards himself as, and make him think and feel and act in a new way, so that he begins to move towards a higher level, towards another state of himself that exists within himself as a possibility. For to pass from one level to another, from the state of an acorn to the state of a tree, everything must be rearranged and altered. All a man's ordinary relations with different sides of himself must alter. The whole setting of his being must change. The whole man must change.[12]

He then went on to write specifically about the Greek word *metanoia*.

> Meeting this higher order of truth a man can no longer be at peace with himself as he is. He must think in a new way—and no one can think in a new way by merely adding some extra knowledge to what he already thinks. The whole man must change—that is, his whole mind must change, first of all. This parable (Matthew 10:34–46) refers to the starting point of Christ's teaching, to metanoia (meta-nous)—to a man beginning to think beyond how he always thought, to think in an entirely new way about himself and his meaning and his aim. It is not repentance, as translated, but new thinking, over and above all that he thought before. In the same way, the righteousness that Christ speaks of is over and above and beyond all that man has justified himself by and regarded as being his righteousness, his idea of being right. It is, indeed, meta-righteousness.[13]

Here we have a problem. All that Nicoll says is correct, but it is easily misunderstood by modern man, specially by those who read quickly and skim over the text, taking in only what they can grasp immediately.

The fact of the matter is that he is correct in saying that a complete remaking of the mind is necessary. But we must understand by that the need for a complete change in the nous. Unless this happens, "ye shall in no wise enter the kingdom of heaven" (Matthew 5:20).

The problem is that, although literally accurate, the meaning has been given a kind of English coloration by taking the idea of *metanoia* intellectually, applying it to the activity of the mind, not to the still nous. This mistake can easily happen, as everyday English language draws little distinction between different kinds of knowledge. Where the Greek used by the Fathers has several entirely different words, all of them are normally translated in English by the one word *knowledge*. Some of these words refer to verbal knowledge, some to direct perception, others to the cognition of the heart that is little understood today in the English-speaking world, but is essential understanding for those who would understand the inner meaning of the Gospels. The "new thinking" implied in the word *metanoia* includes a radical change in the *content* of our thoughts. But this is not all it implies; it also involves a change in the quality of *consciousness* itself. This aspect has been at least partially ignored as the result of difficulties of translating from Greek to modern English—which has no word for the change of consciousness implied.

Even more difficult than the problem of translating words relating to *knowledge* into English is the translation of those concepts that we speak of as reason, intellect, intelligence, and so on. Here, the Greek not only seems to have more words, but sometimes, even today, and almost always in the Greek of the first centuries of Christianity, there is a difference in meaning between these Greek words that is quite clear-cut, while the English equivalents are not clearly distinguished, at least in modern thought.

One word in particular that has caused much difficulty is the Greek word *nous*, which is sometimes translated as "reason," sometimes as "intellect," but is not equivalent to the everyday meanings of either of these words. Because this word with its derivatives is clearly one of the keys to understanding certain gospel ideas, long, vituperative arguments go on among scholars to this day over how this word is to be translated. In fact, taking into account modern usage of the words, it makes more sense to translate *nous* by the word "intelligence" than by either "reason" or "intellect," since intellect and reason are forms or aspects of our intelligence, while the latter word has overtones of *understanding* and of grasping or responding to meaning. The meaning given this word in biological science, where it implies a broad ability to adapt, not on a purely intellectual level, is also appropriate to certain levels of the *nous*.

So what is perhaps implied in his words, but has certainly not been completely understood by the readers of Nicoll's book, is that this *metanoia* involves a very great deal more than a change of mind, much more than a change in our thinking. It does not simply mean taking our thoughts beyond normal limits—although it *begins* in that way. It involves going beyond normal thought and normal knowledge, as in the poetic phrase of

Saint John of the Cross: "transcending reason with my thought." *Metanoia* is a total transformation of the *nous*, an actual change in the "center of gravity" of the intelligence, and it is by studying the nature of this transformation that we can in fact obtain a more complete understanding of both words, *nous* and *metanoia*.

> Lie not one to another, seeing that ye have put off the old man with his deeds;
>   And have put on the new man, which is renewed in knowledge after the image of him that created him (Colossians 3:9–10).

To the extent in our *metanoia* that we achieve *apatheia*, in either a transient or permanent way, we become able to discover the special spiritual stillness (*hesychia*) of the Eastern monks: *hesychia* is to still the nous in God. But there is another paradox here. In the awakening that should follow *apatheia* comes what Theophan calls *zeal*.

This is what Kovalevsky meant when he said, as quoted a little earlier, that "The spirit must be nourished by God and breathe Him."

> And when the men of that place had knowledge of him, they sent out into all that country round about, and brought unto him all that were diseased;
>   And besought him that they might only touch the hem of his garment: and as many as touched were made perfectly whole (Matthew 14:35–36).

As one Athos monk said, the hem of the robe of Christ is within us. If we are humble, then we will see that to touch it is to be made whole. By touching on God within ourselves we are emotionally fed. Emotionally fed, we become inwardly still. This is *hesychia*: one aspect of what Saint Seraphim means when he speaks of acquiring the Holy Spirit.

What is involved was well described by Archimandrite George Capsanis, Abbot of Osiou Grigoriou on Mount Athos. Like many of the twenty Athos abbots, Father George still teaches repentance today in ways that go back to the tradition of the early Fathers. To put this view of *metanoia*, we must first look at the wider, more emotional context within which the Athonite monk approaches these questions, to the idea in Orthodox theology that man, "made in the image of God" (Genesis 1:27), must learn to manifest that image in a "likeness" to God. "In Spirit you shall see the Son, in the Son you shall recognize the Father. In the light of the Spirit you shall see the effulgence of My glory; in the image, the archetype; from your own selves, the superessential."[14]

A few years back, in an address, Father George said: "In order to live authentically, we must live every moment theocentrically." He then added: "If we deny God, we deny and destroy ourselves." Before this in the same address he had said that the idea that we were " 'made in the image of God,' signifies both the origin and the goal of our existence."[15] And a paragraph or so later he added: "Human existence owes its dynamism and its greatness to its 'iconic' character. So far as we 'image forth' the wise and creative God, so far do we discover in ourselves the charisms of knowledge and creativity."[16]

It is a question of discovering God within ourselves, of manifesting faculties previously only manifested at a higher level. By this, humanity evolves and what is truly human—because it is "in the image of God"—emerges in human life. But most of us are not like this: most of us still live in a self-centered way; as it is sometimes put today, "we live in our heads." More than anything else, it is to change this that *repentance* is necessary. And if it is true, as often said, that the strongest force in the ordinary human life is sexuality, then to repent, to turn life around, we have to transform our *natural eros* into a *divine eros*. Then—and only then—this energy that lends its strength to our everyday desires instead will strengthen our desire for the Lord. It is at this point that the Christian life develops its additional emotional power, the force that Theophan the Recluse calls *zeal*. This, according to Father George, is the discovery of the fact that "the sexual urge is an expression of that natural yearning which is implanted within us by our creator, and leads us towards him."[17]

Theophan the Recluse spoke of the same thing, directly linking the motivating force of our lives, the will, with this *eros* as its source of energy. This process of transformation of the eros relates to the Freudian model in a way that explains and radically changes this model, leading to quite different practical conclusions whose implications, in a society now driven by the "Freudian ethic," could be quite enormous.

The Freudian view would appear to be based on a limited view of the classical Greek use of the term *eros*, a use that has been reinforced by the fact that most Christian material on the subject, which was almost all of monastic (or hermetic) origin, was concerned with suppression of the generative forms of *eros*, and said little about any alternative or "higher" forms. There is a strong possibility that Puritan streams of thought, themselves an aberration to the Christian mainstream, had contributed to this narrowing of translations and interpretations, but that requires further investigation. The Puritan model would appear to represent a shift from the transformative to the repressive view . . . a shift that is consistent with the Puritan emphasis on penance, rather than on forgiveness.

The early Christians borrowed the classical Greek term *eros* as they did other key psychological terms, with a subtle but significant change that emphasized the higher of its pre-Christian meanings, the ontological meaning implied in its use as the name of a god. This difference in meaning leads to two fundamental differences in practical use:

1. A difference in meaning, which sees eros as a divine force, a force of the divine love debased by the Fall of man, but a force that can be redeemed and used to lift man to the highest states of spirituality.
2. Implied in this, a difference in practice, which sees the need to transform or redeem the eros, not destroy or suppress it.

This is in part to say, as Boris Mouravieff has said, that the only true emotion is love, but that this love must be purified, for "blessed are the pure in heart."

And the love that draws us to God does not at the same time attract us to selfish interest or advantage. If we realize this, we can be sure that there are different levels or qualities of love.

Everybody knows that the Bible tells us "God is love."[18] But at this point Abbot George takes this idea further by quoting Saint Maximos, who wrote:

> "At times scripture refers to God as desire (eros), and at other times as love (agape), and at still other times as the desirable and the beloved. Being Himself desire and love, He moves towards us while, as desirable and beloved, He moves all those creatures toward Himself who are capable of desiring and loving. It is thus that the great apostle, Saint Paul, having come into possession of divine desire, and become a participant of the ecstatic power, cries out inspired: 'I live, yet not I but Christ lives in me.' He speaks as a lover and—as he says himself—as one caught up in the ecstasy of God. No longer living his own life, but instead that of the beloved, which alone is beauty surpassing speech."
>
> Therefore [adds Abbott George in his own words], we understand the erotic power of the soul, at its deepest level, to be our thirst for the depths of our own being. That thirst can only be slaked when we achieve the goal for which we were made: union with our Archetype, with God—what the Orthodox tradition calls "deification."

He then quotes Saint Nicholas Cabasilas as saying: "The thirst of human souls requires infinite waters."[19]

It is the discovery of these infinite waters that is called *theosis*.

But in most cases we have yet to *recognize* our "thirst for the depths of our own being." And until it is recognized by frequently experiencing it, we will continue to lose sight of it . . . and so forget ourselves.

One of the key passages underlying the ascetic methods of the Eastern Church is found in a letter written by Saint Anthony the Great. This explains that the real work of repentance is done by what Saint Anthony calls the Spirit of Repentance,[20] a spiritual influence that plays different parts at different stages. This first drives us to act in ways that lay the foundations of inner life. With the reinforcement of good teaching from those whose memories of spiritual experience are clear, this can take us on to the point of richer experience, which in its turn leads to the second stage of faith. To understand what happens at this point, we must see that the published translation of this letter, which speaks of mind, is in fact speaking of the discriminating faculty.

Saint Paul and the Ascetic Struggle

I n its Christian form, the possibility of making efforts for repentance, for *metanoia*, was emphasized by Saint Paul when he said that in order to become good Christians we must try our best. He also emphasized that to "win the race" required *temperance*; we must not waste energy, but retain it until we have enough to allow a change in our nature.

> Know ye not that they which run in a race run all, but one receiveth the prize? So run, that ye may obtain.[21]
> And every man that striveth for the mastery is temperate in all things. Now they do it to obtain a corruptible crown; but we an incorruptible (1 Corinthians 9:24–25).

This is the origin of ascesis: ascesis, in the inner, psychological sense, is action that leads to improved ability. Macarius added to this a little: "Christians ought to run the race in the arena of this world with alertness and exactitude, so as to receive the heavenly reward from God and the angels."[22]

The words of Saint Paul confirm the connection of ascesis and repentance. To my mind, the basis of this connection is that true love, the love that originates from Christ, is simple and totally unselfish. But if we are honest with ourselves, if we struggle with and observe ourselves, we will admit that we have the habit of *desiring* what we love. This habitual egotism, which forms a major element in the human personality,[23] is formed early in our lives but continues (and becomes more exaggerated) into old age unless we learn to prevent it. As it takes form it obscures our consciousness, and this in turn makes us more and more rigid and narrow. The process of its formation appears to be complex,[24] and Freud's links of this to infantile and later to erotic reactions obviously contain more than a germ of truth, as it consists of associative memory links between the psyche and the body. This reinforces the power of particular memories or makes them too easily available.

Observation of this whole process is developed below in chapter 14 which discusses the Orthodox monastic view of the process of *provocation*, a practical analysis of the arousing and developing of these egotistic distortions. This is followed by a study of ways of overcoming them, originally given in Evagrius's *Praktikos*, which thus forms one of the most helpful psychological guides for those beginning to engage in the inner struggle. Clement of Alexandria speaks of this: "repentance is high intelligence. For he that repents of what he did, no longer does or says as he did. But by torturing himself for his sins, he benefits his soul. Forgiveness of sins is therefore different from repentance; but both show what is in our power."[25]

Evagrius was most specific. He saw the primary objective of ascesis as being to purify the emotions: "The ascetic life is the spiritual method for cleansing the affective part of the soul."[26] In Evagrius's own terms, this is the pursuit of *apatheia*: of the purity of heart necessary to those who would know God. In the Gospel of Saint Matthew the same idea is expressed in the famous story of the mote and the beam. But most people have wondered at some time how it might be possible to get a great wooden beam in one's eye. The answer is that this is in the language of parable, using inexact and exaggerated terms—a "beam"—to show us that it is analogy for an inner reality.

> And why beholdest thou the mote that is in thy brother's eye, but considerest not the beam that is in thine own eye?
>
> Or how wilt thou say to thy brother, Let me pull out the mote out of thine eye; and, behold, a beam is in thine own eye?
>
> Thou hypocrite, first cast out the beam out of thine own eye; and then shalt thou see clearly to cast out the mote out of thy brother's eye (Matthew 7:3–5).

Monastic Forms of Ascesis

What habits do we have that must change? We can get some idea from this list of ascetic methods of repentance, again provided by Father George and found in the same source. In it he lists methods of repentance, used in Eastern monasticism today, that include:

1. All-night vigil
2. Fasting
3. Prayer
4. Cutting off the will
5. Obedience (to an "elder" as to Commandments)

And of course we must add one he describes but does not include in his list:

6. The struggle with eroticism

"In the practice of these," says our Abbot, "he (the monk) forces himself to deny his private and selfish will, and to love God's will. A monk is 'a perpetual forcing of nature.' The word of the Lord is thus fulfilled: 'The kingdom of heaven is taken by violence, and the violent take it by force.' "[27]

A similar list that differs in detail but not in principle was given by Nicetas Stethatos, a pupil of Saint Symeon the New Theologian, who linked the senses with different forms of asceticism. The comments are mine.

1. Ascesis of the eyes is linked with vigil, perhaps since the eyes are the normal source of distraction by the outside world, and vigil separates us from the normal activities of the world.
2. Ascesis of the hearing is found in many forms of meditation, and this links with the fact that the flood of thoughts "competes" with the hearing of the ear. We cannot listen attentively to sound without becoming deaf to thoughts, and vice versa. (Although we can take in both together in a half-hearted way.)
3. Ascesis of the sense of smell is linked with prayer, which is more difficult to understand.
4. Ascesis of taste is associated with self-control, and I imagine that this is because the pursuit of taste makes fasting impossible.
5. Ascesis of touch links to stillness, and perhaps you can feel why this is so?

In this view, then, prayer is a form of ascesis. For those who cannot live a monastic life, it is one of very few major forms of ascesis possible to them. The other is service: *intentional* persistence in and completion of difficult tasks.

A. Posoff, a Russian who wrote extensively on the subject in German, but has not yet been published in English, wrote:

Prayer is the universal form of asceticism, since it unites the external and interior forms of ascetic practice.

Prayer includes the necessary elements of interior asceticism: attentiveness, concentration and meditation. In the

Mysticism of Reason (speculative mysticism) prayer is regarded as a form of external asceticism since it is often connected with rites, has a verbal form (*logos prophorikos*) and is directed from the Self to the Not-Self,[28] whereas interior asceticism is thought to consist of concentration on the Self. But individual prayer does exist apart from ritual, and there is such a thing as the inner word (*logos endiathetos*), which indeed plays a very important part in noetic prayer. The directing of the Self to the Not-Self benefits the Self, uniting it with the source of life, with fire and light, with the divine Not-Self. In prayer the mind goes beyond the limits of the human into the realm of the divine, and the great power of prayer is in this freeing of the Self from the abyss of subjectivism.

According to Saint Isaac the Syrian, the heart is a spiritual "altar of the Lord," on which the intellect (nous) offers to God the sacrifice of pure prayer.

Along with the intellect, the soul too prays in the heart, and the body is attentive to the prayer. In the Jesus Prayer of the mind and heart, or noetic meditation, all three parts of the human triad are most fully and perfectly unified in one common activity of their powers. This integrating and synthesizing role of prayer is one of its great secrets. In prayer the human triad forms a hierarchical harmony, each member with its parts finding its place and its own voice in the symphony of the whole. Herein lies the great significance of the practice of ascetic prayer; herein lies the great healing role of the true religion of Christ the Logos. There is no other practice in which the powers and functions are so ideally interrelated as in prayer. Disharmonious prayer is not pure, and God, who sees into the heart of man, will not accept such prayer. Temporary at first, the harmony of the heart becomes lasting and stable with practice, until in ascetic perfection it becomes continuous, unending and inviolable, making the perfected man a member of the kingdom of the Logos-Christ while still in this earthly life.

This is why the concentration of the mind in the heart in the noetic Jesus Meditation, the prayer of the mind in the heart which is connected with repetition of the name of Jesus, was regarded by all the eastern church ascetics as the highest form of asceticism. It is a joint activity of the inner and outer man and, as such, is a great unifying force. Noetic prayer, most of all, intimately unites the two, completely overcoming the dyad, the duality of the outer and inner man.[29]

Agrypnia: The All-Night Vigil Service

Monastic methods of asceticism include the *agrypnia* service or all-night vigil. Vigils are for physical and psychological ascesis, since they demand superefforts of remembrance, for keeping watch over oneself, and for re-membrance of God, hence their long but varying duration. A typical monastic joke is what one of the Athos hermits was supposed to have said about an unusually long service: "Fifteen hours is too long. Twelve or thirteen is reasonable, but fifteen hours is just too long!"

Now let me talk about my own experience of these vigils, beginning with the first I ever experienced.

I was not aware of this monastic joke when I emerged from the guest dormitory of the monastery of Simonas Petra within a minute or so of the bell, and hovered, with the evening sunlight streaming into the window, at the top of the staircase down to the *katholikon*. I was simply wondering when the vigil would begin. Had I known this old story, I might have been less eager. It is now clear to me that vigils are composite superefforts: many superefforts in one service.

"Not yet," said the *archontarion*, the guest-house master, just then returned to duty. "Ten minutes, then it rings again. Then you can go in."

We returned to our benches. A tide of activity built up in the mon-astery, and then the bell rang again: three slow strokes, then a repetition of three fast, three more fast, seven fast, a 3–3–7 pattern repeated several times.

As we walked into the narthex of the church, past the big modern frescoes in the covered court beside the door, the tapping of the *semantron* (a wooden sounding-board used to call people to services, first introduced when the occupying Turks prohibited the use of bells) approached down the corridor. Monks ducked through the iron door of the *katholikon* in ones and twos, closing it gently with a solid clunk, and kissed the icons either side of the archway opening into the *litei* (the nave, or second room of the church). Most of them went on into that next room. The service began softly with single voices in the background. The church at this stage was almost entirely dark, with no more than four or five tiny flames to light it.

After a while, the singing began again. Figures came and went. The Royal Doors of the *iconostasis* (the icon screen in front of the sanctuary) were opened and the priests—still in their black monastic robes—could be seen dimly by the light of many candles.

Between the speaking and the singing, it seemed as if they were enacting tableaux, many of them with striking similarities to some of the more common icon designs. "No," said one of the monks recently, "it is the icons that are derived from the liturgy." As I watched, strongly aware at that early stage in my search that I had no chance to discuss what I saw, I remembered what I had once heard and understood about the language of symbolism . . . the language that conveys more than words, and particularly conveys more to the heart. Surely this was an example, but if so, there was no quick way of comprehending; only repeated exposure would do it, especially from the restricted vantage point available to the "unorthodox" that night. One thing that was noticeable was what seemed a degree of precision, of care in posture and positioning, and in getting the tableaux visually correct.

What was very clear was that too much explanation, too much information given in simplified form for tourists, would not help but would prevent any real understanding of whatever "message" was borne in this drama. The heart comes to knowledge without benefit of explanation.

As the hours passed, and the service grew more complex, I noticed that the yellow light was becoming brighter. In the domed *katholikon* church a monk with a long pole was lighting the candles of the great *polyelios* chandelier, one by one. The Greek word *polyelios* is the name given to the great twenty-foot-diameter chandelier that hangs below the central dome of each Athonite *katholikon*. The word means *many suns*, giving a clue to the symbolism of these chandeliers. Watching it swing at key moments during the long vigil one is somehow brought to mind that the uncreated light arises at many points within that darkness of the cave that occurs in so many icons, which symbolizes the true "poverty of spirit," that consciousness without content which can by grace be found within us. This light is also within everyone, "but the darkness comprehendeth it not."[30]

It is met sometimes in prayer, or when we are very close to death. Within the darkness the uncreated light may be found. Meeting it changes us.

Next the monk, with his smoking taper at the top of a long pole, lit the candles of a smaller central chandelier. Then he set both chandeliers swinging, a great symbol showing the emergence of the light within and without: to the stars, to the communicant, as an "infusion" that brings joy and health to every cell in the body. The great brass chandelier, twisted some thirty degrees on its long chains dropped down from the darkness of the dome. Then it checked and swung back. It continually repeated this movement, while within it the smaller chandelier rotated in close circular orbit. Below, the monks passed in their black robes. The chanting continued in the background. The whole pattern conjured up images of the Mevlivi mukhabile, that strange ceremony of J'al addin Rumi's whirling dervishes that celebrates the turning of the planets. They make their pilgrim's escape from self-concern by this strange circling ceremony. In the same way, the great swaying chandelier symbolizes the creation by its "explication" of dancing shadows in a way that echoes Plato's story of the shadows in his parable of the cave, and yet so modern that it would have delighted David Bohm had he seen it.

It is difficult to clearly arrange the memories of that night in proper time sequence. I remember the arrival of the abbot. Some time after the start of the service two monks came in by the door near where I sat. I heard a staff tap the floor once. The new arrivals kissed the icons and passed on, into the nave and then into the sanctuary. Again the staff tapped once.

In instant obedience, the pattern of activity in the church changed. The *geronte* stood there, and dark figures came to him one by one, each helping to transform him, clothing him with rich vestments of gold, a surplice covered with black crosses such as those shown on Athos on the icons of Saint Nicholas and other bishops. The staff, when I saw it later, was black with a Y-shaped head of two leaping golden fish, astonishingly impressive. Now the abbot took charge of the ceremony. His voice sounded loud and sonorous in the intervals between the singing. The priests began to appear in rich vestments instead of their black robes. Another door was opened into a further sanctuary, ablaze with candles. On this first visit to the Holy Mountain, I did not understand much of what was going on, but was struck by the close coordination of the priests at a time when monks were still coming and going to the church, as they did throughout this extremely long ceremony. The whole service became an icon of Orthodoxy, of authority without automatism, of true spiritual unity.

There were recognizably different stages to the ritual, making the whole long vigil into an icon of *theosis* (deification), the entry of man into God through the entry of God into man. At one stage, the priests were kissed on both cheeks by the abbot, one by one, again reminiscent.

There was a great deal of movement between the two sanctuaries. Later I saw one of the monks lighting the candles on the smaller single chandelier in the *litei* (the nave) of the church. The candles in the *katholikon* (choir) had been extinguished, the veil drawn, and the activity and the light moved into the open church. An elaborate stand was placed in the doorway, and an icon placed on it with great reverence. Around this icon, priests circumambulated. For some time just one priest, my friend Father I. Father I., walked with book and candle. Then the age ended, as it were . . . the light in the nave was extinguished, the veil opened, and the great chandeliers were ablaze and swinging yet again. It was about this time that, lulled by the chanting and the penetrating stillness of the service, I fell asleep in my seat . . . leaving all as mystery.

Waking briefly, I crept off softly to bed, to be woken again by bell and *semantron* for the continuation of the service in the early morning.

Vigils surely are a formalized example of what Gurdjieff called *superefforts*. The monks clearly approve the effort one makes to complete the service; indeed, on one occasion, when I had made the effort to walk to Grigoriou— for me almost six hours of walking the mountain paths, extended over two days, only to find that the next night was the night of the vigil—the abbot signified his approval when I completed the vigil on my feet. The sign: when I had to move on to another monastery the next day, as I waited for the little caïque that calls at the coastal monasteries every morning, one of the monks came up to me. "Don't take the boat," he said. "The monastery will provide." Sure enough, I was conveyed to my destination in solitary splendor in the small monastery boat, steered by the barefoot Father Nectarios, the monastery's fisherman—an unheard-of privilege, but a typical example of the reinforcing gestures that on Athos make up an unexplained part of the unwritten tradition.

As I have returned to Athos and experienced many of these vigils, I have begun to discover why that reinforcement was so important, and why the monks welcome these at first sight exhausting services. I cannot find any reference to it in the texts, but experience speaks louder than words. The effect is cumulative, and through the effort to conquer sleep and sustain attention, vigil combines multiple forms of ascesis—physical, psychological, and noetic—to form the foundations of a life of prayer. In this process it clearly reconstructs the solar plexus and counteracts many of the effects of our modern way of life, providing an effective method of restoring what von Durkheim described by the Japanese word *hara*.[31]

Fasting

The truest level of fasting demands the authority of that "other I." For me, fasting has always been a problem. Although there are medical reasons for this problem, and fasting was never intended to become a destructive process, judging by the way I take to the medical excuse to avoid fasting it might just as well have been created by the devil himself. Yet it is clear that intelligent fasting helps people break away from the domineering authority of the body, with its preemptory demands. And I do not mean by "intelligent" fasting that we should give up the fast as soon as it becomes difficult. That is stupid fasting: to go to all that trouble for no result.

Today most churches have standard formulae for fasting, but in fact fasting has a long history; from the Book of Isaiah, for example, it is possible to obtain a much broader view of fasting, one in which the individual chose or formed a resolution on his or her own initiative. Fasting was then *intentional*, but not necessarily always the same; it was an expression of individual intention and individual intelligence. Fasting according to our understanding, instead of according to rule, helps to make sure that the intention comes from the understanding of the heart.

There is another clue about the nature of intelligent fasting. As you attempt to fast, whether successful or not, you will observe that there are two forces that drive you to eat. One is the simple force of genuine hunger. The other is the desire for *pleasure* from your food. A Yoga text advises the pupil not to eat for enjoyment. Many of the early Fathers of the church distinguished between two kinds of desire; we today put it slightly different: we distinguish between *wants* and *needs*.

Needs are physical. If the body is deprived of its needs beyond a certain point, functional harm—what medicine calls functional illness—can be the result. To fast beyond this point, and thus damage the body given us by God, would be *stupid fasting*, but as individuals we can explore to find out what our limits are in reality.

On the other hand, say the Fathers, *wants* are psychological: when we want to enjoy food, this belongs to the *psyche*.

The solution in the more serious monasteries is on fast days to eat food that is not appetizing. Some of the Eastern monasteries make this a general rule except on feast days.

Saint Anthony the Great has this to say about it: "And to those who seek purity in this, the Spirit assigns rules of purification, to eat in moderation sufficient for the strength of the body, but in so doing not to have the taste of concupiscence; and in this way the saying of Paul is fulfilled, 'Whether ye eat or drink, or whatever ye do, do all to the glory of God' " (1 Corinthians 10.31).

For those who must live in the busy world, with neither monastic rule nor the presence of a spiritual guide, to distinguish between *wants* and *needs* can form a practical solution: to try on fast days to eat food that is wholesome but not appetizing and, on other days, or for those who are not subject to a fasting rule, to eat only for hunger and to stop eating whenever you realize that you have had all you *need*, that you are now eating only for pleasure.

But to do this you have to learn to discriminate, to *recognize* the difference between these two ways of eating, and to catch yourself as soon as possible after you stop eating for need and begin to eat only for flavor.

Such an *intelligent fast* is quite different in quality from an enforced fast.

One way in which it is different is that it is more precisely targeted against bitterness and *anger*. Observation will show us that the most common thing that makes us angry is to be deprived of some pleasure. Even the fear of being deprived is sufficient. At the end of his great work on prayer, *The Praktikos*, Evagrius of Pontus quoted a story about a monk near Alexandria who once said about the fast he made from his own understanding: " 'I have this reason for putting aside pleasure—that I might cut off the pretext for growing angry. For I know that anger constantly fights for pleasures and clouds the mind with passion that drives away contemplative knowledge.' "[32]

Here are the mainsprings of our culture of contentment[33] laid bare for those who can see. In our continuous pursuit of pleasure lie sleeping the seeds of the bitterness and anger that fuel our politics. But to overcome this by fasting from the understanding of the heart, we must first understand the possible reasons for fasting. There is more than one such reason. The Gospel of Saint Matthew says:

> Then came to him the disciples of John, saying, Why do we and the Pharisees fast oft, but thy disciples fast not?
>
> And Jesus said unto them, Can the children of the bridechamber mourn, as long as the bridegroom is with them? but the days will come, when the bridegroom shall be taken from them, and then shall they fast (Matthew 9:14–15).

Bishop Germain, successor of Eugraph Kovalevsky, Bishop Jean of Saint Denys, interprets this text in a way that confirms the idea that fasting—from food or from "mental self-indulgence"—is a way of transforming what are now sometimes known as *negative emotions*.

> This passage of the Gospel is at the center of the justification for fasting. It links the absence of fasting to the presence of the Bridegroom, and the fact of fasting to the absence of the Bridegroom. It thus appears that fasting, in general, is linked to a lack, not only to the lack of food, but to a "lack of someone."
>
> As elsewhere, man, taken individually or collectively, is often irritated with himself. It is then that religious and cultural tradition in some parts of the world may suggest to him that he fast; for fasting is not only a religious phenomenon, it goes back to the origins of humanity. One fasts, and the irritation is removed. In retaining these two modes of fasting, fasting in the absence of someone, and fasting to reduce irritation, we trace this act back to the prehistoric cradle of humanity, to discover that Tradition provides it with an unshakable foundation. We will open the book of Genesis: II: 16–17. "You may eat of all the trees of the garden, but of the

tree of Knowledge of good and evil you may not eat, for the day that you eat of that you will surely die."[34]

If all this is true, and it makes more sense the more you consider it, then fasting also relates to the Fall, and in the beginning of the Book of Genesis the connection is made clear. Fasting is a test. Remember that Saint Anthony said that *the Spirit of Repentance* tests us in this way to ensure that we cannot be "turned back." Here, Bishop Germain speaks about the same thing:

> What does this signify, if not a fast of abstinence? It is a demand to abstain from something, a test, not a total fast, and not in a negative sense. No sin here. It is a test whose meaning is that of perfection. God tests man by a passive test because of his perfection. He demands an effort of abstinence from him, a fast: and He expects to be obeyed. Why? Is it to weaken the man? To see how he reacts? That would be a psychological test, not a spiritual test. God wishes to test the inmost heart, to verify the confidence, the faithfulness, the friendship, the love of the creature for his Creator. He faces him with two alternatives: with two influences, the influence of the world, involving a duality of good and evil, of antinomies, and the influence of the Lord, the Tree of Life itself. This is the test.
>
> This fast could be named the test of the love of God. "Man, are you able to love Me without reason, freely?" Do not forget that, in eating its fruit, the tree of the Knowledge of Good and Evil symbolizes union with the world. It is about this union with the world that God says to man: "are you capable of uniting with Me before uniting with the world?" The first question for man is the union with God. After that comes union with the world.[35]

So the first basis of fasting is that it is a test relating to the union of man with his Creator. The second basis is a test of man's ability to rise above the demands of the body, a means of acquiring power over desires and negative emotions. This is exactly described in certain instructions given by Jesus: "But I say unto you, That whosoever looketh on a woman to lust after her hath committed adultery with her already in his heart" (Matthew 5:28) and

> Then came Peter to him, and said, Lord, how oft shall my brother sin against me, and I forgive him? till seven times?
>
> Jesus saith unto him, I say not unto thee, Until seven times: but, Until seventy times seven (Matthew 18:21–22).

Both of these relate to the Fall: the Fall is signified by disobedience to the Creator, and also by captivity to what the Fathers called *passions*; to remembered pleasures that cause us to act "against our better nature," to put it over-simply.

This makes sense of the text from Isaiah that makes something more general of fasting when it says:

> Is it such a fast that I have chosen? a day for a man to afflict his soul? is it to bow down his head as a bulrush, and to spread sackcloth and ashes under him? wilt thou call this a fast, and an acceptable day to the LORD?
>
> Is not this the fast that I have chosen? to loose the bands of wickedness, to undo the heavy burdens, and to let the oppressed go free, and that ye break every yoke?
>
> Is it not to deal thy bread to the hungry, and that thou bring the poor that are cast out to thy house? when thou seest the naked, that thou cover him; and that thou hide not thyself from thine own flesh?
>
> Then shall thy light break forth as the morning, and thine health shall spring forth speedily: and thy righteousness shall go before thee; the glory of the LORD shall be thy rereward[36] (Isaiah 58:5–8).

Obedience and Cutting Off the Will

What does fasting really test: our obedience? What is this obedience that must be tested? Clearly it is not obedience to some man or organization, whatever has been claimed in the long and troubled history of the church. In the inner tradition, the obedience that is needed, the obedience that is tested, is the obedience of the mind, of the soul, to the divine Spirit.

In Russia there was a monk now known as Nils Sorski or Saint Nilus of Sora (1433–1588). He introduced the idea of the *skete* to Russia. And in his *skete* method, because of the shortage of enlightened elders, Nilus of Sora introduced a special method of *cutting off the will*. But the idea is far older than that. In the *Philokalia* we find: "We who live in coenobitic monasteries should of our own free choice gladly cut off our whole will through obedience to the abbot. In this way, with God's help, we shall to some extent become tractable and free from self-will. . . . If we do not cut off our self-will it will become enraged at those who try to compel us to cut it off; and then our incensive power will become abusively aggressive and so destroy that knowledge of the warfare which we have gained only after great effort."[37]

Today, in the monasteries on Athos, the cutting off of the will is done in obedience to the abbot or to some other "Spiritual Father." In the *sketes*, where there is not always a *starets* on hand, Sorski's alternative method of cutting off the will is that every participant becomes obedient to every other. You can see, then, that admission to such a community has a very high initial threshold. To say the least, the chance of making such a *skete* work in the English-speaking world at the moment would be very small. Certainly, you couldn't take people straight into it; they would need several years of preparation.

Think about this as a real question, one that, if answered in a particular way, would mean a complete change in your own way of life. Who would you trust to obey without reservation?

But this method has another application, valuable to nonmonastics because it can be applied to marriage, for instance, where both partners are seriously and sincerely participating on the esoteric path, and that is one interpretation of Boris Mouravieff's doctrine of polar beings.

Obedience to the Commandments

In its early days, Christianity had answers to the inner questions that today lead people to search in other lands, study other times, and go to other faiths for their answers. Our studies have shown that most of those answers still exist in the annals of Christianity. These answers can act in two ways, based on the two "limbs" on which inner Christianity stands.

1. They can change our ideas, our worldview, so that we think in a Christian way and see the world through Christian eyes.
2. They can then influence our actions, either by describing methods of prayer, of charity, and other forms of ascesis, by defining rules or *commandments* by which we might live in a Christian way, or by strengthening our force for this work, our motivation for carrying out those practices.

Commandments and rules provide one form of the obedience that is a key tool of esoteric psychology: they may be the Ten Commandments of Moses, the New Commandment of Christ, or the special rules and exercises of a monastic or another kind of esoteric school.

In practice, our ability to keep the commandments is closely dependent on a change in our worldview. Christian action, in prayer, in charity, or in obedience to Christian commandments, can only occur where we see the world through Christian eyes. This principle of *assent* exists in this Christian psychology at two related levels. Strongly held, an attitude of assent to Christian doctrine has the effect of leading us to assent to actions supported by that belief as we understand it, and prevents our carrying out actions which appear to us to conflict with that belief. Equally, we will not free ourselves from assenting to errors or delusions unless we make the effort intentionally to assent to the rules and doctrines of the church, or to a specific *rule* or code within that church. In our investigation we are discovering why this is so difficult to do today. One reason is a general lack of faith. Another is because today's religious rules and doctrines have often diverged from the early teachings that kept the faith, that remained consistent not only to inner experience but specifically to the intuitions of faith. If we lack this assent of faith, we will find ourselves assenting to anything that takes our fancy: "Blessed is the person who has consented to become the close friend of faith and of prayer: he lives in single-mindedness and makes prayer and faith stay with him."[38]

This hints at a principle the roots of which lie in everyday life, in *engineering knowledge*, as suggested, and in all practical knowledge founded on personal experience. It tells us that we can experience the fact that we can acquire knowledge not based on sensory experience, nor purely on intellectual apprehension. The principle is this: Through faith we assent to the commandment, and keeping the commandment confirms the object of faith, producing the knowledge (*gnosis*) that is the object of faith.

Commandments act to test us: they test the intentions of our hearts and reveal them to us, making us conscious of our state. If we fail to keep a commandment, this will tell us that we do not really believe in our hearts that the commandment is important. If we are weak, then we will learn the importance of commandments and rules only by observing for ourselves the harm done by the actions forbidden by each rule. Observing this helps us rid ourselves of illusions about ourselves and our beliefs.

Certain *rules* can also serve to test our consciousness, in the sense once described by P. D. Ouspensky. Then they act as *alarm clocks*, to use Ouspensky's term: when we find ourselves breaking such a commandment, we realize that our watchfulness, our *nepsis*, has vanished.

Nepsis is another psychological key to repentance. If you seek *metanoia*, ponder at length this passage written by the Blessed Callistus:

> This blessed or rather thrice-blessed water, I mean mental sobriety [Greek *nepsis*] of the soul, is like water gushing forth from the bowels of the earth. Water flowing from the source of the stream fills the stream; the water which gushes forth in the heart and is always, as it were, moved by the Spirit, fills the whole of the inner man with Divine dew and renders the outer man fiery.

> Purified of everything external and having entirely mas-
> tered the senses by active virtue, the mind rests unmoving
> within the heart, its vision established in the center. There it
> receives mental illuminations, like flashes of lightning, and
> thus collects Divine understandings.[39]

There is a more important meaning yet to *assent*: as Benedictine Abbot
Thomas Keating says (using the word *consent* in almost the sense that we
use *assent*), we can *consent* to the presence of God within us. This is the
basis of his method of *centering prayer*, which is very close to the method
described in the medieval *Cloud of Unknowing.*

At this point, the psychology of *assent* and the *assent to faith* become
one and the same thing. And it is in this *assent to faith* that, as Boris
Mouravieff put it in his *Gnosis*, faith through hope can become knowledge,
and then knowledge can become love.[40]

This is confirmed by St. Maximos in a passage alluded to earlier.
"The reward of self-mastery is detachment, and that of faith is knowledge.
And detachment gives rise to discernment, while knowledge gives rise to
love for God."[41]

The Struggle with Eroticism

To change our mind in the ordinary sense of the term is simply to change
how we think. *Metanoia* means much more than this: to change the mind
in unity with the heart. That is, the aim of *metanoia* is *theosis*. How does
theosis come about? By the continual struggle to want God before all else.

Father George says of this: "All the saints live the saying of Saint
Ignatius the God bearer: 'My *eros* has been crucified.' "[42] Then he clarifies
this in its relation to ordinary man, emphasizing that the relation of the
saints to God is erotic only in the sense that it is *a yearning*, not simply
an ethical transformation. It is this which becomes visible, this which
finally transforms even the bones of the saints.[43]

This deification, he says, is brought about by God and "suffered"[44]
by man. "Deified man is purified from the passions. Attending to the
prayers of the heart, he receives an experience of divine grace which
refreshes and comforts him. The most exalted experience of deification is
the vision of the light of Mount Tabor (Matthew 17:1–9), the uncreated
light. Deified people not only see this supernaturally, but indeed they are
themselves beheld within it—as has been witnessed to in the lives of many
saints."[45]

To make our *metanoia* real requires a redirection of *eros*. Boris
Mouravieff's teaching, in his book *Gnosis*, that we each have a "polar

being," is in effect a modern—or very ancient—answer to the question of transformation of eroticism. Fully developed in volume 3 of his *Gnosis*, but in a form that is almost incomprehensible except to those who have read and understood the first two volumes of the work, this touches on ways of transforming erotic love to the higher, theocentric or spiritual form of love sometimes known in the East as *undemanding love*.

Gregory of Nyssa clearly distinguishes the two directions of the *eros*, as well as confirming the doctrine about *diakrisis* and the esoteric interpretation of the Fall, when he writes:

> When the patriarch says to the rich man, "You received your share of good things by your life in the flesh," and concerning the beggar he says similarly, "This man fulfilled his duty by his life in suffering evils." Then he goes on to mention the gulf by which they are separated from each other. These words of his seem to indicate a great doctrine here. In my opinion, the doctrine is this: human life was originally uniform. . . . This opinion is attested by God's first law, which gave to mankind unstinting participation in every one of the good things of paradise, excluding only that which had as its nature a mixture of opposites, evil combined with good (Genesis 2.17). Death was set as penalty for the violator of this law. But man by the impulse of his free will voluntarily abandoned the portion unmixed with evil and took for himself the life compounded from opposites. Nevertheless the divine Providence did not leave our misguided will without the possibility of rectification. When those who had transgressed the law inevitably received the death which had been decreed for their transgression, that death divided human life into two parts, this part in the body and the part hereafter outside the body. The two parts do not have an equal measure of duration; one is circumscribed by a very short limit of time, while the other extends into eternity.[46]

Then he continues, a few lines later, describing the two ways in which man can respond to this situation and, in so doing, defines the Christian path of service in ways that again make it clear that this is very similar to Karma Yoga.

> Those who have not trained their reasoning and have not examined what is better spend gluttonously in the fleshly life the share of good which is owed to their nature, saving up nothing for the life hereafter. But those who manage their life with critical reasoning and self control, although in this short

life they are distressed by those misfortunes which trouble the senses, yet store up good for the subsequent age, so that the better portion is extended for them throughout their eternal life. So this is the gulf, in my opinion, which does not come from the opening of the earth, but is made by the decisions of human lives divided towards opposite choices. He who has persistently[47] pursued pleasure for this life and has not cured his misguided choice by repentance makes the land of the good inaccessible to him hereafter.[48]

By seeing what this teaching and the Athonite form have in common, we can perhaps learn the basic principles of this process. We have already seen (ix) that the monastic method is a "perpetual forcing of nature," in which the monk denies his will to self-satisfaction and attempts to make his whole life revolve around God in order to transform the heart which, no longer receiving satisfaction from any outward source, begins to love only the source of the inner satisfaction that is the grace of God. This is the *hesychastic* "crucifixion of the *eros*." It draws its full force from the successful arousing of prayer of the heart. And this intensity is important: a certain formula of the esoteric tradition says that to succeed, this desire should have the strength of thirst.

The Passions

For those who carry on this struggle in ordinary life, away from the monasteries and hermitages, the form of the struggle changes very slightly: it must continue even though the external situations of the world in which we find ourselves seem as worldly as they ever were. The struggle is still primarily the effort of guarding the thoughts, the effort of preventing uncontrolled response to *provocation*, in the terms used by the Russian Church, for example. It is the struggle with the *passions*, with remembered feelings that make us succumb to provocations for the pleasure they remind us of. Saint Maximos the Confessor defines *passion* in this way: "Passion is a movement of the soul contrary to nature either toward irrational love or senseless hate of something or on account of something material. For example, toward irrational love of food, or a woman, or wealth, or passing glory or any other material thing or on their account. Or else it can be toward a senseless hate of any of the preceding things we spoke of, or on account of any one."[49]

All these little efforts of which we become aware, all of them are "counted," even those that seem to fail. When I attempt to do something necessary instead of something merely distracting, this is counted for progress; for even to perceive what is happening is a success. When I attempt to do what somebody needs, instead of what I want, this too is counted, as also those events when I exert myself, do what I have to do in and for my own life, instead of letting the minutes—or the days—pass in a maze of daydreams. Whenever I do what before I could not do, then I have taken a step on the way of *metanoia*.

But we have to understand that there are two sources of passions in us, those which arise from the body and those which occur in the psyche for purely psychological reasons. Saint Maximos continues: "But I have said that the soul has also other passions apart from the body; and this we will now demonstrate. Pride is a sickness of the soul apart from the body; so also are boastfulness, envy, hatred, impatience, sloth and the rest. But if the soul gives itself to God wholeheartedly, God has mercy upon it and gives it the Spirit of Repentance, which testifies to it about each sin, that it may not again draw near to them; and shows it those who rise up against it and seek to prevent it separating itself from them, contending with it greatly that it may not abide in repentance."[50]

The term *passion* includes what recent teachings have described as *negative emotions*. To be more exact, negative emotions follow the frustration of our wishes, which are the positive side of the passions. They occur, says Gregory of Nyssa,[51] both as a form of "bodily" passion and as forms of purely psychogenic passions, so that, for example, as Fathers such as Evagrius describe, we can feel *anger* as a result of the disappointment of the *desire* for fine foods, or when our avarice or lust is disappointed.

But the Christian esoteric tradition is concerned not to punish these passions—including negative emotions—but to *transform* them. An analysis will show that the passions are a memory, a reflection of love in one or other of its forms. They derive their force from love, although often from remembered love. Their transformation, their redemption made possible by Christ's presence, is again found in purifying that love . . . in feeling it purged of the coloring normally added to it in memory. This begins when we no longer assent to the mere memory of love, but will have the thing itself and no imitation. It is about this that Saint Maximos the Confessor says: "Once the body is moved by the senses to its own lusts and pleasures, the careless mind[52] follows along and assents to its imaginings and impulses. The virtuous mind, in contrast, is in firm control and holds itself back from the passionate imaginings and impulses and instead concentrates on improving its emotions of this type."[53] This occurs when we respond to the impulse to repent. Saint Anthony wrote: "But if it endures and obeys the Spirit which counsels it to repentance, suddenly the Creator has mercy on the weariness of its repentance, and seeing its bodily toils, in much prayer and fasting and supplication and learning of the words of

God, in renunciation of the world, in humility and tears and perseverance in contrition, then the merciful God, seeing its toil and submission, has pity upon it and delivers it."[54]

Even partial success in this has an effect similar to that described by Father George when he defined the New Man by speaking of the change that occurs in the monk whose inner work progresses: "Victory over egoism and the passions makes the monk calm, meek, and humble, in a word— 'poor in spirit'—and a participant in all the virtues of the Beatitudes."[55]

A reminder: *metanoia* is change of heart. Without effort, without struggle, it is incomplete *metanoia*, the "headless axe" that cuts nothing, changes nothing! When it cuts, it produces "the virtues of the Beatitudes." Those who wish to walk the path of salvation, as seen by the esoteric tradition, must learn to make their *metanoia* real.

A Transformed Eros

B efore one gets into the "fine detail" of the struggle, it is helpful to have a broad view of repentance and the transformation of love, and here the present-day view of the monks of Mount Athos, contemporary successors to the early Fathers, is extremely useful, having survived since early times in a stream where continual attempts to apply it in practice have meant that the original meaning has been preserved. The basic principle of this is stated by Father George Capsanis: "Only if the heart of a man is continually being purified of egoism, of selfishness, and of the passions, is it capable through repentance of truly loving God and man. Egotism and love are incompatible."[56]

How is this to be done? Father George wrote a little earlier: "In order for the believer to be joined to Christ and to be made alive, he must first die to the old man by means of repentance. One must crucify and bury the old man (that is, egoism, the passions, and the selfish will) at the cross and tomb of Christ in order to rise with Him and walk in 'newness of life' " (Romans 6:4). This is the work of repentance and the carrying of the cross of Christ. Without repentance, the continual crucifying of the old man, the believer is incapable of believing evangelically.[57] He cannot give himself entirely to God and: 'Love the Lord with all his heart, and all his soul, and all his mind, and all his strength' (Mark 12:30)."[58]

The "redirection of *eros*" has a subtle effect described by one of the Fathers quoted in full in chapter 4, which ends:

> As physical water flows continually from its source, so
> the living water, gushing forth from the soul as soon as it is

opened, never ceases to flow. Flowing in the soul of the holy man Ignatius, it urged him to say: "There is in me no matter-loving fire, but water acts and speaks in me."[59]

Of course, this is not as easy as it seems. In this book we do not say too much about physical ascesis, because this is less a concern of the house-holder, and particularly because most lay seekers, and all those, including many monastics, who do not have the strength, the tremendous dedica-tion to begin with physical ascesis, or who have been too much exposed to life to have the heart for it, can, in general, find it in them to begin only with psychological and noetic forms of ascesis. Although this is more difficult to understand, noetic ascesis at its best introduces energies—the *living water*—which assist in the purification of the body, allowing the struggle with the body to develop more slowly, so that it only "comes to a head" at the very late stage when the student has developed in himself or herself the emotional motivation needed to overcome the body's de-mands. This approach must begin with self-observation, and with a psy-chological struggle that results from observation, and must continue with some form of noetic prayer; but the observation itself may be fueled by and centered about some practice such as the Jesus Prayer, or by some other form of centering prayer.

If we are normal Western men and women, it will take us some time to understand this science of repentance. One reason is because of the subtlety of the noetic process. The other is because most of the time we do not wish to know. There is a quite definite reason for this, and it is because whenever that which we must struggle against is ruling us, it makes us blind to inner truth. If completed, the "end" of either method is the same, but physical ascesis fails if it does not in time lead us to an awareness of the psychological causes of our physical indulgence and, through this, to a psychological transformation of mind and heart, while what begins as psychological ascesis fails if it does not eventually lead to such love of the Lord as to result in almost automatic mastery of the body. Physical ascesis that does not lead on to self-awareness leads to an inflated ego, while psychological ascesis that does not lead to self-control has remained theoretical and therefore ineffectual.

The Hospitality of Abba Moses

Hospitality is not included in Father George's list of forms of ascesis, yet it is a major part of the discipline of his monastery. In fact, one of the great problems of Christian spirituality has been the constant presence of two opposing and entirely valid demands: unworldliness, the demand that one turn away from the world, and responsibility, the equally valid demand that to love one's neighbor means to attend to and care for him or her.

On Mount Athos, these two demands have led to the existence of two different types of monastery. The two types are defined by the following story from *The Gerontikon*[60] about the black Father Moses. According to *The Gerontikon*, I was told, the Fathers consider that there are two ways for the monk: the way of withdrawal, of *hesychia*, and the way of hospitality, *philoxenia*, which was the great Greek virtue until the tourists came. The difference between these ways is described in a parable from one of the early Fathers, who spoke of a dream in which he saw two famous monks who had died.

> They tell the story of a certain brother who came to Scete to see Abba Arsenius, and who went into the church and entreated the clergy to take him to see him, and the clergy said unto him, "Refresh thyself a little, and thou shalt see him." And the brother said unto them, "I will eat nothing before I meet him and see him"; and when the clergy heard this they sent a brother with him to shew him Abba Arsenius, because his cell was some distance away. And when they had arrived there, they knocked at the door and went inside, and having saluted him, and prayed, they sat down and held their peace; and the brother who was from the church answered and said, "I will depart, pray ye for me." But when the other brother saw that he possessed not freedom of speech with the old man, he said unto the brother from the church, "I also will go with thee," and they departed together.
>
> Then he entreated him, saying, "Take me also to Abba Moses who was a thief," and when they went to him, the old man received them with joy, and having refreshed them greatly he dismissed them in peace. And the brother who had brought the visitor to Abba Moses said unto him, "Behold, I brought thee to a man from a foreign land, and to an Egyptian, which of the two pleaseth thee?" And he answered and said unto him, "The Egyptian who hath just received me and refreshed me." And when one of the old men heard what had happened, he prayed to God, and said, "O Lord, shew me this matter; one fleeth from the world for Thy Name's sake, and the other receiveth and is gracious for Thy Name's sake." And behold, suddenly there appeared unto him on the river two great boats, and lo, Abba Arsenius and the Spirit of God were traveling in silence in the one, and Abba Moses and the angels of God were in the other, and they were feeding the monk with honey from the comb.[61]

To the monk, the black Father Moses is the symbol of hospitality, Abba Arsenius the symbol of the *hesychast* who takes the way of the hermit and keeps himself apart from the world. Both ways have equal value, are of equal importance. On Athos, I was told, many of the monasteries are dedicated to the way of hospitality. Father George's monastery of Osiou Grigoriou, for example, where I first heard this story, is dedicated to hospitality, but it actually seems to contain monks of both "types." Certainly they are no foreigners to stillness of heart, although sometimes they seem beset with too many visitors.

There are remote cells and hermitages, particularly on the rocky "deserts" and cliff sides at the foot of Mount Athos itself, at the end of the peninsula, and these remote caves and cottages, once I think described as "The Holy Planet Purgatory," are where many of the *hesychast* hermits live who keep far from the world.

Chapter 11

Prayer

I n a circular relationship, true inner prayer depends on inner separation, and makes it possible, so that both are interdependent. But we should perhaps begin by asking: What is inner prayer? Until you ask this question seriously, everyone knows what prayer is. When you ask, few people know even what is ordinary prayer, and nobody even knows of the existence of inner prayer.

There is good reason for this situation. To a child, prayer is simple petition. To the serious student there are several kinds of prayer. I remember my friend on Athos, Father A., on one occasion, when we were talking about prayer. He mentioned an English book that talked about five different stages of prayer. On Athos, he told me, they only recognize four of these stages; the added stage, that of asking God for things, is not considered to be prayer.

In terms of esoteric Christianity, it is clear that the child's prayer asking for a new toy has no place in the scheme of things, yet other authorities do see a place for petition in the context of handing over command of our lives to the Lord. Eugraph Kovalevsky, for example, as Bishop Jean of Saint Denys, recommends presenting to God our weaknesses, our needs, but as problems, not as desires, not expecting to get what we ask for, but to be helped with the situation in whatever way God knows would help us best in the long run. And we will discover this to be so. This kind of petition becomes more important, not less, as we proceed on the path of Christian esotericism. Indeed, for modern man, it becomes a primary characteristic of this path.

Prayer was well described in an unpublished book by émigré Russian scientist-philosopher Posoff, quoted previously, who wrote about the tradition of noetic prayer:

"Ask and it will be given you; seek and you will find; knock and it will be opened to you" (Matthew 7:7). Seek what? Ask for what? Knock where?

We have a clear answer to these questions: "Seek first his kingdom and his righteousness" (Matthew 6:33).

Where are we to seek the kingdom? This question too is clearly answered: "The kingdom of God is within you" (Luke 17:21).

How can this kingdom be attained? "From the days of John the Baptist until now the kingdom of heaven has suffered violence, and men of violence take it by force" (Matthew 11:12). It is the activity of the spirit in meditative prayer; it is the effort of the intellect in concentrated prayer; it is the power and effort of the soul which thirsts for the peace and bliss of the inner kingdom.

The search for the kingdom in solitary prayer . . . is the "noetic practice" (noera ascesis) which is the prototype of all genuine religious asceticism. . . . Noetic Christ-ascesis consists in contemplation of the Godhead with the aim of passing from the contranatural through the natural to the supranatural.[1]

Noetic ascesis is said to include four elements:

1. attentiveness,
2. concentration,
3. meditation, and
4. prayer.

Ascetics differ as to which position to give to these separate elements. In Eastern Christian ascetic practice, collectedness and concentration of attention lead to prayer in the heart where the nous begins to pray. Pasoff links this with introversion which means "the turning of the eyes inwards," according to Gregory Palamas—and that this refers to the eye or eyes of the soul, not of the body only? Understood in this way, it means that the nous is also drawn inwards.

The One Thing Needful

What role does prayer play in esoteric psychology?

Here we can turn to Evagrius for an answer, when he tells us that "Prayer is the highest action of the nous," and that it is "the rising of the nous to God."[2]

The importance of this noetic prayer or noetic ascesis is described in the gospel story of Martha and Mary, which describes the turning of the nous to God as the "one thing necessary." This early story answers an argument that continues to this day. In the mid-1980s, just before one of my visits to the Holy Mountain, two Englishmen, a clergyman and a social worker, were able to visit the Athos monastery of SimonoPetra. After seeing the demanding regime, they began to ask some very familiar questions, questions that are now being asked of those on the spiritual path by so-called theologians, in Greece as everywhere else in the world. "Why do you bother?" they asked. "How does all this help our fellow man?" they demanded. Then they wanted to know: "Why are you not more concerned with all the sickness and injustice in the world?"

"They did not understand us," a novice told me in quiet simplicity. For these are old questions, although understandable. In medieval times, they were traditionally answered by using the gospel story of Martha and Mary.

This story deals with the same question, but resolves the conflicting pulls by introducing this idea of the "one thing needful or necessary"—a gospel phrase which has become one of the keystones of the inner tradition, and was used by many of the early Fathers in their explanations. This phrase in itself is used repeatedly and has been used in the same way during the past two or three centuries by both Caussade and Theophan in their teachings.

Martha is the well-known symbol of Christian labor in the world, Mary of the monk and the mystic, whose work is essential for mankind yet is necessarily different from that of the world, and for many people difficult to understand. I suspect that this is yet another reason why Mt. Athos is known as Panaghia's Garden: because it is here that Mary's work is done, not that of Martha—a different Mary but the same significance.

But what is the work of Mary: what is the point of all the effort made by the monks? It is the work of remembering God: *mneme Theou*.

In the story, Martha is working in the house and complains that Mary is doing nothing, but simply sitting at the feet of Jesus, which is inwardly an image of prayer:

> And Jesus answered and said unto her, Martha, Martha, thou art careful and troubled about many things:
>
> But one thing is needful: and Mary hath chosen that good part, which shall not be taken away from her (Luke 10:41–42).

The simple form of this is that both Martha and Mary exist in each one of us. Martha is the busy, active circling of our thoughts, Mary the still center that must never be "lost," never forgotten in the hurry of housekeeping, the busy-ness of business. We meet them all the time: Martha the often excitable voice in our heads that never seems to stop talking, Mary the still point from which gentle prayers and simple re- minders issue. In the reality of this, Mary is only heard to speak after something changes in us, when the heart is filled and lit within so that the mind turns naturally back to it. A cold heart, like a cold hearth, lacks the attraction-to-the-center which exists when the fire is full and warm. The struggle we all face is to give this Mary who lives within us the opportunity to tend the fire of the heart, while Martha serves in so many other ways. This, the guarding of the heart by keeping it turned to God, is "the one thing needful."

To understand, to accept, to live entirely by this one thing needful, is very difficult. This state may be the result of successful attempts at *mneme Theou*, and ultimately a permanent state, a change in our center of gravity, is a complete change in the center of our consciousness, a state of *ecstasy*. You can experience it for odd moments: for odd mo- ments you are separate from your feelings, from your body, but espe- cially from your thoughts, from all the activity spinning around in your mind.

Saint John Cassian describes the three renunciations (see chapter 7) as a process of coming out of one life, after which we enter another. The Fathers of the church said that the *nous*, the human intelligence, could be in three different states, described as:

1. against nature
2. its natural state
3. above nature or supernatural

The natural state is that of *inner separation*, in which life passes before us but does not automatically move us. But as we are, we have fallen from that state. When we return to it—by whatever method—we find ourselves in a great stillness, the stillness known by the early church as *hesychia*. In that stillness we can choose what to express. Thoughts arise and fall away. Feelings attract us but no longer insist. Images present themselves but we are not forced to respond to them.

To make this state stable is the first major goal of esoteric Christian- ity, of this ancient therapy.

It is in those moments of *separation* that the intelligence is in its natural state. Fallen man, man as he is, is in an unnatural state. So before we can attain the "supranatural," we have to return to and pass through the natural.

Theocentric Selflessness

The only way to give one's whole life to the one thing needful is to become *theocentric*: God-centered and not self-centered. But how can one become theocentric, how put all one's trust in God, all one's thought toward God? The gospel parable of the lilies of the field gains much of its power from the fact that this question is of such great importance to the Christian life. In understanding the Bible, it is important to see everything in its original context. This particular parable is preceded by the verses:

> But if thine eye be evil, thy whole body shall be full of darkness. If therefore the light that is in thee be darkness, how great is that darkness!
>
> No man can serve two masters: for either he will hate the one, and love the other; or else he will hold to the one, and despise the other. Ye cannot serve God and Mammon (Matthew 6:23–24).

These verses describe the great inner difference that exists between the two states, in the first of which we serve "Mammon," the power of the world as we normally know it, while in the second we serve God. What they describe here concerns the nous.

The nous, the cognitive power of the heart, described by the Fathers as "the eye of the soul," must be transformed or enlightened by "holding" to God and not to Mammon. This is the key to the idea, in the Gospel According to Thomas, that we should "Be passers by. . . . "[3]

To meditate on this passage in the old way of meditating: turn it over in your mind and try to sense what it really means to you, what it would mean to your life if you should do this: if you no longer thought about your own life, but left to God all your daily concerns about food, about clothing, about your job, your relationships, your home . . . imagine, could it even be possible? If you reflect on these words in this way, you will become aware, if you are honest with yourself, of a strange reaction within you. You will find yourself feeling *uncomfortable*. The deeper you reflect on this passage, the more uncomfortable you will become, until you may well feel driven to set it aside. Instead of this, choose, *intentionally* continue your reflections on the same point. The fact is that something in you is unwilling to face the implications of this doctrine, the idea that should you actually leave the details of your life to God, *anything* might happen to you. You would lose control, and with that loss you would also lose the illusion that your control is strong enough to make you safe.

To face reality in this way is a terrifying situation.

Yet this is what it means to live theocentrically. This renunciation is just as possible—just as difficult—to the layperson who lives outwardly the same as before as it is to those who become monks or nuns. This is the renunciation of self, of one's self-concern, self-love, self-centeredness. Just the thought of it causes great fear.

The Just

To be theocentric is to be "justified in the sight of God." The theocentric state of mind is precisely the *righteousness* described in chapter 6 of the Gospel of Saint Matthew. Without this, there is no righteousness. The passage about the fowls of the air describes the attitude that is not only appropriate to but is *normal to* one who has fully accepted the reality of God. It describes the ending of what Gurdjieff called *inner considering*: an end of our continually thinking about ourselves, which is the normal state of man today. The righteous man does not spend his life thinking of himself.

> Therefore I say unto you, Take no thought for your life, what ye shall eat, or what ye shall drink; nor yet for your body, what ye shall put on. Is not the life more than meat, and the body than raiment?
>
> Behold the fowls of the air: for they sow not, neither do they reap, nor gather into barns; yet your heavenly Father feedeth them. Are ye not much better than they?
>
> Which of you by taking thought can add one cubit unto his stature?
>
> And why take ye thought for raiment? Consider the lilies of the field, how they grow; they toil not, neither do they spin:
>
> And yet I say unto you, That even Solomon in all his glory was not arrayed like one of these.
>
> Wherefore, if God so clothe the grass of the field, which to day is, and tomorrow is cast into the oven, shall he not much more clothe you, O ye of little faith?
>
> Therefore take no thought, saying, What shall we eat? or, What shall we drink? or, Wherewithal shall we be clothed?
>
> (For after all these things do the Gentiles seek:) for your heavenly Father knoweth that ye have need of all these things.
>
> But seek ye first the kingdom of God, and his righteousness; and all these things shall be added unto you.
>
> Take therefore no thought for the morrow: for the morrow shall take thought for the things of itself. Sufficient unto the day is the evil thereof (Matthew 6:25–34).

This end to continually thinking about ourselves, of continual inner considering, is of greater practical importance, since it touches on worship and the life of prayer. It depends on real faith, and real faith naturally opens into a relationship with our Lord. We quoted earlier something that Abbot George Capsanis of Grigoriou said a few years back: "When the monk possesses the grace of repentance he knows the true God, not some idea of God." But for most of us, this grace, this living relationship, is continually lost, continually forgotten by us in the activity of our lives, to be restored periodically in moments of recollection that are all too few, in moments aided by sincere participation in the liturgical cycle of the church, in moments of prayer . . . but those "dry" periods in our prayer life; they too reflect the times when that living relationship is absent: when we have lost the sense of the reality of God.

The living relationship is too deep, it exists only in the secret world of the heart, the "closet"[4] into which we must go to pray. When we become superficial, when we exist only in the superficial concerns of our mind, we have lost contact with God: when we have lost contact with God, and cannot restore it, we have limited ourselves to—lost ourselves in—the surface layers of mind. Then we have forgotten ourselves. Elsewhere we quote Father George's comment on the gospel phrase "The truth shall set you free"; the Greek word translated "truth" is *alitheia*. The root is the same as that in Lethe, the name of the river of forgetfulness in Greek mythology, so that *alitheia* is a kind of negative or opposite of forgetting, and truth is an antinomy not of falsehood but of *forgetfulness*. So the practical need is to discover a way of restoring to life that faith that has become dead, cold, superficial. Experience will give us the key here; faith remains dead as long as it remains superficial, that is, until we make the effort to *remember* the whole depth of its meaning, even simply by remembering that its dead form is not the real form.

We will know we have found the real form when we have found an effective form. This is a key.

Without in general remembering what they are for, the church has its methods of achieving this remembering. They are called "mysteries," *mysterion* in the Greek, a word now translated as "sacraments." The primary mysteries form the whole cycle of confession and communion. With the necessary preparation, the necessary forgiveness, these by grace can reawaken the inmost heart.

The problem is that the human mind is so fickle, so easily overlaid by outside events, that even the reality of the mysteries can be forgotten . . . and then: "Ye are the salt of the earth: but if the salt have lost his savour, wherewith shall it be salted? it is thenceforth good for nothing, but to be cast out, and to be trodden under foot of men" (Matthew 5:13).

Epiousion

Ponder the meaning of the Lord's Prayer. "After this manner therefore pray ye":

> Our Father which art in heaven, Hallowed be thy name.
>   Thy kingdom come. Thy will be done in earth, as it is in heaven.
>   Give us this day our supersubstantial bread.
>   And forgive us our debts, as we forgive our debtors.
>   And lead us not into temptation, but deliver us from evil: For thine is the kingdom, and the power, and the glory, for ever. Amen (Matthew 6:9–13).

The Greek Bible has *epiousion*, but the meaning of this word, once translated as "supersubstantial" has been given as "daily" in all or almost all recent translations of this prayer. Even the well-known Strong's Dictionary of Greek has linked it with the need *for subsistence*, and hence justifies the term *daily*. Some early versions have it as "supersubstantial," but translations of this word as "daily" began several centuries ago,[5] so that the original word is today almost entirely unknown. This is just another of those little mysteries that accompany the loss of the inner meaning of the Bible, but at least the fact that something has changed is relatively visible once the facts are known.

Let us make a meditation of this question. What are the possible ways in which prayer could be linked to our need for bread? And what are the roots of the word *epiousion*? *Epi* refers to something being present; *ousia* means substance.

To consider the first question, our bodies need regular food, and if we are expected not to concern ourselves all the time with the needs of our bodies, then it makes sense if we ask this regular or "daily" food of God.

So ponder the meaning of this inner version of the Lord's Prayer. Then ask yourself another difficult one: How can so many people pray *Thy will be done*, if they do not believe it can be done?

Prayer as Relation to God

In the inner tradition we pray not from thought of what we want to obtain for ourselves, but in order to follow Christ's teaching that our lives should become more *theocentric*, in order to learn to leave the solution of our everyday problems in His hands, so as to "Take no thought for your life, what ye shall eat, or what ye shall drink."

The more we understand about prayer, the more difficulty we have speaking about it. But whatever other uses there are for work in our ordinary life, on this Way prayer, worship, and even our everyday work are all forms of ascesis; they are all important for their inner effect. They possess an added value when they help us to turn away from our self-centeredness, help us turn to God; when they help to reveal the intentions of our hearts and help us live by those intentions. If I remember correctly, it was as Athonite monk, speaking to a committee at the European parliament about the nature of Mount Athos, who said "We need prayer and worship to help us remember God. The world is too strong, it takes us away, distracts us, makes us forget." The committee was then told: "The nations today live an anthropocentric life, a life of lethe (forgetting), everyone centered on themselves. We need a 'theanthropocentric' life, a life of 'alitheia' [the word for "truth" in the New Testament]. Living in the world causes the human personality to become fragmented. These anthropocentric, man-centered ideas, attitudes and actions are 'amartia': sin— They divide us internally, and they also divide us one from another."[6]

The point is not that there is no need to care for people in the world. There is much need, but the visibly good work of Martha depends on the secret labors of Mary; to draw a very simplistic analogy, Martha has the car, Mary the petrol. Only spiritual strength can resolve the causes of the problems whose symptoms are so ably and necessarily resolved by the social worker. The priest and the social worker must always serve together, but they should not serve, as they so often do today, in identical ways.

We will discover later that there are two main methods of reaching this "one thing needful." One is to create friction, to bring into being an interior struggle with the associative mechanism of the mind; the other is prayer. They both become effective when they lead to inner separation.

In fact there is little difference between them. In the text of the book *Unseen Warfare* and elsewhere—if not in our own experience— we discover that effort in prayer is an inner struggle, and elsewhere, for example in Theophan, we can discover that all inner struggle with a correct aim is close to prayer; that any kind of struggle with habits of mind, if it is combined with an emotional remembrance of God, is indeed prayer. The latter is the basis of the path of service, which involves what Gurdjieff called "voluntary suffering." A. R. Orage, one of his students, described this once: "This is duty in three languages: it is conscious labour and voluntary suffering. From one aspect it is an intellectual duty to strive to understand the meaning and aim of existence, an emotional duty to feel the weight of the maintenance of everything existing, and a physical duty to make the planetary body the servant of your aim."[7]

This process can be seen in experience . . . but a warning is necessary: seen too simply, the ideas and the experiences to which they refer are
easily attached to the wrong things. The explanation that follows is there
to help us understand, but to avoid the danger of mistaking our objects,
our thought about such experience needs to be "clothed" in precise language. In simple form, without that precision needed to use this knowledge in practice, it says that the awakening of new and higher energies
within our psyche brings joy. At its best, joy brings love and love then
brings greater joy. This, so briefly described, so powerful when tasted, so
hard to find when we seek it—but oh when it seeks us—this is the
shortest and fastest path of the heart, the center lane of the *Royal Road* of
the monks of the Eastern Church.

But as long as the world still pulls us, our fallen past and the circumstances of our lives usually intervene, the joy fades as our attention is
taken by externals. The love fades or turns into disappointment and is
finally forgotten. Then, once again, the Royal Road is a forgotten byway;
a moment in paradise becomes no more than one snapshot among all our
other memories.

Pilgrims leave Athos with tears in their eyes. But what is it they are
crying for?

Seeking to recover this state, the simple view is that monasticism deals
with this situation in one way, by minimizing the external distractions that
remind the monk of the worldly interests that still pull on him. Those who
cannot or will not become monks or nuns may not find this possible if
they have already been "spoiled by the world." If so, they must go about
it a different way . . . a way that is more difficult to understand, so that it
is also harder to find. And when they find this way they discover that the
monk has been there before them: that he too has his psychological needs,
and that in actual fact the more secluded from life we are, the more we
become directly aware of the internal problems and pressures that reside
in the contents of our psyche.

Evagrius, one of the Fathers who knew most about these processes,
also concerned himself with another psychological question. He wrote
about the nous in a way that explains many of humanity's psychological
weaknesses and—properly understood—shows the reason for much of the
ascetic practice of the early church: "The nous wanders when it becomes
passionate, and it is uncontrollable when it obtains the objects of its
desires. But it abstains from wandering when it becomes dispassionate and
has arrived in the company of those who are free of the body."[8]

The problem is to understand this early teaching in a way that fits
in with other doctrines. This is one reason why Evagrius tends to remain

unknown today. In fact, his teachings give valuable clues to the ways in which certain doctrines should be understood—particularly those from gospel sources such as the Beatitudes. When its links to inner experience are registered and the psychological meaning made clear, the meaning of the gospel teaching often seems very different. The Beatitudes—for example: "Blessed are they that mourn: for they shall be comforted" (Matthew 5:4)—can be understood with a whole added dimension when they are linked with the experiences to which they actually refer. These inner experiences come to people particularly on the Path of Service, the path of intentional action. There we must live for a long time with the loss of our personal desires before we begin to awaken to a different sense of emotional interest, so that Gregory of Nyssa taught: "Thus when our Lord says that those who mourn are blessed, the hidden lesson I think He is teaching is this: that the soul should fix its eye on its true good and not be immersed in the illusion of the present life. For it is impossible for a man to live without tears who looks sharply at realities; and we must surely think that man pathetic who allows himself to sink into the pleasures of this world."[9]

Like many such passages, it is easy to read this quickly while registering only part of the meaning. In fact this, like all Gregory of Nyssa's writings, is a statement of great precision, and we need to read it in full to register and then understand everything it is able to tell us. He is speaking not generally, nor morally in a kind of nineteenth-century sense, but here he is giving precise instructions about the use of *attention*. First, he tells us to give our attention to, to keep in the eye of the mind what he calls "the true good," and not be immersed in the present life—which he defines precisely by calling it "the illusion of the present life," therefore telling us that the difficulty with it is precisely that it is illusory. Then he distinguishes precisely between the two ways in which the heart responds to the world, saying first that "it is impossible for a man to live without tears who looks sharply at the realities," which defines the proper perception of the heart, and then defines the different state of the "passion-filled" heart (from the root of which idea the English word *pathetic* is derived), saying: "we must surely think that man pathetic who allows himself to sink into the pleasures of this world."

From this we can learn that by directing the attention toward, turning our mind to, or filling our mind with, that reality—the inner reality that is also the invisible world, once again, that moves us to tears, instead of the illusions that lead to transitory pleasure—we can discover the different state of heart referred to as "magnetic center." There is on the one hand passion, the pathetic, and on the other *apatheia*, dispassion, which is at the same time independence, freedom from the world, the spiritual awakening of the heart, the full awakening of the love which began to wake with this God-given mourning that comes when we begin to realize the realities of our world as it is today. . . or become aware of our own imperfections, our own shortfall against what, in that awakening heart, we intuit[10] we were created to become. Because of this, Evagrius said: "Pray with tears and all you ask will be heard. For the Lord rejoices greatly when you pray with tears."[11]

Degrees of Prayer

Prayer varies in character: there are many ways to pray, so that the common element in different forms of prayer is often difficult to recognize until the practice goes deep into the heart. As suggested earlier, there are also progressive stages in prayer, and proper passage through those stages, leading to awakening of the heart, is governed by the state of that artificial psychological organ known, by modern forms of the tradition, as *magnetic center*.[12] If one makes real efforts to pray, it soon becomes clear that piety is not the only thing needed in this kind of prayer. The development of magnetic center also involves growth in *nepsis*, watchfulness.

This is difficult to achieve. Theophan the Recluse admitted in a letter that to obey the gospel instruction to go into our "inner room" to pray, taken in an inner sense, was too difficult for many people in his time. Because *nepsis* is usually lacking in modern man, many people find it impossible today. Theophan gave a solution in terms of the classical idea of three stages of prayer, describing the entry into the inner chamber as the *third stage* of prayer, although previously he had written about two stages. With this additional stage, he introduced the esoteric idea that the inner room of the gospel was in the heart: that to enter this *inner room* was the stage of mature inner prayer—true prayer of the heart—to which the earlier stages might lead. He began by saying: "Prayer is the devotion of the mind and heart to God, in praise, in thanksgiving, and in petition for the spiritual and material goods we need. The Saviour commanded us to enter into our inner room and there pray to God the Father in secret."[13]

In another letter, Theophan had written about this:

> You can define three degrees of prayer, beginning with reading, prostrations, vigilance, etc. Some people work for quite a long time on themselves before the beginning of prayer: before the gentle movement of the spirit in prayer even starts. Being the highest of gifts, prayer is sent as it were in droplets, in order to teach a man to value it deeply.

In the second degree the bodily and the spiritual are of equal strength. Here every word of prayer is accompanied by corresponding feelings. Inner impulses to prayer arise from within and are expressed in their own words. This is everyday prayer. It is common to almost all people in whom the spirit of devotion is alive.

In the third degree the inner or spiritual prevails and— without words or movements, without bows, without even thoughts—the action of prayer takes place in silence in the depths of the spirit. This kind of prayer is not limited by time or place or any other external thing, and may never cease. That is why it is called the "action" of prayer, something that is constantly present. This is the essence of inner prayer.

Only in this, the third stage of prayer, it is truly possible to obey Saint Paul's instruction that all Christians should "pray without ceasing," so that this instruction is an objective to be achieved, not something to be carried out by repeating words. It is something we cannot "do" with the head, for when we reach this state it is as if it is not we that pray with the mind, but instead Christ prays in our heart.

He (Paul) commands mental or spiritual prayer for all Christians without exception. He also tells all Christians to pray unceasingly. To pray unceasingly is possible only in the heart. Therefore it is impossible to contest the fact that mental prayer is compulsory for all Christians, and if it is obligatory it is also possible—God does not command the impossible.

It is true that this kind of prayer is difficult. Generally speaking, every good is difficult but is not impossible. Prayer is necessarily more difficult, because it is the source of all good, and its surest mainstay. If someone should ask: how am I to pray? The answer is very simple. Fear God.[14]

It is the *fear of God* that brings the heart into our prayer, and this brings the prayer into the heart, arousing the heart to a state in which we become deeply attentive to our prayer. In this, Theophan gives another practical key: "Experience of the fear of God arouses attention and consciousness in the heart. It forces it to stand with devotion before God."[15] Or as Clement put it: "For the fear of God trains and restores to love."[16]

In his introduction to the book *The Art of Prayer*, Bishop Kallistos Ware, an English theologian, a monk of the Greek monastery of Saint John on Patmos, and a bishop of the Greek Church in England, describes these three stages of prayer in contemporary terms: "Just as there are three elements in man, so there are three main degrees of prayer." (A footnote adds a telling note here: "Prayer is a living reality, a personal encounter with the living God, and as such it is not to be confined within the limits of any rigid analysis.") He continues by listing the three degrees of prayer as "(1) Oral or bodily prayer (2) Prayer of the mind (3) Prayer of the heart or ('of the mind in the heart'): spiritual prayer." In this he quotes Theophan as saying: "You must pray not only with the words but with the mind, and not only with the mind but with the heart, so that the mind understands and sees all that is said in words, and the heart feels what the mind is thinking.[17] All these combined together constitute real prayer, and if any of them are absent your prayer is either not perfect or is not prayer at all."[18]

This is probably the most accurate description of prayer with the mind in the heart available, although not an easy one to understand—and this is important because, on this subject, most written descriptions are more confusing than enlightening. This description also makes it possible, with mature consideration, to seek the link between the idea of prayer with the mind in the heart, and modern views of magnetic center.

And although the beginner in prayer must be taught by man, since his communications to God are not yet opened up, the final stages of prayer are taught by God Himself.

Saint Therese of Lisieux wrote about how she began in mental prayer while still a child, and without having yet had any instruction in the "art":

> Up to this time, nobody had taught me the art of mental prayer; I should have liked to know about it, but Marie was satisfied with my spiritual progress as it was, and kept me to vocal prayer instead. One day, one of my mistresses at the Abbey asked what I did with myself on holidays, when I was left to my own devices. I told her that I got behind my bed, where there was an empty space in which you could shut yourself away with the curtains, and there . . . well, I used to think. "Think about what?" She asked. "Oh," I said, "about God, and about life, and eternity; you know, I just think." The dear nun made a great joke of this, and later on she used to remind me of my thinking days, and ask me whether I still thought. I can see now that I was practicing mental prayer without realizing what I was doing; God was teaching me the art in some secret way of His own.[19]

The Inner Room

This "invisible[20] communication" is an essential characteristic of true prayer. But we cannot expect to begin with this or, if we are given a taste of it at the beginning, we cannot expect to be given such rich fare always. However prayer begins in us, we must begin in prayer simply, without expecting too much, but with proper preparation. Theophan put it:

> One must not enter prayer without special preparation. First, a special place is necessary, if possible a solitary place dedicated to this one thing—in front of an icon, with a lighted candle or icon-lamp. Then one should set aside special times morning and evening, and other times too. One should conform to the times of church services. The body should be in a special position—standing or kneeling, with decorum and attentive tension.
>
> On first coming to prayer, one should rein in the mind from its distractions and gather it within. One should shake off all cares or quiet them so far as possible, and bring oneself to the most vivid awareness of the omniscient, omnipresent and all-seeing God. This creates the inner "closet" or prayer room. It was this which the Lord commanded us to enter in order to pray (Matthew 6:6); a temporary sanctuary.
>
> This is the beginning. But then we move on to the gospel definition of the proper conditions for prayer: we must be in the inner room or "closet." Where is this room? It is in our heart. How then can we learn to pray there: if we go there, as well as we are able, God will help us.
>
> According to Saint Demetrius of Rostov, the inner room means the heart. The commandment of the Lord obliges us to pray mentally in our heart to God. This commandment extends to all Christians. The Apostle Paul commands the same, saying that we must pray continually in our spirit.[21]

Theophan repeatedly links the spirit and the heart. There is little doubt that for him the place of the spirit is the inmost heart. But this place in the heart is not so easy to find. Even the meaning of the term is not easy to discover: it took me seven years to discover this answer after I first asked about it.

I learned that it is found in prayer, frequently near death, before the equally often reported meeting with the *light*—it is an ignorance, a forgetfulness, a total darkness of the nous, darkness of mind and beyond mind. This is the Lethe of mythology: it is a quality of the nous; it is *The Cloud of Unknowing* of the medieval English mystics; the darkness of chapter 1 of Saint John, which exists like a backdrop to the active *contents* of our minds, the Cave of the Nativity in the icons of the birth of Christ, the inner room or "closet" of the gospel and of prayer of the heart. If we persist in practices such as that recommended in *The Cloud of Unknowing*, we will at some point find ourselves apparently losing consciousness for blank moments, moments where we are aware of nothing (no-thing) and from which we can remember nothing. Such moments, although producing no detectable effect in our memory, nevertheless leave in us a variety of different kinds of change. Within this inner room the light shines, often unrecognized by us even when we enter *within*, and always hidden from the outside world. The light comes to birth in it just as the haloes of the holy shine in the cave icons. Indeed, the caves in Orthodox icons are consistently shown black inside, with a darkness of mind, not of the senses; a darkness of ignorance, an occlusion of consciousness. Indian teachings call it *dhyana*: Thomas à Kempis speaks of it in the *Imitation of Christ*. Saint John spoke of that which is hidden in the darkness. Reports of near-death experiences describe it. You can experience both in noetic prayer: the darkness first, then the light. "The light shines in the darkness, and the darkness cannot contain it."[22]

This darkness in the heart is one factor of what has been called the magnetic center, the Ark of the Covenant within us. More will be said about this in the next chapter.

Although it shows—to those who know the signs—as a major change in the character of the individual, the idea of *magnetic center* is primarily a description of the psychological "inner room" or "closet" which makes it possible for the layperson to practice prayer of the heart. Linked with this concept are teachings concerning the slow process, often a struggle, by which we create this protective organ within our psyche. One form of this inner struggle was described by Saint Hesychius in a way that underlies the link between prayer and *nepsis*; the approach as described here means we must give *assent* to the Jesus Prayer, instead of responding to tempting thoughts and memories, the *provocations*. This means of beginning prayer of the heart is very similar to contemporary methods of what is known as *centering prayer*. This kind of prayer can only be performed properly if we establish the capacity for great care or *watchfulness*, as otherwise the distractions of the world take over. But this watchfulness can be *built*, when it takes the form of magnetic center. Saint Hesychius wrote about the link between prayer and *watchfulness*: "Watchfulness[23] and the Jesus prayer mutually reinforce one another; for extreme watchfulness follows[24] the content of constant prayer, while prayer follows extreme sobriety and watchfulness of intellect."[25]

The same applies for other forms of centering prayer, since the Jesus Prayer could be regarded as one such. *Watchfulness* is essential in bringing all such methods to fruition. Magnetic center is eventually made stable by the intensity of the combination of prayer and watchfulness, a stage reached very late on the staircase[26] by those who are working in the world. The reason for this is that such methods of prayer either depend on stilling the mind or on separating the awareness from the uncontrolled activities of the mind. This is in fact a description of magnetic center, and *watchfulness* is a fundamental component of this, for without it, magnetic center cannot exist. Saint Hesychius addressed this: "Many of our thoughts come from demonic suggestions, and from these derive our evil outward actions. If with the help of Jesus we instantly quell the thought, we will avoid its corresponding outward action. We will enrich ourselves with the sweetness of divine knowledge, and so will find God, who is everywhere. Holding the mirror of the intellect firmly toward God, we will be illumined constantly as pure glass is by the sun. Then finally the intellect, having reached the limit of its desires, will in Him cease all other contemplation."[27]

Assent to prayer is closely related to two things: one is the idea of assent to faith introduced by Clement of Alexandria. The two forms of assent are mutually dependent, the attitude of *assent to faith* (described in chapter 8) forms a precondition in which *assent to prayer* becomes effective.

Assent must be made in the right way, by the right part of the mind. It is then that it links closely with the idea of consent used in Thomas Keating's method of centering prayer. Assent is possible only to the free: and that freedom, that independence of decision, is possible only to those who habitually break the captivity of the mind and achieve a state of *nepsis*. The *minor liberation* of watchfulness is essential; it puts us in control. Only when we have this degree of control are we able to assent in the moment-to-moment way needed. Otherwise, in the state of captivity of the mind normal to most individuals today, the movements of our attention are limited to the movements of those thoughts and activities that "happen" to be present in us, and that is purely accidental.

The depth of our prayer, according to Saint Theophan, depends on the degree to which we can live our life at other times in awareness of God. As Theophan put it, between us and the world we must wear God's armor, formed by our knowledge of the gospel, by making of God's word the content of our memories. "But if this is so, what is a Christian to do? We must: 'Be strong in the Lord and in the strength of His might.' And [he quotes]: 'Take the whole armour of God, that you may be able to withstand in the evil day' (Ephesians 6:11)." This requires intelligent action to change our own surface nature, and the reference to the "whole armour of God" refers to the need for a *complete* teaching, a teaching that gives full protection. This describes exactly how the acquisition of a complete teaching forms a magnetic center in us that can draw us to God. Elsewhere, Theophan writes: "The farmer not only clears the field of weeds, but sows good seed and vigilantly watches over the seedlings in their growth. It is the same in the spiritual life; in joining battle with passions and bad habits a man must at the same time—with the grace of God—nourish the germ of the higher spiritual life in himself."[28]

With great difficulty our normal condition, the normal condition of modern man, that has been likened to a form of "waking sleep" and in which watchfulness is almost impossible, can be brought to an end. The following passage from Theophan, describing a method of waking up in the morning, may help make clear what is involved: "In the first moment after awakening," he wrote, "as soon as you come to yourself, descend into the heart, and then call, appeal, press into it all the forces of the body and the soul. Do this by attention in the mind, by turning the eyes to it, by a readiness of the will with a certain tensing of the muscles . . . and by watchfulness over the feelings. Repress feelings of pleasure, especially of the flesh, and do this until consciousness has firmly established itself in the heart as on a throne. Remain there all the time you are conscious. Repeat this exercise often in the day, because this ingathering of oneself needs to be continuously renewed and reinforced."[29]

Von Durkheim's studies[30] describe the vivification of the solar plexus, something that happens in the monastic *agrypnia* vigil and is an essential element in a mature life of prayer. Only this state makes possible the prolonged *nepsis*, watchfulness, that is an essential element in the development of prayer towards the state known as prayer of the heart. It was said earlier that *nepsis* is one of the keys to repentance. Without it, we have not the strength to follow through our intention to repent.

In Eastern traditions, this involves special techniques, the exercises of yoga, or a whole range of practices that include the more specific and more widespread practice of development of what is known as hara in Japan. The process is described by von Durkheim in the same book we quoted earlier:

> The task of gaining the right basic center can be fulfilled only by one who, with perseverance and sincerity, without fear of pain and with great patience, overcomes whatever hinders Hara, and furthers that which the developed Hara expresses. To become a complete human being without acquiring the body-soul "center" is not possible. But to acquire Hara through practice means also opening the gate to the way by which Man can become whole.

Only that individual is truly "whole" whose self manifests the Being embodied within him. A man is not "whole" as
long as he fails to accomplish his integration with Being, as
long as, for example, he lives only in the I that is not conformable with Being, but activated always from without. For Western Man the realization of Being within the self is inevitably
connected with the unfolding of the perceiving and creative
mind. But this unfolding also presupposes his re-rooting in the
primal center, which is Hara.[31]

We will perhaps recognize that, apart from specific mentions of Hara, and
apart from specific reference to what von Durkheim calls a primal center,
this whole process has the same properties as what we have described, in
the course of this book, as the Christian inner path . . . and the same
quality of leading to results in the individual human being which appear
to be almost lacking in the Christian world.

In fact, the Eastern Church not only has certain physical exercises,
including exercises of the breath,[32] reported as being known and used only
in certain places, and has its involvement of the body in prayer, particularly
in prostations so common in Eastern monasticism, but it has its own, typically Christian methods of developing this inner center. The problem is that
these methods are among that part of the tradition transmitted *wordlessly,*
and so it seems difficult to find any clear reference to them in the literature.
The development of this primal center is in fact a normal part of the Christian life of prayer but, where somebody is resistant, is too much inclined to
get trapped in the head or in excitement and so on—situations typical of
modern life—the process needs to be "jump-started," to use a modern image,
and for this the primary tool is the monastic vigil service or *agrypnia,* described in chapter 10. In fact, the efforts necessary to complete an *agrypnia* are
remarkably like those described by von Durkheim, when he speaks of how
one who wants to develop hara must work "with perseverance and sincerity,
without fear of pain and with great patience, [until one] overcomes whatever
hinders Hara, and furthers that which the developed Hara expresses."[33]

It is just these qualities that are evoked and, as I now know, developed by the *agrypnia* service. At my first *agrypnia* service (see p. 219) I was
forced to creep off to bed early on. But by the third time I had attended
one of these services, somehow, by that fact alone, I had developed enough
stamina to stay awake throughout the service, although during the previous two days I had walked great distances on the paths between the
monasteries.

The effect on me was quite remarkable. I can only assume it was the
duration of the effort made that produced a significant change in my state
of mind and body, a change I can only describe as a "firming up" of the

solar plexus paralleled to a change in the focus of energy and activity within me. Strangely, this firming up was both physical and psychological in its implications, the latter being of greater significance. It seemed to me that it served in some way as an antidote to stress and to the effects of the laxity of modern life. More than this, it gave me some control over the disorder of my busy mind.

I cannot really explain this effect. But I can thoroughly recommend it to those who find themselves becoming soft in a self-centered world. As a difficult and therefore effective beginning to true asceticism, I suspect it is unmatched.

We have no modern theories that are nearly large enough to contain or explain the power of the *agrypnia*, not even in the work of von Durkheim referred to earlier. Because of this, I suspect it will never enter the life of an intellectually driven West in its complete form, or in its full power.

But if Western members of the Orthodox Church were to perform their very occasional monastic vigils in full, and over the full time normal in the monasteries of Athos, they might discover something that has for far too long been lost to us.

Any serious study of the life of prayer as it is described by the early Fathers—as well as more recently—will reveal the presence of not one but two latter stages in the "firming up" of the inner life, in passing through which the rigor of self-discipline in time becomes the first stage in the "higher" freedom of the rule of the love of God.

But why is this watchfulness not always discussed when we come to the question of a life of prayer? Partially because some books are written for people who have already passed this point in their lives before they get seriously involved in interior prayer, as is true of most monks and nuns of the Eastern Church. At this point, on the monastic form of the Royal Road as it has been described by Boris Mouravieff,[34] the same things can be obtained more easily with little need for special knowledge,[35] but with the emotional force behind them. But for those who must follow the path alone and in everyday life, knowledge of these things helps to protect against falls.

The Jesus Prayer

To see the importance of the two elements in prayer that are my main concern in this chapter, it is first helpful to look again at the overall question of prayer. On my first visit to the monastery of SimonoPetra, on Mount Athos, I mentioned to one of the monks, a Father I., my interest in *Iisus evchi*, the Jesus Prayer, that repetitive *prayer of the heart*, one element of which is the invocation of the name of Jesus in various longer formats. This seems to form the basis of individual practice on the mountain—and it is this which was called by Father George of Grigoriou the "principle export of Mount Athos." In our discussions I used the word *method*. I said that I had in the past tried to use the Jesus Prayer as a method. My memory of his words is imperfect, but I shall try to recapture as much of the sense as possible. "It is not quite that," he told me, "the Jesus Prayer is not a method. Properly, it is a relationship, something personal, emotional. If one treats it as a method, intellectually, then you are missing the whole point, the main point of it, which is a slowly developing relationship with the person of Jesus. Just like speaking to someone in the ordinary way. Only then will it grow, will it change, will it lead to something new. Then everything else will grow from that relationship."

Like many true things, this approach in which things "grow" at their own pace doesn't entirely "make sense" to the Western reason, with its view that the whole significance of human life lies in "doing."

It takes time before we realize that the spiritual life has no methods, that it is not something we do, nor do we achieve anything by it, but instead it is a form of inner growth. The problem is that we have lived in a world in which the normal response to any situation is to "do something," and on Athos one has to learn not to rely on this kind of response. It proves to be a poor guide in this strange country of the spirit. Indeed, the whole idea of using a "method" belongs to what modern thought calls the "left brain" or "dominant hemisphere": the *doing brain* that governs voluntary actions, and whose thinking is shaped accordingly. This part of the mind is in some strange way incompetent in the world of prayer. Prayer as it progresses depends more on a relinquishing of control than on its intensification. Prayer, I have discovered on Athos, requires attentiveness and even purpose, but even so it is not something we do. *Prosevchi*, directed or attentive prayer, the word often used in the passages of the *Philokalia* that talk about prayer, involves a certain directing of attention. But this is difficult to understand because it is not an active control; instead, it involves what one can only call a kind of "effortless effort."

One thing Father S., a monk I met later in the monastery of Grigoriou, was quite definite about. It was that prayer, and especially the Jesus Prayer, was the key. If one was praying in the heart, then everything would be all right, as I have since discovered for myself. The monks also say the same for the liturgy; that it puts things right, and then there is less need to think about one's life and one's work and what should one do, as I had been doing at that time. If one prayed and developed the personal links to Jesus, all this would change in ways one could not predict, and all would be well.

He made no attempt to talk me into joining the Orthodox Church. ("When the apple is ripe!" he said on another occasion.)

The definition of *prayer* given on one occasion by Theophan the Recluse may prove helpful here. "What is prayer?" asked Saint Theophan.

> It is the listening of our mind and heart to God. As soon as any pious feeling starts to move, prayer is there too. To pray seems to bring pious feelings and attitudes into action, leading to a quickening or kindling of life and forming a spirit of devotion. If a person has no devotion, how can he pray? And if devotion is the life of our spirit, we can understand that only a person who knows how to pray can be said to possess spirit. Prayer has been defined as the breath of our spirit—and that is just what it is.
>
> When we breathe, the lungs expand and draw in the life-giving elements of the air, and in prayer the depths of the heart are thrown open, and the spirit ascends to God to commune with Him and receive the gifts this brings. And just as in breathing the oxygen is received into the blood and then distributed to bring life to the body, so, in prayer, what is received from God enters our innermost being and gives new life to everything there.
>
> Prayer is the quickening of the spirit, in a sense its deification. As someone in a myrrh distillery becomes saturated with myrrh, so anyone ascending to God becomes interpenetrated by Divinity.[36]

The Jesus Prayer is essentially *hesychast* in nature, and *hesychia*, the deep stillness of the heart, is not compatible with the active, Western idea of *control*. Overactivity destroys or, to use a modern psychological concept, "masks" it. Watchfulness—*nepsis*—protects it. More to the point, overactivity is a symptom of the absence of true prayer of the heart. And because great care is necessary, the *Philokalia* has a lot to say about this:

> If you wish to pray as you ought, imitate the dulcimer player; bending his head a little and inclining his ear to the strings, he strikes the strings skillfully, and enjoys the melody he draws from their harmonious notes.
>
> Is this example clear to you? The dulcimer is the heart; the strings—the feelings; the hammer, mneme Theou: remembrance of God; the player, mind. By mneme Theou and by remembering Divine things the mind draws holy feelings from

the God-fearing heart, then ineffable sweetness fills the soul and the mind, which is pure, is lit up by Divine illuminations.

The dulcimer player perceives and hears nothing but the melody he enjoys. So the mind, during active prayer, descends into the depths of the heart with sobriety and can no longer listen to anything but God. All his inner being speaks to God with the voice of David: "My soul followeth hard after thee" (Psalms 63:8).[37]

Noetic Prayer

In the esoteric tradition, prayer is not a child's method of asking for what we want. It is a tool for inner transformation, although the churches often underplay this angle, perhaps because people will be attracted to it for selfish motives. Unlike many other aspects of esoteric practice, most of the classical aspects of prayer are well explained already,[38] but I will deal here with certain things which are of great importance in the practice of prayer, yet about which little or nothing seems to be generally known. One is that stages of prayer which seem, at the beginning of the life of prayer, to be so difficult as to be out of reach, can later become relatively familiar and easily reached. This of course requires some kind of progressive and permanent change, and it was for this that Theophan, the man whose researches in the libraries of Middle Eastern monasteries were directly responsible for the extension of Paisious Velitchkovsky's *Dobrotolubyie* (the first Russian version of the *Philokalia*), used the idea of magnetization to God to express the higher stages of hesychastic prayer in which, when the soul reaches a certain point on the path, it is then *rapt in God*, being drawn away from the attraction of the world by the glory given by God within. We also know[39] that Theophan took a great interest in the science of his times, and particularly in magnetic methods then fashionable as a cure for physical ailments; it would not be surprising to find that he himself originated the term. But it would be consistent with his methods to have based it on some earlier idea; and in fact, this is so. Theophan's image of magnetization describes one important aspect of *metanoia*, explaining it by borrowing from the familiar schoolchild's image of the magnetization of iron filings, a graphic image that was in its turn used by Boris Mouravieff. He made it clear that one element of magnetization, in Theophan's sense, is that all the iron filings, representing the desires, have been magnetized so that they all point in the same direction . . . to God. The "magnetic field" which achieves this change: what is this but the state known in the Eastern

Church as *noetic prayer* or prayer of the heart, the inmost and least "intentional" stage of mental prayer?

The second of these almost unknown psychological elements of the life of prayer, an element that actually forms one of the steps in the formation of magnetic center, is the need for a form of what the early Fathers called *nepsis* or watchfulness[40] before prayer can turn inward.

"Watch and pray," says Jesus in the gospel.[41]

Many of the early Fathers spoke or wrote about *nepsis*, but few made it clear that this has a *physical* element or at least requires some kind of definite change in the movement of energy in the organism. Again we find here a familiar pattern: change of thought leads more slowly to change of heart; magnetic center is shown by a life of *nepsis*. Later, unselfish love, the *caritas* of Saint Paul, is added to this *nepsis*.

The third important factor about the life of prayer is the need for *ceaseless prayer*, the need for which was introduced by Saint Paul. On the esoteric path it is necessary to understand the various forms that this can take, depending on the character and lifestyle of the individual. There are in fact two main forms of unceasing prayer which might be described as *spoken* and *unspoken*.

Evagrius made one meaning of this doctrine clearer when he wrote: "Just as bread is nourishment for the body and virtue for the soul, so is noetic prayer nourishment for the nous."[42] Recently, in the terminology introduced by Gurdjieff to fit in with modern thought, the foods for the psyche and the nous have been described as *energies*, in the sense that Palamas said that we cannot know God's essence, but we can know Him by His energies.

Non-Doing

Paradoxically, this question of control without "doing" is linked with another similar difficulty; with the crucial question of how to bring suitable emotions to the point of prayer. A "doing" attitude, an "atomist" or anthropocentric attitude that "I am doing it," "I am praying," prevents this. It has been suggested that it does so by importing inappropriate "active" energies. Unlike these, the correct *hesychastic* energies, to coin a portmanteau term for a concept lacking from the English dictionary, make us sensitive to the personal, the emotional. They make us want to pray, and only when we want to pray can we give attention to our prayer throughout the time of prayer, thus fulfilling one meaning of the biblical idea that we should "pray without ceasing."

Yet these energies, unlike the active energies, convey a certain still-ness, and this paradoxical link of stillness and the will is an essential ingredient of prayer. This comes always with a sense of something greater than ourselves, of dependence on God and on His Holy Spirit.

In simpler terms, one common result of our Western idea that we can "do" almost anything is that normally we confuse control and atten-tion. These are often seen as one and the same, but in fact they are different things, only linked by the fact that attention is needful before we can control something. In prayer, these two are no longer mutually sup-portive. Prayer requires attention without control.

The idea of prayer with the mind in the heart has more than one meaning. It begins, say the Fathers, by concentrating the activity of prayer in the physical heart. It ends in that place to which Saint John of the Cross referred when speaking of "transcending reason with my thought." This itself has two forms:

1. the *imageless* or in Indian terms the *dhyana* stage of prayer or meditation
2. the state of *inner separation*, a major element of *magnetic center*, in which we are detached from and objective to the activities and images of the mind.

This place in the heart is described in the gospels in the images of the pearl of great price and the treasure hid in the field.

Chapter 12

A Nonmonastic Path

For many centuries, almost all the practical work directly linked to the Royal Road has been carried out by monks and nuns, or by laypeople with enough money to live something very close to the monastic life. Seen in this way, this path seems impossible for seekers who are unable to become monks: those who can make little or no change in their external lives. They, like everyone who tries seriously to pray or "meditate"—in either the contemporary or classical sense of this word—will quite early on reach the same problem. The telephone rings. Noises get loud. Somebody needs to talk to you. Worries from everyday life begin to crowd in. The immediate and in a sense correct conclusion—the "obvious" conclusion—is that the two things are mutually exclusive. Attempted solutions vary from soundproof rooms to cottages in the country to booking for month-long retreats. People renounce work for prayer, only to find themselves beset with anxieties caused by lack of income. Yet it seems to them that what they are doing is just what those other men and women did eighteen hundred years ago, when they went off into the desert to seek God.

Some take it further: they approach monasteries simply seeking a refuge from the world, and are surprised when they are not greeted with open arms. They do not understand that monasticism is something more than keeping the world at arm's length.

In fact, renunciation can take outer forms other than monasticism. Other forms have long existed in the church to symbolize the same inner intention and growth in different ways, the most obvious being that of taking *holy orders*.[1] Historically, the great growth of monasticism and the hermetic life, following the establishment of the church under Constantine, suggests that the monastic commitment, with or without formal monastic vows, replaced the taking of holy orders for many people about eighteen hundred years ago, when ordination first became a means to find a career in the world, and the element of renunciation necessary became less important.

Today, certainly, those who are unable, because of responsibilities or temperament or because of the times, to leave the world in the monastic way, need an alternative way of approaching this first renunciation. Although this renunciation need not have any external form, it must in this case be approached directly, taking the form of the internal and psychological process known as *dying to oneself* or to one's old self or false self. The known alternative path by which this is achieved was once described as the Way of the Householder, a way in which our responsibilities become part of the rule or working discipline, and which is based on a particular psychological method that is able to develop inner separation in students with worldly responsibilities. It is this method that is similar to what is sometimes called Karma Yoga.

The householder begins by breaking the illusion of the world, by learning no longer to believe that the world shown by his perceptions and analyses is *real*. For this to occur, he, like the monk, needs to follow exactly the instruction given by Evagrius that "the abandonment of the things of the world is produced by assenting to the science of God." But this assent must take a purely inward form different from that of the monk. This has also been described as a way of living in the world without believing in it. Cassian was perhaps speaking of this when he reminded us that David once wrote: "I am a stranger with thee, and a sojourner, as all my fathers were" (Psalms. 39:12). Thus the Greek word *xenos*, stranger, has great significance in the esoteric tradition, as referring to that little-known part of us which is not at home in the world.

As the gospel says:

> I have given them thy word; and the world hath hated them, because they are not of the world, even as I am not of the world.
>
> I pray not that thou shouldest take them out of the world, but that thou shouldest keep them from the evil.
>
> They are not of the world, even as I am not of the world.
> Sanctify them through thy truth: thy word is truth.
> As thou hast sent me into the world, even so have I also sent them into the world (John 17:14–18).

Monastic and Nonmonastic Ways

S aint Anthony the Great, one of the founders of monasticism and one of the great masters of monastic psychology, wrote that he had discovered that a doctor in a nearby town was more devout than he himself. In a letter he described three types of person: those who seek God out of love, out of fear, or to escape *affliction* (Greek monks and nuns speak of affliction as *thlipsis*, a word that signifies difficulty, suffering, and constriction).[2] The first type progresses rapidly and simply by what has been called, at least in modern terms, "the way of the heart." Taught by certain monasteries, it is sometimes claimed that only this way is known as the Royal Road. But at other times the term seems to have been used to apply to any method that uses the faculty of *diakrisis*, discrimination of spirits, to prevent deviation from the narrow way of the gospel.

The most significant division between the different ways is of course the division between monastic and nonmonastic ways. The difference in the circumstances of individuals between these different ways is such that very different methods are normally used, and the classic descriptions of the Royal Road are certainly based on the monastic life, as are almost all the books on this subject. This is because periods when the nonmonastic way was no longer understood have alternated with periods when it had to "go underground" to avoid persecution, while the outer form of the monastic way has survived intact down to the present time, although its inner content has been lost and restored several times, and indeed, the latest restoration is just now occurring.

The problem is that although at one time many laypeople were able to follow a protected path, giving rise in medieval times to disciplines such as that given in the book *The Sacred Magic of Abramelin the Mage*, which claimed to be possible as a practice only to individuals who could withdraw completely from worldly activity, today the monastic way appears to be unsuitable for those who do not form a firm commitment early in life.

Another ancient statement is that the Royal Road as a term refers to noetic prayer or *prayer of the heart*, a form of noetic ascesis. One Russian émigré thinker wrote about this:

> Although there are other ways and modes of life, and if you like, other practices which have been and are traditionally regarded as righteous, leading to salvation and giving peace to those who follow them . . . this one is preeminently the royal way, surpassing all other practices as soul surpasses body, since it renews the man completely and leads him to sonship of God, miraculously defining in the spirit him who follows it as he should.

Kallistos and Ignatius Tilikoudis call this prayer "prayer
of the heart" and "continuous remembrance of Jesus."[3]

Monastic or nonmonastic, the relation between the Royal Road and prayer
of the heart clearly makes sense, even if there is not complete identity
between them. Prayer of the heart generally has played an important role
on the Way for the larger part of two thousand years, and probably has
roots in apostolic times. But the Royal Road always entails the assistance
of the living God, and this is in general available only to those who
correctly discriminate between "spirits." This discrimination of spirits is
one of the primary characteristics of the esoteric way, since, for someone
of normal human weaknesses, the only way to overcome his own weaknesses is to accept that what is impossible for man is possible for God, and
to ask for and qualify for help. This appears to be the common characteristic of the methods taught by all those who have written about the Royal
Way. Thus the monks of Athos[4] speak about the "grace" of repentance, and
the Athonite tradition advises us to pray for this grace. Saint Isaac the
Syrian, in a prayer, exactly describes the operation of this *medicine*.

O Lord, make me worthy to know you and love you,
not in the knowledge arising from mental exercise
and the dispersion of the mind,
but make me worthy of that knowledge
whereby the mind, in beholding you,
glorifies your nature in this vision
which steals from the mind the awareness of the world.[5]

The Difficulty of Monastic Methods

I n the pursuit of the invisible, the visible world at first appears to be at
least equally important to the inner, so little do we at first know about
the latter. This can be a great hindrance. It is because of this that monasticism—turning away from distraction—often appears to be the most
obvious form of esoteric path. But the fact is that in modern man the
number of psychological ties to the world is normally very large. This is
why Boris Mouravieff and others have claimed that the time of monasticism is over. But at the same time, more knowledge is available about the
monastic form than about other forms of the path, although the latter does
exist. Unpublished writings of Mouravieff speak of the Royal Road in a
monastic form that is simple and direct and requires little special knowledge of those who would follow it. He has also described the methods
used in the monasteries, helping us to understand why such methods

demand monastic conditions, that this is not because monastic methods are easy but because they make such demands on the individual that except in protected conditions they are almost impossible to follow:

> In the working conditions of a monastery, in the kellia and for even stronger reasons in the desert, in solitude, their method proved practical and just. Beyond attendance at services, the rules of this method, called royal, can be summarized in a few lines as follows:
>
> a. Total surrender of the will in favour of that of the master;
> b. Absolute silence;
> c. Youth;
> d. Mastery of sexual energy;
> e. The mastery of the body: struggling against sleep and hunger, genuflections, prostrations, control of the breath.
>
> By these practices—graced overall by silence—one closes the taps through which otherwise, the psychic energy of the monk is lost. From this comes the accumulation in the physical and mental organism of great reserves of fine hydrogens[6] thus saved. Strengthened by this, the disciple practices the prayer of Jesus just as described in the previous chapter.
>
> If the monk, through effective training, came to follow the numbered prescriptions strictly, his prayer acquired an unsuspected strength and, like a flaming arrow, would pierce the veil which separates the I of the Personality from the Real I.
>
> This method is called royal because it is direct, powerful and spontaneous. It does not demand any previous erudition, which in these conditions would serve no purpose.[7]

I can add to this that, on Mount Athos at least, these methods are not simply picked up from books. In addition to the monasteries and the occasional hermitage, the Eastern monastic tradition has this intermediate "circle" of *kellia*—cells or small houses—in each of which a small number of monks work intensively under the direction of an experienced elder. Sometimes these *kellia* exist in villages called *sketes* (see p. 226), but sometimes larger houses with a number of monks are also known as *sketes*, and I suspect, based on very limited meetings with individuals from these houses, that this is because a more demanding discipline is practiced there as in the smaller *sketes*. What kind of discipline? In certain cases, the methods of the tradition are taught to those who later become abbots while they live with specialist masters in *sketes* and *kellia*. Others study in these houses who have no public position.

Each house has a leader, a "spiritual father," and it may have one student or it may have up to eight or nine.

These form the "graduate schools" of the monastic tradition. Their regime is hard. A monk in one of these communities wrote: "According to monastic regulations, the monk sleeps with his cassock, belt, skoufo, and socks on—like a soldier. Just as he must always be found in readiness, where they notify him from the guardhouse for his watch, so the monk also, when called to prayer, he must be ready: he throws off the covers and with one leap finds himself standing. This is repeated every night of his life, because that's when he gets up to fulfill his personal prayer rule."[8] An early reference that gives the background to this situation is fairly readily available in the English language. Saint Anthony's famous *First Letter*, an important document for monasticism, divided seekers of God into three classes, which we might name

1. the just: those who already love God
2. the simple: those who sought God out of fear
3. the rest of us: those who seek God to escape affliction.

Saint Anthony defined these *types*, and showed that they were quite different from one another:

> I think, brethren, that the souls which draw near to the love of God are of three sorts, be they male or female.
>
> There are those who are called by the law of love which is in their nature, and which original good implanted in them at their first creation. The word of God came to them, and they doubted not at all but followed it readily, like Abraham the Patriarch: for when God saw that it was not from the teaching of men that he had learnt to love God, but from the law implanted in the nature of his first compacting, God appeared to him and said, "Get thee out from thy country and from thy kindred and from thy father's house, unto a land that I will show thee" (Genesis 12:1).[9] And he went nothing doubting, but was ready for his calling. He is the pattern of this approach, which still persists in those who follow in his footsteps. Toiling and seeking the fear of God in patience and quiet, they achieve the true manner of life, because their souls are ready to follow the love of God. This is the first kind of calling.
>
> The second calling is this. There are men who hear the written Law testifying of pains and torments prepared for the wicked, and of the promises prepared for those who walk worthily in the fear of God; and by the testimony of the writ-

ten Law their thoughts are roused up to seek to enter into the calling, as David testifies when he says: "The law of the Lord is undefiled, converting the soul: the testimony of the Lord is sure, and giveth wisdom unto the simple" (Psalms 19:7). And in another place he says, "The opening of thy words giveth light and understanding unto the simple" (Psalms 119:130); and much else, all of which we cannot mention now.

The third calling is this. There are souls which at first were hard of heart and persisted in the works of sin; and somehow the good God in his mercy sends upon such souls the chastisement of affliction, till they grow weary, and come to their senses, and are converted, and draw near, and enter into knowledge, and repent with all their heart, and they also attain the true manner of life, like those others of whom we have already spoken.

These are the three approaches by which souls come to repentance, till they attain to the grace and calling of the Son of God.[10]

But the world is changing, and mankind's state of mind has changed with the world in which we must live. In this world now, the proportions of these *types* of men that we meet appear to be different from their proportions among those that Saint Anthony knew. Hence my earlier question asking which of us has met a saint. If there are saints somewhere in the world, there are few in the world we know. Those whom Anthony knew for their innate *love of God* are now few and far between. Even in special places like Athos, such people are now rare. One, perhaps, is my young friend Father P., whose face is perennially softened by his love of God, and who cannot bear too much of the company of worldly individuals like myself; another the saintly Father D., who has been so kind to me, and to whom Christ speaks in simple words, but who has since been troubled by forced contact with our modern world, and has yet to reach the end of the Way. Our world has no place for such men.

About Saint Anthony's second category: at one time, even as late as the end of World War II, such *simple souls* were apprenticed to the monasticism of the Eastern Church in considerable numbers, often coming as young men from peasant backgrounds. Now, with the increasing commercialism of life, there are few such recruits left to come to the monasteries, but I have been privileged to meet some of the last of that earlier generation on Athos, to become friends with one or two of them, and to see that their simplicity hid not an emptiness, but a warmth and fullness that any modern man or woman would envy. Young monks of this kind still do arrive at the mountain, but in their early years there they do not often speak to Western pilgrims, and I think this is because, in their youth, they are kept long hours in the pressure cooker of the Way.

But today there are other kinds of monk in the monasteries of the Eastern Church, and for them the task is not so easy. Most of them are graduates. They include at least one man who was once a pop musician, and several doctors. Some of them, too, are Westerners, and until I read this passage from Anthony, I used to wonder why it was that so many English and American monks that I met on Athos seemed to have failed to reach the peak of that holy mountain which they did so genuinely love. Also, I have met many people who began and sometimes persisted on a path of great difficulty without going off apart from the world; those who have borne *affliction* or *thlipsis*. This thlipsis is something possessed in common by monks who find their monastic life most difficult, and by those laypeople who would perhaps be monks if they were able.

It is thus true that the esoteric path for the layperson is no easier option than that for the monk.

Renunciation of Inner Possessions

N ow perhaps we have a clue. Is there not something in our lives in the West that makes us less suitable today for true spiritual working? And what could it be?

One answer to this is that in the Western world our thinking has become different from what might be called a traditional Christian worldview. To understand this, we need to look with new, more detached eyes at the relation between science and religion as it exists today.

At this point we are suddenly limited in what we can learn from the early Fathers. This is first because most of them were monastic in the broader sense of the term. If they were not monks they were hermits or occupants of small houses that maintained the same monastic isolation from the world. Second, the conditions of modern life are different from any that have gone before in the Christian era. For both these reasons the remainder of this chapter will have to draw more on experience and less on tradition.

At the same time, the Transvolgan Hermits, who for a long time formed the mainstream of Russian spirituality, were once known as the "Non-Possessors." The frugal life of these men (and women) distracts attention from the fact that this name also has an inner meaning: that to give place to God in one's life, one has to be without inner possessions. But inner possessions lead to outer possessions. So the second answer to my question is that we have become dependent—often emotionally dependent—on many things and conditions that people of other times and other places have managed without. Perhaps the best description of this dependency is given by John Kenneth Galbraith in his book *The Culture of Contentment*,[11] a book that suggests, I believe correctly, that the limited worldview that "goes with the territory" of scientific and humanist thought is not the cause but the result of this dependency situation.

But the third thing that makes us less suitable for spiritual working is one that can most certainly be answered by the psychological teachings of the early Fathers. It is that *our minds are overactive* and disobey us, their "owners." Even if we wish to fulfill the Commandments, our minds will not comply. As modern men and women, shaped by Western civilization, this is the place from which we must start our ascesis, the sickness for which we need the medicine that brings repentance. What then can this first renunciation, this *denial of the world*, mean for those outside monasticism? We said earlier that it refers to dying to oneself, and at the first renunciation the self we must die to is the false self that clings to the past and becomes overly concerned with the future. Cassian writes that the first renunciation was described in the biblical call to Abraham, which instructed him to: "Come away from your native land and from your family and from the house of your father. He said first 'from your native land,' that is, from the riches of this world and from the goods of the earth. Second, 'from your family,' that is, from one's past way of life, character and faults, which cling to us from birth and are linked to us by a sort of close relationship and blood. He said, thirdly, 'from the house of your father,' that is, from all worldly memory arising before our eyes."[12]

This is often taken in an external way, so that people leave home and go into "exile" as monks, nuns, or hermits. But it can be understood in an inward way as describing the main sources of our *inner possessions*: community, family, and ancestors. For the householder, the first renunciation means giving up inner possessions. This is the inner meaning of Christ's dialogue with the rich young man. Paradoxically, Christ here says that obedience to the Commandments is not enough. This appears to conflict with the idea that faith replaces the law . . . but a correct understanding of both ideas will remove this apparent conflict.

Higher, timeless knowledge is knowledge that reveals and evokes the memory of authentic experience and guards against false memory, as when I imagine I am what I merely *possess*; as when I imagine I am body, when I merely *possess* a body; as when I imagine I am thought, when I merely *possess* thought; as when I imagine I am feeling, when I merely *possess* feeling; as when I imagine I am imagination, when I merely *possess* imagination; as when I imagine I am knowledge, when I merely *possess* knowledge. The problem is that when I imagine I am what in fact I only *possess*, this leads me to imagine limits to myself, to imagine I am hurt where I am in reality untouched, to imagine I know something which I have only read in a book somewhere, to imagine I cannot do something, when in fact I can do it, and that I can do things of which I am entirely incapable.

In the terms of the gospel, to imagine I am what I only possess is to be *rich*. Rich in illusion.

> The young man saith unto him, All these things have I kept from my youth up: what lack I yet?
>
> Jesus said unto him, If thou wilt be perfect, go and sell that thou hast, and give to the poor, and thou shalt have treasure in heaven: and come and follow me.
>
> But when the young man heard that saying, he went away sorrowful: for he had great possessions.
>
> Then said Jesus unto his disciples, Verily I say unto you, That a rich man shall hardly enter into the kingdom of heaven.
>
> And again I say unto you, It is easier for a camel to go through the eye of a needle, than for a rich man to enter into the kingdom of God (Matthew 19:20–24).

For the householder, the inner meaning of this gospel passage refers to *inner possessions*, the whole passage to those who are inwardly rich. In its inner sense, this term *possession*[13] refers to our possessive attitude toward our thoughts and ideas: they are possessions, and therefore we are *rich*, if we believe that they belong to us, for this leads us to *assent* to them, giving them a kind of authority over us . . . the authority of false personality that makes us believe our thoughts without checking them adequately; makes us want what our desires want without questioning their origin; makes us assent to anger without understanding its causes.

> Thus we lose any freedom of choice in our lives.
>
> And this is a clue to the meaning of this word *assent*.

The way of understanding, in the Gurdjieff terminology the Fourth Way, different from what Ouspensky called the ways of the monk, the yogi and the fakir, begins when conscious influences, first understood as influences not coming from the past, lead to two successive inner actions. First, they lead us to begin discriminating between these *timeless* influences and the influence of the world. This is the preliminary stage of the Way described by Mouravieff as the *Track*. Saint Anthony says of this stage: "Then the Spirit that is his guide begins to open the eyes of his soul, to give to it also repentance, that it may be purified."[14] Second, they lead us to begin to choose between them. Anthony says: "The nous then starts to discriminate between the body and the soul, as it begins to learn from the Spirit how to purify both by repentance. And, taught through this conscious influence, the nous becomes our guide to the labours of body and soul, showing us how to purify them. And it separates us from all the fruits of the flesh which have been mingled with all the members of the body since the first transgression, and brings back each of the members of the body to its original condition, having nothing in it from the spirit of Satan."[15]

Yoga and Discrimination

In the classical teachings of Karma Yoga, which include the same renunciations under quite different terms, this renunciation is traditionally obtained by *discrimination* between the transient, the changing picture of the world, and the eternal, an unchanging and therefore unperceived reality, a discrimination arrived at in Christian terms by *diakrisis*: by clearly distinguishing between the spirit of the world and the Spirit of God. This is a "first step" or first qualification in an ancient system of what have been described as "four qualifications for perceiving reality."[16]

The householder, because he or she cannot follow the path of the monk by outwardly turning away from the world, requires special knowledge, knowledge which will not only inform but convince; which will cause us to *recognize* that the world we perceive and infer is only an incomplete reflection of an inner spiritual reality, and which will reveal to us the uncomfortable truth that our thoughts and beliefs are not our personal property. To know this is to possess *esoteric knowledge*, and practical work on the esoteric path will show that this is identical to the science referred to by Evagrius as the science of God, although the same term can also be used to describe the monastic path as an application of that science. Living in the world, but not being of the world—as this idea has also been put in the past—more normally takes the form described of Saint Anthony's third and most common type of seeker, those who seek God to escape affliction. Yet this too depends on our clearly differentiating inner and outer worlds, inner and outer values, and then learning, under the goad of affliction, to assent to the inner, to the Spirit that comes from God.

The inner process is now clear; psychologically, the first renunciation is approached by means of something similar to the discernment of spirits, spoken of earlier. In this case, it consists of discriminating between what students of Eastern traditions would call the *real* and the *unreal*—did not Blavatsky's *Voice of the Silence*[17] have the phrase: "Lead me from the unreal to the real"? We must choose between the ever-changing and the eternal, whose most important characteristic is that it does not change. For the Christian, this eternal is a "personal God," in the sense that He plays an actual part in our lives, so that we must learn to see as real not only the unchanging, eternal reality that was well known by the Greeks before Saint Paul, but also the changing providence of God: the action of the unchanging in the world of change.

This inner renunciation is possible even for those who cannot or will not be monks or nuns. For the householder the first renunciation begins with assent to something inner, in practice with assent to some good impulse.[18] But as with monastic renunciation, repentance is always a "headless axe" if assent is given indiscriminately, "without *diakrisis*." Experience on pilgrimage shows that in fact the two paths, that of the monk and that of the householder, are virtually the same except in their outward forms— which are of course very different. For the householder, as with the monk or nun, as long as his *diakrisis* turns away from life only *into illusion* it is feeble, and does not cut the bonds of life, so that it can be said, paradoxically, that while the monk turns away from life, the student on the Way of the Householder must turn towards life, towards real life, facing or being forced to face up to those parts of life that we all habitually try to avoid.

Thus, monk or householder, every student on this Way must come face-to-face with the *first renunciation*. But, for the householder, the first renunciation is a purely inner process, yet inner or esoteric science is as aware as "outer science" of the dangers of subjectivism and all forms of self-delusion.

For this reason, even the householder's inner renunciation must be proved in the outside world. For the layperson on the path of the householder, the equivalent of physically leaving the world is that our understanding is *tested in life*. Testing, in this sense, is an apparently spontaneous process whereby circumstances in which we find ourselves will reveal to us how—in simple terms—our actions differ from our ideas. This requires explanation, some of which cannot be given in theory, but only by showing to us the specifically personal meaning of events in our lives.

But some "tests" are triggered by specific ideas within esoteric science, sometimes ideas found in sources such as the gospel. One such idea, which continually reveals us to ourselves, is the idea that on this Way we must pay for what we get: that real progress only comes by giving up something that at the time seems important to us. If we are unwilling to make any real return for something we claim to value, this only reveals the shallowness of our valuation. And so important is money to modern man that it is particularly in our unwillingness to make financial payment for "intangibles" (like esoteric knowledge) that the shallowness of our roots is revealed. As Cassian said: "the appearance of renunciation will be useless for us. It will be merely the body coming out of Egypt. More exalted and more valuable will be renunciation by the heart."[19]

Changing the mind is not enough. There must be a change of heart.

The Two "Legs" of the Tradition

For those on the Way of the Householder as well as for monks, *watchfulness* in the head and *prayer* in the heart both play important roles in esoteric development. The nature of the psychological method is that before we can practice these key elements in the Way, both head and heart must be subject to major changes in the way they perform. These changes are much greater than those who have not experienced them can understand. Saint Maximos the Confessor said that watchfulness keeps the nous pure of provocations while prayer brings grace into one's heart.

In certain modern experiments to find ways of traveling the Royal Road under contemporary conditions, methods are being developed which combine noetic ascesis as a form of prayer with the watchfulness and self-remembering introduced in the psychological method of Gurdjieff and Ouspensky, and these methods are now producing results. We mentioned earlier how it was Maximos the Confessor again who described these two sides as follows: "The reward of self-mastery is detachment, and that of faith is knowledge. And detachment gives rise to discernment [*diakrisis*, discernment of spirits], while knowledge gives rise to love for God. The mind that has succeeded in the active life advances in prudence, the one in the contemplative life, in knowledge."[20] And a little later: "The reward for the labours of virtue is detachment and knowledge, for these become our patrons in the kingdom of heaven just as the passions and ignorance are the patrons of eternal punishment."[21]

There are different degrees of discrimination that are difficult to put into words, and which in most cases can only be distinguished by their psychological effect on us.

Discrimination has to possess a certain depth before it can even begin to lead to the struggle for *metanoia* and so pass on to inner separation and so to *apatheia*. What defines this depth? Discrimination between the body and the world is not enough; it is not enough, for example, to conclude that "*I am my body.*" Discrimination of the ordinary *mind* from the body and from the world is still not enough. Clement of Alexandria writes: "To stones, then, belongs a permanent state. Plants have a nature; and the irrational animals possess impulse and perception, and likewise the two characteristics already specified. But the reasoning faculty (nous), being peculiar to the human soul, ought not to be impelled similarly with the irrational animals, but ought to discriminate appearances, and not to be carried away by them."[22]

The stage that Western man in general is now entering would seem to demand discrimination of the knowing mind (nous) from the activity of mind and from the body. But this is not enough. Discrimination of the unchanging element in oneself from everything that changes is still insufficient, for it leaves one powerless in the world.

Clement describes the qualities that belong to such a person, to the *gnostic*, in his terminology, a Christian man or woman following the inner tradition. This true gnostic has an inner separation which is recognizable by a quality of *apatheia*, while the false gnostic is ruled by the passions so that many of them are what Clement, living at the same time as many of the Gnostic sects, described elsewhere as libertine gnostics. Here Clement describes the *apatheia* of the fully accomplished Christian gnostic: "This is the really good man, who is dispassionate; having, through the habit or disposition of the soul endued with virtue, transcended the whole life of passion. He has everything dependent on himself for the attainment of the end."[23]

Mouravieff's Method

Over two thousand or so years, what was a major factor in early Christendom, an esoteric or inner understanding of Christian tradition, has been progressively forgotten, so that today's Christianity— and today's Christians—are very different from those of two thousand years ago. Yet from time to time, when the need arises, this forgotten tradition has developed a broad form for nonmonastic use, as well as its narrower monastic form. I remember an American monk on Mount Athos complaining to me, on one of my visits to the Holy Mountain, that "the problem with this place is that we [the monks] cannot change anything." One significance of this statement is that even with its variants of *kellia*, *sketes*, and the hermetic life as found on Athos, the monastic environment is more or less standard from century to century. As a result, monastic methods are more easily standardized, and knowledge is not so easily lost.

But knowledge is also needed that is not easily obtainable from monastic sources. Boris Mouravieff, in unpublished texts, has perhaps most clearly described what must be done to obtain results from the nonmonastic psychological method, in which both head and heart must be subject to major changes in the way they perform.

But for those who are not monastics, we must come back to the question of how to achieve this change of heart, and what it could mean to do so. Saint Maximos the Confessor says elsewhere that watchfulness keeps the nous pure of provocations, and prayer brings grace into man's heart, while obedience to the will of God cures the activities of the psyche, and constant watchfulness combined with attentive prayer cures the nous. In his unpublished writings Boris Mouravieff wrote about similar methods, speaking specifically of a formula suited to the needs of householders:

> The method of *Gnosis* is a psychological method, the only method which for active esoteric work does not demand a change in our way of life. This method allows one to progress, and that more quickly compared with in the monasteries. The essential elements of this method are three in number:
>
> a. Prayer;
> b. Doubled attention and thus *presence*;[24]
> c. Constatation.
>
> The simultaneous practice of these three elements involves the whole Personality. . . . This obliges the three centers to assist each other. This is the essential. All the other exercises are certainly useful but are no more than auxiliary to this method.
>   The psychological method . . . in its fullness has many elements in common with Raja Yoga, and moreover with the Orthodox tradition called "the Royal Road." The characteristic as it is presented in *Gnosis* is that it can be applied while we are fully active in the everyday world, and does not demand any change in the way of life demanded of us in that world.[25]

More interesting, inner experience shows that these elements link together in a particular way, and also that they link with both the Fourth Way teachings and the teachings of the early Fathers.

Head and heart, *watchfulness* and *prayer*, are both known to play important roles in esoteric development. Mouravieff's term *constatation* refers to a third element, *diakrisis* or discrimination.

In the terms used by Gurdjieff and others the idea of doubled attention, of attention in and out at the same time, the "two-headed arrow," is clearly associated with the second of these three elements. The relevance of constatation—defined by Mouravieff as perception without judgment—is equally clear. Prayer in this context—prayer of the heart, a form of prayer which begins as a practice but ends as a state—links with these two as a *missing method* whose probable characteristics were described by Ouspensky before his death.

Together these three fulfill the instruction of Boris Mouravieff, given in *Gnosis*,[26] that the student of this path should act as if he or she possessed a complete *magnetic center*. That is, they represent the states—the two "conscious shocks"[27]—needed before the active psyche, what Mouravieff called "the Personality," is able to serve as a vehicle for higher consciousness: for what the Fourth Way teachers would simply describe as Consciousness. Equally, these states exist in the teaching of the Fathers, where we can best understand them by terms such as:

Watchfulness
Noetic Prayer

Watchfulness (Greek *nepsis*) is in fact a union or combination of the two states that form the complete stages of presence and constatation. A typical reference in the early Fathers confirms their belief in the interdependence of watchfulness and prayer, as well as showing how these qualities combine to assist in the struggle with pride, leading to the *humility* that opens the heart to higher powers: "The life of attentiveness, brought to fruition in Christ Jesus, is the father of contemplation and spiritual knowledge. Linked to humility, it engenders divine exaltation and thoughts of the wisest kind."[28]

The therapeutic interpretation of patristic psychology now being developed in Greece emphasizes the doctrine of the early Fathers that again tells us that the cure of the nous requires watchfulness and prayer, mainly the so-called noetic prayer of the heart. It is by these means, it teaches, that the grace of God comes and illumines the nous: "According to the fathers, watchfulness is the restraint or guarding of the reason within the heart so that no thought enters to provoke sin." Saint Paul wrote to Timothy that he should: "Remain watchful through everything" (2 Timothy 4:5).

Watchfulness (Nepsis)

N oetic prayer was discussed in the previous chapter. Watchfulness is both a state and a practice, the practice necessarily preceding and preparing the way for the state. The term originates in a famous gospel quotation: "Watch and pray, that ye enter not into temptation: the spirit indeed is willing, but the flesh is weak" (Matthew 26:41).

The meaning of this idea can be found in modern spiritual methods that combine noetic ascesis as a form of prayer with the self-remembering introduced in Fourth Way teachings. These methods parallel certain methods described by Saint Hesychius the Priest, who wrote,

The great lawgiver Moses—or rather, the Holy Spirit—indicates
the pure, comprehensive and ennobling character of this virtue

[watchfulness], and teaches us how to acquire and perfect it, when he says: "Be attentive to yourself, lest there arise in your heart a secret thing which is an iniquity" (Deuteronomy 15:9).[29]

According to this, watchfulness is both a state and a practice, the practice necessarily preceding and preparing the way for the state. The complete development of *nepsis* is a necessary psychological stage in the Royal Way, an element of the psychological method. During this stage, the primary efforts required are that of *constatation* and the effort to be present, sometimes known as self-remembering.

Since *nepsis* represents an essential stage on the Way, it is not surprising to find it as one of the steps of the Indian system known as the Eightfold Yoga, put into writing in Patanjali's Yoga Sutras. There, this step is called *dharana*, one of a series of words in Sanskrit that belong to the ancient psychological teachings. *Dharana* is generally translated as *concentration* and is often understood to mean concentration *on* something, such as a symbol or mantra, but Boris Mouravieff makes it clear that the idea of concentration has another meaning involving a concentrated remembering or attending to ourselves, done in a certain way that extends what Gurdjieff described as self-remembering to the point where it incorporates an inner-separation. In unpublished writings of Mouravieff recently translated, it is described in this way:

> Now the natural state of the intellect [the nous], concentrated, as we said, is concentrated on the whole of the being of the man, to put it a different way, he concentrates on his *presence in himself*.

Observation suggests that, in all inner traditions, wherever this stage known as *dharana* or *nepsis* is absent, spiritual efforts lead to wrong results. This important concept has no real equivalent in contemporary English thought and language, apart from Fourth Way terminology, where it seems to be referred to, in works such as the commentaries of Maurice Nicoll, as *inner separation*. The lack of a similar term in ordinary English is significant, since such concepts must be understood before they have any practical value. Like the Sanskrit terms *viveka* and *vairyagya*, *pratyahara* has been misunderstood because these words are based on experiences so uncommon in our society that we have no words for them in English. In fact, the words listed here refer to certain changes possible in the relation between awareness and the activity of the mind, normally under specific conditions of reduced mental activity. Only in this condition—only when we are free from distraction—is true *nepsis* possible. In Christian tradition, this is hinted at in the Gospel According to Thomas, in the passage that says: "The fox has his lair, the bird has his nest, but the son of man has no place to lay his head."[30]

In the terms of the Fathers, *nepsis* prevents continued accumulation of intoxicating contents into the psyche, therefore defining the meaning of the term *sleep* in that passage of Saint Matthew. It is clear, too, that it also prevents the waste of subtle energies necessary for our further development. It was Saint Hesychius, again, who said: "Watchfulness is a spiritual method which, if sedulously practised over a long period, completely frees us with God's help from impassioned thoughts, impassioned words, and evil actions. . . . It is, in the true sense, purity of heart, a state blessed by Christ when he says: 'Blessed are the pure in heart, for they shall see God.' "[31]

In fact, *nepsis* demands a dual inner effort that could be regarded as an effort to awake. One aspect is an effort to inhibit our automatic reaction to both internal and external activities. This could be called "breaking identification," or breaking from the associative state in which we spend most of our lives. This change begins—at first briefly—only after we are able to stop "taking the line of least resistance" in our lives. This inner stop must be repeatedly begun, and is begun each time by a definite decision or resolution. This is more difficult than we might assume. The second effort is to be inwardly attentive or present, in a form that also involves the need to remain "in the present moment." The results of these processes over a period of time is the accumulation of *hesychastic* energies in the nous, so that we can perceive in a state of *nepsis*, noetically, that is, in stillness.

Certain methods of prayer, and certain methods of meditation, develop this *nepsis* as a stage in the development of "prayer of the heart," but these are by no means the whole of this practice. In true prayer of the heart, *nepsis* continues automatically so that at a very late stage all the practices are merged into one.

Nepsis also plays a part in the effort of attention necessary for mastery of certain skills, in working at a professional level, and in certain movements and actions that never become easy or automatic. It links with the *Ora et Labora* cycle of periods of work interspersed with periods of prayer. It will be found that these practices can only be carried out to full effect in a state of *nepsis*.

Why is *nepsis* so important? It may be helpful to look at it in a quite different way. There is a shift in us, as we wake up in the morning, where we move out of early morning daydreaming and obtain (relatively) more objectivity and more control over our mind. One of the points of growth in adolescence involves the development of ways to deal with this change by acquiring some freedom from adolescent fantasy—which is an obstacle to clear perception. The same obstacle to perception does not exist in young children, but begins in adolescence, and is therefore connected with misuse of sex energies.

What is learned following this change has an emotional quality that could be described in terms of "learning by heart." This question of learning by heart is absolutely crucial. It is the question of faith.

Faith is never blind belief, it is not learned from words alone, but rests on "the evidence of things unseen" (Hebrews 11:1). "This inner struggle," writes I. M. Kontzevitch,[32] "is vividly portrayed to us by Saint Hesychius of Jerusalem (5th Century), a disciple of Saint Gregory the Theologian." In this quotation, Saint Hesychius wrote:

> Our mind, being something of light appearance and innocent, easily gives itself over to daydreaming and is unrestrainedly subject to evil thoughts, if it does not have in itself such a concept which, like a monarch over the passions, holds itself constantly under control and bridles it.
>
> A ship does not move without water: and there is no progress whatsoever in guarding of the mind without sobriety with humility and prayer to Jesus Christ.
>
> Stones are used for the foundation of a house; but for this virtue (the guarding of the mind), both the foundation and the root are the holy and venerable name of our Lord Jesus Christ. Quickly and easily can a foolish captain wreck his ship during a storm, dismissing the sailors, throwing the sails and oars into the sea, and going to sleep himself; but much more quickly can the soul be drowned by the demons if, when the thoughts begin to emerge, it does not guard sobriety, and invoke the name of Jesus Christ.[33]

And in another place he writes: "Watchfulness is continual fixing and halting of thought at the entrance to the heart. In this way predatory and murderous thoughts are marked down as they approach and what they say and do is registered."[34]

This is a real key. When it is fully matured, the state of watchfulness is quite clearly recognizable. It gives control of the thoughts which, when fast and confused, disturb its stillness. This control, briefly described in the *Philokalia*, is a practical key to the whole psychological method. The first step towards it is to realize that we cannot stop thinking. When we speak of control of thoughts, we do not mean stopping the associative mind from thinking, for thought is its nature; to be more precise, association is the active content of the mind. Without this activity, that layer of the mind does not exist.

But control of thought is possible through a process of developing *choice* or controlling *assent*, a process that leads a long way: "When the soul endowed with intelligence firmly exercises her freedom of choice in the right way, and reins in like a charioteer the incensive and appetitive aspects of her nature, restraining and controlling her passionate impulses, she receives a crown of victory; and as a reward for her labours, she is granted life in heaven by God her Creator."[35]

Choice is acquired with the *neptic state* which arises through the awakening of the noetic consciousness or noetic sense, at which point we become capable of refusing to react or respond to the provoking thoughts. This might be regarded as an inner meaning of freedom of choice. Conversely, as long as the nous *identifies* with the associative processes— as long as its attitude is that the associative activities are personal possessions—the associative movement is communicated to the nous, and disturbs it. The nous then retransmits the disturbing movement to the thoughts, to the feelings, even to the body, as waves on the sea move every ship. Through the medium of the captive or identified nous, movement in one faculty acts associatively on the others, so that disturbance of one part disturbs all. When the identification of the nous ends, these motions are stilled, and so the process of association ceases to act between the different "centers" of the psyche. Then, as one of the Fathers put it, "the heart is delivered from all thoughts."

And here is another key, something that seems difficult before it is passed, but on looking back seems easy, a place which must be found by overcoming certain illusions about ourselves and our lives. Everyone who seeks God will at some time come to this place in themselves: "Although it lacks a few comforts, a life of watchfulness is not an empty life. On the contrary, this life of remembrance of God while following conscience contains an inexhaustible source of spiritual joys, against which earthly joys are wormwood compared to honey."[36] This is *noetic hesychia*, stillness of the nous. It is, sometimes at least, regarded as synonymous with "dwelling in God."

It is also a major element in the self-consciousness of the Fourth Way teachings.

Presence

Most of the time, people find it impossible to "jump"[37] straight into the neptic state. It is at this point that we may have to work at one time on only one or another of the components of this state. One of these components is defined by the fact that unless we are present, a state of watchfulness does not exist.

But what does it mean to be *present*, and who is it who must be present? In prayer we must relax our control but at certain stages must intensify attention so that *prosevchi*, attentive prayer, links with that other Greek word, *prosochi*, which means care and attentiveness in general. The distinction between care and doing is well described by the difference between the different roles played by our two hands during activities like writing or drawing. For a normal right-handed person, the right hand carries out the action, while the left hand fulfills a less active but equally essential role. *Prosochi* and *prosevchi* are "left hand" activities.

Indian teachings continually refer to the *atman* or self, and in Christian doctrine there are certain mentions of an "inner self" in the early Fathers. For instance, at the beginning of chapter 9, we quoted a passage from Saint Hesychius which included the phrase: "the impassioned thoughts of his inner self, which is the nous." Other passages, particularly from Hesychius, also speak of this inner self. Historically, there are several sources that reveal these ideas as a symbolization of the inner relationships more fully expressed in Christianity.

One experiences the necessity for this kind of care in any personal relationship. If one person takes too firm a "right hand" control of a conversation, the other person normally feels shut out of proper communication. Communication requires a certain attentive flexibility which comes when one recognizes someone as a person. It requires a degree of humility. It requires "left handed" attentiveness.

In particular, there is the idea that God cannot be known by the personality, but can be known through the "real Self." God becomes real to me only when I am real or, to put it another way, I can sense the *presence* of a person only when I am at least partially present, only when I am in the "present moment": "There be many that say, Who will show us any good? LORD, lift thou up the light of thy countenance upon us" (Psalms 4:6).

This presence is an essential element in esotericism. Most esoteric teachings can be put into practice only when we are present. At other times, when we come under the rule of the past, giving our thoughts to past and future, we have little possibility of any change in ourselves.

This presence is the "image" that, when fully developed, makes us a "real person." Cabalistic texts[38] use the term *Microprosopus*, related to the Hebrew letter *vau*, as symbol of the Son or Messiah. Modern Greek theology uses the word *prosopon*, the equivalent of the Latin *persona*, as a specialized concept of the *person*, referring to the divine *image* within each human being which must be realized before we can be what God would have us be, and so before we can know God. In Saint Theophan's terms, this is our original good nature which has been overlaid.[39] This is renewed in baptism but is fully revealed only in *theosis*, when we ourselves become godlike. But it begins to be revealed when we are freed, even briefly, from psychological captivity.

Another factor in the same Hebrew system is the "vast countenance," *Macroprosopus*, by which we understand the "world"—the universe—as our glimpse of the countenance of the creator God, the countenance being the manifest, the "small" part we can recognize. These terms may not go back to pre-Christian Judaism, but the idea behind them most certainly does. As we fully understand what we are able to glimpse of *Macroprosopus*, we can come to recognize Him, even though we still will not know "all" about Him. By *Microprosopus*, then, we recognize God by his image reflected in action within ourselves, and the Christ of the gospel not only taught that divine image and spoke as that divine image, but lived it out visibly in His life, making the Father visible to those who had not yet learned to see Him imaged out in the universe.

This recognition is a key step in spiritual growth.

As we are now, if we try to do the will of God, problems arise from our inability to recognize this divine image. The nature of this conflict is expressed, and some solutions suggested, in the parable of the coach or chariot that is found in many spiritual traditions. This image is important in the Bhagavad Gita. But it is no less important in the early Christian *argot*[40] or "language of parable." In Gregory of Nyssa (see chapter 6), the idea of the chariot was linked with certain important facts about the inner life in ways that support the claim of early Christian origin of teachings that came out of Russia with the revolution.

This state of presence is also implied in the following well-known verse from the Psalms: "Be still, and know that I am God: I will be exalted among the heathen, I will be exalted in the earth" (Psalms 46:10).

The Ark As Separation from the World

The human mind, seen broadly, is vastly complex, and as a result the actual process of transforming the mind is if anything more complex than the simplified description given in the previous pages. It is to deal with this complexity and describe the progressive development of this process that the tradition uses an image that in its modern form is known as a *magnetic center*. Boris Mouravieff's *Gnosis* describes this magnetic center as a cage. This image seems at first sight unnecessary, because it seems obvious that a valid image would be the formation of a psychological or inner equivalent of the monk or hermit's *cell*, into which he withdraws from distraction. This latter image is valid, but there are two good reasons for using the idea of the cage. First, in a cage, nothing can enter or leave, yet you can see out quite clearly. The second reason is that this is, in fact, an ancient image. Saint Neilos the Ascetic (died ca. A.D. 430) writes: "Now the food of the passions, as we have already stated many times, consists of sense-impressions. They nourish the passions by attacking the soul with a succession of mental fantasies or idols. That is why Moses put screens of lattice-work around the altar in the tabernacle (cf. Exodus 27:4), signifying that if we wish to keep our mind pure like a tabernacle we should do the same. Just as the lattices around the altar prevented anything unclean from entering, so we should weave a mental barrier against the senses by reflecting on the terrors of the coming judgement, and so bar the entry to unclean impressions."[41]

The ark is another image of exactly the same thing. I wrote earlier of how the monasteries of the Eastern Church call worshipers to church not only with bells but by the hammering of a wooden sounding board they call the *semantron*. They have a myth in which this *semantron* represents Noah hammering the last planks in the ark—a hidden way of saying that *the monastery is an ark*. This refers to the traditional doctrine that the inner teaching serves as an ark to preserve all that is good when mankind is threatened with disaster. But the nonmonastic tradition, as we said, builds its ark in a different way, although the outcome is the same.

What does this image of the ark represent? The story of Moses and of the escape of the Israelites from the Egyptians has been seen since the earliest days of the church as a parable for the escape of the soul from the "Egypt" of worldly life. When Gregory of Nyssa, in his *Life of Moses*, writes about that other ark, in which the infant Moses was set adrift, he does so in terms that clearly express the need to establish certain inner disciplines that take the form of an artificial mental center or divinely created center in the mind.

In this passage from the *Life of Moses*, Saint Gregory wrote about what is called the "second birth," using the image of Moses being saved from the river by Pharaoh's daughter:

> We can most certainly enter upon a better birth into the realm of light, however much the unwilling tyrant is distressed, and we can be seen with pleasure and be given life by the parents of this goodly offspring, even though it is contrary to the design of the tyrant. . . . It is the function of free will both to beget this virtuous male offspring and to nourish it with proper food and to take forethought how to save it unharmed from the water. For there are those who present their children to the tyrant, delivering them naked and without forethought to the

stream. I am speaking of life as a stream made turbulent by the successive waves of passion, which plunge what is in the stream under the water and drown it.

Whenever life demands that the sober and provident rational thoughts that are the parents of the male child launch their good child on the billows of this life, they make him safe in an ark so that when he is given to the stream he will not be drowned. The ark, constructed out of various boards, would be education in the different disciplines, which holds what it carries above the waves of life.[42]

This was spoken of as a discipline, not simply as an idea, and it has also been described as a specific antidote to pride. Saint Therese of Lisieux speaks of the same thing in a quite distinctive way when she tells of how, in preparing for her first communion, she spontaneously formed something similar. She had been given a devotional passage written for her, and wrote about her response to it: "Of course, I'd been preparing my mind for a long time beforehand, but it needed a fresh impetus—it had to be garnished, as it were, with fresh flowers, to make our Lord feel at home. The flowers were the many pious practices which I adopted at the time, only the buds from which they sprang were the aspirations and acts of love, even more numerous, which you'd written down for daily use in my little book."[43]

For ordinary people like you and me, the formation of our own ark is much slower and more elaborate, involving all kinds of intellectualism and mistaken efforts, and one of the mistakes which it should prevent as it begins to be formed would be the mistake of expecting things to go for us just as quickly and easily as they went for the remarkable Saint Theresa.

In his work *Gnosis*, Boris Mouravieff says of this ark: "This is the first key and the effective beginning of esoteric evolution."[44]

Gregory of Nyssa's view is probably slightly one-sided. The other side of the same question is put by Clement of Alexandria, who was a major formative element in the line from which Gregory emerged. Certainly he was the principal spokesman for a premonastic inner interpretation of the Christian doctrine, a psychological teaching that might well be suitable for people who do not have enough time for monastic methods. He wrote: "Before we believed in God, the dwelling-place of our heart was unstable, truly a temple built with hands. For it was full of idolatry, and was a house of demons through doing what was opposed to God."[45]

Applying this to Nyssa's explanation suggests that the new ark or temple reflects the Jewish idea of the Ark of the Covenant, which traveled with the Israelites through the desert; when the temple in Jerusalem was built, the Ark resided in the Holy of Holies, which ordinary men and women were not permitted to enter. Taken personally, such an idea seems no more than a form of elitism, but understood as a parable for an inner process, it has great meaning. In its inner sense, this artificial center, this temple not made with hands, must be a divine influence, a divine presence acting within the human mind, a presence that becomes at the same time a shift of the center of gravity of that life to revolve not around itself but around God: instead of being self-centered, the individual becomes God-centered.

Of course the same distinction, between the instability of a mind founded on knowledge gained by purely human means and the stability of the *nous* that relies on knowledge gained from God, applies to us right to the present day. Higher knowledge stills the mind.

Magnetic Center

In this penetration and transformation of the human soul by higher influences, certain students will recognize an early reference to the magnetic center, which the nonmonastic inner tradition teaches us to construct so as to protect our inner spiritual growth from the external threats of the *tyrant*, the power that "forces the world to labor for empty gains." The basic idea of the magnetic center, the idea of an artificial "center" in the psyche formed of special disciplines as described in Gregory of Nyssa's ark analogy, applies as much to true monasticism as it does to nonmonastic processes; its later stages described by Theophan the Recluse in the middle of the last century, which link it with noetic prayer, were clearly as relevant to monastics as to anyone else. Yet during the past century the idea of magnetic center has been specifically developed in relation to the psychological method, which is of much greater importance in nonmonastic esotericism.

P. D. Ouspensky in the 1930s described how it first appears as a small artificial center within our psychology, whose effects at this stage are to draw us to sources by which it may itself develop further. This development to the point of awakening of the heart is described by Boris Mouravieff. From this, a natural sequence of events leads to the awakening of noetic prayer: "Continuity of attention produces inner stability; inner stability produces a natural intensification of watchfulness; and this intensificaton gradually and in due measure gives contemplative insight into spiritual warfare. This in its turn is succeeded by persistence in the Jesus Prayer and by the state that Jesus confers, in which the intellect, free from all images, enjoys complete quietude."[46] In this condition, a *new life* of the emotions grows within us, which new life, Theophan remarks, must be treated with care until it grows and becomes stronger. From this point on, the student has left behind the "old man," while in this *ecstasy* the new man is transported into the life of God.

Modern interpretations of this idea of the magnetic center appear somewhat different. They fall into two classes. We have seen how P. D. Ouspensky wrote about the magnetic center as a slowly developing "complex" of ideas—"formed from above"—that draw the individual to the esoteric path. Boris Mouravieff a little later extended the idea in a way that shows how the same thing fits Gregory of Nyssa's image of the ark in which Moses was placed by his mother, described earlier. At this stage, the involuntary attraction of the first stage has become an active struggle to overcome past habits of thought, feeling, and action that still rule the student's life. Saint Theophan then describes a third stage, magnetization or gravitation to God, which is presumably the source of the name *magnetic center* which in its character is close to the infused contemplation of Western spirituality.

Passive Unconscious Stage: Attraction to the Way

P. D. Ouspensky wrote clearly about this stage, which is primarily of interest to nonmonastics in whom magnetic center is formed in the way we would today describe as the formation of a "complex," by *diakrisis* or discrimination of certain spiritual influences. This process involves a search for the truth, which is in fact a search for influences that will feed the soul at this stage in its growth; it is clear that Ouspensky was speaking of an earlier stage in the same process described by Theophan, when he writes:

> The results of the influences whose source lies outside life collect together within him, he remembers them together, feels them together. They begin to form within him a certain whole. He does not give a clear account to himself as to what, how, and why, or if he does give an account to himself, then he explains it wrongly. But the point is not in this, but in the fact that the results of these influences collect together within him, and after a time they form within him a kind of Magnetic Center, which begins to attract to itself kindred influences and in this manner it grows. If the Magnetic Center receives sufficient nourishment, and if there is no strong resistance on the part of the other sides of a man's personality which are the results of influences created in life, the Magnetic Center begins to influence the man's orientation, obliging him to turn round and even to move in a certain

direction. When the Magnetic Center attains sufficient force and
development, a man already understands the idea of the way
and he begins to look for the way.[47]

Although neither this description nor the stage it describes has in the past
formed part of the ordinary Christian inner tradition (probably because at
one time teaching began beyond this point), there is no reason why it
should not do so. There is otherwise little need to explain this clear
statement, but it does need to be put into context. The same structure,
formed in the human mind by words coming from "higher levels," not
only makes us aware of the possibility of growth and shows us how to
connect with others who know more about it and have gone further on
the Way, but it then forms the foundation of future growth. It does so
because to have brought us to the stage of finding a "way" it has in
particular demonstrated that it not only possesses but *combines* two qualities in harmony:

1. It has had to bring us knowledge of a particular kind; and
2. it has had to increase our sensitivity to certain subtle forces in life,
   especially emotions.

By continuing to develop these two, thought and feeling, in a harmonious
way, the infant magnetic center plays an ongoing role in our progress on
the way to which it has led us.

Active Stage: The Struggle

This is the stage that forms the substance of Boris Mouravieff's teaching on the subject. Providing an invaluable aid to those seriously attempting inner growth while in the world, he tells us how, as the magnetic center grows stronger, it serves first as a reminding factor, leading
to increasing individual efforts to control our inner and outer activities
in order to enter into cooperation with this process. This is the stage of
the *struggle* between old and new lives, and it begins when we accept
and *assent* to the need to struggle with ourselves, and when this forms
into a lasting resolve. Even then, the struggle still remains in doubt: we
can at any time choose the easier path, temporarily or permanently
giving up the struggle and losing ourselves in outside influences. But if
we do not finally dedicate ourselves to this alternative, says Mouravieff,
our magnetic center slowly grows in strength until it forms the foundation stone of our temple, an artificial center or man-made psychological
organ through which, to the extent that it is formed and balanced, we
become able to connect to the divine.

With the first actions that connect us to others on the Way, the magnetic center has begun a new phase in its existence, for at this point it no longer concerns only thought and feeling. It now begins also to govern our actions and even, although to varying degrees depending on what has influenced us, to modify the way we relate to our bodies, as described earlier.

This stage is largely a struggle with the associative mind, in which we learn not to *identify* with the various impressions in that mind, and by overcoming these *provocations*—described in chapter 14—slowly begin to create the inner separation within us.

Through Knowledge to Detachment

The mature form of *nepsis* that grows slowly during the second stage of the formation of magnetic center—a stage sometimes known as the *staircase*—is a state in which we remain uninvolved while the mind presents various things to us. While in this state, we remain free to choose which of those things we will act upon. The other element of complete *nepsis* is clear and nonreactive recognition of all that is presented to the nous: of thoughts, of perceptions, of physical sensations. This links with Mouravieff's descriptions of what he calls by the French word—also used in English, although rarely—*constatation*. This process of perceiving without reaction or judgment is described in the *Philokalia*: "If we truly wish to please God and to enjoy the grace of His friendship, we should present to Him an intellect [nous] that is stripped bare—not weighed down with anything that belongs to this present life, with any skill or notion or argument or excuse, however highly educated we may be in the wisdom of this world."[48]

It is clear that this is different from our normal way of perceiving either outer sensations or inner contents. Normally we respond to events, real or imagined, by some kind of reaction, and our own reactions bind us, limiting our choice of response and also limiting our awareness. In *nepsis*, this nonreaction is a characteristic of an entirely different state of awareness from that which is normal to us, but this is only developed through practice, and this practice is of perceiving while not reacting.

Underlying this is the fact that how we react to things depends on how we understand them and their relationship to ourselves. Modern psychology has discovered or at least suggested that the way we perceive life has been learned, and that the way we have learned to perceive depends on our worldview: on the way we think about life, about the world, and about ourselves. So deeply is this view ingrained in us over the years that to change it is a slow process and requires special knowledge and special discipline. In the early years of the church it was this special knowledge and special discipline that formed the subject of Christian teachings: an alternative worldview. Today, so far has the mainstream interpretation of Christian doctrine changed that this can best be seen in what we would now call *esoteric knowledge*. If this is expressed in words, but then assimilated to and its mystical content reinforced by direct, mystical experience of that realm, the resulting combination of word and direct experience forms a link between that mind and our higher, spiritual faculties: it begins to cause the emergence of the image or *icon* of God within the soul; this is not just a reflection of, but an active connection to, the *Christ within*. Such an "inner icon" only acquires its transforming power when both elements—word and experiential memory—are present together. Boris Mouravieff wrote about this process that: "When this linkage (the linkage of esoteric knowledge, see earlier) is present, the real 'I' then becomes active. Then the Personality, as well as the 'I' of the body, submit themselves entirely to the real 'I,' who becomes undoubted and absolute master."

To form or develop this link of esoteric knowledge we begin by study, by reading the word of God, by studying texts from the inner tradition. These texts contain a different kind of knowledge, not obtained from the world revealed by the senses, but described in the following passage from the New Testament, part of which was quoted previously in chapter 5, but which is now carefully retranslated into terminology which will make clearer how it relates to what we have been studying:

> Take care that nobody corrupts you through philosophy and vain deceit taken from the tradition of men which is derived from elements of the outside world, and not from Christ. For only in Him the fullness of the Divinity lives in the body. Only in Him is all complete, since He is the source and the power of it all (paraphrased from Colossians 2:8–10).

The method of using this inner knowledge takes different forms at different times. One of those forms was described by Theophan the Recluse in a way suited to those born in the Orthodox community of Russia a little more than a century ago. "You must reinterpret in a spiritual way all that you see around you," he wrote to a correspondent,

> then fight with all your forces to imprint that new interpretation on your mind so that when you look at something, while your eyes see a visible—a tangible object—your mind is contemplating a spiritual one.
>
> This is a tedious and complicated discipline. It aims eventually at a complete re-education of oneself; at a regeneration and a radical transformation of one's materiality. For example, when you look at an immaculate white dress soiled by

black stains, you cannot prevent yourself feeling ill at ease from imagining that dress white and clean as before. The soiled dress is such an unpleasant sight to you. . . . So reinterpret the whole thing and transpose it onto a higher plane. Try to feel how unpleasant it is for the Lord, the angels, and the saints to look at our soiled and crippled souls. We were given immaculately white souls made in the image of their Creator; we have been regenerated and renewed by the vivifying baptismal waters: then we spoiled it all. Sometimes we wash them clean again with the tears of true repentance, only to splash them once again with the mud of darkness. Look at children left alone by their parents and listen to the terrible racket they raise. See how wildly they run, how savagely and carelessly they play, breaking furniture and shouting at the tops of their voices.

This is exactly the chaotic and anarchistic hubbub in the human soul when its attention is wholly turned away from God and from truth; when it has eliminated the fear of God and has forgotten even the taste of His presence.

We enjoy the fragrance of flowers or the delicate aroma of fine perfumes but pinch our nose and turn away quickly when some rotten smell assails us. All of this can be reinterpreted as follows: every soul emanates a specific odour of its own that cannot be likened to any other soul's odour. It was Saint Paul who said, writing to the Corinthians in his second epistle,[49] "You are the aroma of Christ." So purity of soul has its own subtle fragrance.[50]

Theophan described this as a "tedious and complex discipline." In fact, although we need this *result* just as much today, this form of the practice is now virtually impossible to us as we are. Preliminary or different methods are needed.

Why is Theophan's form now almost impossible? Because we do not think in such a way that we are able to carry out this exercise. Our minds do not contain the correct raw materials for such an exercise. We think in a different way from the people for whom Theophan wrote, and as a result we see the world differently. So, although the objective of the transformation of sensations is the same for us today, we must begin this transformation from a different place, using different materials. Fortunately, a form more suited to contemporary man was described by Maurice Nicoll a few decades ago: "In ancient myths many esoteric ideas were introduced in the form of allegories which if taken literally seem nonsense, but if taken psychologically have meaning. You remember when Odysseus landed on the island of Circe he was given by Hermes a magic herb which protected him against her enchantment although his companions were turned into swine by her spells. Do you think this was an actual herb? Maybe—perhaps aconite? But I fancy that this Work,[51] if it were really taken into oneself, would begin to have the same effect—namely, to protect you from the enchantments of life, from its illusions, from its mirrors."[52]

As we are today, we can only learn to *see* the world in a different way by first learning to think of it in a different way, and for this we need to *recognize* first that in general we do not spontaneously discover our ways of seeing the world. We learn them from other people. But in this process there is a possible difference between "thinking fashionably," thinking what everyone around us thinks, and thinking intelligently; we can begin to *choose* what kind of thinking we will allow to take root in us. We cannot choose what we think, but to a considerable degree we can choose what *influences* the way we think. To do this, we have to discover suitably accurate sources of the different worldview . . . an *ortho docis* or correct doctrine. We cannot at first find any substantial proof of the validity of this doctrine, since only by assimilating it will we become able to confirm it. So today, in this time of lack of belief, we face the inherent difficulty that such sources will at first seem untrue, since they do not confirm what everyone believes, nor agree with all that we imagine to be our own belief.

Yet this is a method. We must learn the doctrine of the inner tradition, and "make it our own." That is, we must learn to *recognize* its truth and, in so doing, begin to see the world, and to see ourselves, as described by this doctrine. This is more than an intellectual learning process. Also, the previous view will turn out to be more than an idea. It involves every part of our organism, and every erroneous thought and feeling in a considerable struggle.

The only saving grace, to guard us against error, is that nobody can recognize something that is untrue.

Second Passive Stage: Magnetization to God

The stage of true *magnetization to God*, as the attraction becomes conscious, a stage most clearly described by Saint Theophan, could be called the pull of the spirit. It is here that the relevance of the term *magnetic center* becomes clear in two ways:

1. *metanoia* or change of direction takes form, and thus
2. the individual becomes *wholehearted*.

It is here, of course, when the "iron filings" all point in the same direction, that the gospel teaching that no man can serve two masters[53] actually becomes meaningful. This *magnetization* is the change as seen in the individual. This change applies equally on the monastic way. It becomes an inner realignment that changes the strength and quality of everything that comes from that person. Saint Maximos the Confessor exactly describes this in a way that makes it clear that this is also the "transformation of the eros" which we wrote about earlier: "For the mind of the one who is continually with God, even his concupiscence abounds beyond measure into a divine desire and whose entire irascible element is transformed into divine love. For by an enduring participation in the divine illumination it has become altogether shining bright, and having bound its possible element to itself it, as I said, turned it around[54] to a never ending divine desire and an unceasing love, completely changing over from earthly things to divine."[55]

Seen from the point of view of our way of life, Theophan sometimes used the term *gravitation* instead of magnetization to God. This refers more exactly to the point at which the center of gravity of the life changes, and the individual's life begins to revolve around God.

Clearly there is a connection between this and *apatheia*, so that at first a sensible question seems to be: Which comes first, *apatheia* or magnetization to God? But later, it becomes apparent that the relation of the two is more complex. Magnetization begins weak, long before *apatheia* is achieved. It grows slowly, and remains weak until we begin to approach close to the state of complete *apatheia*. The image of magnetization to God is important for the practical implications it conveys about the way man's relationship to God is formed and depth in prayer obtained. Because of this importance, this section of the book considers the question of magnetization to God from the early stages in which something draws us under new and different influences, to the point where the tension between *prayer* and *metanoia* becomes so intense that it leads to a real change of consciousness.

In the Russian terminology, the definition of prayer is multilevel: it is sometimes—as now—made to extend to what results from prayer. Saint Isaac the Syrian wrote about this: "when men are visited by this ineffable joy, it cuts the very prayer from their lips; the mouth and tongue are stilled; silenced the heart, guardian of imaginings, and the mind, guide of the senses, and the thoughts, swift as boldly soaring birds."[56] Prayer, then, is a "graduated scale" leading from wholly verbal prayer with no real emotion, at one end of the "rule," to wholly emotional prayer—often without words—at the other. Thus one commentator summarized what Isaac the Syrian said next: "Prayer is abandoned, a superior good having been obtained. The mind is in ecstasy, and knows not whether it is in the body or out of the body, as the Apostle says. Saint Isaac also says that prayer is the seed and this is the harvest. . . . The fathers call such a condition prayer because this great gift has its wellspring in prayer, and is bestowed on saints during prayer, but no man knows the real name for it."[57]

Theophan, well versed in the teachings of Syrian Fathers previously unknown in his church, also utilizes this multilevel definition of prayer. The depth of our prayer, according to Theophan,[58] depends on the degree to which we can live our life at other times in awareness of God.

> The aim is to strive towards God; but at first this is done only in intention. It must be made into our actual life—a natural gravitation that is sweet, voluntary and permanent. This is the kind of attitude that shows us when we are on the right track; that God accepts us and that we are moving towards Him. When iron clings to a magnet it is because the power of the magnet draws it. In spiritual matters the same thing is true; it is only clear that God is touching us when we experience this living aspiration; when our spirit turns its back on everything else and is fixed on Him and carried away.
>
> At first this will not happen; the zealous person is still turned wholly to himself. Even though he has "decided" for God this is only in his mind. The Lord does not yet let Himself be tasted, nor is the man yet capable of it, being impure. All he can do is to serve God without tasting Him, so to speak. Then as his heart begins to be purified and set right, he begins to feel the sweetness of a life pleasing to God, so that he begins to walk in His ways gladly and with love. It becomes his natural element, in which he delights. Then the soul starts to withdraw from everything else as from the cold, and to gravitate towards God, Who warms it.
>
> This principle of gravitation is implanted in the fervent soul by divine grace. By its inspiration and guidance the attraction grows in natural progression, inwardly nourished even without the knowledge of the person concerned. The sign of this birth is that where the spirit in someone previously acted compulsively, it now begins to abide in God's presence willingly and quietly without strain, with feelings of reverence, fear and joy. Once the spirit was cramped within him, but now it is settled and stays there permanently. Now it is bliss for him to be alone with God, away from others and oblivious of external things. He acquires the kingdom of God within himself, which is peace and joy in the Holy Spirit. This immersion in God is called "silence of the mind" or "rapture in God."
>
> It may be very fleeting at first, but the ultimate aim is that in time it should become constant.[59]

Saint Macarius the Great, a favorite saint of the *hesychast* monastics, wrote much about this process, for example this description of the fully developed magnetic center: "A conclusion, therefore, is that the soul is united in will with whatever it is joined and bound to as its master. Either it has, therefore, the light of God in it and lives in that light with all of his powers, abounding with a restful light, or it is permeated by the darkness of sin, becoming a sharer in condemnation."[60]

Theophan put it that: "God is in us when our spirit is truly in God. This is not a mental communion, but a living, silent immersion in God in which we are dispossessed of everything else. As a ray of sunlight takes away a drop of dew, so the Lord carries the spirit away as He touches it."[61]

As the doxology of the Eastern Church says: "For with thee is the foundation of life, in Thy light we shall see light."

There are, then, three clear stages that can be recognized in the formation of magnetic center: discovering the reality of the spiritual impulse within us; forming a center of inner separation and control; and the flowering of that fully formed center into a life of spontaneous prayer of the heart. *Prayer as a practice can begin from early in the first stage but only enters fully into the noetic phase during the second stage.*

Together, these stages provide a considerable part of the complete map of the path for nonmonastics. See figure 12.1.

	Type of Inner Work	*Method*	*Stages of Magnetic Center*
4	Union, Eldership	Theosis	
3	Life of Inner Prayer	Noetic Prayer	Theophan's Magnetization to God
2	Struggle to Form Magnetic Center	Psychological Method	Mouravieff's Magnetic Center
1	Beginning Study	Discrimination of the Spiritual Impulse	Ouspensky's Magnetic Center

Figure 12.1 Stages in the formation of magnetic center and related methods of work. The psychological method may also be regarded as incorporating the whole.

Chapter 13

Memory and Discrimination

An early word that has lost its exact meaning is the Greek word *diakrisis*, normally translated "discrimination," one of the most important ideas in all the great traditions of spirituality. But discrimination is a word that has more than one meaning, and its inner, psychological meaning is easily lost. This loss is crucial. If a psychological technique is not exactly understood, it is no more than a quaint idea that has lost its practical effectiveness. In its early stages, the effects of this *diakrisis* are more clearly understandable the better we understand memory. Later they can be more directly understood in relation to *metanoia*, the renewal of mind described by Saint Paul.

Diakrisis and its effect on the content of memory are key factors in the Royal Road as described by the early Fathers. "Without diakrisis," says Saint John Cassian, "the road is easily lost."[1] In terms of the Royal Road, we have to realize that even if *diakrisis*, in its general Greek use, translates as "discrimination," it is one of a number of Greek terms the early Fathers constantly used in specialized ways, in meanings that were both changed and narrowed from the general usage of their time:[2] in modern terms at least, discrimination is a general term for any kind of differentiation, while we will show that *diakrisis* was used, at least by certain of the Fathers, for one specific kind of discrimination that is an essential element—almost a means of locomotion—on the Royal Road. Discrimination is a power of the nous. Saint Maximos the Confessor speaks of this when he says in the *Philokalia*, in the quotation at the beginning of this book: "as the soul's discriminatory power, the *nous*[3] persuades the soul to cleave to the first

295

and to transcend the second" (see p. 49), meaning by these two kinds of influence, one the influence of the world, the other a spiritual influence that draws us out of the ordinary concerns of the world.

This section of our book, then, attempts to describe and restore the correct inner meaning of *diakrisis*, which the early Fathers used in their psychology to describe this discrimination between the two entirely different kinds of *influence* that shape our lives. We will also hope to show how this process of separation can be put into practice in our lives today; how this practice, done correctly, will produce quite definite changes, not only in the way we think of and perceive the world, but in the way we think of and perceive ourselves.

Discrimination, in this special sense, is the means by which the esoteric Christian finds the narrow way of the gospel and, each time he loses it, finds his way back. Without *diakrisis*, no esoteric development is possible to us . . . as Christians, or as members of any of the world's great faiths.

It is by the action of nonverbal discrimination that you can recognize a true conscious influence.

What We Think Determines What We See

Forgotten truths can have little effect on our lives as long as they remain forgotten. For this and other reasons, the *content* and use of *memory* play an important part in the development of spirituality, and we must understand this to fully understand the importance of right discrimination. In the Gospels, most references to memory are by allusion, or are expressed in parables whose meaning is often unclear. In the teachings of the Fathers, as in the modern monasticism that follows their tradition, the question of memory recurs frequently, often using images that, although pictorially different, contain similar elements,[4] supporting the idea that a science of memory existed from very ancient times, although today that early science is almost lost. Before we move on to more familiar aspects of spirituality, it is helpful to consider this question of memory in some depth.

Before real spiritual growth occurs, the struggle for *metanoia* (see chapter 9) must become a reality in our lives. When this has occurred, the effects are slow but cumulative. One of the reasons why the process is slow is the need to make massive changes in the *content* of our memory. It should be clear to most people that perceptions alone do not determine what we remember. Instead, what we remember to a considerable extent determines what we perceive, or at least, it determines what we attend to, what we *register*, and which of our perceptions are meaningful to us. We normally think associatively, and this means that what we think depends on the content of our memory, and on how this has been laid down. Memories become associated because they were laid down at the same moment in time. In our ordinary state, association governs what we can remember, so that to the degree that we remain dependent on associative memory, we live in the shadow of our past, almost totally unable to think for ourselves about things we have not previously thought about. This also means that not only what we think, but whatever new we take in and register, will be registered in relation to what we have already taken in.

Because our thoughts depend on the *content* of our memory, laid down over a lifetime, to make a real change in our thinking simply by replacing this content takes a very long time indeed.

According to G. I. Gurdjieff and others, the traditional model for how this is to be done is the parable of man as a *household*[5] in which control is taken first by a Deputy Steward, then by a Steward, then by the Owner or his Son. It will be noticed here that these "beings" inhabiting the house are similar in having no physical form, although not in character, to the "demons" described by certain of the early Fathers.

The Deputy Steward had the task of bringing some order to the house and its rebellious servants. When he succeeded in doing so, the Owner would send his Steward, who would have the authority to finish the task of bringing the house to order ready for the Owner. Finally, when this stage of the task was finished, it was said, the Owner would arrive, and would take up residence in the house.

The Garden, a Model of Memory

M uch of the psychology of the esoteric tradition is based on a simple but clear model of memory. At least twice, this model appears in different forms in major works of the ancient world, so that, on this information alone, this formulation is probably a major classical element in the traditional psychology that was long ago lost to our modern world. To my knowledge, this model appears in the gospel in the parable of the sower—as well as in a comment on that parable in Gregory of Nyssa, quoted a few pages further on—and it is also found in a slightly different form where Plato uses as his model for memory the image of a wax tablet.

The parable of the sower links this image with the *psychological myth* of the garden, a garden that appears all over the world, and always seems to have the same underlying meaning. In the Genesis version referred to in chapter 7, man is described as having been expelled from a *garden*. In

Jewish mystical mythology, he was also often described as trying to return to this garden, this *pardes*, paradise.

Primitive in feeling, this whole myth can yet evoke in us a strange sense that it is meaningful and significant to us today. It can be interpreted in many ways that are not only surprising in their depth, but fascinating in the way they fit together to present a complete picture. Yet there is one interpretation that would have to be regarded as fanciful but for a few well-hidden clues, and this is the interpretation that regards the *pardes* as a garden in which grow Christian flowers, the "good soil" in which the seed of Christian myth that is more than myth—the seed of that sower who "went forth to sow"—takes root, and may grow, as mentioned earlier and as said in the gospel: "For the earth bringeth forth fruit of herself; first the blade, then the ear, after that the full corn in the ear" (Mark 4:28).

One cannot so much say that this interpretation is *the* original meaning. Psychological myths can rarely be taken in such a narrow way. But we can, I think, say that this myth of the garden expresses things which cannot be said easily in any other way: things beyond the range of logic and yet more true than any theory.

In one sense, this garden exists within us, in the heart, in the soul perhaps. Indian thought uses this image, speaking of the *antakharana* or "inner organ," wherein grow all kinds of seeds, seeds whose results we must reap as they grow to fruition in our lives. Many of them, says this myth, are harmless when small, yet they grow to become thornbushes that fill our lives and restrict our movement: seeds of suffering.

One important aspect of this story is this question of the Tree of Knowledge of Good and Evil, and its relation to the Tree of Life mentioned earlier in the same story. According to Jewish mythology, what grew in *pardes* was *Otz Chyym*, the Tree of Life.

To put it simplistically, knowledge obscures life.

In some way, just as many people suggest, though knowledge helps us in life, in some ways the two things can find themselves in competition, so the great virtue of this myth is that it does in fact put the record straight. It is not, as so many people suggest, that knowledge is itself harmful: it is the kind of knowledge, and the way we react to that knowledge, that can obscure or interrupt life; this prevents the growth of emotional strength proper to man "in the garden."

The mistake we make is to act as if ideas and representations of things were the things themselves. It is then that we no longer see the reality.

Thinking we know, we no longer search.

The garden is the nous as heart, the wordless unifying part of the mind: mind beyond thought, the cave in the icon, the dark water. Here is found "the peace that passeth understanding": "And the peace of God, which passeth all understanding, shall keep your hearts and minds through Christ Jesus" (Philippians 4:7). It was of this that Saint John of the Cross could write: "Transcending reason with my thought . . . " Of this, too, Jacob Boehme said: "He that can throw himself into this, even for a moment, shall hear the unspeakable words of God."[6]

This is symbolized in the gospel by the pool of Siloam. When these waters are troubled by God, something new emerges. But using the image in this way we could say that this does not happen when they are disturbed by desires. Then what emerges is a wish, a *want*.

These wants lie dormant in the garden of the heart as long as we are busy. The first moment we become still, they stimulate thought. If we let these thoughts grow, then the thoughts born of desire will fill our minds and rule our actions. You can observe this happening only when you have actually begun to overcome it. Then, when you have found what you wanted, and the mind falls briefly silent, you will observe in the stillness a brief flicker. Momentarily you will feel that you want something . . . you will begin to imagine what you want, and then mind will be off again on this new pursuit, chasing after your newly discovered want.

Here is a new plant in the garden. If you decide your actions as a result of this growth, then the plant continues to grow. This is the Tree of Knowledge of Good and Evil.

To eat the fruit feels like freedom. But it is the cause of bondage.

The process of eating this fruit and limiting ourselves is described in chapter 14 as a process known by the early Fathers as *provocation*: "By considering the body, attending to that which causes corruption, and so developing self-love, man is exposed continually to the action of pleasure and pain. He eats always from the tree of disobedience—The Tree of Knowledge of Good and Evil—and so in experiencing through the senses takes in knowledge in which good and evil are mixed together. It would not be a lie to say that The Tree of Knowledge of Good and Evil is the visible created world, for this world by its nature is subject to the contradictions that cause pleasure and pain."[7]

There is another fruit that grows in this garden. It is what some call *conscience*. This fruit grows only in a special soil, in a deeper stillness, when our wants too are stilled: "the space between desires." It is of this that it was said: "Be still, and know that I am God: I will be exalted among the heathen, I will be exalted in the earth" (Psalms 46:10).

We eat this other fruit not by doing what we wish, but by doing what we know to be right. This too is a *Royal Way*, because once we learn the taste of this fruit, once we learn to "know what we know," this path can be followed whatever our way of life.

Plato's Wax Tablet Model

The facts behind this view are confirmed by Plato, and it is worth remembering that before the time of Christ he had echoed many aspects of the Christian teaching, although without that *completeness*[8] that led to practical results. The esoteric model of memory, properly understood, will tell us that we must *transform* our memory by increasing its sensitivity so that it *registers* things, other than the merely sensory, by becoming more discriminating, that is, by registering the subtle and meaningful, not the coarse and purely external, and in this way purifying the memory of illusions.

The parable of the sower, written in the time of Christ to describe memory in terms understandable to a population predominantly of farmers, is in fact a model of memory very similar to that used by Plato. Plato conveyed the same basic principles as the gospel parable, but did so by describing the memory as being like one of the wax tablets used for writing. In that Greek analogy, what happens to the "impressions" that fall on the memory depends on the condition or "temperature" of the wax. The similarities of the two models make one suspect that they are different versions of a standard model of memory once used in classical esoteric teaching. Like the parable of the sower, Plato's model described three conditions of memory.

1. If it is too hard, nothing is retained; this is like the seed that falls on the edge of the road, where the earth is too hard-packed and the seeds cannot root. This leads to forgetting of all but the strongest impressions, and so the gentle impressions of spiritual experience are not retained.
2. If it is too soft, too much is retained; the memory is not sufficiently selective, but instead retains irrelevancies and untested delusions, which blanket the memories we wish to retain. In this case the impressions of spiritual experience are usually obscured; a few may survive, but they will not be remembered often enough to lead to any change in our lives.
3. If the wax is in perfect condition, at a perfect temperature, we retain what we wish to retain.

The Parable of the Sower

In this language of parable, another very valuable image is that of Adam in the Garden, and perhaps, paradoxically, the garden as the seedbed in man, the very soil in which "a sower went forth to sow."

Gregory of Nyssa wrote, linking the parable of the sower and that of the tares, and saying that the field in which the tares grow is the heart. Christian tradition retains this not only as an idea, but as experience that extends the idea of the garden beyond that of mere memory to what might be described as states of memory. As the abbot of one of the Athos monasteries once said: "To be in the liturgy is to experience paradise."[9] This is based on doctrine, but it is confirmed in experience, for in an Athonite liturgy one captures again the tears and the joys of that Garden long lost to us, which yet lies all around us: the paradise of the heart which the head can never see unaided. This paradise is approached through tears, through self-doubt, through the penetrating experience of repentance . . . never merely through doctrinal ideas or simple theory. Always, it involves emotional, felt experience, sharp, embarrassing, remorseful, self-revealing, suddenly joyful, often painful, bearing strange undercurrents of sorrow perhaps, but real . . . above all, real: the tears of real people. "Out of the strong came forth sweetness" (Judges 14:14).

And it is in this garden that the sower went forth to sow:

And he spake many things unto them in parables, saying,
>Behold, a sower went forth to sow;
>And when he sowed, some seeds fell by the way side,
and the fowls came and devoured them up:
>Some fell upon stony places, where they had not much
earth: and forthwith they sprung up, because they had no
deepness of earth . . .
>And some fell among thorns; and the thorns sprung up,
and choked them:
>But other fell into good ground, and brought forth fruit,
some an hundredfold, some sixtyfold, some thirtyfold.
>Who hath ears to hear, let him hear (Matthew 13:3–9).

The place where the sower spread his seed, the field where the enemy planted the tares, the wax tablet of Plato's analogy—in the esoteric tradition these are in the spiritual or noetic heart . . . a heart that can be found by beginning from the physical heart, but is in fact something much deeper, the darkness beyond the mind, Saint John of the Cross' thought that transcends reason. This is the field tended by the *householder* of God.

That is why Gregory of Nyssa, quoting his sister Saint Macrina as his teacher, wrote about the parable of the tares that:

> In that story, the householder planted good seed; we are undoubtedly his household. When the enemy had observed the men sleeping, he sowed the useless weeds amongst the nourishing crops, putting the tares in the midst of the grain. And the seeds sprouted alongside each other, for it was inevitable that the seed planted along with the grain would also sprout along with it. . . . We suppose that the Scripture is representing those impulses of the soul by the healthful seeds. If only each of them had been cultivated for good it would undoubtedly have produced the fruit of virtue for us. But since error in the judgement of the good has been sown along with these impulses, that which alone is truly good by nature has also been overshadowed by the plant of deceit growing up with it. . . . This is where the impulse of desire has been led by misjudgment concerning the good. . . . The other emotions in the same way have produced worse plants instead of better. For this reason the wise farmer allows the weed which has grown amongst the seed to remain there, taking care that we do not remove the better part as we might if desire was altogether uprooted as well as the useless growth. For if this should happen to our human nature, what is there which would raise us towards union with the heavenly. So you see that the farmer leaves the bastard seeds in us, not intending that they should permanently dominate the more honourable sowing, but that the field itself, for this is his figurative name for the heart—through the natural power residing in it (which is nous, reason)—should dry up the one part of the plants, but render the other part fruitful and thriving.[10]

Illusory Memories

When this ancient model is used to describe memory, it tells of three states of memory, two of which lead to *forgetting* of the more subtle experiences of life. We forget these things because the matter of memory is "too hard"—not receptive enough—as with the seed that fell by the roadside, so that the impressions left by spiritual experiences begin to grow, but they cannot take root, with the result that the experiences that happen are forgotten, because the memories do not form as a clear impression. Or it is too soft, too receptive, so that too many different kinds of memory are taken in, and the more subtle memories are obscured or overlaid by the coarser and stronger memories or simply by those that come later. Finally, there is memory that is like good soil: cleared or purified, tilled so that it receives a clear impression of the subtle memories and retains them without their being covered over, and kept from excessive "growth" of worldly impressions that would otherwise cover over the spiritual memories.

Psalm 118 (119 in modern Bibles) is recognized by monks of both Eastern and Western churches, and is said by some to be a key to the esoteric tradition. It is an important text for monks in orders such as the Benedictines. The first verse says: "Blessed are the undefiled in the way, who walk in the law of the LORD" (Psalms 119:1; Psalms 118 in the Orthodox version). For this reason, monks in the Eastern Church take care, even today, to quite literally lower their eyes from the world, so as not to take in too many worldly impressions. The conclusions of this can be summarized by saying that, to prevent our forgetting the spiritual, a certain preparation is necessary: we need to eliminate certain impediments to spiritual consciousness. But what are these "impediments"? And how do they link with the *diakrisis* mentioned at the beginning of this chapter? In part, the answer to this question is obvious.

It was Evagrius (again) who wrote about our memories that: "Both virtues and vices make the mind blind, the one so that it may not see the vices; the other so that it might not see the virtues."[11] If our thought determines to what we attend, then one type of obstruction to consciousness exists simply in wrong or *incomplete* patterns of thought. This is exactly what happens today, since the dominant thought held in our times, the misconception which claims that inner experience is unimportant, means that we form the habit of attending only briefly or incompletely to inner sensations. Thus, in self-fulfilling prophecy, we do not find what we expect not to find: giving no attention to the inner world, we find there nothing of importance—if we find anything at all.

Thus, Clement of Alexandria was correct when he put it that what we believe ourselves to know makes us blind to what we might truly know: " 'If any man thinketh that he knoweth anything, he knoweth nothing yet as he ought to know.' For the truth is never mere opinion. But the 'supposition of knowledge inflates' and fills with pride; 'but charity edifieth,' which deals not in supposition, but in truth. Whence it is said 'if any man loves, he is known.' "[12]

Careful self-observation confirms the statement, made by modern commentators on this tradition, that in the normal, unpurified human mind, illusions are as much part of the *content* of memory as is genuine knowledge—perhaps more, since the only knowledge we normally possess is partial knowledge or "knowledge of the world," shaped by man's mind with all the distortions this is prone to. This idea agrees with the Indian tradition of the Vedas, in which *maya*, illusion, prevents *vidya*, knowledge.

Cassian, when we quote his comments on *diakrisis* a few pages further on, refers to this form of discrimination as a means of preventing illusion, and elsewhere it is said that without this the student falls from grace.

But separate from this, in the last quotation from Clement, we can find certain statements about *love* (as charity):

—love does not deal in supposition, but
—love deals in truth, and
—if any man loves, he is known.

This supports the observation that the higher planes of love possess a cognitive capacity which relates directly to the higher planes of memory, and in this we may find a clue to the nature of that seed that I was earlier unable to define.

The Nature of Diakrisis

The stage that Western man in general is now entering would seem to involve the need to learn how to separate the nous from the distractions of the world.[13] This *inner separation* requires that we distinguish or discriminate between the knowledge possessed by the nous and the sensations reaching us from the outside world. To most people who are aware of it, the idea of discrimination seems to be a simple thing with one meaning. In fact, there are a number of different forms, and to find out which of these forms is important, we must look at the whole concept of discrimination in theory, and then, in a very different way, we will look at the practice.

In time, full discrimination leads to *apatheia*. "This is the really good man, who is without passions," says Clement in the passage quoted below in full. This *apatheia* is the test by which effective discrimination can be recognized. The higher knowledge, the gnosis, when first tasted, creates the inner struggle that leads to *apatheia*, but when it is known and assimilated in full it actually ends one's dependence. This is the ultimate unwritten secret, secret precisely and only because it cannot be written, because even when experienced it cannot be immediately assimilated to the mind, but can be assimilated only against appropriate experience: this I consider to be the true Christian meaning of *gnosis*. This kind of dispassion has a certain effect, described here by Clement in terms of the character it produces in the individual:

> For he is prudent in human affairs, in judging what ought to be done by the just man; having obtained the principles from God from above, and having acquired, in order to the divine resemblance, moderation in bodily pains and pleasures. And he struggles against fears boldly, trusting in God. Certainly, then, the gnostic[14] soul, adorned with perfect virtue, is the earthly image of the divine power; its development being the joint result of nature, of training, of reason, all together. This beauty of the soul becomes a temple of the Holy Spirit, when it acquires a disposition in the whole of life corresponding to the Gospel. Such a one consequently withstands all fear of everything terrible, not only of death, but also poverty and disease, and ignominy, and things akin to these; being unconquered by pleasure, and lord over irrational desires. For he well knows what is and what is not to be done; being perfectly aware what things are really to be dreaded, and what not. Whence he bears intelligently what the Word intimates to him to be requisite and necessary; intelligently discriminating what is really safe (that is, good), from what appears so; and things to be dreaded from what seems so, such as death, disease, and poverty; which are rather so in opinion than in truth.[15]

Here Clement again describes the *gnostic* in his terminology, not a student of one of those doctrines known today as the Gnostics, but the Christian man or woman following the inner tradition and so transformed by the kind of knowledge once known as *gnosis*. This knowledge, coming from *real being*, produces in men and women a different stature, first in knowledge, and eventually in a total transformation of character revealing itself in an inner separation recognizable by a growing *apatheia*.

In theoretical terms, to discriminate is to distinguish one thing from another, but we are speaking here about discrimination between different kinds of truth—for instance, between scientific truth and inwardly certain, otherwise ambiguous, experienced or understood truths that cannot be demonstrated. It is to distinguish between something that is true in practical terms for a particular time and situation, and the deeper, more important truths understood by religion when it is in full possession of its abilities.

For our Western civilization, as for the Greek civilization at its peak, Socrates forms the model of this form of discrimination. His example is specifically relevant to the present time in the United States, where vast numbers of individuals are repeating his experience and facing the emptiness of what is ordinarily considered to be knowledge.

Socrates, summarizes Francis Cornford, probably the best translator of Plato, reached the conclusion that the so-called knowledge of the philosophers that had preceded him was faulty in three ways.

1. It was uncertain, and this being so, it was not true knowledge.
2. It was useless to him as a human being.
3. It did not tell *why* things were, only *how* and *where* they were.

So he began to search for and then to teach a different kind of knowledge. An understanding of the ideas of Plato and his times, as developed by Cornford, gives this passage far greater meaning:

> It was not only the man Socrates, but philosophy itself that turned, in his person, from the outer to the inner world. Up to that moment, the eyes of philosophy had been turned outward to seek a reasonable explanation of the shifting spectacle of surrounding Nature. Now their vision is directed to another field—the order and purposes of human life—and, at the center of that field, to the nature of the individual soul. Pre-Socratic philosophy begins with the discovery of Nature; Socratic philosophy begins with the discovery of man's soul.
>
> The life of Socrates found its appropriate motto in the Delphic inscription, "Know Thyself."[16]

We now know that other civilizations possessed that knowledge before Socrates. Other evidence suggests that in human history this kind of knowledge may have *preceded* the narrower form which we now call knowledge.

Esoteric science is inner science, and according to Cornford again,[17] Socrates first turned the attention of Athenian civilization to that inner knowledge which they were ignoring at the time, leaving it to Saint Paul some three centuries later to turn their attention to the fact that their then *unknown god* could in fact be known: that not only could they possess inner knowledge, but in this way it could become *complete*. "For as I passed by, and beheld your devotions, I found an altar with this inscription, TO THE UNKNOWN GOD. Whom therefore ye ignorantly worship, him declare I unto you" (Acts 17:23).

It was this inner knowledge, described by Origen and more fully by Saint Gregory Palamas, as discussed toward the end of chapter 6, which marked the significant difference between pre-Christian Greek thought and Greek Christian thought such as that of the Fathers.

Whatever its origin, personal or from some invisible source, it is clear that this insight attributed to Socrates helped pave the way for the coming of Christianity as understood by the Fathers. It is equally clear that it did so because, although the books which tell us about Socrates, especially those of Plato, have helped to shape the intellect of modern man, the "new" kind of knowledge, taught by and represented by Socrates, was in fact an *emotional knowledge*, a knowledge of the heart or of the nous, a feeling of being. The Fathers, said Werner Jaeger, "led their pupils to that spirituality which was the common link of all higher religion in late antiquity. They began to remember that it had been Plato who made the world of the soul visible for the first time to the inner eye of man, and they realized how radically that discovery had changed human life."[18]

This gives us clues to early church tradition for the simple reason that the early church faced the need to explain itself to a Hellenized world that was already highly sophisticated in just the areas that concerned the church, a world dominated by the classical Greek influence which had by then been shaped or *prepared* by the Socratic insight. As a result, it explained itself by adopting Greek terms and concepts[19] but, as begun by Saint Paul, gave them a distinctly Christian flavor, for instance referring to this *emotional knowledge* specifically in terms of the part it played in the ascesis by which the early Christians struggled for *metanoia*: struggled to transform their nature so as to become more wholly Christian. "For they that are after the flesh do mind the things of the flesh; but they that are after the Spirit the things of the Spirit" (Romans 8:5).

Cassian on Diakrisis

It was Saint Paul, one of the Jews of that time who had been heavily influenced by Greek culture, who linked the study of man with the study of God. *Diakrisis* is one of the *Gifts of the Spirit* that are described by Saint Paul, which are still sought in monasticism today.

In the next few centuries, the Fathers of the church defined *diakrisis* more precisely. In particular, certain of the early Fathers, including Saint John Cassian quoting Saint Anthony the Great, defined this as a specific form of discrimination—*discrimination of spirits*—which fulfills a special and very important role in spiritual growth and life.

This definition touches on questions developed at the beginning of this book, where, for example, we quoted Maximos the Confessor on the significance of the two trees in Genesis—the Tree of Knowledge and the Tree of Life.

Discernment of spirits draws one toward the Tree of Life.

This is the beginning of an entirely different way of living, which begins with an entirely different way of looking at and thinking about life. Without this different view, all spirituality is mere hypocrisy. The different ways of life were described by Gurdjieff not as two trees but as "two rivers," and in these terms, the beginning of true spirituality is a true response to the "influence" of the second river, to what people studying those ideas know as *B influences*. And we should understand that what in that terminology are called A influences and C influences arise from *different worlds*, worlds experienced in entirely different ways, and that B influences also come from and draw us to the world of the C influences. We will begin to look at this question, as does chapter 6 of Boris Mouravieff's *Gnosis*, by trying to define those worlds according to the different kinds of knowledge by which they may be known.

To define the picture at the risk of overcomplexity, Ouspensky divided and then Mouravieff further subdivided the original classifications, so that he described a chain of influences, A, B, C, D and E. Influence A represents the ordinary influences of life in the world, that are in no sense esoteric. Esotericism comes from outside time, which he described as the esoteric influence E. Influences B, C, and D are successive stages toward clarification of the pure influence E. Influences D and C are human beings influenced to different degrees by the direct spiritual influence E. Influences B are influences sown in the world by such people: words, images, music and dance that convey to the person who perceives them an intimation that there exists something beyond the world we know.

The *true* spiritual influences C and D etc. become effective only when they act on this nous, on the eye of the soul. As ideas they have no effect as long as they are only stored as verbal memories in the Personality.

Cassian wrote about *diakrisis:* about discrimination between the A influences and the C, D and E influences regarded as one thing:

> Discrimination, then, is no small virtue, but one of the most important gifts of the Holy Spirit. Concerning these gifts the Apostle says: "To one is given by the Spirit the principle of wisdom; to another the principle of spiritual knowledge by the same Spirit; to another faith by the same Spirit; to another the gifts of healing . . . to another discrimination of spirits" (1 Corinthians 12:8–10). Then, having completed his catalogue of spiritual gifts, he adds: "But all these are energized by the one and selfsame Spirit" (1 Corinthians 12:11). You can see, therefore, that the gift of discrimination is nothing worldly or insignificant. It is the greatest gift of God's

grace. A monk must seek this gift with all his strength and diligence, and acquire the ability to discriminate between the spirits that enter him and to assess them accurately. Otherwise he will not only fall into the foulest pits of wickedness as he wanders about in the dark, but even stumble when his path is smooth and straight.

I remember how in my youth, when I was in the Thebaid, where the blessed Anthony used to live, some elders came to see him, to enquire with him into the question of perfection in virtue. They asked him: "Which is the greatest of all virtues—we mean the virtue capable of keeping a monk from being harmed by the nets of the devil and his deceit?" Each one then gave his opinion according to his understanding. Some said that fasting and the keeping of vigils make it easier to come near to God, because these refine and purify the mind. Others said that voluntary poverty and detachment from personal possessions make it easier, since through these the mind is released from the intricate threads of worldly care. Others judged acts of compassion to be most important, since in the Gospel the Lord says: "Come, you whom my father has blessed, inherit the kingdom prepared for you from the foundation of the world; for I was hungry and you gave Me food" and so on (Matthew 25:34–36). The best part of the night was passed in this manner, taken up with a discussion in which each expressed his opinion as to which virtue makes it easiest for a man to come near to God.

Last of all the blessed Anthony gave his reply: "All that you have said is both necessary and helpful for those who are searching for God and wish to come to Him. But we cannot award the first place to any of these virtues; for there are many among us who have endured fasting and vigils, or have withdrawn into the desert, or have practiced poverty to such an extent that they have not left themselves enough for their daily sustenance, or have performed acts of compassion so generously that they no longer have anything to give; and yet these same monks, having done all this, have nevertheless fallen away miserably from virtue and slipped into vice.

What was it, then, that made them stray from the straight path? In my opinion it was simply that they did not possess the grace of discrimination; for it is this virtue that teaches a man to walk along the Royal Road, swerving neither to the right through immoderate self-control, nor to the left through indifference and laxity. Discrimination is a kind of eye and lantern of the soul, as is said in the Gospel passage: "The light of the body is the eye; if therefore your eye is pure, your whole body will be full of light. But if your eye is evil, your whole body will be full of darkness" (Matthew 6:22–23). And this is just what we find; for the power of discrimination, scrutinizing all the thoughts and actions of a man, distinguishes and sets aside everything that is base and not pleasing to God, and keeps him free from delusion.[20]

But the important thing is that we can discriminate between different things either "horizontally," between things of almost the same importance, but which differ in some way,[21] or "vertically," between things of different value or different subtlety. When Cassian and other early Fathers used the Greek word *diakrisis*, normally translated "discrimination," to describe the process of distinguishing between different *influences* that act on our mind, this is a specific form of discrimination, which is impossible or at least dangerous to define too narrowly, but which we can learn to *recognize*, and that best, perhaps, from Cassian's description quoted above.

The same idea is found many centuries later, in a little text written in England and actually titled *The Discernment of Spirits*. This small book speaks about different kinds of *spirits* that can mislead us, and clearly draws exactly the same distinction as that drawn by Cassian.

One way to approach this is to understand, to remember, to think, in the paraphrased words of an ancient teaching, that: All that I have is from God. I have nothing of my own.

But you must feel this to be true. To begin with you may discover that the idea feels unreal to you, that it does not move you because the idea of God is not sufficiently real to you.

Unless we have reached the second stage of faith (chapter 8), God will remain for us an abstract, intellectual idea. Words alone cannot give us this feeling unless we have already experienced the things to which they refer. Without this feeling of their reality, our *diakrisis* will not be sufficiently real. "This same distinction between different kinds of knowledge was made by Plato—between the 'sensible realm' (aistheton genos) and the 'intelligible or noetic realm' (noeton[22] genos). The first is in constant process of change, the second unchanging. The one consists of phenomena, appearances, destructible things; the other of truly real (ontos onta), indestructible things."[23]

True unity of being is the *necessary* source of unified knowledge. Without unity of being, there is no unity of knowledge. With each moment of unified being, unified knowledge increases.

He must increase, but I must decrease.

He that cometh from above is above all: he that is of the earth is earthly, and speaketh of the earth: he that cometh from heaven is above all.

And what he hath seen and heard, that he testifieth; and no man receiveth his testimony.

He that hath received his testimony hath set to his seal that God is true.

For he whom God hath sent speaketh the words of God; for God giveth not the spirit by measure unto him (John 3: 30–34).

When the early Fathers describe discrimination between the two kinds of knowledge as the "differentiation of spirits,"[24] it becomes clear that the word *spirits* refers not to individual beings, in the modern materialist or spiritualist sense, but to the *influences* that shape our lives: to forces or energies that influence our thoughts and all that comes from them.

This word *spirit*, which is sometimes capitalized as referring to the Spirit of God, represents the one thing in two ways:

1. as an influence in our lives
2. as an energy that "informs" our awareness.

This idea, then, is virtually the same as that introduced in simplified form by Gurdjieff, Ouspensky, and later Mouravieff, presumably in its modern Russian formulation, as "Influences A" and "Influences B." The importance of this is that: "No man can serve two masters: for either he will hate the one, and love the other, or else he will hold to the one, and despise the other. Ye cannot serve God and mammon" (Matthew 6:24). This idea of two spirits or influences is also found in slightly different form in Saint Paul: "For the law of the Spirit of life in Christ Jesus hath made me free from the law of sin and death" (Romans 8:2).

To see that we have nothing of our own is to be free: "Blessed are the poor in spirit."

The early Fathers—and sometimes the New Testament—called the tendencies that influence us *spirits*: they talked about choice between two kinds of spirit: the *spirit of the world*, and the *Holy Spirit*. An English text in the same line as these Fathers wrote about this: "Moreover, that there is a carnal spirit (and not a good one), the Apostle Paul shows when he talks of some men 'vainly puffed up with their fleshly spirit' (Colossians 2:18). And he also makes it plain that there is a spirit of the world, in the passage where he rejoices in God, not only for himself but for his disciples as well, that they had not received the spirit of the world, but that which was sent from God, the Holy Spirit (1 Corinthians 2:12)."[25] This reference to the Holy Spirit will prove of great value to those on the Way. And within this idea of influences, another idea is also implied, that of a different kind of knowledge, of emotionally meaningful knowledge.

All other knowledge is fragmentary. And if we search for knowledge in a fragmentary way, the knowledge we will find is fragmentary.

The true higher knowledge, the heart of knowledge, is the emotional knowledge that is born of direct experience rooted in love.

In modern terms, as we choose to receive the Spirit that was sent from God, this will form in our mind a *clear space*—initially small. We will sense this as a stillness, and it was this stillness, known as *hesychia*, that was taught by the early Fathers, including Saint Augustine, as a sign or test by which we will know when we are touched by the Spirit of God.

The spirit of the world, on the other hand, generates either excitement or apathy, depression, and thoughtlessness. We can *recognize* the difference, and we can train ourselves to recognize it consistently. This begins a clearing away of debris which in time makes us more sensitive to the divine influences, and then the clear space grows.

The Spirit itself is said to exist outside the circle of life.[26]

This process that was called by the early Fathers discrimination of spirits (Greek *diakrisis*) is different from the normal division of things into opposites described earlier. In *diakrisis*, exposure to a higher spirit brings us under a higher law.

This occurs because "you cannot love God and Mammon." Marcarius the Great, in his comments on the parable of the wise and foolish virgins, wrote that the foreign or corrupting element in our souls "must be expelled again by that which is also foreign to our nature, namely the heavenly gift of the Spirit."[27] An essential element of this doctrine is that from verbal description alone we can only occasionally recognize the *spirits* between which we must discriminate. We recognize them only by learning from experience the different tastes of the different *influences*—and this depends on our perceiving the different effects exerted upon us by influences that have different "tastes."

The essential factor is that the way in which we discriminate depends on what part of our whole organism forms the basis of that discrimination. The intellect, when it is tied to the body through the senses, discriminates in one way. The pure nous, when it is free of these ties, discriminates in a quite different way. Saint Maximos the Confessor wrote of this:

> . . . as the soul's discriminatory power, the nous, persuades the
> soul to cleave to the first [a unity of the eternal and spiritual],

and to transcend the second [the sensible, transitory and fragmentary]. The senses have the power to discriminate between pleasure and pain in the body. Or rather, as a power existing in a body endowed with soul and sense-perception, they persuade the body to embrace pleasure and reject pain.

If a man exercises only sensory discrimination between pain and pleasure in the body, so transgressing the divine commandment, he eats from the tree of knowledge of good and evil, that is to say, he succumbs to the mindless impulses that pertain to the senses; for he possesses only the body's power of discrimination, which makes him embrace pleasure as something good and avoid pain as something evil. But if he exercises only that noetic discrimination which distinguishes between the eternal and the transitory, and so keeps the divine commandment, he eats from the tree of life, that is to say, from the wisdom that appertains to his nous, for (then) he exercises only the power of discrimination that belongs to the soul.[28]

To make this distinction that forms the basis of the *discrimination of spirits*, we have to discover the limits of reason: the limits to what intellect can discover with the aid of the body and its senses. These limits are real. Intellect, in our modern sense of this term, can tell us some things, but there are things it cannot tell us. This point is that at which Socrates discovered that he did not know, and because he discovered this he was said to know more than anyone else. In this, the Platonic philosophy comes close to the esoteric tradition; Clement of Alexandria called Plato "Moses talking in Greek."

But when in this we speak of intellect, we do not simply speak of ideas. In this, intellect as dianoia must not only learn words, but as nous must understand their meaning through experience. Without *diakrisis*, experience is incomplete—it is without the sharp edge of *diakrisis* that the "axe" of *metanoia* is "headless." To obtain sufficient experience is a slow matter, even with great persistence in *diakrisis*. The *Royal Road* of the Fathers is the *narrow way* of the gospel. It can be walked only with continual and intense efforts to discriminate. Discrimination then becomes the motivating force for *metanoia*. Repentance leads to *purity of heart*, and purity of heart is the real basis of Christian *psychological development*. In an alchemical process in some ways analogous to the process of photography, the film must first be *sensitized*,[29] and after exposure it must be developed so that the divine image perceived in the purified heart of man emerges spontaneously into the open. The final stage is that it must be *fixed*,[30] or made permanent.

Meat Diet and Milk Diet

As mentioned briefly earlier in the book, Saint Anthony the Great in a letter classified students according to their potential, describing the different characters of three types of seeker.

In terms of their ability to learn, students are sometimes described as falling into two distinct categories. True knowledge, true *gnosis*, is only of use to and only acceptable to the prepared, to those who know how to study it and who can carry out the practices necessary to understand it. Because of this, Saint Paul, and later certain of the Fathers, distinguished between meat and milk diets for instruction of Christians. Saint Anthony the Great was one who used this classification.

Clement of Alexandria used the same classification and elaborated on it rather more fully. "Yet, even in the Church, they fed babes with milk, and the more intelligent with the meat of God's word. What the meat was, we discover in the Stromata, when our author defines the true Gnostic, who follows whithersoever God leads him in the divinely inspired Scriptures. He recognizes many who merely taste the Scriptures as believers;[31] but the true Gnostic is a gnomon of truth, an index to others of the whole knowledge of Christ."[32]

The monks of a century or two ago had a considerable sense of humor. Today on Mount Athos there exists what used to be a house for training novices: the dome over the chapel takes the form of a perfect breast.

Unwritten knowledge in the true sense is different for each individual. In this I am referring not to a concept but to a phenomenon that is almost unknown in the West, where in general everything is mass-produced, even spiritual instruction. Ordinary knowledge is not enough: the mind must be constantly awakened by all kinds of shocks and impulses. One source of these is the precise form of esoteric knowledge known as *meat diet*. This friction must continue until the student learns to make the continuous effort that is needed if he or she is to remain awake, and which is one true meaning of the passage in Saint Paul which tells us to pray without ceasing.

Higher influences come from "outside life as we know it," but when we have changed, we will be able to understand this idea differently from how we now see it.

The "milk diet" of Saint Paul and Saint Anthony the Great—sometimes today known as *influence B*—acts on the purely exterior mind, sensitizing it to the true esoteric teachings, sometimes called *influence C*. Once we are able to receive and recognize the C influences of those qualified to convey the tradition, these begin to waken the mind and strengthen it, making it serviceable to the Lord and giving it the capacity to assimilate and digest the "meat diet," for instance by preparing it to help the heart withstand the struggle that is the outward sign of inner *metanoia*.

The sensitization that occurs in this way is the sensitization of the nous, the discriminating faculty of the mind, making it able to discern and cling to higher and spiritual influences.

Chapter 14

Provocation

I t is necessary to understand more fully the inner struggle that leads to the formation of the *inner separation*, since this is the slow restoration of our power of choice which has been lost to us since early childhood. One of several very different ways of understanding this is in terms of the idea of *provocation*: the idea that the active mind, with its associations, is constantly presenting stimuli to the nous to which the undiscriminating nous habitually responds indiscriminately. Many of the early Fathers, and their Russian successors, have described the process of *provocation* as proceeding through six or more stages of progressive loss of control of one's mind, while Evagrius, in his *Praktikos*, describes eight specific types of provocation.

It might be asked: how does this differ from insanity? A simplistic answer is that the sixth and final stage of *provocation*, which the Russian hermits called *plenenie* (captivity), describes a condition of constant self-gratification and seeking for distraction that today is not only common-place but is now actively promoted in modern teachings of self-expression and assertiveness. This frequently disturbs the body, leading to compulsions, and these can dominate the life of the individual to the point where the individual fails to maintain his or her relation with society, at which point he or she is classifiably insane.

In studying provocation, we must note that modern man differs from those for whom these descriptions were originally written. Almost all Western men and women are subservient to their provocations, simply because they regard those provocations as their possessions, as if they had originated them, which is entirely untrue—as if they were their own ideas, their own feelings, their own beliefs. In fact, these stimuli that drive us are merely "recordings" of the past. Whenever we touch the state of inner separation—which we normally do so briefly that we do not recognize it—we habitually respond to the first energetic (or "exciting") provocation, with the result that we immediately pass out of the state of inner separation again. We then forget ourselves, passing into what Mouravieff calls "confluence," the normal state of modern man. Among other things, this is the reason why we are unable to control our thoughts, and understanding this process of provocation can show us how it is possible to establish control of thought.

Evagrius of Pontus wrote about these provocations: "There are eight general and basic categories of provoking thoughts in which are included every provoking thought. First is that of gluttony, then impurity, avarice, sadness, anger, accidie, vainglory, and last of all pride. It is not in our power to determine whether we are disturbed by these thoughts, but we are able to decide if they are to linger within us or not, and whether or not they are to stir up our passions."[1]

Unstated in this passage of Evagrius is the fact that the "command center," the *magnetic center* at or beyond the stage of inner separation, is the result of special training. It is in effect an artificial or man-made organ in the mind. Until it has been built, we are submerged under continuous provocation, emerging from this state, for short periods only, in intentional action. To develop intentional activities new to our lives is not an easy thing: it will first involve us in a *struggle* with these useless and often harmful thoughts, which tend to accumulate as we grow older—and simple pride, if it leads to our assuming that our thoughts, our feelings, our attitudes to the provoking stimuli are our own, as it normally does, will lead to failure in this struggle. This struggle, however, is far from useless. Not only does it lead to our completing some task previously beyond our capacity, but it increases our capacity for future intentional action and slowly frees us from our recurrent provocations, and so plays a major part in the formation of the magnetic center that makes us serviceable to higher consciousness.

Stages of Provocation

A Russian émigré, I. M. Kontzevitch, wrote about the process of provocation within the *content* of the mind, putting in modern terms ideas first imported to Russia by Saint Nilus of Sora at the end of the thirteenth century. He said first that: "The Holy Fathers, ascetics, discern as many as (six or) seven moments in the development and growth of passions."[2]

These stages, he says, are described by later Russian authorities. Provoking thoughts, the feelings that make us respond to them, and the habitual activities that repeat every time the same provocations occur—all these are predispositions. But as already hinted, there are difficulties in describing the exact way in which these elements act. In observed fact the phases occur differently at different "levels of being"—and indeed, such differences are among the chief means of distinguishing levels of being. Kontzevitch summarizes the way these are described by the later Russian teachers; but the Greek descriptions are not quite the same, probably because of the difference in understanding of those using the ideas. We have said more than once already that provocation is necessary in order to test our character so as to make us aware of what we are like. It tests us by discovering to what we *assent* at a particular moment . . . and this testing sometimes will continue until we have gained control over our moments of assent. Evagrius said about this *peirasmos*, testing or temptation, that:

> Temptation is the lot of the monk, for thoughts which darken his mind will inevitably rise from the part of his soul that is the seat of passion.
> The sin that a monk has particularly to watch out for is that of giving mental consent to some forbidden pleasure.[3]

This is *captivity*: the state of modern man, of fallen man. In the Old Testament, and in authors such as Saint Gregory of Nyssa, this is symbolized by the captivity of Israel under the Egyptians.[4] But as Boris Mouravieff wrote in *Gnosis*: "the passage from Hope to Love is marked by the renewal of the mind, that is, by new Knowledge."[5]

To renew our mind or intelligence—*nous*—we must remove from within us the impediments that hinder spiritual consciousness. That is, our psyche must be *purified*. One important part of this process is the purification of the memory. The outcome of this is described by Saint Macarius: "It is through the renewing of the mind and the tranquillity experienced in our thoughts and the love of the Lord and the love for heavenly things that every new creation of Christians distinguishes them from the men of this world. For this reason did the Lord come in order that he might deign to give these spiritual gifts to those who truly believe in him. Christians possess a glory and beauty and an indescribable heavenly richness that come to them with hard work and sweat, acquired in times of temptations and many trials. All of this must be ascribed to divine grace."[6]

Whether they are monks or householders, *testing* is the lot of all fallen men when they take the path to overcoming the Fall. One form of this testing occurs quite automatically as we begin to become aware of the constant bombardment of provocations, a bombardment that continually tests our emerging consciousness until we become fully conscious of the secondary nature of the provoking stimuli and so separate from them.

This is a major element in what is sometimes known as the "lesser liberation."

Provocation passes through several stages, at each of which it becomes more difficult to "escape" without help. We shall now draw on Kontzevitch's description of these stages, with a little commentary where it can be helpful.

1. Provocation (Russian *prilog*)

Kontzevitch's description of the initial provocation is:

> The first impetus to the emergence of the psychological phe-
> nomenon which may end as passion is known as "provoca-
> tion" or "suggestion" (*prilog*). It is a conception of an object
> or an action corresponding to one of the stained inclinations
> within a person. Under the influence of external impressions,
> or in connection with the psychological working of the
> memory or imagination according to the laws of association,
> this provocation enters the sphere of man's consciousness.
> This first moment takes place independently of man's free
> will, against his wish, without his participation, in accor-
> dance with the laws of psychological inevitability—"sponta-
> neity"—and is therefore considered "innocent" or dispassion-
> ate. It does not incriminate man in sin if it is not caused by
> his "wandering" thoughts, if it is not invited consciously and
> voluntarily, and if a person is not negligent about it. This is
> the touchstone for testing our will to see whether it will be
> inclined towards virtue or vice. It is in this choice that the
> free will of man manifests itself.[7]

The "stained inclinations" he refers to are of course memories of pleasures and dislikes: the term makes it clear that to our natural tendency to enjoy certain things we normally add remembered feeling-impressions, which are evoked from memory by association, for example, by associa-tion with events or with the memories aroused in daydreaming.

In experience, the process of provocation is continual. One after another thoughts and other impressions enter our awareness, and each as it does so arouses feelings, and these provoke us to react.

If we are able to resist this process even for a moment, then a number of alternative provocations appear before us as alternative actions.

Unless we have been through prolonged special training, this state of choice does not occur often.

2. Conjunction (Russian *sochetanie*)

The second stage is a response from our feelings which determines our attitude to the provoking stimulus. Unless the heart is trained, this response will normally be "uninformed," and in this situation many of our responses will lead to two things we do not wish:

1. continuation of the state of confluence
2. mistaken and often self-destructive or self-limiting actions, with the attendant problems these cause in our lives.

In general this second stage occurs too fast for us to stop it. It is colored by past events, and when it occurs unseen, this means that those past events shape our reaction in that moment. The process is described by Kontzevitch:

> Provocation evokes the response of the feeling, which reacts to the impression or image intruding upon the consciousness by either "love" or "hate" (sympathy or antipathy). This is the most important moment, for it decides the fate of the provoking thought: will it stay or will it flee? It is only the emergence of this thought in the consciousness that occurs regardless of the will of the man. If it is not immediately rejected and lingers on, this means that in the nature of a given person it finds compatible ground, which is expressed in his sympathetic reaction to the provocation. Sympathetic inclination attracts attention, allowing the suggested thought to grow and turn into an image of fantasy pervading the entire sphere of consciousness and ousting all other impressions and thoughts. Attention lingers at the thought because man delights in it. This second moment is called conversation or conjunction (*sochetanie*). Saint Ephraim the Syrian defines it as a "free acceptance of the thought, its entertainment, as it were, and a conversation with it accompanied by delight."
>
> In order to cut off the sequence of notions, to remove it from his consciousness, and to terminate the feeling of delight, man needs to distract his attention by the effort of his will. He

must actively and firmly resolve to rebut the images of sin assailing him and not return to them again.[8]

3. Joining (Russian *slozhenie*)

In the personality which lacks a fully formed magnetic center or permanent center, the equilibrium that is destroyed at a moment of provocation is purely transient and depends on momentary efforts which have first had to be learned. When the learned effort ends, the control disappears and is replaced by what Mouravieff calls a state of "confluence," that is, of identification with the *content* of the mind. When not controlled, that content is purely associative in its nature. About this third stage, Kontzevitch says:

> Otherwise, with the absence of willful rejection of the introducing images, the third moment is induced when the will itself becomes increasingly attracted to the thought, and as a result man becomes inclined to act upon what the thought tells him and to get the satisfaction of partaking of it. At this time the equilibrium of his spiritual life is totally destroyed, the soul wholly surrenders itself to the thought and strives to realize it with the purpose of experiencing an even more intense delight.[9]

In modern Western man the breakdown of this control is continual or endemic—indeed, it makes more sense to say that magnetic center as a stable form of control exists only in a very few rare individuals—so that before awakening the magnetic center, the teaching in its contemporary form begins by training aimed at the formation of that center, which is artificial in its nature and is based on disciplines which are in part a result of understanding the factors described in this passage from Kontzevitch.

The formation of some kind of artificial center like the magnetic center was the objective of classical Greek education or *paideia*, and it appears probable that other civilizations, what we would call theocentric, actually formed at their full flowering, and that they may sometimes still form, as in the best of Islam, something similar as part of the higher stages of normal education. Almost certainly this also happened in the early church before the third century, and has happened since then very occasionally in certain very localized Christian communities,[10] so that, in those civilizations, "to be civilized" would imply the possession of magnetic center; but further study is needed before we can be entirely certain of this. Christian communities of this kind probably include some communities in Cappadocia (in Turkey) between the fourth and twentieth centuries, and certain locations in Russia—such as the village where Theophan was born—from the fourteenth to nineteenth centuries.

4 & 5. The Struggle Against Habit

But let us continue with the previous quotation from Kontzevitch:

> Thus, the third moment is characterized by the inclination of will towards the object of the thought, by its agreement to resolve and realize pleasurable fantasies. Consequently, in the third moment the whole will surrenders to the thought and now acts according to its directives in order to realize its fantastic plans. This moment, called joining (*slozhenie*), is the cooperation of the will, which is a declaration of agreement with the passion whispered by the thought (Saint Ephraim the Syrian), or consent [assent] of the soul to what has been presented to it by the thought, accompanied by delight (Saint John Climacus). This state is already "approaching the act of sin and is akin to it" (Saint Ephraim the Syrian). There comes the willful resolve to attain the realization of the object of the passionate thought by all means available to man. In principle, the decision has already been made to satisfy the passion. Sin has already been committed in intention. It now remains to satisfy the sinful desire, turning it into a concrete act.
>
> Sometimes, however, before man's final decision to proceed to this last moment, or even after such a decision, he experiences a struggle between the sinful desire and the opposite inclination of his nature.[11]

Later he quotes Saint Nilus of Sara as writing:

> The best and most successful struggle takes place when the thought is cut off by means of unceasing prayer at the very start. For, as the Fathers have said, whoever opposes the initial thought, i.e. the provocation, will stop its subsequent disposition at once. A wise ascetic destroys the mother of wicked fiends, i.e. the cunning provocation (first thoughts.) At the time of prayer, above all else, one's intellect should be rendered deaf and mute (Saint Nilus of Sinai), and one's heart emptied of any thoughts, even a seemingly good thought (Saint Hesychius of Jerusalem). Experience has shown that the admission of a dispassionate thought, i.e. a distraction, is followed by an impassioned (wicked) one, and that entry of the first opens the door to the latter.[12]

This unceasing prayer can have more than one meaning; it can take the form of constant repetition of a formula such as the Jesus Prayer, or of a simple emotional state of openness to higher levels or higher centers with no specific activity, but all of these become unceasing only when they are stronger than the temptations. This, the action of unceasing prayer giving control over the aimless behavior of the mind, is very close to a fully formed magnetic center. But we must first aim at earlier stages of partial stability, which can only be actively maintained under sheltered conditions, and we must come to understand that when those sheltered conditions are not available, the same stage in the formation of magnetic center becomes instead a continual struggle against loss of control due to outside conditions. This long and difficult struggle with habits is characteristic of this work outside monasticism.

The struggle against habit depends on how deeply the habit is established. Some effort, and particularly long persistence, is needed to struggle against all habits: "However, the last psychological moment of an unstable vacillation of the will between opposing inclinations takes place only when the habit has not yet been formed within the soul, namely, the 'bad habit' of responding to the evil thought. It takes place when a sinful inclination has not yet deeply penetrated man's nature and become a constant feature of his character, a familiar element in his disposition, when his mind is constantly preoccupied with the object of the passionate urge, when the passion itself has not yet been completely formed."[13]

6. Captivity (Russian *plenenie*)

In Kontzevitch's account of the stages of provocation, he writes about stage 6, "captivity":

> When in the power of passion, man gladly and violently rushes to satisfy this passion, either without any struggle at all, or almost without a struggle, he is losing the dominant, guiding and controlling power of his volitional faculty over individual inclinations and the demands of volitional nature. It is no longer the will that rules over sinful inclinations, but the latter rule over the will, forcibly and wholly enticing the soul, compelling its entire rational and active energy to concentrate on the object of passion. This state is called captivity (*plenenie*). This is the moment of the complete development of a passion, of the fully established state of the soul, which now manifests all of its energy to the utmost.[14]

This picture implies that man possesses a degree of control and then loses it. At one time, almost everybody learned control over their own responses in specific situations that varied depending on their early life. Even today, almost all of us[15] have learned not to respond to some temptations. But with modern ideas of freedom, even this occasional self-control becomes less and less common or operates only in specialized and very limited situations, in our profession and elsewhere. This is why the power of the passions grows stronger year by year, something that accounts for the epidemic in the use of drugs and other distractions by which people hide from life. For mankind as a whole this leads to social problems. For the individual, this simply means that the difficulty of overcoming the passions becomes greater so that sanctity seems further and further out of our reach. The fact is that when the process of formation of a passion is complete, the struggle against habit is possible only through intentional suffering; this is not "stupid suffering," taking on suffering pointlessly, but the "useful suffering" of voluntarily refusing to satisfy these passions. This struggle is much more difficult without prayer, although in certain stages it can make prayer itself seem difficult or even for a while fruitless.

Observation of Provocations

In this study I will first repeat Evagrius's description of the particular provocation, then describe my own attempts to observe the same thing under nonmonastic conditions. I must also add that for a layperson committed to a way other than the monastic, someone who has to live in everyday life among people for whom any form of self-denial is often a sign of "weakness" or even stupidity, this kind of struggle often has to be unmentioned and invisible.

When the experiences described by Evagrius and quoted earlier (chapter 9) are interpreted in inner terms, it becomes clear that the demons referred to are no more than complexes or "inner beings": uncontrolled and thus semiautonomous contents of our fallen souls. However, it is easy to understand that those who see everything as outside themselves will also see these demons and similar beings as existing outside themselves.[16] In simple terms, we not only have to recognize the nature of something when it arises, but we need also to remember two other things with the strength of recognition. First, that what we have observed has been seen to exist within ourselves, and second, the harmful results we observe coming from what we have observed within us. Saint John Cassian wrote of this: "Abba Moses replied: 'It is impossible for the mind not to be troubled by these thoughts. But if we exert ourselves, it is within our power either to accept them[17] and give them our attention, or to expel them. Their coming is not with our power to control, but their expulsion is. The amending of our mind is also within the power of our choice and effort."[18]

There is a close relationship between the idea of *guarding the thoughts*, referred to by Father George of Grigoriou, and the idea of self-observation. Before we can guard our thoughts, we must have worked for a long time to form the habit of observing them, and often the only way we will find we are able to observe them is by *trying* to keep guard over them. At first, this *watchfulness* is possible only while we struggle to prevent certain types of thought: in the early stages there is no clear observation without this struggle. Evagrius gave some idea of the level or intensity of observation necessary on both the lay and the monastic paths, when he wrote:

> If there is any monk who wishes to take the measure of some of the more fierce demons, so as to gain experience in his monastic art, let him keep careful watch over his thoughts. Let him observe their intensity, their periods of decline and follow them as they rise and fall. Let him note well the complexity of his thoughts, their periodicity, the demons which cause them, with the order of their success and the nature of their associations. Then let him ask from Christ the explanation of the data he has observed.
>
> The kingdom of Heaven is apatheia of the soul along with true knowledge of existing things.[19]

Based on the Sermon of the Mount, *apatheia*, passionlessness or purity of heart, is seen as the necessary qualification for any awareness of God and therefore, for Evagrius and many other Fathers, to achieve *apatheia* is the same as to attain true spiritual love: "Agape is the progeny of apatheia. Apatheia is the very flower of *ascesis*."[20]

In verse 39 of *The Praktikos*, Evagrius adds what turns out to be an important clue to practical methods of dealing with the passions, although for modern Western man what he describes is no longer commonplace but can only be developed slowly. He wrote: "The psyche will usually flare up against the passionate thoughts at the evil smell of the demons, who are perceived as they draw near and affect the soul with the passion of its assailants."[21] Observation shows that Evagrius uses the term *smell* here, not literally but in the same sense that other esoteric authors use the term *taste*. When we go beyond verbal thought to think in terms of inner experience, we will discover that there is a recognizable quality by which the nous can distinguish the source of different elements in its experience. This is the proper working of the mind of the heart, giving us what has been called the "discernment of spirits," that is, the ability to recognize and so distinguish what comes from a reliable source from what comes from an unreliable or harmful origin. Observation, however, suggests that before the soul can be sensitized against harmful stimuli in this way it must first recognize that the particular type of stimulus is harmful to it.

Evagrius wrote about *recognition* in a passage quoted earlier: "We must take care to recognize the different types of demons and take note of the circumstances of their coming."[22] Recognition is a property of the nous and one of the qualities of *noetic knowledge*. Recognition plays a part in the discernment of spirits. We know the influences that act on us by what in the tradition has been called "taste" and by what Evagrius calls their "smell," in the sense that we say about a situation that "something smells funny here."

Resisting Provocation

Saint Nilus's rule also discusses in detail specific forms of *provocation*, and although it does not actually refer to him, in one part it seems to come very close to the words of Evagrius. Certainly, resisting provocation is one of the most important planks making up Evagrius's psychological ark, as well as the rule of Saint Nilus; that is to say, it is one of the most important disciplines to be learned in building this magnetic center. When we are ready to get down to detail in our inner lives, it is important to learn exactly how this discipline is to be formed, on what we can act. This was made clear at the end of paragraph 6 of *The Praktikos*, which was quoted a few paragraphs earlier. Here, Evagrius clearly defines what we can control and what we cannot—he tells us that we can decide if these provocations will be kept in our minds for a while, and we can decide whether or not they will be free to stir up our passions—and this power of decision is a crucial key to all practical inner work.

But it must be understood that in the state of *confluence* or *identification*, this power of decision is lacking, so that we do not then have this control. One result of this is that today many intellectually devised teachings fail because they are taught to those who cannot carry them out: sometimes "invented" teachings demand that the student control his or her mind in ways that are not in practice possible. At other times ancient teachings which are possible for prepared individuals are given to people who are insufficiently prepared; for example, teachings intended for those who have established magnetic centers may be given to those whose magnetic center is weak or nonexistent. In other words, many attempts to control the mind go wrong through attempting to actively control processes that are not under our immediate or direct control. The teaching about provocation is a case in point. In its classic form as given by Evagrius it can be put into practice only by those who have already built their "ark." In fact, one of the primary uses of the traditional teaching—when properly understood—is to help us distinguish between what we can control directly and what we can only control indirectly as a result of direct control at some other point of action.

The first point is that, once we struggle in the correct way, we will discover that each time we lose the battle by reacting to these provocations we create new impurities—called "passions"—that are formed from our past experiences of the things most attractive to us. It is these powerful images that distract us from reaching the final stages of prayer of the heart. The struggle with provocations aims at preventing the formation of these additional images, and it is therefore crucial to the development of what certain early Fathers, including Evagrius, called *apatheia*, the opening of the heart that occurs in the final stages of development of a mature magnetic center in us. Posoff says here: "The activity of the intellect in the heart begins at the moment when the intellect is strong enough to remain in the heart and not leave it too soon. If the intellect remains in the heart, it means that the passions are overcome and the Holy Spirit is beginning to work in the heart." He also uses the saying Gregory of Sinai quoted earlier: "The Holy Spirit attracts the nous to itself, drawing it into the depth of the heart and preventing its usual wandering about."[23]

This is indeed a key explanation for practical inner work.

What this all means is that after the early experiences we are granted by grace, this activity does not finally go into the heart, and the Holy Spirit does not become active in the heart, until we have become strong enough to resist the provocations that beset us. In fact we will, in the beginning of our inner work, be allowed to taste certain states as a result of our resisting specific provocations. About this the tradition says: "More is asked of those to whom more has been given," so that at a later stage the door in the heart will more often be closed to us until we learn to resist all provocation.

This of course links with the dark nights described by Saint John of the Cross.

At this point it is necessary to remember that we can observe these provocations only when we struggle with ourselves. Our experience of these same provocations is therefore shaped by the kind of struggle we have undertaken, and because we face different struggles from those faced by a monk, our experience of provocations will also be different in character from those of a monk. Yet any effort to struggle against the automaticity of our organism will sooner or later bring us up against one or more of these eight provoking thoughts, and then we will discover exactly how they manifest in our specific way of life. Struggles of this kind are involved in the formation of a magnetic center as an inner and purely psychological "cell" into which our consciousness can withdraw to separate itself from provocation, and a final victory over provocation is a final victory in the formation of this magnetic center. This demands grace, but before this can happen we must build as much as possible for ourselves. This is the rule, as I understand it.

First Provocation: Gluttony

Evagrius describes how the monk experiences this basic form of provocation, because his specific self-imposed effort is to struggle with the demands of the body by limiting what he eats, and his efforts define the character taken by this provocation. At the same time Evagrius's description is recognizable to anybody who has begun to struggle with himself, when it says: "The thought that provokes gluttony suggests to the monk that he give up his ascetic efforts in short order. It brings to his mind concern for his stomach, for his liver and spleen, the thought of a long illness, scarcity of the commodities of life, and finally of his edematous body and of lack of care by physicians. These things are depicted vividly before his eyes. It frequently brings him to recall certain ones among the brethren who have fallen on such sufferings. There even comes a time when it persuades those who suffer from such maladies to visit those who are practicing a life of abstinence and to expose their misfortune and relate how these came about as a result of the ascetic life."[24]

My own observations here link to another paragraph of Evagrius's text, which adds: "For satiety desires a variety of dishes but hunger thinks itself happy to get its fill of nothing more than bread."[25]

Let's be honest: with my age and my long individual and family history of self-indulgence, it is very difficult to struggle against the wish for variety, and even enforced lack of variety forces on me exactly the reactions described by Evagrius as arising from gluttony. This struggle, therefore, leads to exact observation. I must then link that observation to the effects of this demand for variety: that it makes work for others, it limits what I can do and where and when I can do it, it affects me physically. The conclusion of these observations is that I must continue to struggle against this gluttony if I am not to be dominated by it.

Then we must remember, must understand that these provoking thoughts lead to "impurities" of heart, specifically to the desires and negative emotions that are associated with the experiences described above. These impurities of physical feeling are one of the things that close the door in the heart and so prevent the final stages of prayer of the heart.

Second Provocation: Lust

The second observation is described by Evagrius in the following passage:

> The demon of impurity impels one to lust after bodies. It attacks more strenuously those who practice continence, in the hope that they will give up their practice of this virtue, feeling that they gain nothing by it. This demon has a way of bowing the soul down to practices of an impure kind, defiling it, and causing it to speak and hear certain words almost as if the reality were actually present to be seen.[26]

Here again, our experience differs from that of the monk. We are more likely to be stimulated from outside than from the practice of continence. The householder's struggle on this way is not against sex but against trivialization of sex, against the debasing of sex to a purely physical practice. When sex becomes so strong that we forget love, this is the defilement; the struggle is to cleave to love, not to pleasure. When one does so, the quality of one's perceptions will change and one will begin to understand the inner meaning of what Mouravieff writes about the idea of the *polar being*. The slow transformation of sex to Christian love leads to great changes within us, giving us the zeal without which the spiritual is forever out of reach.

Third Provocation: Avarice

Avarice is the desire not only for money but for property and possessions in general. As we grow older, and as we grow more accustomed to our comforts, the power of this provocation grows stronger:

> Avarice suggests to the mind a lengthy old age, inability to perform manual labour (at some future date), famines that are sure to come, sickness that will visit us, the pinch of poverty, the great shame that comes from accepting the necessities of life from others.[27]

Unlike the monk, we are not expected to give up our possessions. The demand we face is to give up our lives in service to a higher will, at first simply taking the form of the need to work for something other than personal gain, to think of something other than our personal needs. But what we will already have discovered is that this desire for possessions is endless. The more possessions we have, the more we feel threatened by their lack. And this is without any intense struggle. With the attempt to serve comes the struggle and the provoking hints that we could do better, that we should take better care of ourselves and those around us, and so on.

Fourth Provocation: Sadness

When the attempt to serve reaches a certain stage of reality, then, as in military service in time of emergency, there come periods when the needs of our service do not allow us time or resources to obtain what we want. At this time we meet the same sadness described by Evagrius in paragraph 10 of his text:

> Sadness tends to come up at times because of the deprivation of one's desires. On other occasions it accompanies anger. When it arises from the deprivation of desires it takes place in the following manner. Certain thoughts first drive the soul to the memory of home and parents, or else to that of one's former life. Now when these thoughts find that the soul offers no resistance but rather follows after them and pours itself out in pleasures that are still only mental in nature, then they seize her and drench her in sadness, with the result that these ideas she was just indulging no longer remain. In fact they cannot be had in reality, because of her present way of life. So the miserable soul is now shriveled up in her humiliation to the degree that she poured herself out upon these thoughts of hers.[28]

This struggle comes to all those who go out of their way to serve, or even to prepare themselves for service.

The method is to learn to recognize the character of these thoughts and be alerted to the effects they will quickly arouse in us. Once this awareness is sufficiently strong, we will begin to be able to turn away from the provocation. But until we are able to control the provoking thoughts, this sadness can simply be borne as long as we are able; then if it is too much, we should not rest in pride, but should take a break from the restriction—should do something we enjoy—in order to recuperate our energies.

This is described by Gregory of Nyssa in his *Life of Moses* as the "bitter water" sweetened by throwing into it a piece of wood, described by Nyssa—with precision but in the language of parable—as a piece of the true cross. On the monastic path, prayer and liturgy fill this place and drive out the sadness with the sweetness of the Spirit. Here, theory is not enough: in the formation of the magnetic center we must discover our own ways of transforming this bitterness, first by turning it positive and so releasing the energy trapped in it, and finally by *mneme Theou*: by finding our own inner communion in remembrance of God, and then by bringing it to a strength sufficient to *transmute* the negative feelings.

Fifth Provocation: Anger

Perhaps the easiest of the provoking thoughts to recognize is that which gives rise to anger. Always in my experience it is based on thought of oneself, the insistent *I* and *me*: he owes *me* this or that; she did so and so to *me*; they ignored *me*; nobody is going to get away with doing that to *me*. We judge others in relation to ourselves, forgetting that Christ said "Judge not, that ye be not judged." In my experience this stems directly from pride, from our sense of our own great worth. Evagrius put it:

> The most fierce passion is anger. In fact it is defined as a boiling and stirring up of wrath against one who has given injury—or is thought to have done so. It constantly irritates the soul and above all at the time of prayer it seizes the mind and flashes the picture of the offensive person before one's eyes. Then there comes a time when it persists longer, is transformed into indignation, stirs up alarming experiences by night. This is succeeded by a general debility of the body, malnutrition with its attendant pallor, and the illusion of being attacked by poisonous wild beasts. These four last mentioned consequences following upon indignation may be found to accompany many thoughts.[29]

There can be little difference here between the experience of the monk and that of the layperson, except that the pressures of life are likely to be stronger in the life of the layperson and nonmonastic, so that once we fall, our anger is likely to be more energetic, although more quickly prevented by interruptions, for which we may thank God. We will discover that the anger which comes alongside the sadness—as described under the previous provocation—is particularly persistent because in such experiences there is always a measure in which we value ourselves and so believe ourselves to be entitled.

Sixth Provocation: Accidie

Evagrius in his description of accidie is directing it so exactly at the monk that it is difficult to see how it can apply to anyone else. He writes:

> The demon of accidie—also called the noonday demon—is the one that causes the most serious trouble of all. He presses his attack on the monk about the fourth hour and besieges the soul until the eighth hour. First of all he makes it seem that the sun barely moves, if at all, and that the day is fifty hours long. Then he constrains the monk to look constantly out of the windows, to walk outside the cell, to gaze carefully at the sun to determine how far it stands from the ninth hour, to look now this way and now that to see if perhaps . . . Then too he instills in the heart of the monk a hatred of the place, a hatred for his very life itself, a hatred for manual labour . . . etc.[30]

How then can this apply to someone who is no monk, whose busy, busy life takes him or her constantly out and about? Some of us will recognize the flavor of this constant provocation that acts in the same way in our very different lives. I sit to study, and immediately I want to be somewhere else, doing something else. I set aside time for prayer, and immediately I remember something else I wish to be doing. It is as if my whole organism resists change, so that the more active I have been in the recent past, the more active I wish to remain. The common view of this is boredom or ennui, but in fact it is the power of habit in the personality, a power whose "wheels" keep spinning long after we have reason for acting. So much is this persistence of activity a characteristic of the personality that Evagrius was able to end his paragraph 12 like this: "No other demon follows close upon the heels of this one, but only a state of deep peace and inexpressible joy arise out of this struggle."[31]

Seventh Provocation: Vanity

Vanity is another provocation that most of us will recognize, although we are not monastics, a provocation that speaks to me again and again. Once it used to tell me that I was someone special and that it was only bad luck or some unfair situation that had prevented my demonstrating this to everyone; then it tells me that I am someone special whenever I have achieved some small thing. This provocation takes so many forms that I am sure you will be able to discover new ones—and that such a discovery too can become a cause for vainglory. Those involved in what we currently call the New Age will particularly recognize Evagrius's description here:

> The spirit of vainglory is most subtle and it readily grows up in the souls of those who practice virtue. It leads them to desire to make their struggles known publicly, to hunt after the praise of men. This in turn leads to their illusory healing of women, or to their hearing fancied sounds as the cries of the demons—crowds of people who touch their clothes. This demon predicts besides that they will attain to the priesthood. It has men knocking at the door, seeking audience with them. If the monk does not willingly yield to their request, he is bound and led away. When in this way he is carried aloft by vain hope, the demon vanishes and the monk is left to be tempted by the demon of pride or of sadness who brings upon him thoughts opposed to his hopes. It also happens at times that a man who a short while before was a holy priest is led off bound and is handed over to the demon of impurity to be winnowed by him.[32]

Of course, this is not the only form vainglory takes. Think of how it has acted on you in your profession. You cannot think how: all your status has been well-earned? That is one form! Think of yourself as a student of this work who is sure you would yourself know what to teach. Think of yourself as a family man, as a good mother, as a person of substance in the community, and so forth, and become aware how you wish people to see you as such! Similar flaws are in us all. Vanity rules: then, when nobody wants to hear what I have to say, it hands me over to the demon of sadness.

Have I given this demon authority in my own mind?

Eighth Provocation: The Demon of Pride

Some say that *pride* is the greatest provocation, that it is the deluded belief of the unredeemed personality in its own absolute reality, its own selfhood, its own ability to *do*, to be cause in every situation. This is supported by Evagrius's description:

> The demon of pride is the cause of the most damaging fall for the soul, for it induces the monk to deny that God is his helper and to consider that he himself is the cause of virtuous actions. Further, he gets a big head in regard to the brethren,

considering them stupid because they don't all have this same opinion of him. Anger and sadness follow on the heels of this demon, and last of all there comes in its train the greatest of maladies—derangement of mind, associated with wild ravings and hallucinations of whole multitudes of demons in the sky.[33]

Pride as a provocation is of course a thought or a series of thoughts. We may recognize some of them: under the influence of pride we habitually claim that everything we do successfully is the result of our own ability, our own action. Subtle indeed are the ways of this type of falsehood, as modern man generally considers it normal and even accurate to make these claims; until we *recognize* them to be *unconscious lies*, they will continue to have power over us. As we recognize the delusory nature of these claims, our willingness to accept praise will slowly reduce, but oh how slowly . . . for these claims are the litany that forms the character of our whole civilization: of you and me and of all those around us.

The Fear of Opening Ourselves to God

Many of the early Fathers include *fear* in their list of passions. Although it is not included in Evagrius's list of *provocations*, fear can be seen to be the "attendant passion" that emerges in response to many provoking thoughts. In my experience, for those who follow the psychological method, this fear generally takes a particular form. This is another way of understanding the fear that resists the surrender of our own autonomy in subordination to God in the final stages of *repentance* (see chapter 10). As we become increasingly aware that to serve God we must take little and sometimes no thought for ourselves, we begin to think of what we would like for ourselves, and then we feel the sadness described above. Or the thought of gluttony raises all its fears and concerns about the threat to health, or impurity raises its head with the thought "just once more" (a variation of Saint Augustine's passage paraphrased "Lord make me good, but not yet"). And these thoughts build up a feeling of fear, a passion of fear in us, and that feeling in turn draws our mind back to these same thoughts time after time.

So not only do these provoking thoughts give rise to the feelings known as passions, but the passionate feelings give strength to the provoking thoughts and keep them uppermost in our minds.

But, as I hinted, the cause of this is simple but it is fundamental to the Christian life: we wish to put the Lord first in our lives, but to give over control we must first relinquish our own control. As quoted earlier: "It is a fearful thing to fall into the hands of the living God." And this is the fearful thing, to put ourselves in "hands" that may put us into a situation in life which we would never allow ourselves to get into. It demands great trust or great freedom from concern for ourselves, and neither of these is easily come by. And the decision is made worse by our awareness that this is the path of the cross, the path of sacrifice, on which we must take up our own cross of sacrifice in order to partake in the life of our Lord. At this point, self-observation has grown far beyond the range of the self-seeking with which it began.

Postscript
Healing the Soul:
Some Conclusions from Matthew 13

The task of the inner tradition is the healing of the human *nous*, sometimes described by the early Fathers as *the eye of the soul*. The *nous* is the garden in which the sower went to sow (Matthew 13:3), the field in which an enemy sowed tares (Matthew 13:24)—as Gregory of Nyssa made clear in the quote found, quite coincidentally, in chapter 13 of this book—the field in which the man planted the grain of mustard seed that became the kingdom of heaven (Matthew 13:31)—and also the field in which the treasure is hid (Matthew 13:44). This *nous* is the background to the whole drama of inner Christianity. The whole struggle between truth and illusion occurs in this hidden place but is imaged out on the visible world. When we believe the illusions of our mind, truth lies bleeding. When we remember a truth so that illusion is put to flight, trumpets sound in heaven—for even heaven is found through the *nous*. When we share our illusions with others the Devil has found allies on the field of battle, and when we accept the invented concept as a divine truth the angels are put to flight and the field is left to dishonor. When *nous* is made pure and empty of the debris of battle, there is "a new heaven and a new earth" (Revelation 21:1). Then we have begun to "put on the *new man*, which is renewed in knowledge after the image of him that created him" (Colossians 3:10).

This is the great myth of our civilization, the struggle between good and evil. Here lies our difficulty, and here is our hope. Against this back drop we must understand the whole inner tradition, and only by interpreting them against this backdrop will we understand the myths and parables of inner reality. Only through this kind of understanding will we become able to unlock the doors of the heart. And only when this is done will everything change, be made new; only then will the kingdoms of man become the Kingdom of God.

But if you will undertake this struggle on your own shoulders, not leaving it to others, this is something that can happen to you at any time.

337

The Barbarians Within

In the logic of history the outward appearance of this struggle has changed over the centuries. The scenario now is that something historically new is happening to Western civilization. All previous great civilizations in the world have been geographically limited. Even Rome, by then rotten to the core and become "easy meat," was several times brought to its knees by so-called barbarians from outside its boundaries. The lesson of history to us is unclear: perhaps that sick giant might have recovered had the vultures not grown impatient. Now this once-Christian civilization is fast becoming equally sick with a sickness that perhaps first appeared with the Weimar Republic in the 1930s but is now becoming universal. The symptoms are the same, and people's unwillingness to recognize them as symptoms is also the same. All around us we see increasing poverty and homelessness; the decay of skills and the inability today to create the things we use today; the disruption of family life; the cult of ugliness and the desire to shock; an interest in excitement and even violence as a way of forgetting what lies around us.

Today, "the gospel of the kingdom has been preached in all the world for a witness unto all nations" (Matthew 24:14) and today Western civilization is molding the world with its technology, its obsession with trade, its gigantic organizations, and the millions of specialists that sustain them, crippled and made dependent by their specialization. Today the barbarians abroad have been turned into customers, but we are threatened instead by a new demon, the *barbarian within* . . . the barbarian within our own *alienated* selves. It is because of this *inner enemy* that so many doors are double-locked, cars are electronically protected, and people hurry home early for fear of the barbarian who lives within our civilization; drugs, crime, street violence, sexual abuse, abuse of authority and wealth, and a tendency to turn our backs on those in trouble, are the most obvious but not, perhaps, the worst forms of this decay.

Corporations, authorities, associations: all the enormous organizations of which our society is composed are formed of specialists. The narrower their specialization, the more it makes them psychologically dependent, not only for abilities not developed in themselves but for satisfactions so often lacking in their lives. It is this mismatch between their lives and their inner needs that frequently leads to *alienation*. It is not surprising, then, that this specialization, having exactly the qualities that have led to this phenomenon of *alienation*, has failed to find an answer to it.

No form of discursive thought can reflect clearly upon itself without the aid of the still and undivided *nous*, and specialization is founded on division.

Specialization silences that potential Socrates which sleeps within each one of us, who, wakened, would first question then rectify the patterns of our thought, and so prevent them crystallizing with age as now occurs. Socrates's thought represented—some[1] say originated—the trend in Greek philosophy that began to question inner meanings providing an alternative viewpoint to the embryonic empiricism of the Presocratics.

Now our only hope is to find ways of analyzing what is happening that do not stem from the kind of thinking that creates the problem. The way I have chosen in years of study and begun to outline in this book is based on the conclusion that every great civilization is the product of its great religion, and that the sicknesses of a culture reveals the failures of the capacity once, I believe, possessed by every true religion to heal the community around it (a belief counter to the immediate evidence of the Christian world today, but still evidenced in its most forgotten corners).

It is also my thesis that the place where one can best investigate these weaknesses is where Christ turned his searching gaze; in the human heart. Just as a forest can only be restored to health by ensuring the health of the individual trees, said the Maharishi Mahesh Yogi, so the health of a society can be assured by assuring the health of individual members of that society. This is logically inescapable, and if so, then the investigation must begin with the individual: *with oneself*; with me, and now with you, the reader, if you will take these thoughts to heart.

Of course, the formation of the individual does depend to a large extent on the society in which he lives. In our society the provision of knowledge depends on the educational system; the transmission of skills on industry and the professions. In ancient Greece the formation of the heart depended on the family and on *paideia* (see chapter 5), on special forms of education that trained the heart as well as head and hand, forms whose still-contentious nature was made visible in the trial and death of Socrates. But it was then transformed and modified in the light of the gospel of love, by those now known as the Fathers of the church. Christian societies grew around this institution of what might be called *emotional education* that was for far more than a thousand years the civilizing influence whose dissemination was a task of the church. This role still survives in a few inner-oriented monasteries, mostly on those fringes of Christendom near where it was originally formulated, but teaching requires teachers, and the churches no longer have such teachers as a function separate from the priesthood, although Saint Paul wrote, about what he called the Gifts of the Spirit: "And God hath set some in the church, first apostles, secondarily prophets, thirdly teachers" (1 Corinthians 12:28).

The big question we can ask is: where today are the teachers of the heart? what teaching was lost when the teachers were lost? The answer this question appears to reveal is surprising. In the introduction to my book, narrowing my study down to a problem that is as much outer as inner, I came in the end to ask of myself one particular question that I felt to be capable of answering the outer need as well as the inner hope. That question: How might I come to feel growing in my own heart the qualities described in the Sermon on the Mount? This is not a new question. For example, in an earlier church, Saint Symeon the New Theologian once wrote.

> He who does not have attention in himself
> cannot be poor in spirit,
> cannot weep and be contrite,
> nor be gentle and meek,
> nor hunger and thirst after righteousness,
> nor be merciful, nor a peacemaker,
> nor suffer persecution for righteousness sake.[2]

Saint Symeon asked this question some time around the end of the last millennium, and despite his importance as one of the major formative influences of the Orthodox Church, this is one of a number of "hard questions" he raised that for a long time have been generally forgotten outside monasticism, even in the Eastern Church. Today, attitudes to this question are divided into two main groups.

Some people claim that Christianity does not work, because few Christians today possess the qualities described in the Beatitudes.

Others, who often regard themselves as Christians, regard this kind of interpretation of scripture, interpretation clearly based on the human situation, as improper and even unchristian.

Today when, in countries like England, so many people have left the churches for the first of these reasons, and when so many Christians and so many whole churches all over the world fall into the second type, all or almost all of which move further and further from the teachings of Christ in their attempts to respond to what they imagine to be popular demand, it seems important to emphasize that there does exist another alternative that gives a different kind of hope: a hope that Christians might again learn to live according to the Sermon on the Mount and that, doing so, they might begin to stem the tide of ethical collapse.

Need for Christian Teaching

To sum up my conclusions from the researches described throughout this book, it has become clear that the loss of emotional training has been crucial to our civilization. Let me put it this way: if it is true that a civilization is formed of civilized beings, to overcome the decay within that civilization demands that we overcome the decay within its individual members. To stem the tide of today's moral collapse requires a new strength within individuals. In our present situation, this demands the restoration of civilized emotions within individuals, and this in turn depends on the restoration of a lost part of the original element of *emotional education* within our civilization. To attain that today would first require a resolution of the weakness of today's church and a return to the empowering capability of the early churches, a task that has long ago been abandoned by most Christian denominations in the progressive breakdown that began with what I called (in the preface to this book) a balkanization of the mind. This was itself one of the decay products stemming from the slow disintegration of the Roman Empire under the onslaught of repeated barbarian invasions, including the Crusades. It is now apparent that the schism that has developed between the Eastern and Western churches has been no more than a staging post in the spread of that balkanizing tendency.

If *paideia* was the emotionally civilizing element that gave Western civilization its strength, as I believe, then the restoration of the necessary elements of this lost emotional education would depend on restoring to active use the main elements of the long-lost Christian *paideia*, with the addition of corrective elements appropriate to our times. To do so would require teachers who were themselves emotionally educated, something that would require inner knowledge, and when we think what kind of esoteric knowledge this might require, we should remember that Evagrius wrote, "The ascetic life is the spiritual method for cleansing the feeling part of the soul."[3] It can be said that emotional education always requires some kind of practice. Both these statements link with what we have said earlier about the survival of esotericism in certain monasteries. At the same time it is clear that on an informal level some survival of this emotional education exists in certain churches in the idea of "taking up one's cross."

Taking Up the Cross

S o Christian *paideia* has survived to this day, but primarily among the more ascetic members of the monastic movement, the rigors of whose methods (asceticism did not always imply hardship in the way it does now) have helped to discredit it with the general public.

Gospel teachings about the *strait gate* and the *narrow way* refer in their simplest sense to the difficult choice that must be taken at this point, where we must go beyond the point which we can see; beyond what we can control. This choice is well described in the gospel verse that says: "And he went a little farther, and fell on his face, and prayed, saying, O my Father, if it be possible, let this cup pass from me: nevertheless not as I will, but as thou wilt" (Matthew 26:39).

This is the point where we "take up our cross." This leaves us *intentionally* exposed to circumstances beyond our control, forced to live out in reality the situation described in the Gospel passage about the "lilies of the field" (Luke 12:22–31). The inner anxiety that results is one of the meanings of the monastic term *exile*. At this point in the Christian life, something in us begins to exert a *resistance*.

The ambiguity of the description used here is normal. These choices are so difficult to define directly that, on the Christian path, they are normally defined indirectly; for instance they may describe the choice that must be made in terms of *indicators* or *signs* whose presence will tell us when we have made the right decision. Some of these signs serve as analogies for what we must observe, but first we must learn to interpret such analogies. Others are simply indicators, but when we observe them this tells us that we are making the right choice. One method is that of negative definition,[4] when we are advised what not to do: not to take the line of least resistance, for example, or not to choose the comfortable or the easy in preference to what we see to be necessary. This method is linked to what is called apophatic theology, which defines God by speaking of what He is not.

Reports of a Lost Esotericism

It is clear that even today lay communities which are directly influenced by what I have called esoteric monasteries—communities that include to my knowledge devout populations within one small seaside town, and in an industrial suburb of a city—show clear evidence of an improved level of emotional education that frees them from many of the problems common to Western populations. It is equally clear that most Westerners who enter esoteric monasteries find the whole thing too difficult. As described in chapter 7, the emotional "luggage" they carry is too much and they, among others, fail to achieve their spiritual goals.

To put it bluntly, you cannot be in two states of consciousness at the same time, and so a general principle of spirituality is that the emergence of a higher state requires the renunciation of the lower. To renounce the lower state requires that we give up all that belongs to it: all the related interests and outer and inner possessions. Many people are unwilling to take up their cross and make this sacrifice. This is the same point which the disciples of Jesus reached and where, as described in chapter 6 of the Gospel of Saint John, many of them left him:

> Many therefore of his disciples, when they had heard this, said, This is an hard saying; who can hear it?
>
> When Jesus knew in himself that his disciples murmured at it, he said unto them, Doth this offend you?
>
> What and if ye shall see the Son of man ascend up where he was before?
>
> It is the spirit that quickeneth; the flesh profiteth nothing: the words that I speak unto you, they are spirit, and they are life.
>
> But there are some of you that believe not. For Jesus knew from the beginning who they were that believed not, and who should betray him.
>
> And he said, Therefore said I unto you, that no man can come unto me, except it were given unto him of my Father.
>
> From that time many of his disciples went back, and walked no more with him (John 6:60–66).

The modern individual carries a large burden of inner possessions. This burden makes conventional monasticism impossible to most of us. It is because of this that chapter 12 of this book addresses the question of an alternative to the monastic method.

It is all very well to write of solutions available at some time in the past. But what do we know today about emotional education? More to the point, what can we do today?

In searching for an answer to this question, my book investigated the forgotten alternatives implied in the psychological teachings of the early Fathers of the church and of their direct successors, with particular reference to teachings such as those of Clement of Alexandria and Origen—and of Origen's pupil Evagrius of Pontus. Clement and Origen were teachers in Saint Paul's sense of the word—they were both successively heads of the school of Christian knowledge in Alexandria in the second and third centuries. This fact may have underlain a certain lack of compromise in their writings which led to both of them, and even their pupil Evagrius, being often discredited in later centuries. Whether or not this is true, as described in chapter 3, there is little doubt that as early as the second century Clement was teaching a more psychological form of Christian ascesis, which ran through the teachings of the early Fathers like a basic pattern, which has been more and more ignored over the centuries, but which has repeatedly surfaced for brief periods in the historical record.

My investigation of these early psychological teachings, detailed in this book, shows that although they appear monastic, in fact they offer a science so complete that it can also provide effective alternatives to the classical monastic method. Their methods aim at the same objectives as do Eastern practices such as Yoga, but after detailed study it seems to me that they do so in a way that, once properly understood, is more suited to modern Western man, in practical forms of Christianity that differ widely from that taught in the West today.

Here, with their origins in the second century but drawing for descriptive data on other older and younger sources, may be the solutions, the hope, so urgently needed by modern man.

The Psychological Method

Underlying my belief in the availability of a solution is another basic fact that becomes apparent only after long study of these ideas: this is the fact that the psychological ideas of the early Fathers form a genuine science, not simply a single system or doctrine, but something much larger. One of the characteristics of a science, in this sense, is that it provides a resource, a seed-bed of techniques from which differing solutions can be drawn for different needs. Thus there are certain key concepts on which what I call the *psychological method* is based. Many of these are held in common by Christianity and the great Eastern faiths. One fundamental resource of this inner science is described in volume 1 of his *Gnosis*, where Boris Mouravieff lists eight methods or forms of *ascesis* or spiritual exercise. These categories are based on a division of our experience of ourselves into eight categories which are in agreement with those in the Indian system known as the Eightfold Yoga, described by Patanjali in his Yoga Sutras. These categories are precise, and observably apply to all normal human beings (or at least all those who possess the potential for inner development), and they therefore appear to form a suitable framework for the study of any kind of development method in any human culture. Following this, it can be said that all exercises, if their purpose is the transformation of the human organism, act in one or other of these eight categories, apart from certain methods such as Prayer of the Heart which have the capacity, when performed to the full, of embracing or acting within two or more of the classes either sequentially or at the same time. Mouravieff describes these categories, in complete agreement with doctrines of Yoga, as:

8. Ecstasy
7. Contemplation
6. Concentration
5. Constatation
4. Breathing
3. Correct Posture
2. Inner Cleanliness
1. Outer Cleanliness

In classical Raja Yoga, the student utilizes these methods sequentially, giving the idea that the eight classes can be regarded as eight steps taken *from the bottom up*, that is, beginning with the coarsest and most external, and ending with the innermost and most subtle. As a science, however, the same framework is used even in India in other ways. It also serves very well to describe the monastic method of the Eastern Church, as described by Boris Mouravieff, although superficially there seems to be a difference between this and Yoga in that the Christian monastic tradition seems to deal with the earlier categories all together, while Indian methods take them more strictly in sequence.

For lay people with little time to spare on exercises, however, the classic bottom up sequence of approach to these steps may be impossible. Their time for prayer and special exercises is normally far too little, and their only possibility is to turn their whole way of life into a continuous exercise. This is a form of *psychological method* very different from the monastic method: in reality it operates *from the top down*, but it *appears* to begin at steps five and six. The reason for this difference between the appearance and the reality is that the efforts made by the student . . . that is to say by his or her Personality, by what Jung would have called the conscious mind, are *psychological efforts* initiated from these intermediate steps, while the actions of the real cause of the process—the real I itself—are for many years invisible to the student.

Real beginning	Ecstasy
	Contemplation
Apparent beginning	Concentration
	Constatation
	Breathing
	Correct Posture
	Inner Cleanliness
	Outer Cleanliness

We have said earlier that the term *psychological method* comes from P. D. Ouspensky, who, between the two world wars, taught the highly simplified psychological form, developed by G. I. Gurdjieff, of what we have now identified as one stream of traditional Orthodox thought. (Although almost certainly with additions borrowed—in ways themselves traditional with the inner teaching—from other forms of inner tradition.) Between them, these two men from an Orthodox Christian world began to define something that my investigations have proved fairly conclusively was based on or identical to—at least in large part—the forgotten psychological teachings[4] of the early church. These teachings form part of the tradition I referred to earlier in the book, a means of healing human beings and restoring them to psychic and spiritual health. This method was one of the two practical supports of early Christianity which together made the early church so different from that of today.

This form of the path, which begins not with external life, nor with the body, but with the *psyche*, is the true *psychological method*. It achieves similar or identical preliminary and final goals to those attained in Yoga, although its methods are very different. The essence of the *psychological method* is that it acts psychologically, as has been said "from the top down," changing the action of the psyche before needing to make massive changes in the student's lifestyle. The way of life of the student then becomes a matter not of obedience to rules but of personal choice, but that choice has to originate from a certain state of mind—sometimes called conscience—based on a change in the way of viewing the world which is attained only as a result of an inner change in the student's psyche, a *change of consciousness* which is the goal of what has been described by certain sources as *waking up*. Such a method requires knowledge, and that knowledge must be understood through direct experience. It was this that led Evagrius to write:

> Knowing, the great possession of man. It is a fellow-worker with prayer, acting to awaken the power of thought to contemplate the divine knowledge.[5]

From the ordinary state of mind, this new way of viewing the world is so different in its goals and concerns that it appears remarkably impersonal, so that it has also been called *objective reason*.

A Method for Today

To consider the psychological method today, we must take into account the actions of the recent teachers to whom we have referred, although, while the results of these modern teachers were sometimes re-markable, they did not equal those produced by the early church. Why do I say this? Because someone who grew up in his household reports that when Ouspensky returned to England in 1946 after six years of war, looked at his English students, and, after a few meetings at which nobody had the kind of real questions that arise when people practice such ideas, said that his teaching had failed, and that it was time to start again from the beginning. The enigmatic and highly capable Gurdjieff, who appeared to be an eccentric teacher of the disciples of an eccentric age, died later than his pupil Ouspensky, but also admitted failure. He did not leave visible behind him anyone of comparable knowledge or ability. "Je vous laissez dans les beaux draps," he said to his students on his deathbed. "I leave you in a fine old mess."

The parallels between these two endings are too strong to be ig-nored. But so was the work of these men too significant to be ignored. Because of Gurdjieff's novel way of explaining things, because of his flam-boyant and apparently egotistical style of teaching that made it too easy to judge him a charlatan and so avoid the searching questions raised by his very existence, and because he disguised or left out certain Christian dogmas whose origin, if admitted, would have been unacceptable to his students, nearly every committed Christian has ignored him. But he is a historical fact, and his influence is indirect as well as direct. The lesson of these teachers, indeed, is not that they were in any way inadequate; far from it, they were the best of their times.

A Christian Origin

Indeed, one of the things that triggered the investigation that led to this book was this almost ignored claim of Gurdjieff to a Christian origin for his system. Further confirmation of the relation (not identity) between the teachings lay in the fact that the *Philokalia*, the great com-pendium of teachings of the early Fathers that has driven Eastern monasticism since the sixteenth century, and which has waited until now to be proven, was translated into English as a direct result of Ouspensky's friendly contact with a hermit on Mount Athos, Father Nikon. After Ouspensky's death, certain of his students made contact with that her-mit, and this contact with the mainstream had considerable effect on Western spirituality, since it was this that led directly to Gerald Palmer's translation into English of parts of *The Philokalia*.[7] The idea came from Father Nikon in conversation with Palmer, once a student of Ouspensky. Palmer's co-translator in this, also co-translator of the *Art of Prayer* and

Unseen Warfare, was Madam Kadloubovsky, who for many years was Ouspensky's secretary.

It was after several years of investigation into sources on Mount Athos that I finally discovered, much closer to home, that only a short time before his death Gurdjieff had arranged for a party to go to Athos in hopes of "reestablishing contact with the tradition" whose doctrines he had taught in such a novel manner. (The search was unsuccessful at that time.) This finally convinced me that this statement that his teachings were esoteric Christianity was correct not just loosely, but in many important details, previously unproved because of the difficulties in carrying out an adequate study. The simplest confirmation of this, indeed, has been the gradually growing awareness that to make this connection has taken us a long way toward the completion of those then still incomplete teachings, so that they lead to results of a new kind.

The new results come from a new understanding of the *psychological method*, and from five conclusions in particular.

1. That the spiritual transformation of man requires as a preliminary condition the temporary and eventually the permanent liberation of the individual *nous* from the activities that normally obscure it.
2. That certain psychological methods described by the early Fathers have the capacity to liberate the *nous* without requiring massive initial changes in our way of life. These changes then follow instead of preceding the change in the nous.
3. That effective use of the psychological method involves the therapeutic use of the specialist knowledge on which the method is based, enabling us to face reality and so overcome emotional delusions and the disturbances of the nous which they cause.
4. That the missing noetic method referred to by Ouspensky actually exists in the form of the noetic prayer used in the inner tradition of the Eastern Church.
5. That noetic prayer and the form of psychological method referred to combine and augment one another to form an effective discipline of inner growth.

If Thine Eye Be Single

But before we can become true Christians, another thing is necessary. If we have read and assimilated the chapters that have gone before, we will by now have understood that a true Christian, in the inward sense, is not someone who lives life according to doctrine, but someone who—

as said by Saint Theophan the Recluse and others (see chapter 2)—lives from an innate, natural goodness.

But even before we can act according to our natural goodness, we have to see not in a fragmented, unnatural way but in a unified and natural way. "The light of the body is the eye: if therefore thine eye be single, thy whole body shall be full of light. But if thine eye be evil, thy whole body shall be full of darkness. If therefore the light that is in thee be darkness, how great is that darkness!" (Matthew 6:23).

In practice, this means that any belief obtained from external sources, which is different from true faith (see chapters 2 and 8), fragments and obscures the natural state of the nous.

Delusion and fragmentation leave us vulnerable to specialization by giving our specialist knowledge, harmless in itself, illusory importance when we treat it as absolute truth, and this leaves us open to dependency on others and on large organizations. In turn this means that we can act as Christians only to the degree that we are able to remain aware that our beliefs, beliefs that, as we will have observed, are drawn from the concensus beliefs of our time, are in a technical sense prejudices[8]—pre-judgments about the nature of things. We cannot avoid this kind of prejudice, but whether we hold anti-religious prejudice or religious prejudice we must remain aware of their imperfection before we can see the world as a Christian should see the world, for it is literally true that in this sense: "For with what judgment ye judge, ye shall be judged: and with what measure ye mete, it shall be measured to you again" (Matthew 7:2).

As long as we believe our preconceptions, we will not understand. But to retain these preconceptions pro-tem while consciously aware of their imperfection, is to render them harmless. A truly Christian view is to accept that only by grace can we finally know, so that in this life prejudgement is necessary. "For now we see through a glass, darkly; but then face to face: now I know in part; but then shall I know even as also I am known" (1 Corinthians 13:12). But Christians understand in some often unstated way that only when we begin to take a detached view of our necessary prejudices; when we begin to be aware that this is all our conceptions are; only then may we begin to select our preconceptions, and from this we may come to see through the unified eye of true faith, the eye of the soul (chapter 9), that becomes in time the eye of love, because this is one of the things it means to be Christian in the inner sense.

To see what this means, we need to look at the question of faith and its relation to observed fact in an inward way, not comparing external evidence, but taking into account the fact that the choice of world view is not based on observation but on assent, and that assent is a decision. To predetermine criteria for truth is always a decision, but that decision may be more or less conscious, and we can learn to make it more conscious. To do so, we must recognize just how it is that we originally decided what is true. If we are honest with ourselves, we will have to admit that whether we interpret our perceptions of the world in a way that agrees with the teachings of the Bible and of Christ, or in a way that is said to be discovered by science, our decision is never finally verified either for ourselves or from our own experience. When we were young we had to accept some kind of consensus view.

What this means is that as we grow older we have never had certain knowledge, but instead we have at some time in the past made a decision. On this decision, on this prejudgement, we have come to Christianity or turned against Christianity. But either way is flawed by dualism, either Cartesian dualism or the legalistic dualism that long ago turned science against the churches, while Christianity is a religion of unity.

Thus to renew our Christianity, to begin again free of the flaw of prejudgement, the answer is sometimes simple. We simply need to decide again; to make the decision, at first sight more Socratic than Christian, that we accept the recognition of our own ignorance; that we acknowledge that we know that we do not know, and so open ourselves to be taught by God in the school of life.

It is in this recognition comes what Boris Mouravieff called constatation.

A Different Kind of Concentration

The form of perception without prejudice called constatation makes possible a special form of concentration. It is at this point that the action of prayer intensifies, and at this point, too, the psychological method becomes more deeply involved in exercises similar to those of certain kinds of Yoga. This is another practical key to the whole process that was given new meaning by Boris Mouravieff in recently translated papers that describe the specific process of concentration referred to earlier (chapter 14).

> The reader will perhaps be astonished if we tell him that the normal state of the intellect [the nous] is the state of concentration. Habitually, man must make an effort in order to concentrate, and he does not know that concentration is possible other than on selected objects. Now the natural state of the intellect, concentrated, as we said, is concentrated on the whole

of the being of the man, to put it a different way, he concentrates on his presence in himself.

Normally, a man should only make his intellect leave
this state, as a Knight draws his sword, for a specific end.

Afterwards, the intellect must return to this state of
concentration like a sword returned to its scabbard. And just
as a Knight will not hold his sword by the blade, the student
must not use his intellect in the wrong way, losing the initiative, but he must dedicate it to the service of the I, that is to
say, to the whole man.[9]

An understanding of this possibility of this differend kind of concentration
is essential to the success of the psychological method. If this is made the
cornerstone of the magnetic center, the culmination of our *diakrisis*, which
is then far from being a headless axe, prayer and contemplation take to
wing and the student finds himself or herself on the Royal Road itself.

Then we will be able to say with Saint Paul:

Lie not one to another, seeing that ye have put off the old man
with his deeds;

And have put on the new man, which is renewed in
knowledge after the image of him that created him:

Where there is neither Greek nor Jew, circumcision nor
uncircumcision, Barbarian, Scythian, bond nor free: but Christ
is all, and in all.

Put on therefore, as the elect of God, holy and beloved,
bowels of mercies, kindness, humbleness of mind, meekness,
longsuffering;

Forbearing one another, and forgiving one another, if
any man have a quarrel against any: even as Christ forgave
you, so also do ye.

And above all these things put on charity, which is the
bond of perfectness (Colossians 3:9–14).

This book, then, is a detailed study of a single Christian inner tradition in several different forms: in its written forms, some of them nearly
two millennia old, and including the Gospels themselves; in its direct
modern form that survives in the monasticism of the Eastern Church; and
in perhaps less complete modern forms, as a lay teaching that in the recent
past has taken on different terminology at different times.

Accepting that these modern forms are incomplete, the book has
also explored what elements in early texts or monastic practice would be
needed to restore something like the original form of this tradition, and

what there was in the psychology of the Fourth Way forms not otherwise available to the West, which might serve as essential replacements for knowledge that has been lost, if ever there is to be a reawakening of spirituality in the Western world.

Notes

Preface

1. The assassination in Sarajevo of Archduke Ferdinand.

2. Allan Bloom, *The Closing of the American Mind.* London. Penguin, 1988.

3. Just as the ancient division between Eastern and Western Roman Empires is the source of the present conflicts in the Balkans area of Eastern Europe, so the division-by-specialization of the ancient esoteric philosophy taught by the early Fathers of what was then one Church has led to persistent misunderstandings between the related specializations.

4. Boris Mouravieff, in an article in a European magazine, reports how he asked Gurdjieff where he obtained his esoteric teaching, and Gurdjieff replied: "Maybe I stole it." *Revue Syntheses*, No. 138, Brussels, 1957.

Introduction

1. Referred to in books such as *The Illness and Cure of the Soul in the Orthodox Tradition*, by Archimandrite Hierotheos Vlachos. Greece Birth of Theotokos Monastery, 1993.

2. A factor which has sometimes, somewhat naively, led to the conviction in theological circles that if an unwritten tradition cannot be documented it cannot be proved and is therefore "unreal." Scientific anthropology, on the other hand, has long been forced to study unwritten traditions, since in many cultures key traditions have little or no written form. Hence in our studies we have been forced to learn certain lessons from the latter discipline.

3. Although the monastery of Saint Andrew on Mount Athos (officially known as a *skete*, but larger than some of the main monasteries) has been closed for many years, the twenty ruling monasteries of the peninsula are all still fully functional today.

4. See Thomas Merton, *The Wisdom of the Desert.* London. Sheldon Press, 1961.

5. Boris Mouravieff, *Gnosis, Study and Commentaries on the Esoteric Tradition of Eastern Orthodoxy.* Newbury, MA. Praxis Institute Press, 1990.

6. Himself a student first of C. G. Jung and then of Ouspensky.

7. According to Bishop Kallistos Ware, one of the translators of the Greek *Philokalia* into English, the structure of this work is intentionally fragmentary, having been put together with a technique common to the early Fathers and today known to scholars as the "scatter technique," a method used to prevent certain ideas being linked together before they were properly understood.

8. Including the little book about the Jesus Prayer, *The Way of the Pilgrim*. Anon. Trans. R. M. French. London. S.P.C.K., 1930.

9. See Jacob Needleman, *Lost Christianity*.

10. A. Posoff, *The Inner Kingdom*. Trans. Esther Williams, as yet unpublished in English.

11. Archimandrite Hierotheos Vlachos, *The Illness and Cure of the Soul in the Orthodox Tradition*, Greece. Birth of Theotokos Monastery, 1993, p. 47.

12. A view in exact opposition to that which the church had reached by those medieval times when it put Galileo on trial and burned Bruno for his thinking.

13. Archimandrite George Capsanis, *The Eros of Repentance*. Trans. Alexander Golitzin. Newbury, MA. Praxis Institute Press, 1992.

14. In events described in Eusebius, *Ecclesiastical History*. Trans. Kirsopp Lake. Cambridge, MA. Harvard, 1926.

15. At this point the translator wrote: "bred from the intellect, the mind, and its reason." This comment is easily misunderstood as referring to normal intellectual processes or to those by which Plato defines the intellectual recognition of the ideal, although it is probable that the passage originally referred to the *nous* or "intellect of the heart" just as the *nosis* of *gnosis* appears to come from the same root as the word *nous*. The *nous* may also receive knowledge that is not sensory in origin, but comes from God.

16. Translator's note in *The Ante-Nicene Fathers*. Grand Rapids, MI. Eerdmans, 1986.

17. Clement of Alexandria, *The Stromata*, Book VI, chap. 7 in *The Ante-Nicene Fathers*. Grand Rapids, MI. Eerdmans, 1986.

Chapter 1

1. The Narrow Way (Matthew 7:14): "Lord, how can we know the way"; (John 14:5) and the answer, "I am the way, the truth and the life" (John 14:6), the Way of Righteousness (2:Peter 21).

2. "Because strait is the gate, and narrow is the way, which leadeth unto life, and few there be that find it" (Matthew 7:14).

3. The basic idea is that Christian doctrine may differ from denomination to denomination, but that Christian experience is one. I first met this idea at a conference of the Society of St. Alban and St. Sergius, where it was said that the churches were *"doctrinally divided but charismatically one."*

4. Archimandrite Hierotheos Vlachos, *The Illness and Cure of the Soul*, p. 30.

5. Metropolitan Anthony of Sourozh, in an unpublished talk.

6. The present abbot and community of the Athos monastery of Simono-Petra once occupied the Great Meteora monastery in central Greece, but were driven out by tourism and so came to Athos.

7. P. D. Ouspensky, *The Cosmology and Psychology of Man's Possible Evolution*, Newbury, MA. Praxis Institute Press, 1989.

8. See chapter 13.

9. St. John Cassian, *On the Holy Fathers of Sketis*, in the Philokalia, pp. 98–99. Developed in full in chapter 13.

10. Clement of Alexandria, *The Stromata*, in *The Ante-Nicene Fathers*. Grand Rapids, MI. Eerdmans, 1986. Book I, chap. 18.

11. Ibid. Book VI, chap. 7.

12. Referred to directly in Pierre Caussade, *Abandonment to Divine Providence*, a title which, as a concept, is itself a very important part of the esoteric way. Trans. J. Ramiere, S. J. Exeter. Catholic Records Press, 1921.

13. Sometimes known in the West as "Pseudo Dionysius," because although his teachings are highly valued in the East and the West, the name is clearly a pseudonym in a form commonly used at that time.

14. Pierre Caussade, *Abandonment to Divine Providence*.

15. Morton Smith, *Clement of Alexandria and a Secret Gospel of Mark*. Cambridge, MA. Harvard, 1973.

16. St. Mark the Ascetic, in *The Philokalia, the Complete Text*. Trans. Palmer, Sherrard and Ware. London. Faber, 1981, Vol. 1, p. 138.

17. St. Macarius the Great, from Homily 5 in *Pseudo-Macarius, Fifty Spiritual Homilies and the Great Letter*. Trans. G. Maloney, S. J. New York. Paulist Press, 1992.

18. This psychology existed alongside the similar psychological doctrines of the Stoic philosophical school, which was a major force almost throughout the Roman Empire during the early centuries of Christianity and whose teachings were in some ways identical with those of the Fathers, and in other ways very different.

19. The greatest work of Aquinas. See Etienne Gilson, *The Philosophy of St. Thomas Aquinas*. Trans. Edward Bullough, New York. Dorset Press.

20. G. P. Fedotov, *A Treasury of Russian Spirituality*. Belmont, MA. Nordland, 1975, p. 95.

21. Cf. St. Gregory Palamas, *The Triads*. Trans. Nicholas Gendle, New York. Paulist Press. 1983.

22. Obviously the same as the Greek *nepsis*, sometimes translated "sobriety," and sometimes "watchfulness."

23. Quoted in G. P. Fedotov, *A Treasury of Russian Spirituality*, p. 95.

24. Discussed in detail in chapter 14.

25. G. P. Fedotov, *The Russian Religious Mind, Vol. 2*. Cambridge, MA. Harvard, 1966, p. vii.

26. For those who are unaware of him, Gurdjieff was a Greek Armenian spiritual teacher who is known to have taught in Moscow before the revolution, and who finally reached as far West as California. Gurdjieff told the students of his strange system that "this is esoteric Christianity," but without revealing his sources for this information, although a clue is given by the fact that at the end of his life he suggested an attempt to contact those who originated the teaching, and directed that attempt to specific Christian sources. Not surprisingly, this statement had little or no effect: his students continue to seek for the source of his teachings in the Sufi masters of the Middle East.

27. It has been said that even the gargoyles of a cathedral such as Notre Dame de Paris contained hidden meanings. (Cf. Fulcanelli, *The Mystery of Cathedrals*. Trans. Mary Sworder. London. Neville Spearman, 1971.)

28. But this would be a lack of valuation at least partially due to lack of real knowledge.

Chapter 2

1. The Greek word is *synergia*.

2. A definition that is not a direct result of scientific research but rather a part of the popular belief system that has come into being alongside the teachings of science itself.

3. *A poem of Saint Andrew of Crete, The Great Canon*. Trans. Derwas J. Chitty. London. Fellowship of Saint Alban & Saint Sergius, 1957. Verses 6 and 7.

4. Although in a Christian context it is important not to interpret that inner experience simplistically, or in a shallow way, but to move slowly toward a deeper understanding of what it tells us. This accords with Aquinas's description of *revelation*.

5. Detailed study of the Old Testament will show that the prophets are classified by being the medium *by which the Word of God* reached to Israel. If this is kept in the back of our mind as we read the book, an understanding will emerge.

6. Boris Mouravieff in *Gnosis* used the French term *contenir*, to contain, saying that ordinary mind is unable to *contain* these truths.

7. Saint Symeon the New Theologian, *Discourses*. Trans. C. J. de Catanzaro. New York. Paulist Press, 1980.

8. The Jesus Prayer, as expressed in its original source, Luke 18:13.

9. Saint Symeon the New Theologian. *Discourses*.

10. Ibid.

11. Saint Maximos the Confessor, *The Philokalia*. Vol. II, pp. 194–195.

12. For that intellect which discriminates between different intellectual content can also discriminate between different sensations.

13. Saint Maximos the Confessor, in *The Philokalia*. Vol. II, pp. 194–195.

14. Ibid.

15. Ibid., p. 195.

16. See chapter 3.

17. "But while men slept, his enemy came and sowed tares among the wheat, and went his way" (Matthew 13:25).

18. Saint Isaac the Syrian, Homily 3: *The Ascetical Homilies of Saint Isaac the Syrian*. Boston, MA. Holy Transfiguration Monastery, 1984, p. 19.

19. For information on Gurdjieff and Ouspensky, see Postscript.

20. Karlfried von Durkheim, *Hara, the Vital Center in Man*. New York. George Allen & Unwin, 1962, p. 33.

21. See p. 53.

22. Quoted from Saint Cyril of Alexandria.

23. Saint John Climacus, *The Ladder of Divine Ascent*. Trans. Colm Luibheid and Norman Russell. New York. Paulist Press, 1982.

24. The original translation has "intellect" here, but we have given the Greek word *nous*, because the meaning of this is different from the English word *intellect*, and this difference is quite essential to the esoteric meaning.

25. Saint John of Karpathos, in *The Philokalia*. Vol. I, p. 299.

26. See particularly his *Essay on Contemporary Events*.

27. A work by Jacob Bronowski, *The Origins of Knowledge and Imagination*. Yale. New Haven, CT. 1978, suggests that in the so-called language of certain species there is no distinction between the transmission of knowledge and the giving of commands. Legalistic interpretations of higher teachings are a fall into this kind of *command language*.

28. Echoing what was said during 1993, in an article in the London *Times* by Lord Rees-Mogg, one-time editor of the *Times*, about the way that inner experience is undervalued in our times.

29. According to Pieper, certainty of intellect comes as a result of *assent*.

30. G. P. Fedotov, *The Russian Religious Mind*. Cambridge, MA. Harvard, 1963, p. 271.

31. Ibid.

32. St. Maximos the Confessor, *Four Hundred Chapters on Love*. Trans. George C. Berthold. New York. Paulist Press, 1985.

33. The Fathers sometimes wrote of those among their number who actually sought out certain kinds of suffering, and although of course some of this was stupid or unnecessary suffering, at other times this was a result of genuine understanding and an awareness of what was necessary to restore balance to their lives.

34. St. Gregory of Nyssa, *The Life of Moses*. Trans. Abraham J. Malherbe and Everett Ferguson. New York. Paulist Press, 1978, pp. 19–24.

Chapter 3

1. *Liturgy of Saint John Chrysostom*, in various translations.

2. Archimandrite Placide of the monastery of SimonoPetra, in an address. Around 1990.

3. The title *Christian* denotes a level of *being*. It was only such an individual, whose Christian potential was fully developed, in whom the Fall had been overcome, who was known as Christian to certain of the early Fathers such as Macarius the Great.

4. St. Gregory of Nyssa, *The Life of Moses*, pp. 47–50.

5. Constantin Cavarnos, *The Hellenic Christian Philosophical Tradition*, Belmont, MA. Institute for Byzantine and Modern Greek Studies, 1989, p. 109.

6. Self-referential or self-illuminating, and so different from what Saint Paul calls "human knowledge," which is descriptive: each element is described in terms of something else, just as in modern physics, in which energy is described in terms of space and time.

7. Clement of Alexandria, *Stromata*, p. 318.

8. St. Gregory of Nyssa, *The Life of Moses*.

9. Morton Smith's book is based on similarities between the writings of Clement of Alexandria and a letter referring to the existence of a secret, esoteric version of the Gospel of Saint Mark, see further details, pp. 108–109 below.

10. Morton Smith, *Clement of Alexandria and a Secret Gospel of Mark.* Cambridge, MA. Harvard, 1973, p. 34.

11. Michael Talbot, *The Holographic Universe.* New York. Harper Collins, 1992, p. 40.

12. Ibid.

13. Ibid., p. 41.

14. Ibid.

15. Which, according to Gregory of Nyssa, should have no boundaries. See p. 69.

16. "For now we see through a glass, darkly; but then face to face: now I know in part; but then shall I know even as also I am known" (1 Corinthians 13:12).

17. St. Isaac the Syrian, *The Ascetical Homilies.* Homily 3.

18. Andy Gaus (translated), *The Unvarnished New Testament.* Romans 3:10–12.

19. But we must remember that at one time this word meant the same as *uncover.*

20. Clement of Alexandria, *The Stromata.* Book 1, chapter 13.

21. St. John Cassian, *On the Holy Fathers of Sketis.* In *The Philokalia*, pp. 98–99. Quoted more fully in chapter 13.

22. St. Maximos the Confessor, *Four Hundred Chapters on Love.*

23. Greek *Theoria*, contemplative knowledge obtained direct from God, akin to the *gnosis* of the gospel.

24. Evagrius, *The Praktikos* in *The Praktikos and Chapters on Prayer.* Kalamazoo, MI. Cistercian Publications, 1972. V 56.

Chapter 4

1. St. Gregory Palamas, *The Triads.*

2. Evagrius. *The Praktikos.* V 101.

3. St. Joseph the Visionary, quoted in *The Syriac Fathers on Prayer and the Spiritual Life*, by Sebastian Brock. Kalamazoo, MI. Cistercian Publications, 1987.

4. St. Macarius the Great, *The Fifty Homilies.* Homily 5.

5. Ibid.

6. Evagrius, in *The Philokalia.* Vol. 1, p. 52.

7. This in spite of the fact that Gurdjieff and Ouspensky both emphasized the idea that "man cannot do."

8. Clement of Alexandria, *The Stromata*. Book VI, chapter 7.

9. The great mystical text of the Cabala.

10. There are reasons why it is never conveyed fully in writing, and what more nearly complete explanations do exist go into the question at great length and either use extremely obscure terminology such as that of alchemy, or the modern terms of Gurdjieff groups, neither of which belong in an introductory text for Christian readership.

11. In the sense of not normal to . . .

12. St. Macarius the Great, *The Fifty Homilies*. Homily 5.

13. This defines Palamas's great contribution to the theology of the Eastern Church, described by Abbot George Capsanis as follows:

> The distinction between God's hidden being and his active presence has always been maintained by the Orthodox church. However, while it appears in the works of many Fathers, it was the Athonite Saint, Gregory Palamas, who first taught it systematically in the fourteenth century, in order to defend the reality of the saints' experience of God as light. . . . We feel it no exaggeration to say that this saint's teaching is a great blessing for the world. Why? Because it insists that the believer, once having become cleansed of the passions and having become a participant in the holy sacraments, is capable of receiving a direct experience of God, of seeing the uncreated light of the Holy Trinity—the same light which the Apostles beheld at the Lord's trans-figuration on Mount Tabor (Archimandrite George Capsanis, *The Eros of Repentance*, pp. 22–23).

14. St. Macarius the Great, *The Fifty Homilies*. Homily 5.

15. The translation originally had: "beyond natural power."

16. St. Macarius the Great, *The Fifty Homilies*. Homily 5.

17. In Greek the same word is sometimes translated *accepted* and some-times *received*. In most translations of the Bible it is given as *accepted*. In this case the use of the word *received* would have given the passage greater inner meaning.

18. St. Macarius the Great, *The Fifty Homilies*. Homily 5.

19. This test is not one hundred percent reliable, because human error has sometimes entered into the statements of doctrine as well as often entering into understanding of the same doctrine.

20. St. Macarius the Great, *The Fifty Homilies*. Homily 5 V 4.

21. Nicholas Zernov, *Moscow the Third Rome*. New York, NY. Macmillan, 1937.

22. St. Joseph the Visionary, in *The Syriac Fathers*.

23. Blessed Callistus, *Texts on Prayer* in *The Philokalia*.

24. St. Macarius the Great, *The Fifty Homilies*. Homily 5.

25. One should not assume from this that self-reliance is wrong: in the tradition it has been said in many different ways that before we will have a will of our own we cannot do the will of God.

26. Note how this echoes the teaching emphasized by Theophan—himself a great admirer of Macarius, whom he frequently quoted—on the fact that our present state is unnatural.

27. This particular paragraph of what is throughout a remarkably cogent translation would clearly make more sense if it read: "*as though custom and long habit made it the same as an actual part of our nature.*"

28. St. Macarius the Great, *The Fifty Homilies*. Homily 5.

29. St. Joseph the Visionary, in *The Syriac Fathers*.

30. Archimandrite Vasileios, *Abbot of Stavronikita, Hymn of Entry*. Crestwood, NY. Saint Vladimir's Seminary Press, 1984.

31. Evagrius of Pontus, quoted in Kallistos Ware, *The Orthodox Way*. London. Mowbrays, 1979, p. 12.

32. *Panaghia* means All-holy in Greek, and is used as a name for the Mother of God; Athos is called the Garden of *Panaghia* because of a legend that Mary was once there, and was given the peninsula as her garden.

Chapter 5

1. Although it may not have been borrowed specifically from the church, as many technical terms in this tradition were generally current in the Greek thought of the time.

2. A gentle key that this statement has been hermetized to hide its meaning from the uninitiated. The last three lines give an accurate description of the kind of knowledge obtained only through this friction or *thlipsis*, the theological term used for this in Greek monasticism.

3. Clement of Alexandria, *The Stromata*, in *The Ante-Nicene Fathers*. Grand Rapids, MI. Eerdmans, 1986, Vol. 20.

4. To understand the part played by circular definition, consider modern physics, in which everything is defined in terms of space and time, and space and time are measured by reference to each other.

5. A case in point is the *filioque*, the addition made to the Nicene Creed by the Western Church, which states that the Holy Spirit proceeds from the Father *and the Son*.

6. As for example defined by Karl Popper in his book *Objective Knowledge*, which refers to knowledge in the form that can be written down. That is, in modern terms, *information*.

7. Clement of Alexandria, *Stromata*.

8. Clement of Alexandria, *Stromata*. Book VI, chapter 7.

9. St. Isaac the Syrian, *The Homilies*.

10. In fact, it almost certainly existed throughout the church and even before the time of the church.

11. Morton Smith, *The Secret Gospel*. New York. Harper and Row, 1973, p. 15.

12. The importance of wearing no more than a cloth over a naked body is that this was the traditional baptismal costume in a church that baptized—and still does in some places—by total immersion in water, repeated three times. To those who understood, it would therefore appear to convey an additional meaning to the event described.

13. Morton Smith, *The Secret Gospel*, p. 17.

14. Two things about this are certain: that Origen was Clement's successor as head of the Alexandrian Catechetical School, and that Origen began to write a text named the *Stromata*, in imitation of Clement's *Stromata*.

15. Clement of Alexandria, *Stromata,* but re-entered for clarity by Robin Amis.

16. In the sense defined by Aquinas in his *Summa Contra Gentile*, where Josef Pieper summarizes his conclusion as that "revelation is simply the communication of a spiritual inner light whereby human cognition is enabled to observe something that would otherwise remain in darkness." See Josef Pieper, *Belief and Faith*.

17. St. Macarius the Great, *The Fifty Homilies*. Homily 5: 11–13.

18. St. Therese of Lisieux, *Story of a Soul*. London. Collins Fount, 1977, p. 39.

19. By Lord Rees-Mogg in an article in 1993 in the London *Times*.

20. The best example of this circular definition is given by a study of physical constants. During the heyday of physics this gave rise by imitation to the use of circular arguments of the same kind in every discipline that wished to emulate the success of physics (see note 6 to this chapter).

21. *Population Growth and Resource Consumption and a Sustainable World*. London and Washington. U.S. National Academy of Sciences and the Royal Society, 1992.

22. See Saint Theophan the Recluse, *The Heart of Salvation*. Trans. Esther Williams. Newbury, MA. Praxis Institute Press, 1992.

23. Werner Jaeger, *Early Christianity and Greek Paideia*. Cambridge, MA. Harvard, 1965, p. 153.

24. Not all subtle sensations have spiritual significance, nor do the highest mystical impulses equate with any ordinary sensations, yet even here an increase in sensibility is valuable—although we should be warned that it has its problems.

Chapter 6

1. John 3:3, the "from above" is a literal rendering of the Greek; the difference between this and the common modern translations is of great importance in the inner tradition.

2. St. Macarius the Great, *Fifty Homilies*. Homily 30.

3. The Orthodox *Festal Menaion*, Trans. Mother Maria and Kallistos Ware. London. Faber, p. 82.

4. St. Macarius the Great, *Fifty Homilies*. Homily 15.

5. St. Maximos the Confessor, *Four Hundred Chapters on Love*: 1st Century, #36.

6. Ibid. #43.

7. St. Macarius the Great, *Fifty Homilies*. Homily 4.

8. The archaic Greek term used for the passport needed by all visitors to Athos.

9. The monastery's residence on the fringes of Karyes, a long, low house in the woods kept for its representative on the central Holy Community of Athos.

10. "Good day."

11. "Sit down."

12. A kind of cottage occupied by several monks working together under a spiritual father.

13. It is *nous* in the Greek.

14. St. Gregory of Nyssa, *Life of Moses*, p. 83.

15. See Genesis 1:28.

16. As described by Father George Capsanis.

17. St. Gregory of Nyssa, *The Soul and Resurrection*. Trans. John Meyendorf. Crestwood, NY. Saint Vladimir's Seminary Press, p. 57.

18. The translator of the quoted work adds in a footnote that to free their hands for whip or sword, charioteers would wrap the reins round their waist. If they fell, they would then be dragged behind the equipage with no control over their situation—a fit simile for the normal state of the human mind.

19. St. Gregory of Nyssa, *The Soul and Resurection*, p. 57.

20. St. Gregory of Nyssa, *Life of Moses*, pp. 82–83.

21. See St. Theophan the Recluse, *The Heart of Salvation*.

22. Boris Mouravieff, in unpublished papers.

23. Morton Smith, *The Secret Gospel*.

24. It will be noticed here that what today is often called "speaking with tongues" is reported as meaningless or *incoherent*.

25. St. Gregory Palamas, *The Triads*.

26. Archimandrite George Capsanis. *The Eros of Repentance*.

27. Boris Mouravieff, *Gnosis*. Praxis Institute Press, Vol. I, p. 43.

28. Paraphrase from St. Isaac the Syrian. *The Homilies*.

29. Eugraph Kovalevsky, *A Method of Prayer for Modern Times*. Trans. Esther Williams. Newbury, MA. Praxis Institute Press, 1993.

30. Ibn Aribi. Quoted in Boris Mouravieff, *Gnosis*.

31. This usage of the term almost certainly began in the early sixties with the transcendental meditation movement begun by the Maharishi Mahesh Yogi, who was faced with the need to translate the term *dhyana* into an English language with no direct equivalent term.

32. In both its modern sense of *learn*, and its ancient meaning of *uncover*.

Chapter 7

1. Evagrius of Pontus, *Kephalia Gnostica*. Now in translation.

2. St. John Cassian, *The Conferences*. Trans. Colm Luibheid. New York. Paulist Press, 1985.

3. Ibid. *Conference 3*.

4. Ibid.

5. Definition taken from St. Gregory Palamas, *Triads*, p. 82.

6. Evagrius, *Kephalia Gnostica*.

7. Evagrius, *Kephalia Gnostica*.

8. St. John Cassian, *The Conferences*.

9. Evagrius, *Kephalia Gnostica*.

10. St. John Cassian, *The Conferences*.

11. Ibid.

12. Evagrius, *Kephalia Gnostica*.

13. The original has "a will for."

14. See chapter 13.

15. St. John of the Cross, *Bk. I, the Dark Night of Sense and Desire*, from *The Ascent of Mount Carmel. The Complete Works of St. John of the Cross*, Vol. 1. London. Burns Oates & Washbourne, 1947.

16. The ritual pilgrimage to Mecca.

17. See the book of the same title by J. K. Galbraith, *The Culture of Contentment*. New York. Houghton Mifflin, 1992.

18. See G. I. Gurdjieff, *All and Everything*. Aurora, OR. Two Rivers Press, 1993.

19. Archimandrite George Capsanis, *The Eros of Repentance*.

20. St. Gregory of Nyssa, *The Life of Moses*.

21. Evagrius, *Kephalia Gnostica*.

22. St. Macarius the Great, from the introduction to *Fifty Homilies*.

23. To use the term used by Gurdjieff.

24. Evagrius, in *The Philokalia*. Vol. 1, p. 52.

25. Different translations here use *knowledge* or *reason*, and by contrasting them we make the point that the meaning is not exactly the same as the most common meaning of either of these English words.

26. Anon., *The Cloud of Unknowing*. London. Watkins, 1956, p. 63.

27. Evagrius, *Kephalia Gnostica*.

28. St. John of the Cross, *The Dark Night of Sense*.

29. Paraphrasing St. Paul.

30. St. John Cassian, *The Conferences*. Conference 3, p. 86.

31. St. Cyprien of Carthage, quoted from Eugraph Kovalevsky, *A Method of Prayer*.

32. St. John Cassian, *The Conferences*. Conference 3. p. 87.

33. St. John of the Cross, *The Ascent of Mount Carmel*.

34. Gurdjieff often used the term *it* in this way to describe activities occurring in us but not actually part of our own nature.

35. St. Theophan the Recluse, *Commentary on Psalm 118*. Part translated and serialized in *Living Orthodoxy* magazine.

36. Beryl Pogson, *Maurice Nicoll, a Portrait*. Fourth Way Books. New York, 1990.

37. St. Maximos the Confessor, *Four Hundred Chapters on Love*. 2nd Century. 13.

38. The best known are not strictly Christian: See *The Book of the Sacred Magic of Abramelin the Mage*. Trans. S. L. MacGregor Mathers. New York. Dove, 1975.

39. Shantanand Saraswati, then Shankaracharya of the North, in unpublished teachings.

40. St. John Cassian, *The Conferences*. Conference 3. p. 2.

41. St. Symeon the New Theologian, *The Discourses*. Trans. C. J. deCatanzaro. New York. Paulist Press, 1980.

42. St. John Cassian, *The Conferences*. Conference 3. p. 86.

43. See the quotation from St. John Cassian at the beginning of this chapter.

44. Ibid.

45. Ibid.

46. I have seen the term in Orthodox texts that originated before Gurdjieff's time.

47. St. Gregory of Nyssa, *On the Beatitudes*. Quoted in *From Glory to Glory*. Trans. Crestwood, NY. Saint Vladimir's Seminary Press, 1979.

48. Who died in 1993.

Chapter 8

1. For a study of *provocation* see the last chapter in the book.

2. Described in more detail later in this chapter.

3. Or did he simply express an existing trend? It is often impossible to distinguish between concepts that create a trend and those that express an existing trend.

4. Clement of Alexandria, *Stromata*.

5. St. Theophan the Recluse, *The Heart of Salvation.*

6. Josef Pieper, *Belief and Faith.*

7. Ibid.

8. Saint Maximos the Confessor, *Four Hundred Chapters on Love*, 2nd Century, V25.

9. I. M. Kontzevitch, *Acquisition of the Holy Spirit.*

10. Clement of Alexandria, *Stromata.* Vol. II, chap. 3.

11. It was presumably this that was rendered, I think, by P. D. Ouspensky as "You cannot understand and disagree."

12. Clement of Alexandria, *Stromata.* Vol. II, chap 3.

13. The term *subconscious* is used here to refer to memories which are not normally accessible to consciousness, specifically in this case those which can be raised into consciousness by keeping a verbal reference to the experience in the field of attention for a certain brief period of time.

14. St. Anthony the Great, *The Letters of Saint Anthony the Great*, Trans. Derwas J. Chitty. Oxford. SLG Press.

15. Ibid.

16. The same conflict based on two related doctrines exists in Zen Bhuddism, in which many people are confused by the association of the doctrine of sudden illumination with the idea of preliminary purification.

17. The medieval name for Dionysius the Areopagite, often known in the West as Pseudo-Dionysius.

18. St. Gregory Palamas, *The Triads.*

19. Using this term *Being* in the sense it was used by Gregory of Nyssa, in the sense that a true, theological existentialism would use it: as one of the qualities of the divine in a more than Platonic sense, which is also the root and reality of everything.

20. St. Isaac the Syrian, *The Ascetical Homilies.* Homily 3, p. 19.

Chapter 9

1. In *The Philokalia.* Exact source untraced.

2. St. Hesychios the Priest, in *The Philokalia.* Vol. 2, p. 174.

3. Attributed to St. Anthony the Great in *The Philokalia.* Vol. 1, p. 346.

4. *Gospel According to Thomas.*

5. The reference to the eye of the soul shows that the word translated here as "mind" must have been the Greek word *nous*, which was commonly described as the eye or eyes of the soul.

6. G. P. Fedotov, *A Treasury of Russian Spirituality*, p. 95.

7. Gospel of St. John, end of chapter 3. From A. Gauss, *The Unvarnished New Testament*.

8. Kallistos Ware, Praying with the Body, *Sobornost, Eastern Churches Review*. No. 2, 1992.

9. *The Prayer of Joseph the Visionary*.

10. Archimandrite George Capsanis, *The Eros of Repentance*.

11. Ibid.

12. Plato in his dialogues uses the stranger (Gk. *xenos*) as one of the speakers. Modern scholars of this tradition regard this as a reference to real I, the divine self within us which sometimes speaks as *conscience*, a connection which puts hospitality in terms of compassion, of seeing our own selves in the stranger.

13. St. Theophan the Recluse, *The Heart of Salvation*.

14. The original translation has *intellect* here, but we have again given the Greek word *nous*, because the meaning of this is different from the English word *intellect* and this difference is quite essential to the esoteric meaning.

15. St. John of Karpathos, *The Philokalia*. Vol. 1, p. 299.

16. In the Greek New Testament it is *nous*, in the King James Bible and many other English translations it is the less precise term *mind*.

17. This is the basis in Yoga of the *Method of Cause and Effect* or Karma Yoga. See H. P. Shastri, *Triumph of a Hero*. London. Shasti Sadan.

18. See Boris Mouravieff's *Gnosis*.

19. *The Golden Book*, quoted in Boris Mouravieff's *Gnosis*. Vol. 3, p. 217.

20. Or to be more precise than the original translation, of the qualities it evokes in human character.

21. Boris Mouravieff, *Gnosis*. Vol. 3, p. 217.

22. Maximos the Confessor, *Four Hundred Chapters on Love*. C 30.

23. Archimandrite Cherubim Harolambas, *Recollections of Mount Athos*. Brookline, MA. Holy Cross, 1987.

24. Evagrius, *The Praktikos*, V 43–44.

25. *Constate*: A rare English word implying to perceive and register something without judging.

26. Allan Bloom, *The Closing of the American Mind*. London. Penguin, p. 71.

27. Morton Smith, *Clement and a Secret Gospel of Mark*, p. 34.

28. Ibid., p. 35.

Chapter 10

1. St. Neilos the Ascetic, in *The Philokalia*. Vol. 1, p. 220–21.

2. N. A. Motilov, *A Wonderful Revelation to the World*. Seattle, WA. St. Nectarios Press, 1985.

3. "And Jesus said unto them, I am the bread of life: he that cometh to me shall never hunger; and he that believeth on me shall never thirst" (John 6:35).

4. Eugraph Kovalevsky, *A Method of Prayer*.

5. St. Theophan the Recluse, quoted in *The Heart of Salvation*.

6. Included again later on (chapter 14) in a commentary on part of the Praktikos of Evagrius, St. Gregory the Sinaite. Trans. David Balfour, from *Theologia*. Athens, 1982.

7. See Alister Hardy, *The Spiritual Nature of Man*. Oxford. Clarendon Press, 1979.

8. See Abram Maslow, *Towards a Psychology of Being*.

9. We say that knowledge is light because to know something makes it more possible for us to *register* it.

10. I say normally because there is no use expecting the Lord always to conform to rules understood by humans: "The wind bloweth where it listeth, and thou hearest the sound thereof, but canst not tell whence it cometh, and whither it goeth: so is every one that is born of the Spirit" (John 3:8).

11. In Matthew 5.20.

12. Maurice Nicoll, *The New Man*, p. 62.

13. Ibid.

14. St. Gregory the Sinaite. *Discourse on the Transfiguration*.

15. Archimandrite George Capsanis, *The Eros of Repentance*, p. 1.

16. Ibid., p. 2.

17. Ibid., p. 3.

18. "He that loveth not knoweth not God; for God is love" (1 John 4:8).

19. Archimandrite George Capsanis, *The Eros of Repentance*, p. 4.

20. See St. Anthony the Great, *The Letters of Saint Anthony the Great*. Letter 1.

21. Often translated: "So run that you may obtain it."

22. St. Macarius the Great, *The Fifty Homilies*. Homily 4.

23. In the sense in which this term was used by Gurdjieff, P. D. Ouspensky and Boris Mouravieff, among others, who used it to refer to the *content* of the "ordinary" mind of thoughts, feelings, etc.

24. Part of the process is described by St. Theophan the Recluse, quoted in *The Heart of Salvation*, published by Praxis, and also in *Raising Them Right*, published by Conciliar Press.

25. Clement of Alexandria, *Stromata*.

26. Evagrius of Pontus, *The Praktikos*, V 78.

27. "And from the days of John the Baptist until now the kingdom of heaven suffereth violence, and the violent take it by force" (Matthew 11:12).

28. Despite its capitalization, the use of the word Self here clearly refers to the ordinary ego, which benefits from having its attention taken away from itself but even then remains limited in sensibility.

29. A. Posoff, *The Inner Kingdom*.

30. "And the light shineth in darkness; and the darkness comprehended it not" (John 1:5).

31. Karlfried von Durkheim, *Hara*, p. 12.

32. Evagrius, *The Praktikos*, V 99.

33. J. K. Galbraith, *The Culture of Contentment*.

34. Bishop Germain, *Essai sur le jeûne de l'oeil ou jeûne visuel. Présence Orthodoxe*. Paris.

35. Ibid.

36. The archaic word *rereward* refers to a protector or shield to protect the back of a man in battle.

37. St. Hesychios the Priest, *The Philokalia*. Vol. 1, p. 166.

38. Saint Ephriam the Syrian, *The Syriac Fathers*, p. 36.

39. Blessed Callistus, *Texts on Prayer. In Writings from The Philokalia on Prayer of the Heart.* Trans. Kadloubovsky and Palmer. London. Faber, 1951, p. 272.

40. Paraphrased from Boris Mouravieff's *Gnosis*. Vol. 1.

41. St. Maximos the Confessor, *Four Hundred Chapters on Love*, 2nd Century, v25.

42. Archimandrite George Capsanis, *The Eros of Repentance*.

43. The bones of many saints have been found uncorrupted after many years in the ground.

44. In the old sense of the word *suffered*, as referring to something that is not done by man but simply happens to him.

45. Archimandrite George Capsanis, *The Eros of Repentance*.

46. St. Gregory of Nyssa, *The Soul and Resurrection*, p. 70.

47. The translation had "definitively."

48. St. Gregory of Nyssa, *The Soul and Resurrection*, p. 71.

49. St. Maximos the Confessor, *Four Hundred Chapters on Love*.

50. Ibid.

51. St. Gregory of Nyssa, *The Soul and Resurrection*.

52. The mind is at that moment without intention and so still subject to accidental forces.

53. St. Maximos the Confessor, *Four Hundred Chapters on Love*.

54. St. Anthony the Great, *First Letter*.

55. Archimandrite George Capsanis, *The Eros of Repentance*.

56. Ibid.

57. Here this term does not refer to external evangelism, an idea foreign to the thought of Mount Athos, but to a *glorification*, a visible transformation that acts outwardly as well as inwardly.

58. Archimandrite George Capsanis, *The Eros of Repentance*.

59. Blessed Callistus, Texts on Prayer, in *The Philokalia*.

60. *The Gerontikon* is a collection of stories in Greek about the *gerontes* or early Fathers of the church. There are several English translations and renderings available.

61. G. A. Wallis Budge, *The Gerontikon*. London. Chatto & Windus. 1907.

Chapter 11

1. A. Posoff, *The Inner Kingdom*.

2. Evagrius, *On Prayer* in *The Philokalia*, p. 60, v35–36.

3. *Gospel According to Thomas*.

4. "But thou, when thou prayest, enter into thy closet, and when thou hast shut thy door, pray to thy Father which is in secret; and thy Father which seeth in secret shall reward thee openly" (Matthew 6:6). This gospel teaching about going into our closet to pray has more than one meaning, since it refers not only to the need to find an undistracted place in which to pray, and a place where one is not concerned what others think who may be watching, but it also can be seen in an inner meaning as referring to prayer of the heart, which can only occur in a "secret" place within our heart.

5. See Eugraph Kovalevsky, *A Method of Prayer.*

6. Exact source uncertain.

7. From A. R. Orage, *Commentaries on Gurdjieff's All and Everything*, Aurora, OR. Two Rivers Press.

8. Evagrius, *Kephalia Gnostica.* Century 1: v85.

9. St. Gregory of Nyssa, *The Life of Moses.*

10. Here we must take great care not to confuse this concept of intuition with what is called "Kantian intuition," and in fact to remember always that this intuition of the heart has to do with our ability to learn things that are not showed to us in man-made ways through the senses.

11. Evagrius of Pontus, *On Prayer* in *The Philokalia.* Vol. 2, p. 58, v6.

12. Described in some detail in the next section of this chapter, and in even more detail in Boris Mouravieff's *Gnosis.* Vol. 1.

13. St. Theophan the Recluse, in *The Heart of Salvation.*

14. Ibid.

15. Ibid.

16. Clement of Alexandria, *Stromata.*

17. Others have put this by saying that when we pray we must be aware of the meaning of what we say.

18. Kallistos Ware, in the Introduction to Igumen Chariton of Valamo, *The Art of Prayer.* Trans. Kadloubovsky and Palmer. London. Faber, 1966, p. 21.

19. St. Therese of Lisieux, *The Story of a Soul*, p. 79.

20. Or "unspeakable," in the words of Jacob Boehme.

21. St. Theophan the Recluse in *The Heart of Salvation.* Praxis Institute Press, 1992.

22. Freely rendered from Saint John, chapter 1.

23. Greek *nepsis*, translated "watchfulness."

24. The original translation had "goes with."

25. St. Hesychius, *On Watchfulness and Holiness. Philokalia.* Vol. 1, para. 94.

26. A term introduced in the West by Gurdjieff but almost certainly a reference to the "ladder" of St. John Climacus.

27. St. Hesychios, *On Watchfulness and Holiness.* Vol. 1, para. 88.

28. St. Theophan the Recluse, *Four Sermons on Prayer,* in *The Path of Prayer.* Trans. Esther Williams. Newbury, MA. Praxis Institute Press, 1993.

29. St. Theophan the Recluse, *The Heart of Salvation.*

30. Karlfried von Durkheim, *Hara.*

31. Ibid., p. 34.

32. Certain methods of chanting, used on Mount Athos, are backed by a long almost unchanging "drone" note. Boris Mouravieff reports the use of such music in Russian monasteries as a breathing exercise.

33. Karlfried von Durkheim, *Hara.*

34. In unpublished writings of Boris Mouravieff on file with Praxis Research Institute.

35. Only those responsible for guiding the other monks need much knowledge.

36. St. Theophan the Recluse, *The Heart of Salvation.*

37. Blessed Callistus, *Texts on Prayer.* In *Writings from* The Philokalia *on Prayer of the Heart.*

38. In the works of many of the Fathers, and of more recent saints, such as St. John of the Cross and St. Theophan the Recluse.

39. St. Theophan the Recluse, *The Heart of Salvation.*

40. See details in the next chapter.

41. Matthew 26:41, referred to on p. XX.

42. Evagrius of Pontus, *The Praktikos,* V 101.

Chapter 12

1. Certainly holy orders symbolized not only inner intention but inner performance to Saint John Cassian, who wrote: "The one who anoints his mind for the sacred contests and drives away passionate thoughts from it possesses the

character of a deacon. The one who illuminates it with knowledge of beings and obliterates counterfeit knowledge possesses that of a priest. Finally, the one who perfects it with the holy perfume of the knowledge of a worshipper of the Holy Trinity possesses that of a bishop." St. John Cassian, from *The Philokalia*, Vol. 1.

2. Echoing one of the qualities of the *intervals* in a musical octave, although not one of the properties of this that is usually studied.

3. A. Posoff, *The Inner Kingdom*.

4. Specifically referring to Archimandrite George Capsanis, Abbot of the Monastery of Grigoriou.

5. A very good definition of *ecstasy* from St. Isaac the Syrian, *Daily Prayers*, in *The Syriac Fathers*, 1, v1.

6. A technical term used in Boris Mouravieff's *Gnosis*, and in previous books, including those of P. D. Ouspensky.

7. Boris Mouravieff, in a publication of his Center for Esoteric Christianity, out of print in French since the center closed after Mouravieff's death in the late 1960s.

8. Archimandrite Cherubim Harolambas, *Recollections of Mount Athos*.

9. We will understand by now that this has an inner meaning: that the "country" that Abraham was to leave was inside him, as was the land that God was to show him, a land within him but then still unknown to him.

10. St. Anthony the Great, *First Letter*.

11. John Kenneth Galbraith, *The Culture of Contentment*.

12. St. John Cassian, *The Conferences*. Conference 3.

13. And this usage of the term *possession* applies to the inner meaning of the idea of demonic possession, an idea which has no outer meaning.

14. St. Anthony the Great, *First Letter*.

15. Ibid.

16. See the many translations of Shankaracharya: *Vivekachudamani: The Crest Jewel of Wisdom* or *Crest Jewel of Discrimination*.

17. H. P. Blavatsky, *The Voice of the Silence*.

18. This assent to some good impulse also requires discernment. Readers are referred to a warning given in the medieval English book *The Discernment of Stirrings*, by the author of the *Cloud of Unknowing*. In this book its author warns the reader, originally supposed to be a specific individual: "I say all this to show you how far you still are from a real knowledge of yourself, and to warn you not to give up too soon, and not to follow the special impulses of your youthful heart for fear of being deceived. Moreover, I say all this to let you see what I am thinking

about you and your impulses as you have asked me to do. For my opinion is that you are quite capable of, and indeed eager for, sudden impulses to do particular things, and quick to hold onto them once you get them—and that is a very dangerous thing!

" . . . potentially this can be a very good thing, . . . but that can only be if a soul so disposed will diligently, day and night, humble itself before God and take sound advice; if it will take steps to offer itself up; if it will give up its own mind and will in these sudden, special impulses and state categorically that it will not follow them, however attractive, uplifting and holy they may be, unless it has the full approval of its spiritual masters . . . " By the author of the *Cloud of Unknowing*, in *The Discernment of Stirrings*, published in *A Study of Wisdom*. Fairacres, Oxford. SLG Press, 1980.

19. St. John Cassian, *The Conferences*.

20. St. Maximos the Confessor, *Four Hundred Chapters on Love*, pp. 25–26.

21. Ibid., p. 34.

22. Clement of Alexandria, *Stromata*, p. 371.

23. Ibid.

24. The last two of these three points are defined later in this chapter.

25. Boris Mouravieff, unpublished writings from the French.

26. Boris Mouravieff, *Gnosis*. Vol. 1.

27. See P. D. Ouspensky, *The Psychology and Cosmology of Man's Possible Evolution*. Newbury, MA. Praxis Institute Press, 1989.

28. St. Hesychius the Priest, in *The Philokalia*, Vol. 1, p. 187, v147

29. Ibid., p. 163, v2.

30. *Gospel According to Thomas*.

31. St. Hesychius

32. I. M. Kontzevitch, *The Acquisition of the Holy Spirit*. Vol. 1, p. 163, v2.

33. St. Hesychius, quoted p. 42. Op. cit. also in different translation in *The Philokalia*.

34. Ibid., Vol. 1, p. 163, v6. The translation has *noted*; we have changed the term to fit the terminology being developed in this book.

35. Attributed to St. Anthony the Great, in *The Philokalia*, Vol. 1, p. 351.

36. Ibid.

37. Taking a term from the teaching of Krishnamurti.

38. The texts referred to are not pre-Christian so that we can only draw limited conclusions from this.

39. St. Theophan the Recluse, *The Heart of Salvation*.

40. The alchemist Fulcanelli links this term *argot* with *Art Gothique*—thus tying it to the cathedral builders who, centuries ago, formed the Christian basis of alchemy. See Fulcanelli, *The Mystery of Cathedrals*. London. Neville Spearman, 1971.

41. St. Neilos the Ascetic in *The Philokalia*, Vol. 1, p. 234.

42. Gregory of Nyssa, *The Life of Moses*.

43. St. Therese of Lisieux, *The Story of a Soul*.

44. Boris Mouravieff, *Gnosis*.

45. Clement of Alexandria, *Stromata*.

46. St. Hesychius the Priest, in *The Philokalia*, Vol. 1, p. 163.

47. P. D. Ouspensky, *In Search of the Miraculous*.

48. St. John of Karpathos, in *The Philokalia*, Vol. 1, p. 310.

49. 2 Corinthians 2:15.

50. St. Theophan the Recluse, *The Heart of Salvation*.

51. Used here as a term for the Fourth Way teaching, for which we can substitute some more general term describing the ongoing inner tradition.

52. Maurice Nicoll, *Commentaries on the Teachings of Gurdjieff and Ouspensky*. Vol. 3. London. Vincent Stuart, 1957, p. 862.

53. "No man can serve two masters: for either he will hate the one, and love the other; or else he will hold to the one, and despise the other. Ye cannot serve God and mammon" (Matthew 6:24).

54. A reference to *metanoia*.

55. St. Maximos the Confessor, *Four Hundred Chapters*. 2nd Century, v48.

56. St. Isaac the Syrian, *The Homilies*.

57. G. P. Fedotov, *A Treasury of Russian Spirituality*.

58. St. Theophan the Recluse, *The Path of Prayer*.

59. St. Theophan the Recluse, *The Heart of Salvation*.

60. St. Macarius the Great, *Fifty Spiritual Homilies*. Homily 1.

61. St. Theophan the Recluse, *The Heart of Salvation*.

Chapter 13

1. St. John Cassian, *Conferences*.

2. A case in point is their adoption of technical terms originally used by the Stoic school of philosophers and psychologists that existed in many places in the Roman Empire in the early years of the church. Another such term is *prolipsis*, predisposition, which had one technical description in Stoic thought, to which the Fathers then added their own slightly different if more precise meaning.

3. The translation originally had "intellect" at this point. We adhere wherever possible to the growing consensus to use the word *nous*—which has already come into English usage. We use the word untranslated to distinguish it from translations of other Greek words which come closer to the English concepts of intellect and reason.

4. E.g. the "hard wax" of Plato's memory image, and the roadside in the gospel parable of the sower.

5. A term that gives new meaning to the name sometimes given to the esoteric path of *The Path of the Householder*.

6. Jacob Boehme, *Dialogue on the Supersensual Life*.

7. St. Maximos the Confessor.

8. This term we have introduced to define the point at which the doctrine becomes effective: when sufficient of it is known and applied. Some elements are more important to the completeness of a teaching than others. For some, alternatives exist. The same "effective completeness" has now been lost to Christianity, and it is the purpose of this book amongst other activities to attempt to restore it.

9. Archimandrite George Capsanis, *The Eros of Repentance*.

10. St. Gregory of Nyssa, *The Soul and Resurrection*.

11. Evagrius of Pontus, *The Praktikos*, v62.

12. Clement of Alexandria, *Stromata*, p. 312.

13. As distinguished from the previous stage sometimes associated with what scientific anthropologist Levy-Bruhel called "participation mystique."

14. Placed in the context of the whole of Clement's *Stromata* it is clear that this refers to the soul which contains gnosis, not to a member of the gnostic sects, against which Clement was actively opposed.

15. Clement of Alexandria, *Stromata*, p. 371.

16. F. M. Cornford, *Before and After Socrates*.

17. Ibid.

18. Werner Jaeger, *Paideia*.

19. As mentioned earlier, many of the technical terms used by the early Fathers are identical with those used by the stoic school of philosophy.

20. St. John Cassian, *On the Holy Fathers of Sketis*, in *The Philokalia*, pp. 98–99.

21. We can even discriminate between otherwise identical objects because they differ in *position*, and this factor plays a part in modern philosophical thought.

22. I.e. "of the *nous*."

23. Constantin Cavarnos, *The Hellenic Christian Philosophical Tradition*, p. 21.

24. Sometimes this idea emerges in modern translations as *demons*.

25. Anon. *The Discernment of Spirits*.

26. Boris Mouravieff, *Gnosis*. Vol. I.

27. Macarius the Great, *The Fifty Sermons*.

28. St. Maximos the Confessor, in *The Philokalia*. Vol. 2, p. 194.

29. Early photographic films had to be *sensitized* immediately before use.

30. The idea of *fixing* was used in alchemy before it was applied to photography.

31. The Faithful.

32. Clement of Alexandria, *Stromata*.

Chapter 14

1. Evagrius of Pontus, *The Praktikos*, v6.

2. I. M. Kontzevitch, *The Acquisition of the Holy Spirit*, p. 39.

3. Evagrius of Pontus, *The Praktikos*, v74–75.

4. St. Gregory of Nyssa, *Life of Moses*, p. 33 and below.

5. Paraphrased from Boris Mowaviff, *Guasis*. Vol. 11, p. 61.

6. St. Macarius the Great, *The Fifty Homilies*. Homily 5, v5.

7. I. M. Kontzevitch, *The Acquisition of the Holy Spirit*, pp. 39–40.

8. Ibid., p. 40.

9. Ibid., p. 41.

10. See references to education in Theophan the Recluse, *The Heart of Salvation*.

11. I. M. Kontzevitch, *The Acquisition of the Holy Spirit*, p. 41.

12. St. Nilus of Sora, quoted in I. M. Kontzevitch, *The Acquisition of the Holy Spirit*, p. 42.

13. I. M. Kontzevitch, *The Acquisition of the Holy Spirit*, p. 41.

14. Ibid., p. 42.

15. Apart from those who believe that they should be free to do whatever they want.

16. This is a state of mind that has not only existed in modern times, when it manifests in statements such as: "Demons do not exist," but when this state existed in certain past eras, it led to the *projection* (in a very Jungian sense) of all inner contents: of ourselves and of the world outside us, as external beings that today we sometimes call "mythical." This form of projection appears today to be evidence of the *superstition* of the past, and gives us the illusion that today we have become wiser.

17. I.e., to *assent* to them.

18. St. John Cassian, *On the Holy Fathers of Sketis*, in *The Philokalia*. Vol. 1, pp. 97–98.

19. Evagrius of Pontus, *The Praktikos*, v50.

20. Ibid., v81.

21. Ibid., v39.

22. Ibid., v43.

23. A. Posoff, *The Inner Kingdom*.

24. Evagrius of Pontus, *The Praktikos*, v7. The addition [that provokes] was made in place of the word *of* to link to the content of this chapter.

25. Ibid., v16.

26. Ibid., v8.

27. Ibid., v9.

28. Ibid., v10.

29. Ibid., v11.

30. Ibid., v12.

31. Ibid., end of v12.

32. Ibid., v13.

33. Ibid., v14.

Postscript

1. Such as F. M. Cornford, *Before and After Socrates*.

2. St. Symeon the New Theologian, *Three Methods of Attention and Prayer*, in *Writings from the Philokalian Prayer of the Heart*. Trans. Kadloubovsky & Palmer, London. Faber, 1951, p. 158.

3. Evagrius of Pontus, *The Praktikos*, v78. The original translation has *affective*, for which we have substituted *feeling*.

4. Perhaps demonstrated best by Dionysis the Areopagite, the Saint Denys of the medieval European mystics.

5. This term for the method was originally coined by Ouspensky.

6. Evagrius of Pontus.

7. A later and augmented version of this *Philokalia*, the Russian *Dobrotolubiye*, was edited by the same Saint Theophan to whom we have already referred and its publication arranged by the Moscow house of the great Russian monastery of Saint Panteleimon, whose mother house is on Mount Athos. As yet only extracts from the complete work exist in English translation, although much of the content is identical with that in the Greek *Philokalia* now partially completed.

8. "All we can hope to have today is critical theory, i.e., the theory that constantly uses methodological doubt to examine all our accepted prejudices in order to see whether better ones cannot be conceived. . . ." Paulos Mar Gregorios, *Science for Sane Societies*, rev. ed. 1987. New York. Paragon House, p. 117.

9. Boris Mouravieff, from unpublished material.

Index

Abandonment to Divine Providence, 24, 38
accidie, 333
Adamantius, Origen, 14, 33, 53, 110,
    135, 306, 343, 362n. 14
agrypnia, 215, 217–20, 252, 253–54
alitheia, 241
all-night vigil. *See agrypnia*
Andrew, Saint (of Crete): Canon of, 42,
    43–44
anger, 332
Anthony, Saint (the Great): on ascesis,
    138–39, 213; on faith, 177–78; on
    fasting, 221; on purifying the nous,
    184; on three types of seekers of
    God, 263, 266–67, 314; on
    transforming the passions, 230–31
Anthony of Sourozh, 21
apatheia, 85, 193, 206, 292, 304, 326,
    328
Apocrypha, 32
Arabi, Ibn, 137
Argonauts, 85
ark, 282 86
Ark of the Covenant, 284
Arsenios, Saint (of Cappadocia), 12
Art of Prayer, The, 6, 247
ascesis, 67, 213; as work on oneself,
    137–40; doctrine of, 85; definition
    of, 137–38; noetic, 23, 138–39, 184,
    198, 236; physical, 138; psychologi-
    cal, 138
assent, 171–72, 225–26, 227, 280;
    categories of, 344–45; to faith, 185,
    227, 251; monastic forms of, 214–
    31; philosophy of, 172–75; psychol-
    ogy of, 175; to prayer, 251

atman, 281
attention, 245
avarice, 330–31
avidya, 134

balkanization of the mind, xiv
Barlaam (the Calabrian), 29, 106, 135
Basli, Saint (the Great), 67
Benedict, Saint, 37
Blavatsky, H. P., 271
blind belief: as opposed to knowledge
    or real faith, 180–81
Boehme, Jacob, 299
Bohm, David: on nature, 71, 72
born from above, 84–85
bridegroom: image of, 83–84
Brownowski, Jacob, 357n. 27
burning bush: analogy of, 45

called: vs. chosen, 85
Callistus (Blessed), 94; on *nepsis*, 226–27
Cappadocian Fathers, 33
Capsanis, Abbot George, 53, 135, 241;
    on aescetic forms of repentance,
    214–15; on finding God in our-
    selves, 211; on Gregory Palamas,
    360n. 13; on love, 212, 231; on
    metanoia, 188, 210
captivity, 317, 319, 324–25
Caussade, Pierre, 19, 24, 38
Cavarnos, Constantin, 66
chanting, 373n. 33
chariot of fire: parable of, 126–30
Chariton, Abbot, 6
choice, 280
chosen: vs. called, 85

Christ: as icon of God, 123; light of, 136
Christianity: and natural law, 186; as opposed to deist worldview, 104–05; as state of being, 90; inner tradition of. *See* inner tradition
church Fathers: written teachings of, 33–36
Clement (of Alexandria), 15, 19, 22, 24, 33, 67, 68, 72, 110, 173, 303, 343; on the ark, 284; on assent, 175; on division of esoteric path, 201, 202; and gnosis, 16, 70, 107–11, 135; on the gnostic, 274, 305; on love, 304; on Plato, 313
Cloud of Unknowing, 38, 157–58, 227, 249–50
coherence, 132
commandments: as test, 226
communion, 98
concentration, 277, 350–52
Conferences, 142
conjunction, 321–22
conscience, 9, 123, 299
consciousness: transformation of, 26
constatation, 94, 275, 276, 277, 288, 350
contemplation, 77–78; infused, 77
contemplative knowledge, 158
Cornford, Francis, 306
Crest Jewel of Discrimination, 156
Culture of Contentment, The, 269
Cyprien, Saint (of Carthage), 159–60

daath, 107
deification, 165–67, 212, 227; summary of process of, 53
demons, 162, 198–200, 325
detachment: through knowledge to, 288–91
dharana, 277
dhyana, 61, 250; and meditation, 138
diakrisis, 77, 106, 137, 139, 146, 192, 193, 198, 201, 205, 207, 273, 275, 295, 326–27; and Karma Yoga, 271–73; nature of, 304–07; Saint John Cassian on, 307–13

diet: meat vs. milk, 314–15
discernment of spirits. *See diakrisis*
Discernment of Stirrings, The, 374–75n. 18
Discernment of Spirits, The, 310
discrimination, 273–74, 295; emotional, 195; horizontal, 310; vertical, 310. *See also diakrisis*
dispassion. *See apatheia*
Dobrotolubyie, 257
Durkheim, Karlfried von: on hara, 52–53, 252; on vivification of solar plexus, 252–53
dying to oneself, 262
dynamis. See energy

Eccles, Sir John, 201
Ecclesiastical History, 32
Eddington, 3
education: emotional, 116, 117; religious, 115–17
effort: and salvation, 184–86
Einstein, Albert, 3
Elizabeth, Saint: icon of, 55
emotion: blindness to, 141–42; negative, 230
energies, 46, 53, 79–80, 86–87, 258–59; *hesychastic*, 278; quest for, 80–82; and virtue, 82
Ephriam, Saint (the Syrian), 175; on conjunction, 321
epignosis, 68
epiousion, 242
epistemi, 180
eros, 211–12; transforming natural into divine, 87, 193–98, 211, 227–28; 231–32
eroticism: higher, 185; struggle with, 215, 227–29
esotericism, 73–74; as unwritten tradition, 105–06
Eusebius, 32
Evagrius, 80–81, 83, 99, 244–45, 343; on anger, 332; and ascesis and *apatheia*, 214; on contemplative knowledge, 77, 134, 346; on

demons, 162, 198–99; on fasting, 222; on levels of renunciation, 142, 143–44, 156, 158; on memory, 303; on observation, 326; on prayer, 236; on provocation, 317, 318, 319; on recognition, 327
exegesis by practice, 58
experience, xviii
eye of the soul. See nous

faith, 104, 105, 171, 175, 279; assent to, 185, 227, 251; common ground of, 181–82; confirmed, 176; of consciousness, 178, 179–81; natural or innate, 176; real as opposed to blind belief, 180–81; that becomes knowledge, 177–78; without works, 178–79
Fall, 25–26, 42, 54; inner reality and, 72–73; New Testament on, 74–75; outer and inner interpretations of, 74; restoration from, 63–64; Saint Maximos on, 48–51
fasting, 215, 220–24; history of, 220–21; intelligent, 220; as related to the Fall, 223; stupid, 221
Fedotov, G. P.: on Saint Nilus of Sora, 55
fighting cock: parable of, 162
First Letter, 266
Fourth Way, 139, 270
Francis, Saint (of Assisi), 37
Freud, Sigmund, 214

Galbraith, John Kennedy: on dependency on possessions, 269
Garden of Panaghia, 148
George, Abbot (of Grigoriou), 61; on guarding the thoughts, 326
Germain, Bishop: on fasting, 222–23
gerontes, 91
Gerontikon, 6, 37; on two types of monastery, 233
Gifts of the Spirit, 19
Gilson, Etienne, 28, 173
Glorification of the body, 81
gluttony, 329–30

gnosis, 16, 67, 68, 70, 76, 77, 101–02, 134; Alexandrian tradition of, 107–11; definition of, 105, 106; and diakrisis, 137; as differs from Gnosticism, 28, 101, 105–07; experiential, 102–03; lack of in modern world, 114–15
Gnosis: Study and Commentaries on the Esoteric Tradition of Eastern Orthodoxy, xiii, 135, 227, 228, 276, 284, 344; magnetic center as cage in, 282
Gnosticism, 28, 101, 105–07
God, 166; biblical kingdom of, 185; doing the will of, 123–26; fear of, 247, 335–36; knowledge of, 134–37; limitations of, 112–13; magnetization to, 190, 291–94; omnipotence of, 111–13; surrender to, 121–22
Golden Book, The, 194
Gospel According to Thomas, 32, 73
grace: and salvation, 184–85
Gregory (of Nyssa), 3, 15, 64, 65, 68; on attention, 245; on the burning bush image, 58–59; and the chariot parable, 126–30, 282; on the image of the ark as magnetic center, 284, 285, 286; on negative emotions, 230; on the parables of the tares and of the sower, 301–02; on renunciation, 152–53; on sadness, 331–32, on second birth, 283–84; on self-calming, 169; on two directions of eros, 228–29; on virtue, 71, 72
Gregory Palamas, Saint, 20, 29, 46, 53, 55–57, 79, 106; on energies, 81, 135; on inner knowledge, 306; on knowing God, 136; on theology, 180
Gregory, Saint (of Sinai), 206, 328
Gurdjieff, 23, 36, 52, 66, 139, 161, 185, 346; on changing memory content, 297; Christian origin of system of, 347–48, 356n. 26; on energies, 81; on influences, 311; on inner considering, 240; on intentional or voluntary suffering, 169, 243; on two ways of life, 308

habit: struggle against, 323–24
hara, 52–53, 252–53
Hardy, Alister, 207
headless axe: parable of, 203–04
heart, 103–04; path of, 20–23; purity
    of, 313
Heart of Philosophy, The, 176
hesychia, 46, 189, 210, 238, 312;
    noetic, 280
Hesychius (of Jerusalem), 30; on
    magnetic center, 250; on *nous*, 183;
    on watchfulness, 250, 251, 276–77,
    278, 279
History of the Tree of Life, 50
Homer, 85
hospitality, 232–34
human nature: distortion of, 51–54
humility, 188–89
Huxley, T. H., 27

Ignatius, Saint (of Loyola), 37
Iisus evchi. See Jesus Prayer
Imitation of Christ, The, 38, 250
influences: A, 308, 311; B, 139, 308,
    311, 314; C, 308, 314–15
inner considering, 240
inner experience, 1, 57–58
inner life: as therapy, 9–11; inability to
    remember, 54–55
inner self, 281
inner separation, 184, 238, 277, 304
inner tradition, xiii–xiv; history of, 3–4;
    loss of ancient knowledge of, 27–30;
    as tradition of interpretation, xvii
inner world: as window, 71–75
Isaac, Saint (the Syrian), 52, 73, 112;
    on knowledge and faith, 181; prayer
    of 69–70, 92–93, 264; on prayer as
    multilevel, 292; on unwritten
    tradition, 108
Isaiah: on fasting, 224

Jackson, Hughlings, 44, 133
Jaeger, Werner: on Greek philosophers,
    116, 307
James (brother of Jesus): on faith, 177

Jean (bishop of Saint Denys): on love of
    God, 136; on prayer, 235
Jesus Prayer, 61, 254–57
jnana, 134
John Cassian, Saint, 22, 106, 262, 325–
    26; on *diakrisis*, 304, 307–13; on
    holy orders, 373n. 1; on the
    renunciations, 142, 144, 165, 167,
    238
John, Saint (of Kronstadt), 12, 37
John Climacus, Saint, 175
John, Saint (of the Cross), 24, 38, 70;
    and *metanoia*, 210; on the renuncia-
    tions, 147, 157, 158, 161; on
    transcending reason with thought,
    259, 299
John, Saint (of Karpathos): on *metanoia*,
    191
joining, 322, 323
Joseph, Saint (the Visionary): prayer of,
    81–82, 92–93
Josephson, Brian, 72
Jung, C. G., 54, 143
Justification by Faith, 177

Karoulia, 150–51
Keating, Father Thomas, 61; on
    consent, 227, 251
kellia, 265
Kephalia Gnostica, 142
knowledge, 209; inner, 105; esoteric,
    289; kinds of, 66, 70–71; modern
    view of, 50; role of in spirituality,
    75–77; theory of as barrier to faith,
    55–58; through, to detachment,
    288–91
koinonia, 97, 130
Kontzevitch, I. M.: on assent to faith,
    175; on provocation, 318–24
Kovalevsky, Eugraph. *See* Jean (bishop
    of Saint Denys)

Lewis, C. S., 102
liberation, 9
Life of Moses, 15, 58–59, 64–65, 128,
    152–53, 283–84, 331–32

lillies of the field: parable of, 239
liturgies, 38
living water, 94
logos, 76
Logos ton Theon, 76
Lord's Prayer, 242
love. *See* eros
lust, 330

Macarius the Great, 26, 119–20, 130;
and ascesis, 213; on being, 90; on
Christ as icon of God, 123; on
energy, 82–83, 86–87; on the five
virgins, 86–87, 94–96; on God, 111–
12; and influences, 312; on magnetic
center, 294; on renewing the mind,
319; on renunciation, 155; on
sanctification, 87–88
Macrina, Saint: on the parable of the
tares, 302
Macroprosopus, 282
magnetic center, 246, 250, 251, 318,
322, 324; active stage, 287–88;
staircase stage, 288–91; ark as, 282–
85; passive unconscious stage, 286–
87; second passive stage, 291–94
Maloney, Fr. George: on renunciation,
155
Mark, Saint: Gospel of, 104, 109–10
Maslow, Abram, 207
Matthew, Saint: on fasting, 222, 223;
on possessions, 270; on righteousness, 240; on secret prayer, 372n. 4;
on Tradition of the light, xvi
Maximos, Saint (the Confessor), 57,
174, 227; on contemplation, 77–78;
on demons, 162, 163; on discrimination, 295–96, 312–13; on the Fall,
48–51; on love, 196, 212; on
passion, 229, 230; on prayer and
watchfulness, 273, 275; on temptations, 122; and transformation of the
eros, 292
meditation, 138
Mehat: on division of esoteric path,
201–02

memory: changes in content of, 296–
97; as a garden, 297–99; illusory,
302–04; three conditions of, 300
Merton, Thomas, 6
metanoia, 6–7, 150, 186, 188–89, 227–
28, 291; as change of being, 206–13;
definition of, 203; modern solutions
to, 131–34; modern views of, 204–
06; struggle for, 191–93; work on
oneself as effort of, 130–31
microprosopus, 281
mneme Theou, 122, 189–91
monastic rules, 37
monasticism: difficulties of methods of,
264–68; and nonmonastic ways,
263–64; unwritten teachings of
Eastern, 36–37
Moses, Father: and hospitality, 232–34
Moses: as example of resurrection in
life, 26
Motilov, N. A., 205
Mouravieff, Boris, xiii, 4, 6, 15, 19, 36,
64; on the ark, 284; on assent to
faith, 227; categories of ascesis of,
344–45; on concentration, 277,
350–51; on constatation, 94, 275,
276, 288; on esoteric knowledge,
289; on gnosis, 275; on influences,
308, 311; on knowing God, 135; on
love, 194, 195, 212; on magnetic
center, 285–86, 287; on monasticism, 131, 264–65; polar being of,
193, 227–28; on prayer, 275; on
presence, 275, 276; on renewing the
mind, 319; on the renunciations,
168

narrow way, 19–20, 22, 160, 313
Needleman, Jacob: on faith, 176
needs, 221
Neilos, Saint (the Ascetic): and
magnetic center, 283; on *metanoia*,
203
Nektarios, Saint, 12
nepsis, 226, 246, 250–51, 252, 258,
273, 276–77; importance of, 278–79

New Man, The, 207
Nicholas Cabasilas, Saint, 212
Nicodemus (of the Holy Mountain), 6
Nicoll, Maurice, 7, 162, 205, 277; on *metanoia*, 208; on repentance as change in psychology, 207–08; on transformation of sensations, 290–91
Nikon, Father, 6
Nilus, Saint (of Sora), 17, 28, 55; and eye of the soul, 184; monastic rule of, 29–30, 37; and provocation, 318, 323; and *sketes*, 224
nous, 55, 183–84, 337; definition of, 106; liberation of, 69; light of, 110; illumination of, 19, 48, 51, 239; three stages of, 238; translations of, 209

obedience, 215, 224–25; to the commandments, 225–27
oil: of gladness, 87; of the supernatural grace of the Spirit, 87
one thing needful, 237–38; methods of reaching, 243
Orage, A. R., 243
oral tradition, 23–24
Origen. *See* Adamantius, Origen
Ouspensky, P. D., 10, 36, 52, 66, 89, 139, 161, 185, 207, 275, 347; on influences, 308, 311; on limitations of God, 112–13; on magnetic center, 285–87; on path of the heart, 22; and psychological method, 346; on rules, 226
paideia, 117, 341
panaghia, 361n. 32
Paphnutius, 142
passions, 143, 229–31, 328; transforming, 230–31; two sources of, 230
Patanjali, 184, 344
Paul, Saint, 19; and ascesis, 137–38, 213–14; and meat or milk diet, 314; on turning toward reality, 146
pearl of great price: parable of, 143, 159
peirasmos, 319

Perennial Philosophy, 67
Perennial Philosophy, 26, 27
Philokalia, 6, 25, 35, 37, 54, 257, 347, 354n. 7, 380n. 7; on cutting off the will, 224; on discrimination, 77, 295–96; on the Fall, 48–50; on the parable of the headless axe, 203–04; on prayer, 256–57
philosophy: in early Eastern church, 65–69; esoteric, 66, 67; exoteric, 66, 67; Greek, 29; mesoteric, 66
Philotheus (of Sinai), 28; and eye of the soul, 184
philoxenia, 189
Pieper, Josef, 174
pilgrimage, 148–50
Plato, 111, 116, 306, 368n. 12; concept of One, 71, 72; on three conditions of memory, 300; wax tablet model of, 300
plenenie. See captivity
Polanyi, Michael, 174
Polycarp, Martyr, 32
Posoff, A.: on intellect and the heart, 328; on prayer and asceticism, 215–16, 235–36
possessions, 145
Praktikos, The, 214; on passions, 326; and provocation, 317, 327
prayer, 138–39, 215–16, 235–36; as relation to God, 242–46; assent to, 251; centering, 61, 227; definition of, 256; degrees of, 246–48; of the heart, 61, 77, 92, 273, 263–64, 372n. 4; inner, 235, 249–54; link of with watchfulness, 250; noetic, 257–58, 276. *See also* Jesus Prayer
presence, 275, 276, 277, 280–82
pride, 334–35
prilog. See provocation
Principiis, de, 53, 136
Problems of Pain, The, 102
prodigal son: parable of, 23, 186–88
prosevchi, 255
prosochi, 281
prosopon, 281

provocation, 35, 214, 317–18; observation of, 325–27; resisting, 327–36; stages of, 318–25

psychological method, 346; and concentration, 351, of early Fathers, 344–46

psychology: abnormal, 10; loss of, 28; of the social sciences, 10

purification, 178

reality: turn toward, 145–46

rebirth, 8, 85

recognition, 10–11, 139, 177, 198–202

redemption, 41

renunciation: first, 143, 144, 145–50, 272; fourth step in, 144–45, 165; modern understanding of, 167–69; nonmonastic, 261–62; of possessions, 268–71; second, 143–44, 147–50, 154–57; stages of in India, 148; third, 144, 147–50, 158–64; three levels of, 142

repentance, 204

Republic, 116

resurrection, 63

Resurrection: General, 25–26, 63

righteousness, 240

Royal Way. *See* Royal Road

Royal Road, 9, 13, 19, 22–23, 92, 197, 313; compared to Yoga, 20; as oral tradition, 24; as prayer of the heart, 263–64

Russian Religious Mind, The, 36

Ruysbroeck, Jan van, 136

Sacred Magic of Abramelin the Mage, The, 263

sadness, 331–32

saints, 11; list of recent, 11–12

salvation: and effort, 184–86; and grace, 184–85

sanctification, 196; wholeheartedness as requirement for, 88

Schroedinger, E., 3

second birth, 283–84

self-calming, 169

self-remembering. *See* presence

semantron, 283

senses of the soul: control of, 93–94; five virgins as, 94–96

Seraphim, Saint (of Sarov), 12, 91; and *hesychia*, 210; on *metanoia*, 205

Shankara, 156

Silouan, Saint (of Athos), 12, 169

skete, 224, 225, 265

slozhenie. See joining

Smith, Morton, 24–25, 70, 109, 132, 201–02

sochetanie. See conjunction

Socrates, 313; on knowledge of philosophers, 306

Sophrony, Father, 169

Sorski, Nils. *See* Nilus, Saint (of Sora)

sower: parable of, 297–98, 300, 301–02

spirit, 311; and energy, 80

spirituality: role of knowledge in, 75–77

starchestvo, 91

startsi, 91–92

Stethatos, Nicetas: on senses and asceticism, 215

Stromata, 24, 85, 362n. 14; on reuniting fragmentary knowledge, 75–76

suffering: intentional or voluntary, 169–70, 243

superefforts, 121, 122, 197–98

Symeon, Saint (the New Theologian), 29, 30, 42, 55, 340; on inner experience, 47–48; prayer by, 166–67

Symeon (the Studite), 29

synergy, 84

Talbot, Michael, 71–72

tares: parable of, 133, 301–02

Teilhard de Chardin, Pierre, 64

temptations, 122

testing, 319–20

theocentric selflessness, 239–40; as justification, 240–41. *See also* renunciation: second

theology, 180; apophatic, 164–65

Theophan, Saint (the Recluse), 5, 6, 11–12, 36, 37, 39, 83, 124, 128, 161; on assent, 172–73; defines prayer, 256; on depth of prayer, 251–52, 293; on inner prayer, 246–47, 248, 249; on magnetic center, 285–86, 294; on magnetization to God, 190, 257–58, 291; on result of the Fall, 206; on using inner knowledge, 289–90; on zeal, 210, 211
theoria, 76, 77, 134, 180
theosis. See deification
Therese, Saint (of Lisieux), 12, 113; on the ark, 284; on inner prayer, 248
Thomas Aquinas, Saint, 171; on distinction between knowledge and blind belief, 174
Thomas à Kempis, Saint, 136, 250
transcendental meditation, 61
Transvolgan Hermits, 268
treasure hid in the field: parable of, 143
Tree of Life, 298
Tree of Knowledge of Good and Evil, 298
truth: unchanging, 26–27

uncreated light, 47, 159
unity of being, 310
Unseen Warfare, 6, 243
unwritten Christian tradition, 108

vairyagya, 192
vanity, 333–34

Vasileios, Abbot, 99
Velitchkovsky, Paisious, 6, 55, 91, 257
Vespers of the Transfiguration, 53
vidya, 134
virgins: parable of the wise and foolish, 83–84, 86–88
virtue, 79–80; and energy, 82
Vivekachudamani, 156
Voice of Silence, 271

waking sleep, 52
wants, 221
Ware, Bishop Kallistos, 354n. 7; on prayer, 185, 247–48
watchfulness. See nepsis and provocations: observation of
Way of the Householder, 262
Whitehead, A. N.: on assumptions, 72
wholeheartedness, 89–90, 121, 291; as requirement for sanctification, 88
will: cutting off, 29, 215, 224–25
work on oneself, 130–31; ascesis as, 137–40

xenos, 262, 368n. 12

Yoga: Eightfold, 184, 277, 344; Karma, 130, 146, 262, 271–73; Raja, 345

zeal, 210, 211
Zernov, Nicholas: on starchestvo, 91
Zohar, 84, 85